HUNTINGTON LIBRARY PUBLICATIONS

THE FIRST GENTLEMEN OF VIRGINIA

INTELLECTUAL QUALITIES OF THE EARLY COLONIAL RULING CLASS

BY

LOUIS B. WRIGHT

THE HUNTINGTON LIBRARY
SAN MARINO, CALIFORNIA
1940

Printed in the United States of America by the Adcraft Press, Los Angeles, California

TO

MAX FARRAND

AND

EDWIN F. GAY

TABLE OF CONTENTS

PREFACE

THE transition from England to America of ideas of aristocracy, with the historical implications of that social development, is a theme for a book much larger than this one. The present discussion attempts an interpretation of only one phase of that problem: the evolution of a ruling class of gentlemen in Virginia. And, even in that limited field, it has been impossible to treat all the aspects of the life of the gentry. It has seemed desirable to concentrate chiefly upon the relatively neglected problem of the intellectual qualities and attributes of the group who became the leaders of the colony in the first two or three generations. The broader fields of social history can be better left to others; indeed, much has already been done to reveal the external life of colonial Virginia. But there is still need for an analysis of the inner life, of the spiritual and intellectual natures, of our ancestors, because an understanding of their development helps to explain the later course of history.

Evidences of the intellectual interests of colonial Virginians are scarce, but not altogether lacking. If there is very little that can be called literature, that dearth is not proof that the men who established their power in Virginia were devoid of mental development and left no mark on intellectual history. They bought and read books; they wrote letters; they talked and made speeches; they practiced the game of politics and at times graduated from politics to statesmanship; and they shaped a cultivated social order. Their record is written in the history of the colony, and sufficient documents have survived to indicate something of the mental life of the leaders in this evolution.

The present discussion is concerned with the earlier colonial period, when the patterns of life were being fixed. The biographical sketches illustrative of the temper of the Virginia gentry have been confined to the first and second generations in America. Only in the case of William Byrd II does the discussion extend much beyond the first third of the eighteenth century. By that time the colony had acquired the social and intellectual characteristics that it would display for generations to come. The period of this first crystallization of social attitudes is the period covered by this book. The individuals discussed were chosen because they are representative of several different types of the Virginia gentleman, and because sufficient evidence survives to permit generalization about their qualities.

The discussion, in the pages that follow, of the qualities of the gentleman does not attempt a neat and compact definition. There is every reason why one should be skeptical of such definitions of elastic and variable social qualities—qualities which are not precisely the same for any two individuals. It is possible, however, to arrive at a sort of common denominator of what a gentleman must be. The word has acquired so many different connotations in modern usage that it is well to bear in mind that the writer is attempting a description of the conception of the gentleman of the seventeenth and early eighteenth centuries, not the gentleman of the nineteenth and twentieth centuries. Under the influence of sentimentalism, evangelical Christianity, and theories of political equality, fundamental changes took place, in the nineteenth century, in the popular conception of the qualities of the gentleman. It is difficult for us in the twentieth century to divest ourselves of notions of the gentleman that have been inherited from the previous century.

In the interest of clarity and readability, all contemporary quotations have been normalized in spelling and punctuation, in accordance with current practice. The preservation of the peculiarities of the whimsical orthography of earlier generations is a doubtful virtue in an exposition of this sort.

To the staff of the Huntington Library I am indebted for unfailing courtesy and help in the preparation of this volume. From Miss Mary Green, Mrs. Clara Buck, Miss Marjorie Shepard, Miss Edith L. Klotz, and Mrs. Marion Tinling, I received assistance with innumerable troublesome details. The skill and special knowledge of the reference librarian, Miss Mary Isabel Fry, made possible the identification of scores of almost unintelligible book titles in Virginia inventories.

From my colleagues on the research staff of the Huntington Library I have received much valuable advice and criticism. Professor Godfrey Davies, Mr. Merrill H. Crissey, Professor Edwin F. Gay, Professor Robert G. Cleland, and the Director, Dr. Max Farrand, have all been unsparing of their time. From scholars in other institutions I have received further aid and suggestions, and I am especially grateful to Professors Allan Nevins and John A. Krout of Columbia University, Professor Thomas J. Wertenbaker of Princeton, Professor Howard M. Jones of Harvard, and Professor Avery Craven of the University of Chicago. The shrewd criticism of Mr. James A. Hawken has been exceedingly helpful. To my wife I am indebted for critical opinions that never spared the writer's vanity.

L. B. W.

The Huntington Library
San Marino, California
October 27, 1939

CHAPTER I

ENGLISH PATTERNS FOR VIRGINIA PLANTERS

VIRGINIA has never hid her light under a bushel, nor let others forget the contributions of her sons to the development of the social, political, and intellectual life of the nation. And Virginia's pride in her past is well justified. Particularly in statecraft, in the early periods of our history, Virginia was surpassed by no other region in the number of leaders possessed of good breeding, intelligence, and wisdom. Even yet the tradition of a cultured and intelligent leadership has not completely disappeared from the political life of that commonwealth, for the tradition is fortunately tenacious, and ancient as such things go in America. Virginia, moreover, in the seventeenth and early eighteenth centuries developed a way of life and a certain aristocratic outlook which, if not always acceptable to other localities, nevertheless profoundly influenced the course of American history. An inquiry into the background and qualities of the founders of this aristocratic society, with particular emphasis upon evidences of their intellectual interest, is my present purpose.

Despite Virginia's contribution to political thought and political leadership, nineteenth-century historians, particularly New Englanders, often taunted her with the barrenness of her intellectual achievements in the seventeenth and early eighteenth centuries, or damned her with faint praise in statements that are accurate so far as they go but do not tell the whole story. For example, Moses Coit Tyler politely, but with a shade of contempt for the mental qualities of Virginians, describes the colony's dominant social class as composed of "country-gentlemen, loud-lunged and jolly fox-hunters, militia heroes, men of boundless domestic heartiness and social grace, astute and imperious politicians, fiery orators, and by and by, here and there, some men of elegant literary culture, mostly acquired abroad; here and there, perhaps after a while, a few amateur literary men; but no literary class, and almost no literature."[1]

Barren indeed is Virginia, in the early period, of notable monuments of literature, and of formal documents recording the thoughts of her people. But to imply that the men who ruled the destiny of the colony were almost wholly indifferent to intellectual matters, or devoid of an interest in literature, is to miss a true understanding of the society they were founding. Their ambition was to reproduce in the wilderness of Virginia the county life of England, not the atmosphere of the literary clubs of London. Moreover, although to them religion was a very important matter, it was not the chief end of life, and they were not driven to search their souls and pour out in crabbed prose confessions of their spiritual state, or to wage controversial war with those who differed from them, as were the more introspective and industrious penmen of New England. If seventeenth-century Virginians wrote little, it is not altogether proof of intellectual atrophy. Their ways were not the ways of New England, nor, let it be repeated, of literary London. They were trying to be country gentlemen in the English manner, and country gentlemen, for better or worse, they became.

The tight little aristocracy that developed in Virginia in the later years of the seventeenth century quickly gained a power and influence far in excess of the numerical importance of its members, who were vastly outnumbered by the yeoman class.[2] Planter-aristocrats ruled Virginia as by prescriptive right, and from the ranks of their descendants came statesmen who helped weld thirteen rebellious colonies into a nation. The mental

[1] Moses Coit Tyler, *A History of American Literature during the Colonial Period, 1607-1765* (New York, 1909), p. 92.

[2] See Thomas J. Wertenbaker, *Patrician and Plebeian in Virginia* (Charlottesville, Va., 1910), *passim.*

qualities of Virginia's Revolutionary leaders depended upon something more than the mere demand of a great emergency. Back of them lay a tradition of training for leadership—the tradition of the country gentleman who had learned to assume as his natural obligation certain political and social responsibilities. Because of the later importance of this aristocratic class and the influence of its ideals, some inquiries into its background and the qualities of its founders are needed.

Such inquiries, it is needless to say, necessarily must be of an archaeological nature. The tradition in question has perished in the tide of modern progress, and has been swept away by the sea of democracy. If an occasional voice has sounded an elegiac note over the end of gentility, few have heard and none has heeded. Two or three years ago Mr. Henry Dwight Sedgwick, in a sad, ironic little book, reviewed the life and death of the gentleman and concluded that the genus was extinct. A few years earlier a South Carolina newspaper editor wrote a book to express his own bitter regret over his state's "surrender to democracy" and consequent descent into mediocrity.[3] In general, however, we have shed few tears over the passing of such aristocratic ideals of gentility as we had developed. They were incompatible with the necessities of specialization, the scientific outlook, the creed of commercial success, and humanitarian notions of the brotherhood of man. Nevertheless, the ancient history of aristocratic development in America has a certain amount of archaic interest, as it has a greater significance than is likely to be remembered in this day of scorn for old and unproletarian traditions.

The contemplation of the origins of the characteristics and qualities of an aristocracy that once exerted a great influence in the formation of a new nation is perhaps of more importance than the question of the ancestral derivation of Virginians.

[3] Henry Dwight Sedgwick, *In Praise of Gentlemen* (Boston, 1935); W. W. Ball, *The State That Forgot: South Carolina's Surrender to Democracy* (Indianapolis, 1932).

Buckets of ink have already been employed in the latter cause. Many books and a still greater number of earnest essays have been written by loyal Virginians in a pious effort to make manifest their descent from noble or aristocratic English houses. Occasionally, having fallen short of credible fact, these efforts have prompted satirical comment from unsympathetic readers who find it hard to believe that so many descendants of Edward III—and even of William the Conqueror—should have found their way to a single colony in the New World. One historian, callously surveying the lists of emigrants in the seventeenth and eighteenth centuries, sardonically suggests that the archives of Newgate Prison and the Old Bailey might prove a more fruitful source of genealogical information than the records of the peerage.[4] The truth, however, is in neither extreme. No one well informed in colonial history is so naïve as to maintain that Virginia was won from the forest and the Indian by aristocratic settlers in silken doublets. Nor can the view be substantiated that jailbirds and the scum of English port towns played any important part in the colonial settlement. As was the case in most of the other colonies, the majority of the Virginia settlers were hard-working folk bent upon bettering their economic lot. Though Virginia probably attracted more emigrants of gentle birth than any of the other North American colonies, unimpeachable proof of important social connections in England cannot be found for most of the so-called First Families.[5] The significant fact is not the social position of their ancestors, but what they became in a world of their own making.[6]

The pattern of life which the ruling class of Virginia planters sought to follow was an ancient heritage dependent upon the

[4] Marcus W. Jernegan, *Laboring and Dependent Classes in Colonial America, 1607-1783* (Chicago, 1931), p. 49.

[5] For facts and arguments on the question of the origins of the Virginia aristocracy, see Philip Alexander Bruce, *Social Life of Virginia in the Seventeenth Century* (2d ed., Lynchburg, 1927); Thomas J. Wertenbaker, *The Planters of Colonial Virginia* (Princeton, 1922), and *Patrician and Plebeian in Virginia, passim.*

[6] For a discussion of the rise of the Virginia aristocracy, see Chapter II, *infra.*

possession of land, with sufficient income to maintain one's position with dignity and honor. During the Renaissance the state of the gentleman was outlined and his code prescribed according to fairly definite standards. The seventeenth century inherited most of the Renaissance conceptions of gentility, subject to such modifications as gradual change had brought about. It was this inherited pattern of behavior as accepted by seventeenth-century English gentlemen that profoundly influenced the upper planter class in Virginia.

The precise definition of a gentleman—even a gentleman of the sixteenth, seventeenth, or eighteenth century, when the term had less vagueness than it has with us—is difficult, for there are no immutable laws to determine membership in that caste, no flaunting marks of undeniable identity, like the tail feathers of the lyrebird, which immediately set it apart from other fowl. Certain qualities which the gentleman in 1540 regarded as essential in all who claimed social brotherhood with him were less important to the gentleman of 1640. And his grandson in 1740 had still different standards. Moreover, even in the same generation, wide differences in quality were discernible. Two men unquestionably accepted as gentlemen would vary in manners, and even in morals. Nevertheless, a few fundamental requirements were recognized, and, even if one generation placed greater emphasis upon a certain quality than the next generation might see fit to accord it, there gradually grew up a sort of code of what made a gentleman, though, like the British Constitution, it was unwritten, subject to much debate, and withal flexible enough to change with new conditions.[7]

[7] A mine of information upon this subject is to be found in an unpublished dissertation by Professor Virgil B. Heltzel, "Chesterfield and the Tradition of the Gentleman" (University of Chicago, 1925). I am indebted to Professor Heltzel for permission to read and use his work.

Valuable published works on this theme are: Ruth Kelso, *The Doctrine of the English Gentleman in the Sixteenth Century* ("University of Illinois Studies in Language and Literature," XIV [1929]); John E. Mason, *Gentlefolk in the Making* (Philadelphia, 1935); and William H. Woodward, *Studies in Education during the*

The very basis of the gentleman's status was the recognition of an inherent inequality in mankind. Some men were set apart to lead and to rule as a natural and inherited right, while others were foreordained to labor in humbler stations. The upper class, the gentry, had certain rights and privileges, and in return they had particular responsibilities for their inferiors and owed definite obligations to society as a whole. The two classes were complementary to each other. The gentry ruled, not as dictators and tyrants, merely for their personal glory or aggrandizement, but as the wiser and better-trained element in a harmonious society. The lower classes, in their turn, contributed to the well-being of the whole by conscientious attention to their trades and vocations. When each class remembered its own obligations and duties and acknowledged the position of the other, then the body politic was healthy—as Shakespeare and many another writer before and after him were careful to point out. The recognition of this sort of class distinction was the first essential in determining what a recent writer has called the Guild of Gentlemen.[8]

The gentry, in theory, were born to their privileges and responsibilities. There is an often-repeated story that the old nurse of James I besought the King to make her son a gentleman. "A gentleman, I could never make him, though I could make him a lord," was the reply of her royal master. Yet such was the flexibility of the social organization in England, that the ranks of the gentry were being constantly recruited from the families of wealthy merchants, and even, in rare cases, from the prosperous yeomanry. The process of evolution was gradual, it is true. A gentleman was not made by the sudden acquisition of wealth and the assumption of aristocratic manners. A tadpole does not become at once a frog, though he may be placed in a

---

Age of the Renaissance (Cambridge, 1924). A recent essay on the general subject is Esmé Wingfield-Stratford's *The Making of a Gentleman* (London, 1938).

[8] Sedgwick, *op. cit., passim.*

perfect frog pond with the most inviting of lily pads. In time, if the resident frogs do not devour him, he evolves into a little frog, and from that state into a bigger frog, until at last he can sit on the cool bank and croak with the best of them. The evolution of the gentleman was somewhat similar, though slower. It usually took more than one generation. In the sixteenth and seventeenth centuries, many a wealthy merchant, having made his fortune in London or Bristol, gave up trade, bought a manor house from some indigent gentleman, acquired a pew in the parish church, and felt himself launched on the road to gentility. Indeed, he may have fancied himself a gentleman, but the older county families knew better. In the fulness of time, however, the tradesman's children grew up with the children of the older families in the neighborhood, and perhaps intermarried with them, and were accepted as gentlemen and gentlewomen. After a generation or two, only a few old ladies in the county who treasured their genealogical lore remembered to scoff discreetly at the origins of the newer families. Though it was generally conceded that gentlemen must be born and could not be made, a generation's remove from the countinghouse or shop might work a transformation. In a new land, such as Virginia, it was even easier of accomplishment than in an English county where social life followed more closely the conventional grooves.

If wealth did not make a gentleman, it was impossible in poverty long to hold a place amongst the gentry. Younger sons of the gentry therefore constantly passed into the ranks of tradesmen and the lower orders of society. For some of these, Virginia was a godsend, since, with a little money, they could acquire property and become landed proprietors as befitted their inherited station. Many a poor youth, who might have been apprenticed to a shopkeeper if a colonial life had not beckoned, was equipped by his family with sufficient capital to become somebody in the New World. Many a tradesman's son also found it easier to rise to gentility in Virginia than at home.

The most apparent characteristic denoting the gentleman was attention to manners. Grace and dignity of deportment at once distinguished a person of gentle breeding from the yokel. Manners, moreover, were not a veneer that could be laid on any foundation. The manners of the gentleman came from an inner consciousness of a position to uphold, a dignity to maintain, and an example to set. The first essential in the code of manners was courtesy—a courtesy that had become instinctive, that was not ostentatious, that was natural and unassuming. If, indeed, manners tended to crystallize into stiff formalities, the gentleman knew how to adapt himself to the formalism required of any situation. Through training, the natural instincts of the gentleman were sharpened and refined. Through training, he acquired grace of body, dignity of bearing, a polished speech—in short, all the conventions of behavior that made for decorum. These conventions might vary from generation to generation, but, whatever they were, the gentleman was expected to know them and be guided by them—guided, be it noted, and not fettered, for only the social climber need be a slave to the rules; your true gentleman knows when and how to disregard convention without transgressing good manners. Such was the general theory of manners that the country gentleman accepted. In details, the manners of the seventeenth-century squire were a far cry from those prescribed a hundred years later, or those acceptable in a similar society today.

On the surface, the morals denoting a gentleman were less distinctive than the manners, though there was a fairly consistent code of conduct to which gentlemen subscribed if they did not always adhere. Truth and honor were the basis of this code. The code, in theory, would not permit a gentleman to lie, be guilty of meanness, commit a theft, cheat at cards, betray a friend, or show cowardice. Such offenses were unpardonable.

But sins of the flesh might be forgiven. If he drank too deep and got himself fuddled, his friends thought none the worse of him. If he could not resist the temptation of illicit love, it was no more than had happened even to Solomon. But his sins must not be gross; he must not appear as the seducer of innocence; and he was required to provide for his illegitimate offspring. Even in his iniquities the gentleman was expected to remember the rules of decorum and the laws of justice.

The virtues of the gentleman owed more to Aristotle than to Christian writings, though, from the middle of the seventeenth century onward, the religious note grew stronger. Fortitude, temperance, prudence, and justice were the four cardinal qualities that Aristotle and succeeding classical writers laid down as fundamental to the gentleman. The Renaissance accepted these entire, and added liberality and courtesy. These six virtues were described by Sir Thomas Elyot in *The Book Named the Governor* as those requisite in all who would occupy positions of leadership in the state.[9] Out of justice, according to Elyot, grew an allied virtue, the sense of fidelity, which included loyalty. These virtues were the core of the gentleman's code in all periods. Piety was often commended in the conduct books, even assumed in some degree, for the gentleman must set an example of religious observance to lesser folk. The aim most frequently recommended was to seek Aristotle's golden mean between extremes—a goal which led to moderation in everything, including religion. Though the interpretations placed upon these abstract virtues varied somewhat from generation to generation, and from locality to locality, they remained a fairly constant ideal toward which the gentleman was expected to aspire, even if he did not reach the lofty heights of perfection which their attainment might imply.

The question of what constituted the honor of a gentleman —that quality which was the very mainspring of his actions—

[9] Kelso, *op. cit.*, pp. 75-76.

troubled all the writers of courtesy books, and their answers are vaguer than one might wish. An early-seventeenth-century work observes that "honor in his true definition is a certain reverence, which one man yieldeth to another extraordinarily, for his virtuous merit, and worthy desert, so that it should not be wealth, but virtue, which should make an honorable man."[10] Others leaned toward the notion that honor and reputation were equivalent. More than a century later, Chesterfield defined honor as reputation derived from distinguished virtue.[11] Though a gentleman might have trouble reducing his honor to a definition, he was always conscious of possessing it, careful not to lose it, and quick to defend it. The seventeenth- and eighteenth-century gentleman's concern for the preservation of his honor resulted in an increase in dueling, but the approval given this practice has been exaggerated in the popular imagination of later times. Indeed, there is a surprising amount of condemnation of the practice, from the time of King James onward. A gentleman was required to preserve and defend his honor, but was constantly warned by writers from Montaigne to Chesterfield that the duel was a futile way of achieving this desirable end.

The accomplishments believed proper for a gentleman were partly a result of his code of manners and morals; at least, they cannot be separated from them, for they exemplify the code in action. The art of pleasing—which from the sixteenth to the eighteenth century the gentleman was enjoined to study—was the key to the politer graces. Dancing, fencing, riding, ability in conversation—these were expected of all men who moved in the beau monde. Some ability in music was creditable, but not required; stringed instead of wind instruments were preferred, because the latter "puff out the face in vulgar fashion." In nothing must the gentleman appear too proficient. If he

[10] *The Rich Cabinet* (1616), quoted by Kelso, *op. cit.*, p. 97; see also pp. 98 ff.
[11] Heltzel, *op. cit.*, p. 44.

danced well, that was expected; if he could execute with extraordinary dexterity all the fancy steps in the manual, he proved himself too much the dancing master. The seeking after personal perfection, which from the time of the Renaissance had dominated the conception of the gentleman's training, had for its ideal the keeping of proportion in all things; hence, the gentleman was expected to remain an amateur in his accomplishments, lest the endeavor to become too expert in any particular field of knowledge or skill destroy the nice balance and symmetry so much praised by writers on aristocratic education.[12]

The sports of a gentleman were those in keeping with his dignity. Though he might fence with one of his own class, he might not wrestle with a country peasant, partly, it seems, because of the risk of being thrown—a thing most undignified. In all his sports, he must invariably remember that fair play distinguishes the gentleman from the uncouth clown. If he engaged in dangerous sports—which he did, despite the warnings of reformers—he must never betray a timid or a fearful nature. A display of courage and daring was expected in sports, as in all other encounters of life.

Hunting was naturally the most popular sport of country gentlemen, but was not always approved by writers of conduct books, and lacked many of the hard-and-fast conventions and much of the social glamor of the present-day hunt club. Indeed, writers from Sir Thomas More to Chesterfield objected to excessive indulgence in hunting, for a variety of reasons, but chiefly because it was a notable devourer of one's fortune and was conducive to cruelty. Francis Osborne in his *Advice to a Son* would exclude hunting altogether, as an illiberal sport, beneath the notice of a gentleman—a cause of undignified extremes of temperament.[13] Notwithstanding these opinions, hunting, with hounds, with hawks, and with guns, was greatly favored among

[12] Kelso, pp. 84-85.
[13] Heltzel, pp. 236-40.

English gentlemen. The keeping of a deer park was one of the rare privileges enjoyed by the gentry, and deer hunting, from time immemorial, had been regarded as one of the peculiar blessings of the well-born. The prestige of owning a deer park, no less than the love of hunting, was something to be richly valued. When city merchants dreamed of owning landed estates, one of the pleasures that loomed largest in their imaginations was the thought of being able to send fat bucks to friends and neighbors whom they wished to impress. Only gentlemen—and an occasional poacher—could make free with such a royal animal as a buck. Fox hunting, though not unknown, had not yet attained any great social importance in England, for foxes were still regarded as vermin to be caught by any means and knocked on the head as a pest. The rules for the protection of the fox, one should remember, are chiefly a nineteenth-century obsession.[14] Love of field sports carried over to Virginia, but the abundance of wild life and the freedom of the wilderness prevented any form of hunting from becoming a monopoly of the gentry.

The problem of the sort and amount of learning that a gentleman was expected to encompass is important, since upon that depends some of the qualities of mind and intellectual leadership which he displayed. From the sixteenth to the eighteenth centuries treatises on conduct, as well as observers of English life, complain of the ignorance of the gentry and exhort gentlemen to give more attention to learning. These complaints have been taken perhaps too literally as evidence of a widespread and sodden ignorance. Actually, many country gentlemen were not only well-read, but possessed of broad learning.

Learning, indeed, had long been recognized as a highroad to gentility. Many a simple man's son had risen to a position of authority and dignity in church or state by way of the uni-

[14] A serious study of the fox in England, and the changing attitude toward it, would provide a revealing and significant bit of social history.

versity. A well-beaten path to an improved social position was through the university, or through the Inns of Court to the profession of law, and ultimately—if fortune smiled—to a landed property in the country. A period of residence in one of the Inns of Court was particularly useful. There a youth could acquire some knowledge of polite behavior, as well as an acquaintance with law French and legal mysteries hidden therein. Learning undoubtedly made social climbing easier, if it did not always insure success.

The gentleman's learning, as conventionally prescribed, was expected to be extensive rather than deep. The doctrine of amateurism insisted that a gentleman should wear his learning lightly, that he should not smell of the lamp, that he should flee from the pedantry of the schoolmaster as from the plague. Yet he should know—at least well enough to quote in English, on occasion—the great authors of Greece and Rome. The belief that an educated person should be able to read the classic tongues, Greek and Latin, extended into the eighteenth century, though Daniel Defoe in *The Compleat English Gentleman*, written in 1729,[15] protested vigorously that it was not "worth any gentleman's while, as Oldham says, to go seven year to the grammar Bridewell (the school) and there beat Greek and Latin, as whores beat hemp."[16] But Defoe, be it remembered, was merely a tradesman, and therefore an outsider when writing about gentlemen. He insisted that a knowledge of the classic authors in translation was sufficient, but the very violence of his protest indicates a persistence of Greek and Latin grammar in traditional education. Some knowledge of other languages, particularly French, was desirable, though Englishmen were content to speak their foreign tongues as Englishmen and not

[15] Daniel Defoe, *The Compleat English Gentleman*, ed. Karl D. Bülbring (London, 1890). Written by Defoe about 1729, this work remained in manuscript until published by Bülbring.

[16] *Ibid.*, p. 210.

as natives. Perhaps it smacked too much of the specialist to learn French after the school of Paris instead of Stratford-at-Bow. But the backbone of the gentleman's academic training, of course, was the humanities. In some way, it was felt, an acquaintance with classic authors, either in translation or in the original tongues, would induce wisdom. To this end, the ancient historians and orators were particularly favored. By the last third of the seventeenth century, however, scientific discoveries and investigations attracted the interest of virtuosi, who hailed science as the *summum bonum*. Though, by 1729, Defoe was commending scientific study to gentlemen, many writers on education, in the late seventeenth and early eighteenth centuries, warned against too much preoccupation with the new subject. Even John Locke, who thought a certain amount of natural science valuable, expressed the fear that it would possess the mind, exclude humanistic thinking, and dwarf man's spiritual perceptions.[17] If writers like Locke could have looked further into the future, their warnings might have been more direful. The most recent writer to discuss the plight of the gentleman in modern civilization attributes to science and its "rejection of traditional values" one of the deathblows given the Guild of Gentlemen.[18]

Specific advice on study, with suggestions of books to be read, are frequently encountered in treatises on conduct. One of the best-known of such works, Henry Peacham's *Compleat Gentleman* (1622), a treatise long read on both sides of the Atlantic, devotes much space to counsel on the best means of cultivating the mind. Books are a necessary means to mental improvement, but they must be used, not merely possessed, Peacham points out. "Affect not as some do," he warns, "that bookish ambition to be stored with books and have well-furnished libraries, yet keep their heads empty of knowledge; to desire to have many

[17] Heltzel, pp. 104, 164-65.
[18] Sedgwick, pp. 149-52.

books, and never to use them, is like a child that will have a candle burning by him all the while he is sleeping."[19]

Wide reading in the classic authors, especially the historians, is recommended by Peacham. Among the authors favored by him are Tacitus, "the prince of historians," Livy, Quintus Curtius, and others of like quality. Of Plutarch, he observes: "For morality and rules of well living, delivered with such sententious gravity, weight of reason, so sweetened with lively and apt similitudes, entertain Plutarch."[20] Poetry he commends, praising Virgil as the greatest of the Roman poets. "To sweeten your severer studies," he advises, "by this time vouchsafe poetry your respect, which howsoever censured and seemeth fallen from the highest stage of honor to the lowest stair of disgrace, let not your judgment be infected with that pestilent air of the common breath, to be an infidel."[21]

Although Peacham awards to history first place among the studies recommended to gentlemen, he urges that attention be given to cosmography, to mathematics (particularly geometry), surveying, music, drawing and painting, heraldry, and related subjects. Every gentleman, Peacham thinks, should be able to blazon his own coat of arms and understand the devices. Many books are named by title as suitable for the attainment of the knowledge required, and, in the chapters on drawing and on heraldry, the author provides detailed technical information. Like earlier Renaissance treatises, Peacham's book also has a chapter of counsel on physical training and the proper development of the body. His *Compleat Gentleman* sums up the ideal of education that developed in the sixteenth century and persisted for more than a hundred years.

Somewhat similar, though more tinged with bourgeois notions, was the educational advice in Richard Brathwaite's *The English Gentleman* (1630). Like Peacham, he emphasizes the

[19] Henry Peacham, *The Compleat Gentleman* (1622), p. 54.
[20] *Ibid.*, p. 52. [21] *Ibid.*, p. 78.

value of historical reading, and finds a very practical reason to commend it: "For in this treasury or storehouse of history you shall find better means than all the *Helps to Discourse* which our weak pamphleteers can publish to enable you to discourse in all companies." History he calls "the sweetest recreation of the mind," and thinks it better to read history than "to entertain time in nothing but the cry of dogs or flight of hawks." [22]

Roughly a century after the treatises of Peacham and Brathwaite, Defoe's *Compleat English Gentleman* took for its thesis the need of a sound education for the country gentleman who expected to assume his proper place in the community. Like his predecessors, he emphasized the importance of a well-stocked library, which the owner should have the wit to utilize, and he stressed the value of history, geography, philosophy, and the classics in translation. If he broke with some of the traditional authorities in refuting the idea that a knowledge of the Greek and Latin languages was necessary, he did not underestimate the good to be found in the translated works of ancient authors. And his commendation of the study of the natural sciences showed the influence of the new scientific movement. Gentlemen who failed in their youths to gain the proper background of learning might remedy the defect by self-instruction, Defoe insists. This procedure, it is clear, was followed by some of the leaders who established themselves as gentlemen in the New World.

If critics from Sir Thomas Elyot to Daniel Defoe condemn ignorance in the country gentleman,[23] their criticism indicates recognition of the obligation of the gentry to fit themselves for intellectual as well as social leadership. In Defoe's treatise, a lively dialogue between an ignorant squire and his better-educated neighbor shows the former's chagrin over the disgrace of being an empty-head. The implication is that unlearned

[22] Richard Brathwaite, *The English Gentleman* (1630), p. 220.
[23] Woodward, *op. cit.*, p. 302.

squires were not altogether content with their state. Though that diligent journalist, Defoe, the sometime hosier of Cornhill, may not have had a great intimacy with the genteel tradition, he made many shrewd observations on the social conditions of his day.

So much for the theory of what a gentleman ought to be, how he ought to act, and what he ought to know. Such, in general, were the qualities prescribed by theorists from the sixteenth to the eighteenth century. More important, perhaps, is the way in which the theory of gentility made itself manifest in practice, or, in other words, what manner of men were the English country squires, the models imitated in Virginia.

Macaulay's description of the gentry, in his famous chapter on the "State of England in 1685," would lead one to believe that the typical squire was an ignorant Tory, with scarcely "learning enough to sign his name to a mittimus," his chief pleasures "commonly derived from field sports and from an unrefined sensuality"—a boor living in dirty unconcern of the barnyard filth piled outside his window, a lout eating swinishly and guzzling himself into a daily drunken stupor.[24] In Macaulay's picture, the country gentleman can hardly be distinguished in language, bearing, or accomplishments from the veriest yokel on his land. "Few knights of the shire had libraries so good as may now perpetually be found in a servants' hall, or in the back parlor of a small shopkeeper," Macaulay asserts. "An esquire passed among his neighbors for a great scholar if *Hudibras* and *Baker's Chronicle*, *Tarlton's Jests*, and the *Seven Champions of Christendom* lay in his hall window among the fishing rods and fowling pieces."[25] Having rarely been out of his county and knowing nothing of the world, Macaulay's squire was full of hates and prejudices born of provincial ignorance. If this picture even approaches the truth, surely all the treatises on aristocratic

[24] Thomas Babington Macaulay, *The History of England* (London, 1860), I, 331 ff.

[25] *Ibid.*, p. 408.

behavior must have been written by windy theorists inspired only by wishful thinking.

But here, as elsewhere, Macaulay was swept away by the brilliance of his rhetoric, and, as Sir Charles Firth has pointed out, his picture is no more than a caricature. A few sentences from Firth's appraisal of Macaulay's description will help to correct a view that has too long colored our thinking about the seventeenth-century gentry:

> At the period of which he [Macaulay] wrote, the class as a whole was much larger than it is now; the land was divided amongst more owners, and large properties were fewer. Gregory King estimated that the landed gentry consisted of about 16,000 families, and the class included rich knights and baronets, whose ancestors for generations had represented the county, and the 'little gentlemen of two hundred a year' that a dramatist laughs at. The level of culture varied as greatly as the average amount of wealth. The smaller gentry were naturally less cultivated than those who could afford to spend liberally on the education of their children and to travel. In the remoter parts of the country the gentry were less educated and less civilized than those who lived nearer to the capital. In the picture which Macaulay draws of the class as a whole these shades of difference are suppressed; he generalizes too much from the lower half of the class and makes no adequate allowance for the large number of educated and intelligent men it contained.[26]

If many lords of manors from among the 16,000 families were boors of the sort described by Macaulay, others were intelligent leaders, educated in the universities, living lives of dignity and usefulness. The administration of local government was in their hands, and many of them were their people's spokesmen in Parliament. Provincial they may have been, but they were not incapable of shrewd political and social leadership. Nor were gentlemen even of modest means strangers to the

[26] Sir Charles Firth, "Macaulay's Third Chapter," *History*, XVII (1932-33), 214; repr. in Firth, *A Commentary on Macaulay's History of England* (London, 1938), p. 132.

amenities of a cultured life.[27] Their houses, if not fine or richly decorated, were usually furnished in a style befitting their prestige; there they dispensed hospitality with a liberality that sometimes went ill with their purses. Furthermore, many references in letters, and lists of books in wills and inventories, show that country squires were not unconcerned about the state of their minds. They wrote urgently for books and made thoughtful provision for their bestowal after death.[28] If some country gentlemen had only a few tattered old volumes lying among their fishing rods and fowling pieces, others had carefully-selected libraries from which less fortunate neighbors might borrow books. The condition of the country gentleman, in short, was such that it excited the envy of those who had not been born to that station. If the gentry as a whole had lived the dully sodden lives pictured by Macaulay, it is singular indeed that well-to-do merchants and prosperous tradesmen should have looked forward to the day when they might emulate the state of the gentry.

Fortunately, we do not have to deduce the picture of the country gentleman by logic, or to depend upon sheer conjecture. Letters, diaries, journals, and family records provide abundant evidence of the kind of life he led. Fine examples of the substantial county families who made no pretensions to unusual grandeur, yet were the backbone of English aristocracy, were the Verneys in Buckinghamshire, the Oxindens in Kent, and the Holleses in Nottinghamshire, for all of whom there are voluminous records easily available. These families, it is true,

[27] See Mary Coate, *Cornwall in the Great Civil War and Interregnum, 1642-1660: A Social and Political Study* (Oxford, 1933), pp. 3-9; Alfred C. Wood, *Nottinghamshire in the Civil War* (Oxford, 1937), pp. 8-9.

[28] In the Stowe MSS, Accounts, in the Huntington Library is an interesting list of books ordered between 1660 and 1695 by Sir Richard Temple. Although Temple was an unbookish person, as were most of his family, this list shows fairly frequent orders for useful and current publications. I am indebted to Professor Edwin F. Gay for calling my attention to this list. Contemporary letters of families like the Verneys and Oxindens show fairly frequent requests for books.

represent the upper stratum of the country gentry, but their wealth was not great; and, though at times they served their king at court, they were county people rather than courtiers.

Though it would not be difficult to gather, among the country squires of the seventeenth and eighteenth centuries, a gallery of rogues and ignorant bumpkins to match against the more cultivated country gentry, rascals and ignoramuses were not the models that Virginia planters remembered with envy and sought to emulate. If some planters did reproduce the ignorance and debauchery of the boors among the English gentry, it was the result of frailty and predisposition rather than conscious imitation. The qualities of men like the Verneys, the Oxindens, and the Holleses were the characteristics that intelligent members of the Virginia ruling class wished their children to possess; hence it may be instructive to see what manner of men were the better class of English gentry during the formative period of Virginia's growth.[29]

Of the seventeenth-century Verneys, Sir Edmund and his two sons, Edmund and Ralph (both of whom were also knighted), led lives that might be considered symbolic of similar families much later in Virginia. The father and his two sons took part in the stirring events of the Puritan Revolution: Sir Edmund and his namesake on the side of the King; Ralph on the side of Parliament. The two Edmunds lost their lives in battle—the father at Edgehill and the son at the siege of Drogheda. Ralph lived through the Puritan Revolution and the

[29] See, for example: Frances Parthenope Verney, *Memoirs of the Verney Family during the Civil War* (4 vols., London, 1892-99); *Letters and Papers of the Verney Family down to the End of the Year 1639*, ed. John Bruce (Camden Society, LVI [1853]); *The Oxinden Letters, 1607-1642*, ed. Dorothy Gardiner (London, 1933); *The Oxinden and Peyton Letters, 1642-1670*, ed. Dorothy Gardiner (London, 1937); *Memorials of the Holles Family, 1493-1656*, by Gervase Holles, ed. Alfred C. Wood (Camden Society, 3d Ser., LV [1937]). For information about another group of English country gentlemen, not mentioned in the discussion in this chapter, see Sir George Reresby Sitwell, *The Hurts of Haldworth and Their Descendants at Savile Hall, the Ickles, and Hesley Hall* (Oxford, 1930), especially pp. i-li.

Restoration. If the family was politically divided, the father and these two sons were nevertheless moderates, eager to preserve their traditional rights and liberties, loyal to ideals they had inherited.

Sir Edmund the elder, knight marshal and royal standard-bearer, was a fine gentleman who never forgot his county connections even though his duties took him to court or to foreign countries, as when he traveled as attendant to Prince Charles on the unfortunate marriage expedition to Spain. Educated at Oxford, he had a "mind accomplished in all active, useful, and manly knowledge." Sanguine in financial matters, he lent his king money and received in payment two portraits by Van Dyck—one of himself and one of his royal master. His contemporaries regarded him as "a generous friend and liberal landlord. He was 'a ready and complete man for the pleasures of ladies,' and his family was said by the king to be 'the model he would propose to gentlemen.' "[30] Though he had no heart in the quarrel with Parliament, he had served the King too long to be disloyal, and he died defending the royal standard at Edgehill, when he might have saved his life by surrendering this symbol of loyalty.

Sir Edmund the younger was a true son of his father. Although he ran into debt at Oxford and left without a degree, he paid off his obligations with the first money he received after serving with the King's army on the Scotch border in 1639. A little later, while a member of Sir Thomas Culpeper's company in Flanders, he utilized his time in winter quarters at Utrecht to study Latin, French, and history, and thus repair the gaps in his learning. Like his father, he gave his life in a cause for which he had no enthusiasm, because his code of loyalty demanded it.

But curiously it is Sir Ralph Verney, the anti-royalist member of the family, who best illustrates the qualities of the wise

[30] *Dictionary of National Biography, sub* Sir Edmund Verney.

and cultured country gentleman, so unlike the squires described by Macaulay. If Sir Ralph's conscience made him espouse the cause of Parliament at the beginning of the struggle with the King, he had little more enthusiasm for his side than his father and brother had for theirs. He had opposed Laud and the bishops, but, when the parliamentary faction tried to force him to subscribe to the Solemn League and Covenant, he chose rather to go into exile.

From Sir Ralph's letters, written at home and abroad, we get illuminating flashes that reveal the ideals and conduct of the country squire. They show us a man who never forgot the classical training he received at Magdalen College, Oxford—a man who retained an interest in books and things of the mind until his dying day in 1696. They also show us a gentleman exceedingly careful of decorum, eager to maintain the dignity and position of his family, always conscious of his own obligations to society. In exile in France during the Puritan Revolution, he was constantly writing home for books, chiefly theological and political works, including such things as Hooker's *Of the Laws of Ecclesiastical Polity* and Milton's *Eikonoklastes*.[31] So punctilious was he of decorum in dress that when he went into mourning he wore a black nightshirt and black nightcap, and he owned a black-draped mourning bed which circulated in the family as it was needed.[32] Even amidst the hardships of exile, he strove to dress in the fashion he had known in England. In one letter he writes for a new wig, inclosing a specimen lock of hair and ordering that the wig "be well curled in great rings and not frizzled," and that it be made "handsomely and fashionably, and with two locks and let them be tied with black ribbon."[33]

Fearful lest his sons should fail to receive a training befitting their station during the troublous times of the Interregnum, Sir Ralph constantly sends them advice. To his son Edmund he

[31] F. P. Verney, *Memoirs,* II, 221-22. [32] *Ibid.,* III, 38. [33] *Ibid.,* II, 234.

sends a sharp reproof for a slovenly letter, reminding him that "your very French phrase might teach you to write better sense, and English too."[34] Edmund apparently was something of a trial to his father, for a little later Sir Ralph in exasperation comments that "Mun confesseth to me he hath scarce looked at a book since his coming from Utrecht; if he hath neglected his exercises as much as I believe, he may come home and keep sheep, for he will be fit for little else."[35] Although Edmund never became the scholar his father desired, he developed into an intelligent country squire, particular about his dress and accouterments. "He plays the lute and guitar," says an account of him, "and has generally a book on hand: the story of the siege of Buda, the last French treatise on the art of war, Mr. Dryden's verses, sermons, political squibs and pamphlets, besides the news letters which come down by the carrier. On his study table there is a 'very little brass mathematical instrument about the length of a pen to draw lines with ink, and also an ebony ruler.' He writes excellent letters, keeps copies of them, and dockets those he receives."[36] Sir Ralph's admonitions had evidently made a good letter writer of his son, and if he fell short of great learning he at least was not devoid of intellectual interests.

During his exile, Sir Ralph demonstrated the liberality that was expected of a gentleman, by giving generously to those less fortunate than himself, particularly to distressed Anglican ministers. On his return to his manor house at Claydon in Buckinghamshire, he once more became the openhanded landlord his tenants had known before the days of trouble. Claydon again became a center where the amenities of the gentle life were observed. The manor house was comfortably furnished; the library was adequate; and to the picture gallery containing the likenesses of a long line of Verneys was added the portrait of

[34] *Ibid.*, III, 232-33. Letters dated June 11, 1655.
[35] *Ibid.*, pp. 241-42.
[36] *Ibid.*, IV, 166-67.

Sir Ralph, painted by Cornelius Jannsen. At Claydon there was music and laughter and good manners, but nothing of the brutality that Macaulay attributes to country squires—not even the brutality of field sports, for, though Sir Ralph was a skilled rider, he never liked hunting. In useful and intelligent occupations, the squire of Claydon lived out his long life—an example to his contemporaries for honesty and integrity. Though he accepted a baronetcy from Charles II, he remained true to his political principles, and was one of the few Whigs in the Parliament of 1680, thus demonstrating that independence which has always been one of the distinguishing qualities of the country gentry.

The Verneys, like many another seventeenth-century family, from time to time looked toward Virginia as a land where their pattern of life might be duplicated. Indeed, in 1635, when Tom Verney, a younger brother of Sir Ralph, found himself in trouble over a love affair, his family equipped him with supplies and servants and shipped him to Virginia to establish the Verney name on the James River.[37] But Tom, ever an unsteady soul, before a year was out had abandoned his supplies and was back in London. Although several years later he again planned to become a colonist—this time in the West Indies—and armed himself with Jeremy Taylor's *Holy Living and Holy Dying*, Lewis Bayly's *Practice of Piety*, the "Turkish History," and some Westphalian hams, Tom Verney was not the sort to establish the family name in America.[38] Ne'er-do-well that he was, however, it is worth noting that he also had an interest in books—so great an interest, indeed, that, when preparing to go to sea in 1654, he wrote Sir Ralph a begging letter requesting particularly a copy of Raleigh's *History of the World*, "it being a book I extremely fancy."[39] Not even the black sheep among the Verneys was so mutton-headed—if one

[37] *Letters and Papers of the Verney Family*, pp. 160-64.

[38] F. P. Verney, *Memoirs*, III, 139.

[39] *Ibid.*, p. 163.

may strain that metaphor—as the seventeenth-century country gentleman too often has been made out to be. Nor do we have to believe that the Verneys were extraordinary among their kind for manners, culture, and learning.

The seventeenth-century Oxindens of East Kent were representative of the fairly prosperous county families. Their letters indicate much the same pattern of life as that described in the Verney papers. And, it might be added, this pattern of life closely resembles that established in Virginia.

The country gentleman of the seventeenth century followed a traditional routine in the education and disposition of his family—a routine illustrated by the Oxindens and imitated, with necessary modifications, by the Virginia gentry. This traditional practice prescribed, observes the editor of the Oxinden letters,[40] "university training for his eldest son, beginning perhaps at fourteen, followed often by a call to the Bar. For one other son, the second, if gifted enough with brains, Oxford or Cambridge likewise, ordination to the Church's ministry, and to crown all, a family preferment; for any other sons, a London apprenticeship, leading to a merchant's or shopkeeper's career." The sons of Richard Oxinden of Barham are examples of the pattern. Henry attended, for a time, Corpus Christi, Oxford, where he received a background of learning before becoming head of the family on his father's death in 1629. He was acquainted with the poets to a certain degree, wrote a little not-very-good poetry himself (in both Latin and English), and quoted in his letters Ovid, Warner's *Albion's England*, John Donne, and a few other writers, both ancient and modern. James went to St. John's, Cambridge, though Henry engaged in some wirepulling in an effort to procure him a fellowship at his own college of Corpus Christi. After receiving a degree at Cambridge, James spent a term or two at Oxford pursuing theological studies, and at length got a living in Kent. Richard,

[40] *The Oxinden Letters, 1607-1642*, p. xxiv.

the third brother, was apprenticed to a cloth merchant in Fish Street, London, but later went off to join his uncle, Colonel Proud, as a soldier in Gelderland. The youngest brother, Adam, was also apprenticed to a London merchant, and a sister, Katherine, married Thomas Barrow, a mercer in Cheapside. The Oxindens thus demonstrate a social characteristic of the English gentry that prevented the growth of a rigid caste system: the constant absorption of younger sons and daughters in the ranks of trade. If proud old country squires occasionally spoke scornfully of tradesmen and sometimes resented their daughters' marrying shopkeepers or even prosperous merchants, their scorn overlooked younger brothers apprenticed in London. Colonial Virginia gentlemen, as we shall see, had even less prejudice against trade. Like the Oxindens, most wealthy Virginia families were glad to have sons engaged in mercantile pursuits—sons who often lived in London and did business as Virginia merchants.

If the life led by Henry Oxinden at Barham was somewhat provincial, in general it was pleasant, gracious, dignified, and useful. His correspondence with neighbors and friends proves him a hearty man, devoted to field sports, but not unmindful of intellectual matters, or negligent of his duty to the community. In a letter to his cousin Henry Oxinden of Deane, he requests two books concerning the Sabbath, "for I desire to read them before they be as much out of request as the Sabbath itself now is." And he adds a postscript: "I would have certified you that my beagles did run down a hare on Saturday, but that I would not have you think it any news for them to do so." [41] In another letter he requests a copy of the new edition of *Leicester's Commonwealth*, "to see how it differs from ours." [42] Throughout his correspondence there are references to

[41] *Ibid.*, p. 116. Letter dated Jan. 8, 1636. It might be mentioned that, in his old age, Henry Oxinden of Barham took holy orders and in 1663 received the living of Radnage in Buckinghamshire—a step dictated by his financial necessities at that time.

[42] *Ibid.*, p. 267. Letter dated Dec. 29, 1641.

books ordered from London; and occasional literary allusions indicate a gentlemanly interest in polite literature as well as in the controversies that got into print. But Henry Oxinden doubtless shared the aversion to pedantry expressed in a letter sent him by his neighbor, Sir Thomas Peyton, who asserts: "I read sometimes to satisfy my own private quaeres and ignorance, not to confound learned men and their books and friends with words newborn."[43] In books, as in other things, a gentleman was not expected to have the knowledge of a specialist. Though the squire of Barham spent most of his time on his estate, he was conscious of the demands of fashion—particularly so when he began to pay court to his ward, Katherine Culling, and we find him writing urgently for a "high black fashionable hat," a gold and silver hatband "if it so be in the fashion," a dozen and a half gold and silver buttons for a short coat "such as you think will be suitable to the lace you bought to my scarlet suit," and "one of the best new fashion plain bands and cuffs you can get."[44] No spendthrift is he, however, for he displays a commendable thrift by fixing a limit to the prices to be paid. Practical shrewdness and a zeal to see other members of his family properly settled are frequently shown in his letters, as in a note to his dull brother James (who had just taken orders), advising him to get a great deal of help at Oxford on a sermon he had been invited to preach at the marriage of a Kentish cousin, to buy himself a new black suit, and to announce loudly that the sermon had been hurriedly prepared so that it would seem as good as circumstances would permit, in order that he might make a favorable impression and obtain a living in the community.[45] But in all his letters Henry Oxinden shows himself a lover of justice, cognizant of his own obligations of leadership in the community, as may be seen in a letter protesting with great rationalism and good sense the accusations of witchcraft brought against a

[43] *Ibid.*, p. 162. Letter dated Apr. 20, 1640.
[44] *Ibid.*, p. 251. Letter written in 1641.
[45] *Ibid.*, pp. 168-70. Letter written in 1640.

certain Goodwife Gilnot.[46] In Henry Oxinden of Barham we have another country gentleman who might have been a model for any Virginia planter to emulate. And, as his correspondence effectively shows, there were numerous others like him. Here was no ignorant boor, but a civilized if provincial aristocrat, conscious of his own dignity and position.

Another country gentleman, representative of his class, was Gervase Holles of Grimsby in Lincolnshire, who wrote out the *Memorials of the Holles Family, 1493-1656*,[47] a document that provides some of our clearest pictures of the lives and habits of county people, for Holles was unselfconscious, and described in his simple, unadorned narrative the frailties as well as the virtues of his ancestors and their family connections in Nottinghamshire and Lincolnshire.

Born in 1607, Gervase Holles as a youth was taken into the household of his more opulent cousin, John Holles, later the first Earl of Clare, who supervised his bringing up, even taking the trouble "to read logic and philosophy to me himself."[48] Subsequently he entered the Middle Temple and was eventually called to the bar. From that time onward, Holles played the role expected of an influential country squire. In 1638 he settled at Newark-on-Trent and three years later became a justice of the peace in Nottinghamshire. A loyalist member of Parliament in 1641, he was suspended for a speech displeasing to the Parliamentarians. During the Civil Wars, he fought under the Earl of Newcastle, and went into exile from 1651 to 1660. After the Restoration, he became Master of Requests and represented Grimsby in Parliament. At various times he was also mayor of Grimsby. The sense of public service characteristic of the country gentleman made Holles accept such duties even when they proved burdensome.

[46] *Ibid.*, pp. 220-23. Letter dated Sept. 23, 1641.

[47] *Memorials of the Holles Family* has been recently edited by Alfred C. Wood; see n. 29, *supra.*

[48] *Ibid.*, p. 228.

From Holles' chronicle of his family, we get many glimpses of the quality of the country gentry as interpreted through seventeenth-century eyes. For example, a brief description of his father, Frescheville Holles, who died in 1630, throws light on both manners and morals.

> He was the true heir of his grandfather's hospitable disposition. . . . He would never set down to meals unless he had some of his friends or neighbors with him, and in case they came not he would send for them. Accordingly he was charitable to the poor and very prompt to do any civility or courtesy to a stranger. . . . To his friends of the gentry he had always a most hearty kindness, and to his neighbors (even the poorest) an answerable affability which rendered him beloved of everybody.[49]

Frescheville had his faults, however, for he was overfond of gaming, and died in debt. He was also of a violent temper and given to loud swearing. But he was of an exemplary continence —something which "the males of our family have not been too ambitious of," his biographer confesses.

If we may believe the family chronicler, the Holleses were all fond of good living and generous in their hospitality. Sometimes their impetuosity led them into duels—a fact deplored by Gervase, who condemned dueling as "both brutish and damnable" and a custom threatening to "divide the union betwixt a Christian and a gentleman."[50] Although most of the Holleses took delight in following the hounds, they made no fetish of field sports and did not let sports and pastimes interfere with duties of public service. If, as Gervase frankly declares, love sometimes outran discretion, they showed a certain decorum in their iniquities. Like many of the older county families, they had a fine disdain for the new-made aristocracy brought in by James I— a disdain which caused Sir John Holles for a time to live aloof on his country estate, though he at length cynically bowed to

[49] *Ibid.*, p. 201.
[50] *Ibid.*, p. 81.

the custom of the times and paid the sum necessary to advance him to the first step toward an earldom.[51]

The Holleses had more than a smattering of learning, as Gervase is at pains to emphasize in a description of his patron, Sir John. Indeed, so clear a picture does this passage give of some of the noteworthy characteristics of the country gentlemen, that it is worth quoting at some length:

> But his mind was yet the far nobler part, which was adorned with all the ornaments the University, Inns of Court, Court, camp, travel, and language could enrich him with. . . . He had a felicity of conversation beyond all other men; no person (of what condition soever) that came to him parted away uncontented; for he would quickly find the bottom of his capacity and which way his genius lay; then he would discourse with him civilly in his own element, so as all men took their leave of him with a great deal of satisfaction.
>
> His table was in effect a continued *Convivium Philosophale;* for after he had reasonably well checked his appetite, he would ever start some discourse either in divinity, philosophy, or history, in all which he was excellent. So that every man at his table had his mind as well as his body feasted. It hath often repented me that I have not gathered and preserved those apothegms which fell from him at several times which really would have weighed with the best of the ancients.
>
> His table was always good and his retinue answerable, having ever the sons of some gentlemen or other of good quality to follow him, who would send their sons to him as to a school of knowledge, virtue, and temperance. For he hated drunkenness and debauchery, nor would he endure excess in his buttery, which caused his housekeeping (in this lewd age where no entertainment is valued that does not swim in drink) to be the less commended. The gentleman of his horse once took the liberty to tell him that his table was good, and a little charge more would make his housekeeping without exception and much to his honor—namely, an hundred pounds more yearly in his cellar and as much in his stables. He replied, 'Watson, Watson, look you to my profit. I will look to my honor myself.'

[51] *Ibid.*, pp. 94, 99.

> He was exceedingly eloquent, and in his familiar letters had one of the best styles that ever I yet met with. One discourse he was writing (and I believe finished before he died, but I have seen but a part of it). It was an answer to some passages in Sir Francis Bacon's *Essay of Empire*. . . .
>
> He was of a most courteous and affable disposition, yet preserved exactly the grandeur and distance of his quality. . . . His youth was lively and spiritful, and he would say that it was a preposterous thing to see a young man old. But his age was ever accompanied with a cheerful gravity.[52]

Like the personification of advice laid down in a conduct book is this description of Sir John Holles, who possessed grace of body and skill in fencing, horsemanship, and dancing, as well as the proper accomplishments of the mind.

Though the Holleses respected learning and possessed their share of education, they subscribed to an accepted belief that the gentleman should preserve his amateur standing even in the acquisition of knowledge. This attitude is expressly stated in a passage describing Sir Gervase Holles, grandfather of the chronicler:

> He was as well furnished with learning as in his own opinion befitted a gentleman; for I have heard him say he would have a gentleman to have some knowledge in all the arts but that it did not become him to be excellent in any of them. He was no stranger to the softer muses. I had a book of his poems (which I have lost amongst other manuscripts) which discovered no vulgar but a very sprightly fancy, such an one as might have marched with the foremost in these days; they were written about the beginning of Q. Elizabeth. Excellent company he was and pleasant, and certainly of his own times one of the best chroniclers. In his youth (as I have observed before) he was exceeding wild, but that his reason and riper age reduced to a far different temper; which showed him a great example of temperance and sobriety, though not of continency.[53]

The lack of continency mentioned here, we might note in passing—this one vice among many virtues and accomplishments—

[52] *Ibid.*, pp. 111-13. [53] *Ibid.*, pp. 125-26.

was not a serious blot upon the reputation of a gentleman, in the eyes of that generation; moreover, the grandson makes the extenuating observation that the two illegitimate children of this honorable ancestor were "begot after his wife's decease." [54]

The manners, the customs, and the ideals of the Holles family, as revealed by the contemporary chronicler, are a clear indication of the relation of seventeenth-century life to the theories of behavior laid down in the conduct books. The Holleses, furthermore, seem to have represented, in their virtues and their frailties, the norm rather than the exception among the upper stratum of the country gentry.

The lives of other seventeenth-century country gentlemen show a similar adherence to a tradition of dignified conduct befitting their station, a similar recognition that learning had its place among the gentleman's accomplishments, and an identical belief in their obligations of public service. In formal biographical sketches, we must make allowances for the practice of eulogizing the subject, but the very fact that biographers chose to emphasize qualities and virtues traditionally recommended to gentlemen is significant. The lives of Sir John Digby, Sir Henry Gage, and Major General John Smith, written by Edward Walsingham near the middle of the seventeenth century,[55] read like summaries of the qualities prescribed for gentlemen by Henry Peacham or Richard Brathwaite. All three of these men came from substantial county families. Sir John Digby, for example, belonged to the Digbys of Buckinghamshire and was a brother of Sir Kenelm Digby, whose interest in the New World led him to send books to Harvard and to correspond with John Winthrop, Jr. To read the sketch of

[54] *Ibid.*, p. 125.

[55] Edward Walsingham, *Life of Sir John Digby (1605-1645)*, ed. George Bernard (*Camden Miscellany*, XII; Camden Society, 3d Ser., XVIII [1910]); *idem, Alter Britanniae Heros: Or The Life Of The Most Honourable Knight, Sir Henry Gage, Late Governour of Oxford, Epitomiz'd* (Oxford, 1645); *idem, Britannicae Virtutis Imago. Or, The Effigies Of True Fortitude, Expressed to the life, in the famous actions of that incomparable Knight, Major Generall Smith* (Oxford, 1644).

Sir John, one would think that Walsingham had opened Peacham's *Compleat Gentleman*, and had filled in the description of the accomplishments and virtues of his subject from what he read there. Sir John had been grounded in "the liberal sciences, music, and French," and had been polished by travel in Flanders, France, and Italy. At home in the country, he "followed the most laudable and best gentleman-like sports and recreations with knights and gentlemen, his kind neighbors."[56] He was skilful in arms, courageous, and quick to defend his honor. A lover of justice, he gave orders during the Civil Wars that his men were not to wrong anyone of the countryside, on pain of being cashiered and fined. Temperate in all things, he amazed the Scotch, who captured him on the border, because "they had never seen nor met with such a man whom they could neither see moved to indignation and wrath, enticed to drink, nor allured to speak ill of others, and free from other vices incident to many men."[57] Preserving a stoical calm in spite of all calamities, he further excited the admiration of spectators when, as a prisoner of Parliament, he and certain of his colleagues were conducted through the streets of London, and "the courageous prisoners, nothing deceited by this disaster, changed not their countenance, but rode on confidently, so that one might read in the serenity of their visages, the quiet of their minds, nothing amated at so coarse treating by their enemies."[58] Walsingham's sketches of Gage and Smith follow the same pattern, though both of these men are described as even more accomplished in learning. Smith had shown himself studious of books in military science and a diligent reader of history, believing that a "complete soldier" ought to know both the theory and practice of military science and be acquainted with the course of human history. Gage likewise was a student of history and military science, as well as heraldry. Being a master

[56] Walsingham, *Life of Sir John Digby*, p. 81.

[57] *Ibid.*, p. 77. [58] *Ibid.*, pp. 100-101.

of Latin, French, Italian, and Spanish, and having some knowledge of Greek and Dutch, "he bestowed himself in translating books, which he exceeding well performed." [59] Even though we must discount Walsingham's eulogistic praise, we can be certain that his descriptions of the qualities of these country gentlemen were not made up out of the whole cloth but had some basis in fact.

Without overmuch diligence, one could compile a long list of able and cultured men who were a credit to the country gentry of England during the seventeenth and early eighteenth centuries. So well known are some of these names that the mere mention of them calls up pictures of dignified bearing and civilized living during years of social change which taxed the stability of lesser men. Despite upheavals affecting the whole social order, the strong tradition of what a gentleman should be, what he should know, and how he should conduct himself in all his relations continued to mold the lives of members of county families. If some adopted the stricter views of the Puritans, they did not let fanaticism destroy the symmetry of the gentleman's way of life, however much religious views might affect certain aspects of behavior. John Winthrop, for example, though he became one of the Puritan fathers of Massachusetts Bay, remained an English country gentleman—albeit a somewhat grave one—who was greatly concerned to prevent the children of the colonists from falling into barbarism. Colonel John Hutchinson was the perfect pattern of a Christian gentleman, but one who did not let his Puritanism betray him into the folly of the zealots: he wore his hair long and curled according to fashion; he loved music, painting, and sculpture; and he entertained hospitably and graciously.[60]

By the same token, the tradition of the gentleman was a stabilizing influence in the Restoration period. Not all aristo-

[59] Walsingham, *Alter Britanniae Heros,* p. 3.

[60] *Memoirs of the Life of Colonel Hutchinson . . . By His Widow Lucy,* ed. Sir Charles Firth (London, 1906); see especially pp. 43, 95-96, 295.

crats were dissolute courtiers with the morals and manners of the Earl of Rochester, as we are sometimes led to believe. We should remember men like John Evelyn, who, one biographer declares, "typifies better than anyone else, culture and enlightenment in the Stuart epoch." [61] If any one reason accounts for this quality in Evelyn, it is the fact that he never forgot that he was a gentleman with all the obligations that his position entailed. Although he disliked the moral corruption of the court, he believed that the gentleman's place was to remain a servant of the state and not retire from his duty. But when his public services permitted, Evelyn liked nothing better than the life of a squire, at Sayes Court and later at Wotton. Another gentleman, scholar, and public servant who typifies the finest in the tradition was Sir William Temple. Like Evelyn, he found the greatest satisfaction in retirement to his estate, first at Sheen and then at Moor Park, Surrey, where he played tennis, looked after his orangery and garden, reread the classics, discussed philosophy, and set an example of noble living to his neighbors.[62] This retirement, however, was after he had performed his duty to the state as one of Charles II's most brilliant ambassadors, and he again emerged for active service in the crisis of 1679. Life according to Aristotle's golden mean was an ideal he set himself. Describing his habitual temperance and his love of simple things, his sister, Lady Giffard, remarks that he "said he was made for a farmer and not a courtier, and understood being a shepherd and a gardener better than an ambassador." [63] He was inclined to intemperance only in eating fruits; he drank wines regularly (commonly those not best for him) but never to excess. He liked gaming, but after several years he counted

[61] Arthur Ponsonby, *John Evelyn* (London, 1933), p. 324.

[62] Clara Marburg, *Sir William Temple, a Seventeenth Century "Libertin"* (New Haven, 1932), p. xiii.

[63] *The Early Essays and Romances of Sir William Temple, Bt., with the Life and Character of Sir William Temple by His Sister Lady Giffard*, ed. G. C. Moore Smith (Oxford, 1930), p. 29.

his losses and decided that it was an extravagant waste. He thought no man should make love after forty, or stay about affairs of business after fifty. In all things he essayed to be "correct." Sir William Temple's life, like that of the more religious Colonel Hutchinson, was a pattern of decorum, an example of adherence to a code writ large in many a courtesy book.

Many social changes took place in England during the period we are considering, but the position and prestige of the country gentry were not greatly altered. If the Puritan Revolution caused hardships and great losses to many loyal gentlemen, they were compensated later in the century, when "once again land and political power were synonymous terms."[64] Despite civil commotion and political upheaval, the landed gentry remained the backbone of the social order. Although the quality of life altered in some degree, as economic and political changes tended to make the country gentry less provincial and more worldly-wise,[65] county families adhered to ancient traditions of social responsibility and local leadership which underwent little essential change from generation to generation. The position of the landed families who lived on their estates and took seriously their obligations to society remained an envied one. As we have seen, the acquisition of land which would in time bring the prestige of social position, was the dream of every tradesman and merchant who had accumulated wealth. And, having acquired land, such newcomers to the soil set themselves the task of emulating the manners, customs, and way of life of the gentlemen who seemed most worth imitating. Even if boors and drunken louts did disgrace their birthrights in some manor houses of England, they were not looked upon as models for imitation. The pattern of behavior was set by the well-bred, cultured, and responsible types who lent distinction to the English gentry.

[64] Mary Coate, *Social Life in Stuart England* (London, 1925), p. 12.
[65] *Ibid.*, pp. 21-23.

As social-climbing citizens at home sought to imitate the landed gentry, so Virginia colonists who had the opportunity of acquiring land and accumulating wealth attempted to duplicate the manner of life led by that most envied of mortals at home, the proud and powerful country squire. And the particular kind of squire imitated was not, of course, the loutish bumpkin ridiculed by satirists, but the well-brought-up, educated, and accomplished gentleman of the type illustrated by the Verneys, Oxindens, and Holleses that we have noticed. Since Virginia was far distant from cultural centers, colonial fathers among this new landed aristocracy were concerned lest their sons grow up into ignorant boors, and they did what they could to prevent it by importing books, employing tutors, and, whenever possible, by sending their sons to English schools.

The intellectual heritage transmitted to the Virginia ruling class by the tradition of the gentleman's training was of incalculable consequence in the development of American ideas and social concepts. As an aristocratic upper class developed and gained authority and social prestige, its members became increasingly conscious of their inheritance from the English tradition. While they developed an independence of spirit and became Virginians instead of Englishmen in a distant colony, they had a dream of being Virginians like the fine gentlemen of the older civilization. That dream helped to shape the thinking and the cultural ideals of the Virginia ruling class throughout the seventeenth and eighteenth centuries.

CHAPTER II

THE DEVELOPMENT OF A VIRGINIA ARISTOCRACY

DESPITE realistic facts produced by a generation of hard-working historians, an imaginary concept of colonial Virginia has taken shape in popular belief. In this fanciful picture—a picture frequently drawn in nineteenth-century fiction—rich and romantic Cavaliers lived in feudal splendor, surrounded by multitudes of retainers. Great houses, filled with furniture and finery brought from England, provided a background for these barons of the Virginia rivers. There the lords and ladies of the new dispensation spent their leisure in cultivating the social graces. With dancing, gaiety, and decorous flirtation they passed the time in Arcadia. Only dueling disturbed the idyllic dream, for in Arcadia gentlemen were touchy about their honor and a duel at dawn under the oaks beside a dark river was the invariable method of settling personal disputes—in the novels that described the dream world of early Virginia. These silken-coated grandees were all descended from some ancient and distinguished family of England—preferably from some knight who came over with William the Conqueror—and titles in the family trees of the colonists were thicker than dogwood blooms in spring. Thus have romancers imagined Virginia in colonial days, and so firmly has the idea become established that some patriotic antiquarians have struggled vainly to prove its truth. Contributors to the genealogical magazines of the South too often have had an obsession concerning the nobility of their ancestors.

Romantically absurd as some of the notions of colonial Virginia have been, there is nevertheless a germ of truth in the imaginary picture of life there. Virginia did develop an aristocracy of wealthy planters, who, in time, came to live in considerable splendor, who established a pattern of life modeled after the English gentry, who ruled the destinies of the colony as by inherited right. Even though this development was gradual, and the more magnificent manifestations of this aristocracy came late in the colonial period, the seventeenth century saw the evolution of a hierarchic social order with a few great planters at the top. If realistic historians, revolting at the nonsense of many genealogical claims, have been moved to emphasize the essentially plebeian quality of the vast majority of Virginia settlers, we must not forget that the men who ruled the colony from its inception made up an aristocracy whose power and influence were out of all proportion to their numbers.[1] If the majority of Virginia colonists were simple, hard-working folk of no ancestral pretensions and little wealth, the families who controlled them and their destinies soon became both wealthy and proud. It is not necessary to assume, however, that even these members of the ruling class were aristocratic in their origins. A few were, most were not. But, having reached Virginia and become possessed of great tracts of land which assured them wealth, power, and social recognition, they quickly assumed all the prerogatives of the aristocratic order they had known in England. Though latter-day worshipers of democracy may discern the seeds of popular government in colonial Virginia, actually the government, from the first settlement to the Revolution, was aristocratic, even oligarchic.

[1] See *passim* in Thomas Jefferson Wertenbaker, *Patrician and Plebeian in Virginia* (Charlottesville, Va., 1910), *The Planters of Colonial Virginia* (Princeton, 1922), and *The First Americans, 1607-1690* (New York, 1927); Philip Alexander Bruce, *Social Life of Virginia in the Seventeenth Century* (2d ed., Lynchburg, Va., 1927), *Institutional History of Virginia* (2 vols., New York, 1910), and *Economic History of Virginia in the Seventeenth Century* (2 vols., New York, 1907); Charles M. Andrews, *The Colonial Period of American History: The Settlements* (New Haven, 1934), I, 208-9. A stimulating and worth-while discussion of the development of social distinctions in the various colonies is to be found in Dixon Wecter, *The Saga of American Society* (New York, 1937), chaps. 1-2.

The English origin of this aristocracy is a question that has provoked endless arguments. Debates over the gentility of the First Families of Virginia have been waged in countless antiquarian articles, often with more enthusiasm for a particular point of view than historical logic justifies. But no longer do even amateur historians hold the opinion that the founders of the aristocratic families were without exception dispossessed Cavaliers, or adventurous younger sons of the nobility, or, in the technical sense, even "gentlemen" at all. Indeed, the reaction against such a belief has been so strong that we are likely to forget that a considerable number of the seventeenth-century settlers did come from families of the gentry—enough, perhaps, to serve as leaven for the developing aristocracy, enough to set an example of the manners and behavior of English country gentlemen.

Full of good sense is a statement, on this subject, made in 1705 by Robert Beverley, the Virginia historian. The first permanent settlers were men of low circumstances, he comments, and adds: "Nor was it hardly possible it should be otherwise; for 'tis not likely that any man of a plentiful estate should voluntarily abandon a happy certainty to roam after imaginary advantages in a new world." Beverley is careful, however, to explain that other sorts of settlers also came:

> But this way of peopling the colony was only at first. For after the advantages of the climate, and the fruitfulness of the soil were well known, and all the dangers incident to infant settlements were over, people of better condition retired thither with their families, either to increase the estates they had before, or else to avoid being persecuted for their principles of religion or government. Thus, in the time of the Rebellion in England, several good Cavalier families went thither with their effects, to escape the tyranny of the usurper, or acknowledgement of his title. And so again, upon the Restoration, many people of the opposite party took refuge there, to shelter themselves from the King's resentment. But Virginia had not many of these last, because that country was famous

for holding out the longest for the royal family, of any of the English dominions.[2]

Throughout the period of settlement, a constant stream of younger sons of the English gentry came to Virginia. Of this there can be no question,[3] though the size of the stream may have been exaggerated. Some of these younger sons were little better than remittance men, and proved failures even with the opportunities that Virginia offered. Others succeeded in establishing themselves and founding families that duplicated the traditions of country gentlemen at home. An illustration of the process is provided by Henry and William Randolph, who founded one of the colony's most distinguished families. Henry, who arrived in 1643, was the half-brother of Thomas Randolph the poet, and a nephew of Sir Richard Lane.[4] His own nephew William Randolph, who reached Virginia a little afterward and became the earliest of the Turkey Island Randolphs, was the son of a country gentleman of Warwickshire.[5] The first two Randolphs immediately asserted themselves as leaders in the new country, and William's descendants included such leaders as Thomas Jefferson, John Marshall, and Robert E. Lee.[6] Other gentlemen also came; one or two families, like the Wests and Fairfaxes, could even boast descent from peers; but of the background of most of the settlers who were careful to sign themselves "gent." we know next to nothing.

The cold truth is that the English origins of nearly all of the

[2] Robert Beverley, *The History of Virginia*, ed. Charles Campbell (Richmond, Va., 1855), pp. 232-33. See also Hugh Jones, *The Present State of Virginia* (1724), ed. Joseph Sabin (New York, 1865), p. 22.

[3] See Bruce, *Social Life in Virginia*, *passim*, and Robert A. Brock, *The Colonial Virginian: An Address Delivered before the Geographical and Historical Society of Richmond College, October 13, 1891* (Richmond, Va., 1891), *passim*.

[4] *The Virginia Magazine of History and Biography*, XXVIII (1919-20), 363-64.

[5] William G. Stanard, "Major Robert Beverley and His Descendants," *Virginia Magazine of History and Biography*, III (1895-96), 261-68. See also William Clayton Torrence, "Henrico County, Virginia: Beginnings of Its Families," *William and Mary College Quarterly*, XXIV (1915-16), 202-10.

[6] Brock, *The Colonial Virginian*, p. 13.

colonists, even those who founded aristocratic families, are unknown. Many of the most impressive family trees depend upon such feeble phrases as "an old tradition declares," or "the subject of this sketch is believed to descend from a family of the same name in Buckinghamshire." Though the First Families of Virginia may have in their veins the bluest blood in all England, the proof of their descent will rarely stand in either a court of law or a council of scholars.

If the use in England of the term "gentleman" after a name was not proof of hereditary gentility, the assumption of that appellation in faraway Virginia was even less conclusive. Nor was the claim to coat armor convincing. In England the granting of coat armor merely indicated that the bearer of such an honor had attained sufficient respectability and prosperity to obtain from the College of Heralds the necessary privilege. Pedigrees could be obtained in that day, as in this, on the payment of a fee. It is significant that Shakespeare desired of the College of Heralds a coat of arms for his father, the tradesman of Stratford, that he might claim to be a second-generation "gentleman." In Virginia, the pretensions to coat armor were often most tenuous. As the authentic genealogies of Virginia families show, many emigrants who signed themselves "gentleman" were sons of merchants or tradesmen of London. For instance, a certain Richard Wright, who became a large landowner in Northumberland County, Virginia, is listed indifferently as "gentleman," "merchant," and "captain." As a matter of fact, he was a merchant-ship captain out of London before he found it profitable to settle on his Virginia estate. His son, Francis Wright, described as major of the militia, sheriff, justice of the peace, and gentleman of Westmoreland County, served on the bench of the county court for thirty years and was regarded as one of the aristocracy.[7] In a new country, the assumption of the

[7] Charles Arthur Hoppin, "Some Descendants of Richard Wright, Gentleman, of London, England, and Northumberland, Virginia, 1655," *Tyler's Quarterly*

title of gentleman was even easier than at home, and we may reasonably suppose that most men who had attained prosperity were certain to claim the distinction of a social station higher than that of the rank and file of the colonists.

Although many of the ruling families were descended from ancestors who could boast no better heritage than a successful connection with trade, this ancestral shortcoming did not prevent their gaining positions of honor in the new land, provided they had land and money to support their claims. For it was capital, which enabled settlers to bring in servants and clear rich tracts of tobacco land, that determined the Virginia aristocracy of the seventeenth and early eighteenth centuries.[8] Later, when nineteenth-century imaginations were dazzled with the heroics of Scott's novels, Virginia was peopled in fancy with the descendants of chivalrous peers and fair ladies of the court much nobler in blood than the settlers of reality.[9]

Virginia, from the very start of the colonial venture, was regarded as a land of opportunity, where men might accumu-

---

Historical and Genealogical Magazine, I (1919-20), 127-41; "The Washington-Wright Connection and Some Descendants of Major Francis and Anne (Washington) Wright," *ibid.*, IV (1922-23), 153-314.

A curious commentary on the advantages of being of the gentlemanly class is to be found in the public records of Northumberland County. One Alice Atkinson accused Richard Wright, "aged 22 yeares or thereabouts," of ravishing her. In a deposition she testified that she told a certain Mrs. Salisbury of her misfortune and that Mrs. Salisbury replied "that Mr. Wright was a gentleman and it was a pity." In Record Book No. 2, under date of Aug. 20, 1655, there is the following entry (spelling modernized and abbreviations expanded): "Whereas it appeareth unto the Court that Alice Atkinson hath in a most infamous manner defamed Mr. Richard Wright in taxing him of ravishment and no proof thereof, the Court do therefore order that the said Alice Atkinson shall have twenty stripes upon her bare shoulders forthwith." Apparently Wright, probably a rowdy young blade just arrived in the colony, had been mixed up in a drinking brawl, and the evidence is vague as to precisely what happened. The clues are to be found in Beverley Fleet, *Virginia Colonial Abstracts. Vol. II. Northumberland County Records, 1652-1655* (Richmond, Va., 1937), pp. 62, 129-31.

[8] Ulrich B. Phillips, *Life and Labor in the Old South* (Boston, 1929), p. 27.

[9] Samuel E. Morison, *The Oxford History of the United States, 1783-1917* (Oxford, 1927), II, 19-20.

late wealth. All types of Englishmen, from the poorest laborer, who came over as an indentured servant, to wealthy merchants and cadets of ancient families, looked upon the tobacco lands of the Virginia rivers as a potential source of enrichment.[10] During most of the first fifty years of the colony's growth, the price of tobacco was high, the supply of fresh land seemed inexhaustible, and money-making required neither extraordinary acumen nor specialized skill in agriculture. Indentured servants, when their term of servitude expired, took up land and established themselves as small planters. From such humble beginnings rose a few families who in time acquired a certain prominence, but the political and social importance of ambitious indentured servants has been exaggerated by historians who have reacted—sometimes a little too violently—against the follies of overzealous ancestor worshipers.[11] While individual hard work and thrift during the period of high tobacco prices insured economic advancement, the cards were all stacked in favor of the colonist with sufficient initial capital to bring over servants and procure large tracts of land. By purchase and by the headright of fifty acres of land, with which the importer of servants was rewarded for each immigrant, prosperous men acquired large plantations which quickly enriched them. Even though Virginia was soon dotted with thousands of small holdings that in their total acreage exceeded the baronial estates, the great planters, relatively few in number, managed to gain and keep political and social control in the colony.

After the Restoration of Charles II, economic and political changes at home and abroad further increased the advantages

[10] See William E. Dodd, "The Emergence of the First Social Order in the United States," *The American Historical Review*, XL (1934-35), 217-31.

[11] All students of the colonial history of Virginia are much in the debt of Professor Wertenbaker for his stimulating studies. His efforts to correct certain romantic views of Virginia life were greatly needed. In emphasizing the importance of the yeoman class in *Patrician and Plebeian*, however, he sometimes seems to imply a greater political and social importance for the freed men than they actually attained. See Andrews, *The Colonial Period in American History*, I, 209 n.

that the large Virginia planter had over the small farmer. The enforcement of the Navigation Acts under Charles gave English merchants and shippers a monopoly of the tobacco trade and kept prices so low that it was next to impossible for a farmer any longer, by the labor of his own hands, to become economically independent. While the large planters with unlimited areas of fresh land and plenty of servants could make money when tobacco was low, the plight of freed servants and other poor men grew steadily worse. About this time, for a variety of reasons, negro slavery received a fresh impetus. With the great trading companies pushing the sale of negroes in the colonies, the more well-to-do planters contrived to buy as many as they could afford. When the British government in 1665 placed restrictions on the sale of white indentured servants, the demand for African slaves became still more insistent. By the end of the century, negro slavery was firmly established, and slave labor on large plantations was creating an economic situation conducive to the growth of an aristocratic social order. By the end of the first quarter of the eighteenth century, a society founded on slavery and almost feudal in character had developed.[12]

The introduction of the African slave system was the most important single factor in the evolution of the Virginia aristocracy, for it enabled wealthy planters to crush, perhaps unconsciously, the economic power of small landowners who depended upon their own labor. Wealthy men, able to take up increasing acreages of new land and farm them profitably with slaves, succeeded where poor men, confined to lesser holdings, soon exhausted their farms by overcultivation of tobacco, and either had to face failure or push on into frontier regions.[13]

[12] Dodd, *op. cit.*, pp. 220-26; Wertenbaker, *Planters of Colonial Virginia*, pp. 96, 130.

[13] Avery O. Craven, *Soil Exhaustion as a Factor in the Agricultural History of Virginia and Maryland, 1606-1860* ("University of Illinois Studies in the Social Sciences," XIII, No. 1 [1925]), *passim;* Wertenbaker, *Planters of Colonial Virginia*, pp. 144-47.

The influence of slavery upon the social structure of colonial Virginia was far-reaching, extending even to subtle changes in manners and behavior; but that is a theme for later discussion. Its immediate effect was to make possible an aristocracy of rich planters who in time learned to value the amenities of a genteel life.

During the period of settlement, let it be repeated, the fundamental fact determining social status was capital. That some families were founded by the sons of gentlemen was of far less importance at the moment than whether they had money enough to bring over servants and take up large tracts of land. The tradesman, the merchant, and the gentleman who were adequately financed at the start gained a similar foothold in the economic structure of the colony, and, if they prospered sufficiently, they all became members of the ruling class, and, in the course of time, developed similar ideas about family, position, and social obligations. All of them had definite notions of what they would do with wealth, once they had attained it: they would become landed proprietors as much as possible like the country gentry of England, but they would adapt their "gentility" to the requirements of new conditions. And, whatever their background, that is what they did.

In England, merchants were constantly buying land and retiring to the country to lead lives of leisure—the ultimate reward of their industry and thrift. In Virginia, that reward came easily to the owner of fat lands and numerous servants. It is small wonder, then, that a constant stream of London merchants, or their sons, migrated to Virginia to invest their capital. Not only were they reasonably certain of profit in pounds and shillings, but they could also look forward to a social position of dignity and honor. "It is known," observed John Hammond, writing in 1656, "such preferment hath this country rewarded the industrious with, that some, from being wool-hoppers and of as mean and meaner employment in England, have there grown great merchants and attained to the most eminent advancements the country afforded."[14] Certainly, during the seventeenth and early eighteenth centuries, no colonist who succeeded in procuring large tracts of land and properly establishing himself thereon failed to become an accepted member of the developing upper class, whatever his social position may have been in England. It should be added, however, that, despite John Hammond's comment on the low origins of some high-placed Virginians, few except substantial settlers with money to aid them reached this good eminence.[15]

Some of the most enterprising and prominent families of colonial Virginia were descended from merchants and tradesmen. Thomas and Philip Ludwell, Nicholas Spencer, Thomas Stegg, William Byrd I, Robert Bolling, Richard Booker, Miles Cary, George Brent, John Chew, and many others who might be named, belonged to trading families distinguished for their industry and shrewdness. Most of them grew rich in Virginia and begot sons to add luster to their names. As planters, they utilized every opportunity to increase their wealth and improve their status. But their social ambitions, one should always remember, were subservient to their financial interests, and no seventeenth- or early-eighteenth-century Virginian was so foolish as to despise trade. Conditions of life in the colony prevented the growth of towns and placed a monopoly of trade in the hands of the great planters. For this blessing they thanked God, and violently resented any coasting schooner from New England that came up their rivers to traffic with their poorer neighbors, tenants, or slaves. The only trade the planters despised was the petty traffic of interlopers.[16]

[14] John Hammond, *Leah and Rachel, or, The Two Fruitful Sisters Virginia and Maryland* (1656), in Peter Force's *Tracts* (Washington, 1844), III, 20.

[15] Andrews, *The Colonial Period in American History*, I, 208.

[16] John Spencer Bassett, "The Relation between the Virginia Planter and the London Merchant," *Annual Report of the American Historical Association for the Year 1901* (Washington, 1902), I, 553-75.

Colonial Virginians, unlike some of their more romantic descendants, were less concerned over the ancestry of their fellow colonists than with whether they were sufficiently well off in present possessions to maintain themselves with comfort and dignity. Though class consciousness was evident from the start, invidious distinctions based on the status in England of settlers' families were rarely—if ever—made. As in most frontier sections, respect was paid to men of prowess and enterprise, and it was of little consequence in seventeenth-century Virginia whether a planter's father was a cloth merchant of London or the knight of his shire, provided the planter himself was successful and prosperous. Although the higher planter group soon became acutely conscious of class distinctions, in pre-Revolutionary days they never developed into a true caste. As in England, there was a constant ebb and flow in the ranks of the upper class, as small planters grew prosperous and worked themselves into a better station, or as old planters fell on evil days and lost their possessions.

The economic development of Virginia made for the division of society into three main groups: servants and slaves, yeomanry, and a ruling class of great planters. During the first fifty years conditions were most favorable to white servants' graduating into yeomen—that is to say, into small independent farmers who worked their tobacco plots with only such aid as their families could give them. A few of these yeomen—fewer than one might suppose—rose to positions of some consequence as members of the House of Burgesses or as holders of county offices; but, from the later years of the seventeenth century, as large plantations multiplied and great planters became more powerful, the yeomen had less and less political or social importance.

Virginia's preoccupation with tobacco culture to the exclusion of other sources of wealth discouraged the growth of towns until very late in the colonial period and prevented the development of a commercial middle class like that of New England. In Virginia, the one goal of every settler was to get land and raise tobacco. Since tobacco exhausted the soil in a few years, fresh land was constantly needed; hence, for successful farming, larger tracts were required than was the case in New England, where farmers lived close together in compact villages and usually shared common wood lots and pasture land. In Virginia, on the contrary, there was no incentive, even among small farmers, to live together in villages, and the size of the larger plantations made for scattered homesteads, each more or less economically independent of the others. Since the great planters, with shipping connections in England, imported all the commodities needed for themselves and their less opulent neighbors, and had the goods delivered directly to their wharves along the rivers, there was little opportunity for the development of a class of middlemen—importers, merchants, shopkeepers, bankers—the people who normally make up the population of trading centers. London and Bristol were the trading towns of Virginia planters. In the early days, even craftsmen were exceedingly scarce. Carpenters, blacksmiths, weavers, shoemakers, and other artisans who managed to reach Virginia, more often than not abandoned their trades to become growers of the profitable Indian weed. Instead of settling in villages and developing industries as they did in New England, they, too, scattered up and down the rivers as small farmers. With no organized independent middle class to check the power of the wealthier planters and with a yeomanry that became steadily weaker and less assertive as slave competition increased, the growth of a dominant aristocracy was inevitable.

By the mid-seventeenth century, the progress of the wealthier planters toward the prosperity and power that became so marked a few generations later had already begun. If not many planters at this time had much to boast about in the way of houses and furnishings, at least a few were already well established, with comfortable homes. One of the most prosperous Virginians of his day was Captain Samuel Matthews, a trader who early acquired large tracts of land above Newport News and established a manor that was almost a village in itself. He was "an old planter above thirty years' standing, one of the Council, and a most deserving commonwealth's man," says an account published in 1649. Captain Matthews' riches were sufficient to enable him to win the daughter of a London knight, we are further informed by the same author, who was evidently pleased over the good man's prosperity:

> He hath a fine house, and all things answerable to it: he sows yearly store of hemp and flax, and causes it to be spun; he keeps weavers, and hath a tan-house, causes leather to be dressed, hath eight shoemakers employed in their trade, hath forty negro servants, brings them up to trades in his house. He yearly sows abundance of wheat, barley, &c. The wheat he selleth at four shillings the bushel, kills store of beeves, and sells them to victual the ships when they come thither: hath abundance of kine, a brave dairy, swine great store, and poultry; he married the daughter of Sir Thomas Hinton, and in a word, keeps a good house, lives bravely, and a true lover of Virginia; he is worthy of much honour.[17]

Matthews' position in the colony was such that during the Commonwealth period he was made governor and, despite opposition, ruled with justice and liberality.

Another early planter who established himself with some degree of sumptuousness was George Menefie, a merchant in origin. By 1634 his homestead, Littleton on the James River, was noted for its pleasant surroundings. "His large garden contained the fruits of Holland, and the roses of Provence," says a later historian, "and his orchard was planted with apple, pear, and cherry trees, and here the peach was cultivated for the first time in North America. Around the house were rosemary, thyme, and marjoram, favorites of that age."[18]

[17] *A Perfect Description of Virginia* (1649), in Peter Force's *Tracts* (Washington, 1838), II, 14-15.

[18] Edward D. Neill, *Virginia Carolorum* (Albany, 1886), p. 112.

Although a few settlers in the early period managed to build comfortable houses and develop "estates," as these glimpses of life on the Matthews and Menefie plantations suggest, in the first years most planters, great and small, devoted their energies less to procuring the pleasures of a gentle life than to wringing a cash profit out of their tobacco crops. While they were establishing themselves, even the richer planters made shift to get along with very simple clapboard houses, the only kind then available. As the strain of clearing land and building houses relaxed somewhat, and as wealth increased, planters improved their homes, laid out gardens, and gradually began to surround themselves with some of the amenities of life. Moreover, though tobacco was always a main source of profit, the wasteful methods employed in the first heyday of high prices had to give way to thriftier processes of farming, and the planters who prospered most were those, like Captain Matthews, who utilized every opportunity for profit that their plantations afforded. Although as early as Captain Matthews' time, the richer planters were becoming a class-conscious aristocracy, shrewd trading and thrifty management were not only compatible with their notions of gentility but were also necessary. This attitude prevailed throughout the colonial period. In a comment on Larkin Chew, mentioned in the Virginia Council Journals, 1726-53, the editor comments:

> He was evidently an energetic man, a large buyer and seller of lands and with other irons in the fire, for though in his deeds he is always styled 'gentleman,' in the various grants to him he is called variously, 'gentleman,' and 'builder' or 'carpenter.' He no doubt took contracts for building houses. Our ancestors of the colonial period, no matter what their overseas ancestry may have been, would have laughed at some of the foolishness talked by their descendants, who state with pride that *their* forefathers were never in trade or mechanical pursuits. The fact is that these same forefathers engaged in any kind of business they thought would be profitable. Being men much engaged in business they did not often

do the practical work, but they supervised it. Mr. Cocke did not stand behind the bar in the tavern he owned at Varina, and Charles Carter, of Cleve, and Nathaniel Harrison, of Wakefield, did not actually work at the oven in their bakeries of ship biscuit, nor did Henry Cary and Larkin Chew have time to saw and plane; but they would not have understood any one who thought that owning any kind of business was discreditable.[19]

The rise of the Byrd family from a background of business and trade further illustrates the kind of aristocracy that a frontier life produced.[20] Other families of the highest social standing had much the same history.[21] William Fitzhugh, for example, got rich partly by reason of his trade as agent for ship captains who left goods with him for disposal.[22]

From the first, the control of most governmental offices was in the hands of men of rank and position.[23] If a few yeomen by superior ability and unusual industry managed to obtain offices, the vast majority of political posts were filled by the higher order of planters.[24] "In Virginia, as in England," says Philip A. Bruce, the historian of Virginia institutions, "the large landowner carried so much weight that he found no difficulty in securing the election of a son to the House [of Burgesses], especially if that son had shown that he possessed decided abilities. . . . The broader the plantation, and the more numerous the proprietor's slaves and herds, the more extensive was the influence exercised by him among voters belonging to his own calling, and the more easily he obtained the advancement of any person of his own blood aspiring to enter public life."[25] The chief planter in each county was designated commander over

[19] *The Virginia Magazine of History and Biography*, XXXII (1924), 49.

[20] See Chapter XI, *infra.*

[21] Bassett, *op. cit., p.* 557. For a discussion of a similar development in South Carolina of an aristocratic society from wealthy merchants, see Mrs. St. Julien Ravenel, *Charleston: The Place and the People* (New York, 1912), pp. 91 ff.

[22] Bassett, pp. 558-59.

[23] Bruce, *Institutional History of Virginia, passim.*

[24] *Ibid.*, II, 426.

[25] *Ibid.*, p. 424.

military and naval forces in his jurisdiction and given the title of "colonel."[26] Not merely was he responsible for drilling the militia in time of peace and leading it in time of danger, but also, among other things, he was intrusted with some of the duties of law enforcement. The office of sheriff, carrying with it a dignity unknown in modern times, was likewise held by men of prominence. Since the county courts were the backbone of legal administration, the commissioners (or justices of the peace, as they were called after 1662)[27] had great power and influence. These officers were, of course, chosen from the ranks of the large planters.

At the top of the hierarchy of government officials were the members of the Council of State, generally called simply "the Council"—a small body of the highest-ranking men in the colony. Their power was so great and their offices and duties so multifarious that a recital of them sounds like a burlesque of government in a Gilbert and Sullivan opera. They constituted the Upper House in the Assembly, corresponding to the House of Lords in England; they sat as a General Court to hear the most serious criminal and civil cases in the colony; as members of the Council, they were exempt from arrest and from certain levies; and they had many individual offices and duties.

> It is not going too far to say [observes Bruce] that the members of the Council appropriated to themselves all those higher offices of the colony which were attended with the largest salaries, or presented the most numerous chances for money-getting. They deliberately disregarded the fact that the concentration of these offices in so few hands brought about serious damage to the public interests whenever the Councillor was required by his incumbency of two separate positions to perform two sets of duties really in conflict with each other; a Councillor, for instance, was called upon to pass upon the correctness of his own accounts as collector; as collector, he was obliged, for his own enlightenment as a judge

[26] *Ibid.*, pp. 15 ff.
[27] *Ibid.*, I, 488.

of the General Court, to inform himself of all violations of the Navigation Acts; as a farmer of the quitrents, he practically owed the success of his bid to himself as Councillor; as escheator, who was a ministerial officer, he took and returned the inquisitions of escheats to himself as a judicial officer, and as such, passed upon points of law coming up in his own inquisitions.[28]

Naturally offices of such power and profit were kept in the hands of the most important planters. Membership in the Council conferred Virginia's highest cachet of aristocracy; it gave the privilege of writing "Esquire" after one's name and commanded the deference of all lesser folk. On occasion the Council even felt strong enough to lord it over the royal governors. In the course of time, a few families came to look upon membership in the Council as theirs almost by hereditary right. In a letter to the Earl of Dartmouth, dated March 9, 1713, Governor Spotswood complains about the interlocking nature of family connections on the Council:

> This winter hath [been] fatal to three gentlemen of her Majesty's Council here, who all died in little more than a month, and the number of Councillors falling thereby under nine, I have in their place (according to the power given me in my commission), called to that board Mr. Nathaniel Harrison, Mr. Mann Page, and Mr. Robert Porteus, who are all men of good parts, loyal and honest principles, and of plentiful estates; and, indeed, I know no others so fit for that post, except some who enjoy places of profit in the government, and, without losing them, are incapacitated to be of the Council, or else others, who are related to one particular family, to which the greatest part of the present Council are already near allied.[29]

Virginia had no titled aristocracy, but it had an equivalent in the great ones who sat in the Council of State.

By the later years of the seventeenth century, the evolution of a Virginia aristocracy had progressed to a point where a

[28] *Ibid.*, II, 360-61.

[29] "The Official Letters of Alexander Spotswood," ed. Robert A. Brock, in *The Virginia Historical Society Collections*, II (1885), 54-55.

small ruling class not only monopolized public offices but also, by that very fact, dominated the economic life of the colony. Officeholders, from members of the Council down to the lesser officials of the counties, were often able to use their posts for personal profit. Nor does this mean that they were necessarily dishonest. Legitimate emoluments and perquisites of office, such as fees received by collectors of customs, helped to enrich officials. Occasionally, however, great men added to their possessions by highhanded, if not culpable, methods. For example, Edward Hill, the lord of Shirley, was charged in 1677 with appropriating public property to his own use but claimed that the charges were made by malicious persons, spiteful because of his part in suppressing the Bacon rebellion.[30] With the haughtiness of a Coriolanus, Hill, in a lengthy defense, expresses the aristocrat's contempt of "that hydra the vulgar"—the ignorant "rout of people" who clamor against him. He may have had too little of the sense of public responsibility that went with the gentleman's position, but at least he had the pride of place which became such a notable characteristic of the Virginia aristocracy.

By the end of the seventeenth century, the aristocracy was supreme. Headed by the members of the Council, the ruling class monopolized land to such an extent that immigrants had difficulty finding homesteads, and poor farmers in need of fresh land had to migrate to the frontier. The abuses of the ruling class in monopolizing land was the subject of a report made to the Board of Trade, in 1696, by the British commissioner, Edward Randolph. Discussing the sparseness of the settlers and the widely scattered nature of the holdings, Randolph remarks:

> The chief and only reason is the inhabitants and planters have been and at this time are discouraged and hindered from planting

[30] The charges against Hill and his answer are printed in *The Virginia Magazine of History and Biography*, III (1895-96), 142-47, 239-52, 341-49; IV (1896-97), 1-15. See Phillips, *Life and Labor in the Old South*, p. 27.

tobacco in that colony, and servants are not so willing to go there as formerly, because the members of the Council and others, who make [*sic*] an interest in the government, have from time to time procured grants of very large tracts of land, so that there has not for many years been any waste land to be taken up by those who bring with them servants, or by such servants, who have served their time faithfully with their masters, but it is taken up and ingrossed beforehand, whereby they are forced to hire and pay a yearly rent for some of those lands, or go to the utmost bounds of the colony for land, exposed to danger and often times proves the occasion of war with the Indians.[31]

Powerful as was this ruling class of wealthy men, it was numerically small at the beginning of the eighteenth century. "In the seventeenth century not one planter in fifty could be classed as a man of wealth," Professor Wertenbaker points out, "and even so late as 1704 the number of well-to-do was very narrowly limited. In a report to the Lords of Trade written in that year Colonel Quary stated that upon each of the four great rivers of Virginia there resided from 'ten to thirty men who by trade and industry had gotten very competent estates.' Fifty years later the number had multiplied several times over."[32] In the years around the turn of the century, membership on the Council was held by such men as Dudley Digges of Bellfield, Benjamin Harrison of Wakefield, Matthew Page of Timber Neck, John Custis II of Arlington, Edmund Jenings of Ripon Hall, Robert Carter of Corotoman, Lewis Burwell of Carter's Creek and King's Creek, and William Bassett of Eltham —all great landowners with manorial establishments so distinguished that the very names of the plantations are still familiar wherever Virginia history is known.[33] That an ancestor of John Custis had kept a victualing house did not matter. The descendant of the victualer was now a lord of the land, a great

[31] Quoted by Wertenbaker, *Planters of Colonial Virginia*, p. 142.

[32] *Ibid.*, p. 157.

[33] William G. and Mary Newton Stanard, *The Colonial Virginia Register* (Albany, N.Y., 1920), pp. 43-44.

man, and a member of a proud aristocracy.[34] These men and their kind, perhaps numbering in all fewer than a hundred families, were the political, economic, and social rulers of the colony. In the later years of the eighteenth century, their descendants were a numerous company from whose ranks came powerful leaders who exerted tremendous influence in the councils of the rebellious colonies and the new republic.

So vast were the acquisitions of land by the great families that it was unnecessary to invoke the law of primogeniture to insure an adequate landed estate for the head of the family. The eldest son, it is true, usually inherited the homestead and often received the largest portion of land, but younger sons were amply provided with broad acres. Thus it was that an aristocracy of landed proprietors multiplied until tidewater Virginia in the eighteenth century was dotted with lordly estates, and prolific families like the Carters could take pride, not in one family seat, but in many baronial establishments.

The independence of plantation life, the responsibilities for the direction of affairs, and the necessary social obligations in the community served to make leaders of the larger landowners. Their duties were like those of the country gentry of England, with many added responsibilities, and they soon occupied the position of country gentlemen, whatever their fathers had been in the mother country. Describing the influences of the plantation upon this evolution, Professor Wertenbaker has commented:

> As for the wealthy planters, even in the seventeenth century they were being molded by the influences under which they lived into that type of Southern gentleman which in succeeding generations became so distinctive a feature in the nation's history. The boy who was reared upon a plantation of several thousand acres, tilled perhaps by forty or more slaves and servants, was taught the various duties which were to fall to his lot when he grew to be a man. When still quite young he exercised authority over the work-

[34] Neill, *Virginia Carolorum*, pp. 208-9.

> men and directed them at their tasks, so that he might develop the habit of command. He acquired versatility by performing the hundred and one tasks required in the conduct of the plantation—the raising of stock, the planting and tending of tobacco, the laying out of orchards, the building of fences, the purchasing of goods from the English importers, the care of the sick, the superintendence of plantation manufacture. While his mind was thus trained to business, his body was developed by an active out-of-door life—by hunting, fishing, swimming, and racing. From his father and his guests he became acquainted with the political life of the colony, and no doubt kept fairly well abreast of the chief happenings in England. All in all, the plantation life tended to make him practical, inquiring, robust, and self-reliant, even though it seldom instilled into him the inventive spirit or inspired him to literary effort.[35]

The planters developed a pride in the life they led, in their estates, and in all that these represented. In their interest in the details of farm life, they were far from the dandies they have been pictured. The eighth Duke of Devonshire, a fine gentleman of a later day, is said to have declared that the proudest moment of his life "was when my pig won the first prize at Skipton Fair."[36] In a similar fashion, Virginia planters were the kind of aristocrats who took pleasure in their contacts with the soil. Furthermore, they were actually "working gentry." Although they may not have labored with their own hands, as did the small farmers, they kept a close personal watch on the details of farm management. Overseers might control the slaves in the fields, but the owners made the plans, selected seeds and livestock, saw that proper fields were laid out, ordered the clearing of new ground, acted as their own veterinarians and doctors (dosing their animals and slaves when necessary), wrote innumerable business letters to merchants in London, kept a close watch on expenditures and sales of farm products—

[35] Wertenbaker, *The First Americans*, pp. 259-60.

[36] Quoted from Chester Kirby, *The English Country Gentleman: A Study of Nineteenth Century Types* (London, 1937), pp. 237-38.

in short, led the life of hard-working business men. They were a landed gentry with the heavy responsibilities that the possession of great estates entailed. Amidst such labors it is remarkable that they made a place for any of the pleasures and graces that go with gentility. Their preoccupation with the practical concerns of life was conducive to the evolution of farmers in buckram rather than elegant silken aristocrats. Yet, despite their labors, the ruling class found time for some appreciation of books, learning, and a cultivated way of life. That fact speaks volumes for their determination to be a race of gentlemen.

The members of this upper class were eternally conscious of their superiority, and were diligent to see that the lower orders of society observed distinctions in rank. As early as 1674, evidence of social stratification is provided by the case of a tailor, James Bullock, resident of York County, who scandalized the gentlemen of that district by presuming to enter his mare against a horse owned by Dr. Matthew Slader in a race for a purse of two thousand pounds of tobacco. For such presumption, the tailor was fined one hundred pounds of tobacco by the justices, who declared that racing was "a sport for gentlemen only." [37] Deference was demanded and generally received as a right by the upper classes; when some rude yokel failed in the respect he was supposed to show to superiors, he might be fined. More serious than contempt of court was the offense of William Hatton when, in 1662, he declared that the justices of the peace of York County were a lot of "coopers, hog-trough makers, peddlers, cobblers, tailors, weavers, and not fitting to sit where they do sit." Because he had reflected upon the social status of the gentlemen of the county, he was made to eat his words.[38] Gentlemen were quick to invoke the law against common fellows who so far forgot themselves as to be impudent toward their betters.

[37] "History of York County in the Seventeenth Century," *Tyler's Quarterly Historical and Genealogical Magazine*, I (1919-20), 264.

[38] *Ibid.*

Having acquired the estate and dignity of country gentlemen, Virginia planters soon began to yearn for coats of arms—for recognition from the College of Heralds of their ancient lineages. The eagerness of the Virginia gentry for coat armor is significant of their desire to be of the gentry, to be like the aristocracy in the mother country. During a period of hard times in Virginia in the winter of 1687, William Fitzhugh was less concerned over the falling price of tobacco than over the procurement of a copy of his coat of arms, as he indicates in a letter to his brother, Captain Henry Fitzhugh, then residing in London:

> I thank God I am plentifully supplied with servants of all conditions to serve me in all my occasions, therefore would not have you put yourself to the charge or trouble of procuring or sending me any in, well knowing it lies out of the course of your business and concerns. But again, as I said last year, I should be heartily glad of your picture and our coat-of-arms fairly and rightfully drawn, not as on the steel seal that came here, if you cannot find any advantageous opportunity of shewing me the original. Since my last God has pleased to help me with one son which not long since was christened by the name of Henry. We live here very plentifully without money, and now tobacco is low I shall be very hard put to it to purchase £10 for to supply our mother.[39]

The ruling class, of whom Fitzhugh may be taken as a typical example, nearly all managed to lay claim to coat armor. According to one Virginia antiquarian, over one hundred and fifty colonial families had a "vested right" to it.[40] Although such a statement would be hard to substantiate, the truth is that, by the beginning of the eighteenth century, nearly every family of any social pretension could boast a copy of its coat of arms. Prosperous planters wanted not only the position and prestige of the ancient gentry but also the visible tokens of this much-desired state.

[39] "Letters of Henry Fitzhugh," *The Virginia Magazine of History and Biography*, II (1894-95), 16-17.

[40] Brock, *The Colonial Virginian*, p. 12.

By the first quarter of the eighteenth century, there were enough families of aristocratic standing to make something of a show in the "society" of the little capital of Williamsburg. Of these, the Reverend Hugh Jones, writing in 1724, observes:

> Here dwell several very good families, and more reside here in their own houses at public times. They live in the same neat manner, dress after the same modes, and behave themselves exactly as the gentry in London, most families of any note having a coach, chariot, berlin, or chaise.[41]

The "civilized" behavior of these planters, who kept up with the latest fashions of London, impressed Jones, for he comments further concerning them:

> The habits, life, customs, computations, etc. of the Virginians are much the same as about London, which they esteem their home; and for the most part have contemptible notions of England, and wrong sentiments of Bristol, and the other out-ports, which they entertain from seeing and hearing the common dealers, sailors, and servants that come from those towns, and the country places in England and Scotland, whose language and manners are strange to them; for the planters, and even the native negroes generally talk good English without idiom or tone, and can discourse handsomely upon most common subjects; and conversing with persons belonging to trade and navigation from London, for the most part they are much civilized, and wear the best of clothes according to their station; nay, sometimes too good for their circumstances, being for the generality comely handsome persons of good features and fine complexions (if they take care), of good manners and address.[42]

The urbanity of the great planters—induced, in Jones's opinion, by frequent contacts with London—was such that clergymen going out to Virginia were advised of the necessity of conducting themselves as gentlemen:

[41] Jones, *The Present State of Virginia,* p. 32. A few years earlier, Beverley, in *The History of Virginia,* p. 239, had condemned his countrymen for their lack of industry because they ordered everything, even their wooden ware, from London, "to the eternal reproach of their laziness."

[42] Jones, *op. cit.,* p. 43.

> Clergymen for Virginia should be of such parts, tempers, and notions as these [orthodox Anglicans]. They likewise should be persons that have read and seen something more of the world than what is requisite for an English parish; they must be such as can converse and know more than bare philosophy and speculative ethnicks, and have studied men and business in some measure as well as books; they may act like gentlemen, and be facetious and good-humored without too much freedom and licentiousness; they may be good scholars without becoming cynics, as they may be good Christians without appearing stoics.[43]

When Jones made these observations, the evolution of the Virginia gentry had reached its first stage of maturity. The lines of social stratification that were to persist for generations were now plainly marked. A few great families that in future years were to influence the destiny of the whole country had already risen to power. Traditional attitudes toward the various social groups had had time to become established. Virginia had developed the social characteristics that largely shaped its history for the next century.

[43] *Ibid.*, pp. 96-97.

CHAPTER III

THE QUALITY OF THE GENTRY

By the end of the seventeenth century Virginia's aristocracy had already begun to take on certain definite characteristics, to adopt a pattern of life agreeable to its members, to develop conventions peculiar to the class, and to evolve a fairly consistent type of gentleman. The members of this order of colonial aristocracy, having much in common with their brethren in spirit, the English country gentry, both consciously and unconsciously followed the models provided by English tradition. Although many Virginia planters were new to the dignities and honors of their station, even the newest gentleman soon fell into the pattern set by the leaders. Their ideals of conduct, their actual manners and behavior, their hopes and aspirations, their way of life, were not always precisely the same as those of their counterparts in England, but they paralleled them as closely as Virginia conditions permitted.[1]

During the early period of settlement the stern business of fighting off Indians and making livable homes in swamps and wildernesses was not conducive to gallantry or the refinements of drawing-room manners, but these very hardships helped to bring out some of the more solid qualities that distinguished the gentry; and, in a surprisingly short time, the colony was sufficiently civilized for the wealthier planters to begin thinking of the virtues of genteel manners.

Although Captain John Smith had many hard things to say about the laziness and unruliness of the adventurers who were writ down as gentlemen in the lists of the first planters, some of these early settlers demonstrated qualities of character which

[1] See the concluding chapter in Philip A. Bruce, *Institutional History of Virginia* (New York, 1910), II, 605-36.

the upper class has usually managed to show in times of necessity. During the second year of the Jamestown settlement, when there was urgent need for felling trees and making clapboard, Captain Smith chose for a woodcutting detail two gallants, Gabriel Beadell and John Russell, "both proper gentlemen." Although this labor was strange to their condition, "within a week they became masters" and set an example to all the others, albeit "the axes so oft blistered their tender fingers that commonly every third blow had a loud oath to drown the echo." Let no man think, the chronicler observes, that these gentlemen spent all their time as "common woodhackers" or that they "were pressed to anything as hirelings or common slaves," yet such was the example they set that the writer was led to believe that "30 or 40 of such voluntary gentlemen would do more in a day than 100 of the rest that must be pressed to it by compulsion."[2] The capacity of the gentleman to adapt himself to the necessities of his environment and to assert his leadership may be symbolized by the industry of Master Beadell and Master Russell, the woodchopping, swearing gallants.

Since the wealthier planters who developed into the aristocracy controlled the affairs of the colony from the outset, they early gained experience in political leadership and learned to perform one of the first duties of the gentry—service to the state. From time out of mind, that had been considered part and parcel of the gentleman's life. In Virginia the leading planters assumed the obligations and duties of office, and, though the honors and emoluments were often a sufficient inducement to make officeholding attractive, many onerous and tedious duties were performed simply as civic obligations.

[2] *The Proceedings of the English Colony in Virginia . . . Till This Present 1612*, in *Travels and Works of Captain John Smith*, ed. Edward Arber (Edinburgh, 1910), I, 126-27. It may be worth mentioning that the swearers were punished at the end of the day by having for each oath a can of water poured down their sleeves.

The great planters expected to serve as sheriffs, justices of the peace, and members of the House of Burgesses; if they were peculiarly fortunate or richer than most, they could look forward to becoming members of the all-powerful Council. Like the holders of similar posts in England, the colonial gentry received for their labors a full measure of respect and honor.

No Virginia gentleman would have thought of shirking his civil duties, though many a planter must have found the demands of office irksome. Year in and year out one finds the Lees, the Corbins, the Fitzhughs, the Carters, the Ludwells, the Burwells, and others of the ruling families carefully performing the duties of public offices, even those which offered little reward in material things. Although voting privileges were reasonably democratic in Virginia throughout this period,[8] the electorate returned to office for term after term leaders from the upper class. The higher appointive places, of course, were monopolized by the aristocracy. The gentry could not escape experience in leadership, and sons of the great planters found themselves inevitably trained for positions of honor and trust in the government of the colony. If in time they came to look upon such posts as prerogatives of their birth and social inheritance, they also learned to regard them as serious obligations.

In military affairs the upper class also gained experience as leaders. Since the greater planters were the commanders of the militia in their respective counties, they had the responsibility of insuring their localities against Indian attacks and of protecting outlying regions in time of danger. Though the

[8] Bruce, *op. cit.*, II, 630: "The basis of the suffrage, however, down to the Restoration was more democratic than that of England; except during one short interval, the right to vote was governed by manhood alone; but after the reaction following the return of the Stuarts had set in, that right was restricted to freeholders and leaseholders; and towards the end of the century was further confined to freeholders. Thus, as time went on, the basis of the suffrage came to resemble more and more closely that of the Mother Country; and in doing so to drift further and further away from the landmarks of democracy."

hazards of Indian warfare lessened as the colony became more thickly populated, the militia continued to hold musters, and occasionally, even in the eighteenth century, there were Indian forays that gave an opportunity for the display of the military prowess and courage expected of the gentleman-leader. Nor was war the only concern of the military commanders. The colonels of the militia, observed Francis Louis Michel, a Swiss traveler in 1701-2, "are conspicuous, rich men, who allow themselves to be used for police as well as military duty."[4] So great was the sense of duty felt by the gentry for the maintenance of order in the commonwealth, that the colonels of the militia were willing to give their personal attention to the enforcement of the law.

Not merely in civil and military affairs but even in religion the planters felt an obligation to set themselves up as leaders. No one can pretend that their piety was always remarkable, but, like the best of the English gentry, they looked upon religion as necessary to decent and respectable living and as essential to a well-ordered state. Since the members of the ruling class, almost without exception, were orthodox Anglicans, they labored to maintain conformity in the colony. The control of the Church was in the hands of the great planters, who served as vestrymen and church wardens and took a serious view of their duties. Throughout the colonial period, these officials, though chosen by "free election," were selected from the best families in the colony.[5] They had the duty of guard-

[4] "Report of the Journey of Francis Louis Michel from Berne, Switzerland, to Virginia, October 2, 1701-December 1, 1702," tr. and ed. William J. Hinke, in *The Virginia Magazine of History and Biography*, XXIV (1916), 26.

[5] Bruce, *op. cit.*, I, 63-64: "Even more controlling was the influence which the vestrymen exercised from a social point of view. As the first gentlemen in the county, apart from the prestige they derived from being the principal guardians of public morals, they were looked up to as the models of all that was most polished and cultured in their respective parishes. It was one of the happiest features of that early society that each community possessed in its vestry a body of men prompted as well by every instinct of birth, education, and fortune, as by every dictate of

ing public and private morality, of presenting to the county courts offenders against decency, of seeing that the laws requiring church attendance and Sabbath observance were obeyed, of presenting clergymen to the governor for induction to the parish—in short, of maintaining religion and the Church.[6] Planters at times served as deacons and read the prayers when the parish was without a minister. On the plantation itself, many a planter conscientiously held prayers for his household and acted as the spiritual as well as the secular head of his little community. Rarely were even hard-drinking, hard-swearing, slave-driving plantation masters without a reverence for religion. If in the twentieth century it is sometimes difficult to realize the place occupied by religion in the lives of these seventeenth-century men and women, we should not forget that the Puritans and others of the stricter sects had no monopoly of religious feeling, and that Virginians in their own way were often as religious as dwellers in the Massachusetts Bay Colony.

Although the adventurers and gallants who came to Jamestown in 1607 could not be described as searchers after spiritual truth, it is worthy of note that the tradition of religion as an essential of community decency was so strong that one of the first buildings erected was a church, and that, by the governor's command, prayer was held daily. When four years later Sir Thomas Dale laid out Henrico, farther up the James River, he built, "at each corner of the town, a high commanding watch-house, a church, and storehouses: which finished, he

their official duty, to set the people at large a good example in their personal deportment and in their general conduct. To their influence is directly traceable a very large proportion of what was most elevated and attractive in the social life of the seventeenth century; and to that influence, we are, in no small degree, indebted for the character of the distinguished men of Virginia who cast such renown over the great era of the Revolution."

[6] *Ibid.*, pp. 28-33, 73, 82, 97, 132 ff., 215 ff. It is sometimes forgotten that Virginia passed laws requiring Sabbath observance, and in 1699 placed on its statute books a law making failure to attend worship on Sunday punishable by a fine of five shillings; see *ibid.*, p. 35.

began to think upon convenient houses for himself and men."[7]

In later years the gentlemen of the colony followed the example of the first settlers by promoting the erection of churches; by the end of the century, the Swiss traveler Michel observed that in every county there were "one, two, or three churches according to the population, whether it is thickly settled or scattered," but so distant were the plantations that churchgoers sometimes rode as much as thirty miles to attend the services—"not a great hardship," he adds, "because people are well mounted there."[8] Occasionally a great planter supported the parish church practically singlehanded, as in the case of Robert Carter, who rebuilt Christ Church in Lancaster County at his own expense and paid most of the rector's salary. Though the lords of the land in Virginia did not hold in their hands the patronage of the parish churches, as did English squires of similar station, they had much the same attitude toward the clergy.

The religious responsibilities of the great planters could not fail to influence their characters. The constant exercise of an oversight of the church, with all that this supervision implied, created in them a sense of moral obligation that was almost as keen as the recognition of their civil duties. Virginia gentlemen, like men in every age and class, fell short of perfection, it is true, and sometimes they sinned grievously before the Lord, but in general they tried to remember their adherence to an orthodox, if somewhat liberal, Anglican faith. And not even the

[7] Captain John Smith, *The General History of Virginia* (1624) in the *Travels and Works*, II, 509.

[8] "Report of the Journey of . . . Michel," pp. 21-22. Hugh Jones, *The Present State of Virginia* (1724), ed. Joseph Sabin (New York, 1865), pp. 68 ff., reported in 1724 that "Their churches were formerly built of timber, but now they build them of brick, very strong and handsome, and neatly adorned." But Jones was not too pleased with many conditions in the colonial Church. Owing to the distance, weddings and funerals were often held in homes. Burials frequently were in plantation graveyards instead of the churchyard. The ceremonies and government of the Church were not altogether to Jones's liking; see his comment, p. 97.

most godless member of the aristocracy would have denied that he ought to set an example to lesser folk.

The responsibilities of civil and religious leadership naturally produced in the members of the upper planting class a sense of their power and importance, and engendered that pride of family and position which, in later generations, has so often provoked comment from observers of Virginia life. If pride is the first of the Seven Deadly Sins, Virginia aristocrats from an early date stood constantly in danger of damnation. The meek had not inherited the good earth of Virginia, and the exigencies of life in the colony all combined to accelerate a normal disposition of the upper class to become proud rulers of their little principalities. "There are no lords, but each is a sovereign on his own plantation," said a certain Monsieur Durand, an aristocratic Huguenot visitor in Virginia in 1686-87. "The gentlemen called Cavaliers are greatly esteemed and respected, and are very courteous and honorable. They hold most of the offices in the country, consisting of twelve seats in Parliament [the Council], six collectors, the rank of Colonel in each county, and Captains of each company. It is not necessary to have studied law to be a member of Parliament. They sit in judgment with girded sword."[9] It is natural that the sovereign rulers of the tobacco kingdoms should have become men of definite opinions and strong wills, occasionally possessed of original minds—men so accustomed to rule that they looked upon questioning of their power as an impudence. The wonder is that they were not more arrogant. A plantation master who could live like a lord of creation, commanding his servants to do his will, and, more often than not, inducing his lesser neighbors to act in accordance with his wishes, could not be expected

[9] *A Huguenot Exile in Virginia*, tr. and ed. Gilbert Chinard (New York, 1934), p. 110. The writer of this narrative is known simply as one of "the noble stock of the Durand of Dauphiné." The "Parliament" to which he refers in the passage quoted is of course the Council, which sat not only as an Upper House of the legislative assembly, but also as the highest colonial court.

to acquire qualities of meekness and humility. If Robert Carter was the only one whose haughty sway over a vast domain won the sobriquet of "King," others were not far behind in their pride and power. Even in death they sought to perpetuate the remembrance of their position. Robert Newman in 1655 specified that he was to be buried with regard for his "rank and quality,"[10] and many tombstones proclaimed the earthly pomp and circumstance of the occupants of the graves beneath.[11]

But pride was not the only quality begotten by the planters' power. The habit of commanding men exercised many subtle influences on the characters of colonial aristocrats and helped to prepare them for the leadership which Virginia provided in crises in our later history. Powerful and free as were the great planters, they were not above the law, and they had inherited the notion that their position required them to set an example to the multitude. Their code prescribed rules of behavior which a gentleman felt compelled to obey. While the possession of slaves and servants made overbearing tyrants of a few small-minded men, more often the responsibilities of rule enforced the necessity of restraint and self-discipline. Though much has been made of the injurious effects of slavery on slaveowners, there was something to be said on the other side, as an anonymous apologist in the early nineteenth century pointed out: "The high sense of personal dignity with which the habit of authority and command inspires him [the slaveholder], makes him courteous in his manners, liberal in his sentiments, generous in his actions. But, with his disdain of all that is coarse and little and mean, there often mingle the failings of a too sensitive pride; jealousy of all superiority; impatience of contradiction; quick and violent resentment. His liability to these vices is so obvious that it is often an especial purpose of early instruction to guard against them; and thus is formed in happy natures such

[10] Mary Newton Stanard, *Colonial Virginia: Its People and Customs* (Philadelphia, 1917), p. 343.

[11] *Ibid.*, pp. 347 ff.

a habit of self-command and virtuous discipline as to make them remarkable for their mildness and moderation."[12] Edmund Burke in his famous speech on conciliation with America had earlier made a somewhat similar observation concerning the influence of slavery on Southern planters. If the ownership of slaves did not always induce in their owners the desirable virtue of moderation, nevertheless the command of a subservient race imposed many checks and required the exercise of a self-control that proved of great value in the training of leaders. Not even the complete cynic can fail to observe the effort of the seventeenth- and eighteenth-century Virginia gentry to live up to the obligations that their power imposed. The occasional failures only emphasized the seriousness with which planters in general took their responsibilities.

Riches came so easily to the large tobacco growers that surprisingly early they developed a love of luxury which was reflected in their houses and furnishings. For was it not fitting that the lordly few who had climbed to the top of the social ladder should display the external trappings of honor, that they should maintain estates in keeping with their position, that their station should be apparent in the magnificence of their surroundings? Indeed, something of the Renaissance notion of the virtue of magnificence as a quality of the gentlemanly estate is evident in the care which plantation lords took to provide themselves with settings worthy of their rank.[13] If undiscrimi-

[12] Quoted by Ulrich B. Phillips, "Plantations with Slave Labor and Free," *American Historical Review*, XXX (1924-25), 744-45, from an article in the *American Quarterly Review*, II (1827), 251-52. For an opposite view, emphasizing the danger of slavery to the slaveowner, see Worthington C. Ford, "A Sketch of Sir Francis Nicholson," *Magazine of American History*, XXIX (1893), 499-513. "In itself slavery was sufficient to undermine the real strength of the rulers, and morally produced important results on the character of the slave owners," this writer comments (p. 503). "They were a proud, stiffnecked, and overbearing race, restive under restraint, and little inclined to dictation from others."

[13] Stanard, *op. cit., passim*, provides a mine of information about the amenities of life in colonial Virginia. See also the works by Bruce and Wertenbaker, cited in the preceding chapter.

nating romancers have drawn an exaggerated picture of colonial Virginia as a region of white-colonnaded mansions, we should avoid the opposite extreme of imagining that rich planters even in the first century of settlement would be content to dwell in frontier cabins. The Huguenot Durand noticed in 1686-87 that large quantities of brick were being manufactured, and out of them the better houses were being built, with separate kitchens—a clear indication of an adequate number of house servants.[14]

The desire of the richer planters for a setting in keeping with their position in the colony prompted them to import from London fine furnishings for their houses, Turkey rugs and tapestries, great quantities of pewter and silver plate, tables and chairs of the latest fashion, pictures for their walls, books for their libraries, and jewels and fashionable clothes for their persons.

Evidence of the taste of the aristocracy in their household furnishings is to be found in wills, inventories, and letters. We learn that rich Oriental rugs were used as table covers and hangings as well as floor coverings;[15] that expensive tapestries were not unknown; and that large sums were spent for silver plate to adorn the dining rooms of great houses. Colonel Francis Eppes of Henrico County, for example, had in 1679 "a suit of tapestry hangings" worth £18 17*s*. William Fitzhugh of

[14] *A Huguenot Exile*, p. 119. A little later, describing the houses in Williamsburg, Robert Beverley, in *The History of Virginia* (Richmond, Va., 1855), comments (p. 235): "The private buildings are also in his [Governor Spotswood's] time very much improved, several gentlemen there having built themselves large brick houses of many rooms on a floor; but they don't covet to make them lofty, having extent enough of ground to build upon; and now and then they are visited by high winds, which would incommode a towering fabric. They love to have large rooms, that they may be cool in summer. Of late they have made their stories much higher than formerly, and their windows larger, and sashed with crystal glass, adorning their apartments with rich furniture. All their drudgeries of cookery, washing, dairies, etc., are performed in offices apart from the dwelling houses, which by this means are kept more cool and sweet."

[15] Stanard, p. 82.

Stafford County in 1683 ordered tapestry hangings for a room twenty feet long, sixteen feet wide, and nine feet high; and elsewhere he refers to other rooms hung with tapestry.[16] So early as 1656 John Hammond observed the "good store of plate" in planters' houses,[17] and later in the century the quantity of plate possessed was an index to a planter's wealth and position. William Fitzhugh regarded silver as such a good investment, both socially and financially, that he made large purchases of plate in London and had it adorned with his coat of arms.[18] The eagerness of Virginia gentlemen to keep up with the latest fashion in household furnishings is evident in the record of Colonel Richard Lee's difficulties with English customs officials over a trunkful of silver plate which he took to England in 1655 to have remodeled in the newest style. When the trunk was seized as Colonel Lee started to return, he testified that most of the silver had been brought from Virginia, and, to prove that it was for his personal use, he pointed out his coat of arms engraved on each piece.[19] The purpose for which much of the planters' silver was designed is an indication of their convivial natures. For instance, David Fox of Lancaster County in 1662 drew up a deed giving to his daughter Hannah, after his death, a notable collection containing a sillabub dish, a large dram cup, a sack cup, a wine bowl, a tankard and caudle cup, and a gallon basin, besides sundry other cups and dishes.[20]

[16] *Ibid.*, p. 73.

[17] *Leah and Rachel* (1656), in Peter Force's *Tracts* (Washington, 1844), III, 16.

[18] Stanard, p. 100. Mrs. Stanard, commenting upon the silver plate owned in the colony, says (p. 96): "I find in my own incomplete notes names, with dates, of nearly two hundred owners of silver–sixty-odd in the seventeenth century and the rest in the eighteenth."

[19] *Ibid.*, p. 98.

[20] *Ibid.*, p. 99. See also the will of David Fox, dated Sept. 14, 1664, in Beverley Fleet, *Virginia Colonial Abstracts, Vol. I. Lancaster County, Record Book No. 2, 1654-1666* (Richmond, 1937), p. 86. Fox bequeathes to his son David and his daughter Hannah, besides land, slaves, horses, etc., rich household furnishings, jewelry, many silk garments, etc. The deed of 1662 is given by Fleet, p. 72.

The family-consciousness of the aristocracy frequently manifested itself in collections of portraits and in the display of coats of arms. Contemporary portraits of a fair number of seventeenth-century settlers survive, as do a few earlier ancestral portraits, which they brought with them.[21] When rich Virginians visited London, they often sat for their portraits. A well-to-do planter of Jamestown, one Edward Jaqueline, on a visit to England in the early years of the eighteenth century sought out "an artist of the greatest merit he could find" and had painted individual pictures of himself, his wife, and five children, with his coat of arms on each picture.[22] Not uncommonly families who could claim coat armor (and perhaps some who could not) had their household and personal objects decorated with armorial bearings. Sometimes coats of arms were painted and framed for hanging. Occasionally a commander of the county militia had his coat armor painted on his drum, as we know from the inventory made in 1677 of the personal property of Colonel William Farrar of Henrico.[23] Besides portraits, some planters collected other pictures. An inventory of property of Governor Spotswood shows an early-eighteenth-century acquisition of "26 prints, Overton's Theatrum Passion, one Scripture piece of painting, The History of the Woman Taken in Adultery, valued at £36."[24] About 1690 David Fox, whose father had owned many silver drinking vessels, possessed "3 pictures in the parlor and 25 Pictures of the Senses in the hall."[25] Colonel Fox's great hall was probably an eminently appropriate place for allegorical pictures of the senses. Colonel William Byrd II gathered a collection of portraits of English noblemen—a piece of vicarious social climbing that aroused the democratic spirit of a certain Mr. Waltham of Williamsburg,

[21] Stanard, pp. 314 ff.
[22] *Ibid.*, p. 315.
[23] *Ibid.*, p. 134.
[24] *The Virginia Magazine of History and Biography*, VIII (1900-1901), 108-9.
[25] Stanard, p. 316.

who bequeathed Byrd a diamond ring, "upon condition that he would permit his portait to hang up in the same room with those of the noblemen, with his hat on." [26] Portraits, pictures, and painted coats of arms clearly lent an atmosphere of gentility to a Virginia planter's house.

Since the social leaders of an aristocracy in a new country naturally felt it incumbent upon them to keep up with the fashions, planters were constantly ordering from their London agents expensive clothes and other personal finery, including jewelry of considerable value. Rich personal adornment was not a matter of vulgar display; on the contrary, it was evidence of the aristocrat's recognition of what was suitable and proper in dress. A gentleman, even a gentleman on the upper reaches of the Rappahannock, might not dress like a churl when he met with his fellows on social occasions. Accordingly he and his lady had to have proper clothes of the latest cut; old garments of good quality, however, were not discarded, but were often bequeathed to grateful heirs. The elder David Fox, for instance, left to his daughter Hannah a great array of fine silk garments that had belonged to her mother.[27] From the seventeenth century onward, Virginia wills frequently mention bequests of silver-hilted swords, an essential of the gentleman's dress on formal occasions. Likewise, from an early date, colonists owned a considerable quantity of diamonds and other jewels.[28] Clearly the ladies and gentlemen of this frontier society were not content with the simple adornments that the wilderness afforded. When Francis Louis Michel was selecting a stock of merchandise to take to Virginia, he was advised to include plenty of such luxuries as "shoe buckles, hair powder, especially amber, all kinds of perfumes and laces," and, of course, a large supply of wearing apparel.[29] Though Virginia

[26] W. S. Morton, "The Portraits of Lower Brandon and Upper Brandon, Virginia," *William and Mary College Quarterly*, 2d Ser., X (1910), 338-40.

[27] Fleet, *op. cit.*, p. 86.

[28] Stanard, pp. 206 ff.

[29] "Report of the Journey of . . . Michel," p. 5.

in the seventeenth century was on the uttermost verge of English civilization, the gentry of that colony constantly took thought of what was proper in dress. The concern over decorum is particularly evident in their care to observe the conventional customs of mourning, to wear proper black clothes, and to provide the friends of the dead with mourning rings and gloves.[30]

The royal governors, as representatives of the court and of fashionable London, exerted no little influence upon the social life of the Virginia aristocracy. Although the colony was not always happy in the King's choice of a viceroy, and political quarrels were frequent, nevertheless the social influence of the governor—usually a knight, sometimes a courtier, and occasionally a peer of sorts—was considerable; for American "society" has ever loved a lord, and colonial Virginia was no exception. If some of the governors were less noble than their titles, Virginians overlooked their shortcomings as long as possible. The governor who exerted the greatest influence was Sir William Berkeley, who ruled Virginia for nearly a quarter of a century, his various terms falling between the years 1642 and 1677. Since this was the most critical period in the crystallization of an aristocratic social order, the influence of a courtier having the gallantry and polish of Sir William cannot be doubted. One should remember that not until his last years did he become an unpopular tyrant, and even then, during the Bacon Rebellion, most of the conservative ruling class stood by him. He was an aristocrat of a noble family, a former member of the Privy Council, a courtier who had stood high in the favor of Charles I. Furthermore, he had shown his interest in letters, and had achieved some reputation as a gentleman-playwright. As governor of Virginia he entertained graciously at his manor house at Green Spring, near Jamestown, and set an example of courtly manners that gentlemen of more rustic backgrounds were pleased to imitate. In a letter to Lord Arlington, on May

[30] Stanard, pp. 341 ff.

1, 1666, Governor Berkeley observed that they in Virginia "live after the simplicity of the past age; indeed, unless the danger of our country gave our fears tongues and language, we should shortly forget all sounds that did not concern the business and necessities of our farms."[31] But Berkeley was thinking of the gaiety of the court in London and comparing plantation life with it. His own little court at Green Spring helped to introduce some of the urbanity that he missed. And Berkeley was rather proud of the aristocracy who surrounded him, for he wrote in *A Discourse and View of Virginia* (1663) that "men of as good families as any subjects in England have resided there, as the Percies, the Berkeleys, the Wests, the Gages, the Throgmortons, Wyatts, Digges, Chicheleys, Moldsworths, Morrisons, Kemps, and hundred others, which I forbear to name, lest I should misherald them in the catalogue."[32] A little further on he refers to the way good families have become established in Virginia, where "a small sum of money will enable a younger brother to erect a flourishing family in a new world, and add more strength, wealth, and honor to his native country than thousands did before that died forgotten and unrewarded in an unjust war."[33] Though Berkeley's reputation has suffered as a result of his revenge on the Bacon rebels in his irascible old age, his earlier contribution to courtly manners and fashionable social life should not be forgotten.

The qualities of the gentry that we have been describing pertain largely to their public relations and to the external manifestations of gentility. In their private lives they showed a similar consciousness of their station and the obligations that it entailed. They subscribed to the traditional code of gentlemanly conduct and endeavored to acquire the traditional accomplishments.

[31] Quoted in *The Virginia Magazine of History and Biography*, XIX (1911), 29, from the *State Papers, Colonial.*

[32] Ed. of 1663, p. 3.

[33] *Ibid.*, p. 9.

Of all the virtues of the Virginia aristocracy, hospitality was perhaps the most notable, and it carried in its train most of the other social graces and accomplishments. Hospitality embraced the virtue of liberality, that cardinal virtue so much commended in Renaissance courtesy books; and the grand scale on which the great planters entertained showed something of the spirit of magnificence that had also been greatly praised in treatises on the conduct of gentlemen. The hospitality of Virginians early attracted the notice of observers of colonial life. John Hammond in 1656 found the inhabitants "generally affable, courteous, and very assistant to strangers";[34] thirty years later Durand observed that the Virginians spent most of their spare time visiting each other—unlike Frenchmen, who used their leisure in lawsuits.[35] Strangers traveling in the colony had little use for inns, since planters of high and low degree alike graciously offered entertainment, as Durand found to his surprise: "They cordially gave me to eat and to drink of whatever they had, and if I slept in a house where they owned horses, on the morrow some were lent to me to use for the first half of the next day's journey."[36] At the turn of the century Michel declared that the hospitality of the planters was such that it was "possible to travel through the whole country without money except when ferrying across a river," and, if a stranger offered pay, "they are rather angry, asking whether one did not know the custom of the country."[37] The two early historians, Robert Beverley and Hugh Jones, also testify to the hospitality of their countrymen. Conditions all conspired to make hospitality easy: food was abundant,[38] serv-

[34] *Leah and Rachel*, p. 15.

[35] *A Huguenot Exile*, p. 111.

[36] *Ibid.*, p. 136.

[37] "Report of the Journey of . . . Michel," pp. 114-15. For a discussion of the hospitality of Virginians see Stanard, pp. 118 ff., and Philip A. Bruce, *Social Life of Virginia in the Seventeenth Century* (2d ed.; Lynchburg, Va., 1927), pp. 174 ff.

[38] See the comments of Durand (*A Huguenot Exile*, pp. 113, 123-24) and Michel ("Report," pp. 36-37) on the subject of food.

ants were plentiful, and the isolation of the plantations made a chance visitor, especially one from afar, more than welcome, for he provided a delightful diversion from the routine of country gossip. Planters cordially received all comers, regardless of whether they were relatives, friends and neighbors, or strangers. Nor was it necessary for the traveler to be of the same social station to claim entertainment in a great house, for not even a humble wayfarer was turned away. In their hospitality, the planters continued the kind of openhearted, generous "housekeeping" that had been characteristic of English country gentlemen for generations; the decay of this housekeeping in England, as the nobility crowded to London in the late sixteenth and seventeenth centuries, had caused many a lamentation from pamphleteers who would have been pleased to see how Virginians had re-established the tradition of hospitable entertainment and liberality.

The amenities of plantation life encouraged the cultivation of the social graces expected of the gentry. Gentlemen and ladies followed the traditional training that would develop in them the art of pleasing. They were expected to pay proper attention to their manners, to learn the technique of polite compliment and pleasant conversation, to be graceful in dancing, and to be at least moderately conversant with music and polite letters.

Good manners were the distinguishing mark of the gentleman. Though certain moral lapses might be forgiven, and rudeness under stress of great provocation might be overlooked, consistently boorish behavior marked a man as one outside the pale. Colonel Daniel Parke, a dashing gallant and a member of the Council, who left Virginia for England in 1697, was guilty of lapses in both morals and behavior, yet he stoutly advocated the code of manners that he thought the gentry should have, and prescribed for his daughter rules of conduct that throw light on the gentleman's conception of his obligations to others. Commissary James Blair, who hated Parke bitterly, describes him as a "handsome young man of that country [Virginia], one . . . who, to all the other accomplishments that make a complete sparkish gentleman, has added one upon which he infinitely values himself, that is, a quick resentment of every the least thing that looks like an affront or injury. He has learned, they say, the art of fencing, and is as ready at giving a challenge, especially before company, as the greatest Hector in the town." Colonel Parke, Blair charged, "doth entertain a gentleman's lady, one Mistress Berry, whom he had conveyed away from her husband in London, in 1692, and carried her to Virginia along with him, calling her by the name of his cousin Brown." Incensed at sermons preached in Bruton Church against adultery, Parke would have challenged the commissary to a duel, Blair asserted, had not respect for the cloth forbidden it. Instead, on a Sunday he dragged the commissary's wife from a pew, where she sat with Parke's own father-in-law, Colonel Ludwell.[39] Yet this same Parke, who could break the moral law and forget his manners in so violent a fashion (if we can believe Commissary Blair's prejudiced account), wrote a wise letter to his daughter Frances, reminding her of the manners expected of her social station and of the obligation of the gentry to their inferiors. "Mind your writing and everything else you have learnt," Parke enjoins her, "and do not learn to romp, but behave yourself soberly and like a gentlewoman. Mind reading, and carry yourself so that everybody may respect you. Be calm and obliging to all the servants, and when you speak, do it mildly, even to the poorest slave. If any of the servants commit small faults that are of no consequence, do you hide them. If you understand of any great faults they commit, acquaint your mother, but do not aggravate the fault."[40] This does not sound like the advice

[39] "Virginia Gleanings in England," *The Virginia Magazine of History and Biography*, XX (1912), 373-75.

[40] *Ibid.*, p. 375.

of a man who would drag a clergyman's wife out of her pew. Parke a little later impressed both England and Virginia with his courtier's manners and gallantry. As aide-de-camp to the Duke of Marlborough, he brought to the court the news of the Blenheim victory but, as a gallant Virginia gentleman, declined the reward of £500 usually given the bearer of such tidings; instead, he requested a little picture of Queen Anne.[41]

Insistence upon decorum in social relations was characteristic of the Virginia aristocracy from the time it developed as a social order, and from an early date the higher planting class were noted for their courteous manners. The desire to give their children opportunities of learning the formalities of genteel behavior and acquiring the polish that only comes through experience in formal "society" induced a few of the wealthier planters to send their sons and occasionally their daughters to England to be educated. Faith in the value of training in good manners, rather than belief in the worth of academic learning, was undoubtedly the controlling influence in persuading some parents to let their children go on this hazardous journey. But relatively few could attain to a finishing course in England. Parents, therefore, had to be all the more diligent to bring up their children carefully and to set an example of correct behavior. The necessity for vigilance lest children grow up with rude rustic traits made colonial parents particularly sensitive to their duties. It is not without significance that books on manners and etiquette are frequently found in the library catalogues of the planters. Nor is it strange that skilful dancing masters should have been in demand in the colony.

Plantation festivities provided an opportunity for experience which helped to give even stay-at-home planters poise and grace in their social contacts. Ease of life and love of pleasure combined to make the planters a sociable people who delighted in attending balls and similar gatherings. To provide

[41] *Ibid.*, p. 378.

a place for "assemblies," four prominent planters, Henry Corbin, Thomas Gerard, John Lee, and Isaac Allerton, signed an agreement on March 30, 1670, to build a "banqueting house" so that "each man or his heirs yearly, according to his due course" might make "an honorable treatment" for the entertainment of their wives, sweethearts, and friends, "to begin the 29th of May, which will be in the year one thousand, six hundred seventy and one," and to continue in regular rotation forever.[42] The house was built, and there for a time Corbins, Gerards, Lees, and Allertons entertained their neighbors on festive occasions.

Throughout the colonial period dancing was the most popular of the social amusements, and not to know how to dance was to display one's lack of good breeding. To music furnished by servant-fiddlers, the ladies and gentlemen of the colony danced the nights away. On one occasion in the last decade of the seventeenth century the zest of the company was so great that they kept dancing through the night until eleven o'clock of the next day, which unfortunately was the Sabbath; the scandal was the greater because the dance had been given by Margaret Teakle in the absence of her father, the Reverend Thomas Teakle, a wealthy clergyman of Accomac County.[43] The Reverend Mr. Teakle would have forgiven a dance in his absence, as well as the borrowing of a negro fiddler, but dancing on the Sabbath morning to the very hour of church service was shocking even to a liberal Virginia clergyman. From an early date dancing masters and musicians were in request, and by the beginning of the eighteenth century the colony was well supplied with dancing teachers. In 1716 the Board of Visitors of William and Mary College granted

[42] The text of the agreement is given in *The Virginia Magazine of History and Biography*, VIII (1900-1901), 171-72. See also Bruce, *Social Life*, pp. 185-86.

[43] *Ibid.*, pp. 187-88. Bruce (p. 189) calls attention to three indictments at one term of court in Princess Anne County, in 1691-92, for fiddling and dancing on the Sabbath.

William Levingstone permission "to make use of the lower room at the south end of the college for teaching the scholars and others to dance until his own dancing school in Williamsburg be finished." [44] When Levingstone completed his school, he also used it as a theater, with Charles and Mary Stagg in charge. After the death of her husband, who had directed the theater, Mrs. Stagg conducted fashionable "dancing assemblies" there.[45] Since dancing occupied so large a place in the social life of the period, it was an essential part of the training of ladies and gentlemen. The Reverend Hugh Jones in his advice on the improvement of William and Mary College even recommends that the college take a hand in this phase of the social training of its students. "As for the accomplishments of music, dancing, and fencing," he says, "they may be taught by such as the president and masters shall appoint at such certain times as they shall fix for those purposes." [46]

Social gatherings which brought men and women of the upper class together with a certain degree of formality naturally tended to increase attention to manners, and to develop in the men a chivalrous attitude toward women. Furthermore, the relative scarcity of women in the seventeenth and even in

[44] "Proceedings of the Visitors of William and Mary College, 1716," *The Virginia Magazine of History and Biography*, IV (1896-97), 169.

[45] Stanard, pp. 230-31.

[46] Jones, *op. cit.*, p. 87. Records of the insistence upon adequate instruction in dancing are frequent in the eighteenth century. In the 1730's Mary Mason was sent for a year and a half to dancing school. (*William and Mary College Quarterly*, IX [1901-2], 241.) In his will dated Sept. 10, 1762, Charles Carter of Cleve provided that, among other things, his sons be taught dancing, and that his daughters might "be maintained with great frugality and taught to dance." (*The Virginia Magazine of History and Biography*, XXXI [1923], 62-63.) Frequent notices of dancing teachers are to be found in the *Virginia Gazette*. The Reverend Andrew Burnaby, in his travels in Virginia in 1759, observed that the women were "immoderately fond of dancing," but he did not think they showed so much grace as English women. (*The Virginia Historical Register*, V [1852], 90.) The most formal and graceful dances were the minuets, but, even among upper-class Virginians, jigs and reels were common. Seeing Virginia ladies dancing jigs and reels, Burnaby seems to have concluded that they were a somewhat rustic lot.

the eighteenth century magnified the esteem in which they were held. Although there were fewer artificial conventions in the courtesy shown women in the colonial period than in the early nineteenth century, chivalric deference was nevertheless considered the gentleman's proper demeanor where women of his own social class were concerned. This deference was deeper than the mere externals of behavior. If Virginia gentlemen were not invariably the very models of morality, the amount of overt sexual misconduct among the gentry was slight. Divorce was extraordinarily rare,[47] and, if there was marital infidelity among the upper classes, little of it was sufficiently notorious to be recorded. As in England, however, a man could transgress the Seventh Commandment and still be a gentleman. Colonel Daniel Parke, in 1710, willed the greater part of his fortune to an illegitimate daughter in the Leeward Islands, on condition that she take his name and assume his coat of arms—an action that greatly offended his legitimate children in Virginia and their friends; but it would be hard to say whether the father's violation of conventional morality or the exclusion of his rightful heirs from their inheritance was regarded as the greater sin.[48] Parke's conduct, however, was the exception

[47] William Fitzhugh, writing on June 8, 1681, to Kenline Chiseldine, attorney-general for Maryland, discusses "the cruelty of Mr. Blackstone towards my sister-in-law"—which had become so unbearable that she had several times attempted suicide. He suggests precedents for a separation, citing them from Coke on Littleton. "I think," he says, "there is some means to be used for a separation because of his continued cruelty which in England is practical; here in Virginia it is a rare case, of which nature I have known but one, which was between Mrs. Brent and her husband Mr. Giles Brent." Mrs. Brent was granted a legal separation by the Governor and the Council, on charges of extreme cruelty preferred against her husband. (*The Virginia Magazine of History and Biography*, I [1893-94], 40.) Another of the rare cases of separation was that of Mrs. Motram Wright, who was granted a legal separation from her husband, in Lancaster County, on Oct. 12, 1694. She had been the widow of Wright's uncle when she married him ten years before, but in that time had come to be troubled in her conscience for marrying one within the prohibited degrees of affinity. (*Ibid.*, XIII [1905-6], 201-3.)

[48] *The Virginia Magazine of History and Biography*, XX (1912), 379. Bastardy

rather than the usual behavior of Virginia gentlemen, who, as a whole, appear to have walked the path of sexual rectitude a little more scrupulously than did their contemporaries in England.

Like country squires in every English county, the Virginia gentry were lovers of sports and pastimes. Hunting, fishing, horse racing, cockfighting, and cardplaying occupied much of their time. And, if their propensity for gambling was notorious, that was nevertheless accepted as a respectable vice.

Hunting was a hearty rather than a formal sport. Not yet had riding to hounds become a conventionalized social event. Throughout the period, the colony followed the practice of the mother country in hunting foxes as vermin.[49] In the early

---

was not uncommon, of course, but there seem to have been few cases involving the more prominent families. Statutes were enacted, from time to time, dealing with the delinquencies of servant women and with provision for their offspring. For example, the House of Burgesses in 1662 passed an act reading as follows: "Whereas by act of Assembly every woman servant having a bastard is to serve two years, and late experient show that some dissolute masters have gotten their maids with child, and yet claim the benefit of their service, and on the contrary if a woman got with child by her master should be freed from that service it might probably induce such loose persons to lay all their bastards to their masters; it is therefore thought fit and accordingly enacted, and be it enacted henceforward that each woman servant got with child by her master shall after her time by indenture or custom is expired be by the churchwardens of the parish where she lived when she was brought to bed of such bastard sold for two years, and the tobacco to be imployed by the vestry for the use of the parish." (William W. Hening, *The Statutes at Large, Being a Collection of All the Laws of Virginia,* II [New York, 1823], 167.) Later, in the mid-eighteenth century, the Reverend Theodosius Staige, of Charles Parish, York County, was charged before the Council with "not executing his office in not christening of bastard children and opposing the singing the new version of Psalms." The Council, meeting on May 4, 1743, ordered him to fulfil these duties or remove himself from the parish within six months. (*The Virginia Magazine of History and Biography*, XVI [1908], 27-28.)

[49] Fairfax Harrison, "The Genesis of Foxhunting in Virginia," *The Virginia Magazine of History and Biography*, XXXVII (1929), 155-57. Beverley, *op. cit.*, p. 255, comments on the kind of fox hunting practiced in Virginia at the beginning of the eighteenth century: "They have another sort of hunting, which is very diverting, and that they call vermin hunting; it is performed afoot, with small dogs in the night, by the light of the moon or stars. Thus in summer time

days shooting quail, wild turkeys, deer, and bear was more popular than fox hunting. While visiting Robert Beverley, the historian, in 1715, John Fontaine was entertained with field sports. "We took our guns and went ahunting," he records in his *Journal* for June 18, 1715. "We killed some squirrels and partridges but did no hurt to the wild turkeys nor deer, though we saw several. Today we went to some of the planters' houses and diverted ourselves for some time, and so returned to our friend's house and passed away the evening merrily." [50] The aftermath of a hunt was frequently a merry party at the house of one of the participants, as Fontaine implies. Beverley himself in his history describes the various sorts of "hunting, fishing, and fowling with which they entertain themselves an hundred ways." [51] Of the abundance of fish, he comments: "I have sat in the shade at the heads of the rivers angling, and spent as much time in taking the fish off the hook as in waiting for their taking it." [52] Among the more exciting sports was hunting wild horses, "which they pursue sometimes with dogs and sometimes without."[53]

Skill in horsemanship was expected of every gentleman; in fact, even the poorest planters took pride in their horses and their ability as riders. Hugh Jones commented somewhat sarcastically that "they are such lovers of riding that almost every ordinary person keeps a horse; and I have known some spend the morning in ranging several miles in the woods to find and catch their horses only to ride two or three miles to church, to the court house, or to a horse-race, where they generally appoint to meet upon business." [54] Speaking of the "common planters," he further observes that they "don't much admire labor, or any manly exercise, except horse-racing, nor diversion,

---

they find abundance of raccoons, opossums, and foxes in the corn fields, and about their plantations; but at other times they must go into the woods for them."

[50] Ann Maury, *Memoirs of a Huguenot Family* (New York, 1872), p. 266.

[51] Beverley, p. 254. [52] *Ibid.*, p. 256. [53] *Ibid.*, pp. 257-58. [54] Jones, *op. cit.*, p. 49.

except cock-fighting, in which some greatly delight."[55] The popularity of horse racing began early in Virginia and increased in its fascination throughout the colonial period. From the first it was regarded as a sport for gentlemen, and, though the whole countryside could be spectators of races, only gentlemen could enter their horses in the contests.[56] The races were usually for a purse, and betting was heavy; lawsuits resulting from controversies over infractions of racing rules or quarrels over the settlement of wagers were not infrequent and provide much of our information concerning the sport.[57]

Interest in athletic exercises and marksmanship prompted Sir Francis Nicholson, the governor, to proclaim in 1691 an annual field day at which "the better sort of Virginians only, who are bachelors," should engage in contests of skill and strength for prizes offered by the governor. Whether the annual celebration which Nicholson designed for St. George's Day became as popular as the governor hoped is not quite clear, but similar celebrations were common.[58] The younger gentry took part in such sports as wrestling, but it was considered improper to wrestle publicly with social inferiors.[59]

Like horse racing, cockfighting was a sport which gentlemen enjoyed, though the gentry could not make it their private monopoly. Anybody with a brace of fighting cocks could invite his neighbors to attend a spectacle of this sort. Not many records of cockfights as social events date from the earlier period, but by the mid-eighteenth century elaborate cockfights, followed by a ball at night, were not uncommon. As at horse

[55] *Ibid.*, p. 48.

[56] For the celebrated case of James Bullock, the tailor, who was so presumptuous as to enter his horse in a race with a gentleman's horse, in York County, on Sept. 10, 1674, see Chapter II, p. 59.

[57] See W. G. Stanard, "Racing in Colonial Virginia," *The Virginia Magazine of History and Biography*, II (1894-95), 293-305.

[58] M. N. Stanard, *op. cit.*, p. 257.

[59] Wrestling was frowned upon by some English writers on the accomplishments of the gentry. See Chapter I, p. 11.

races, the gentry bet heavily, often putting up livestock as stakes when cash was scarce.[60]

The favorite vice of the gentry was gambling, particularly gaming at cards, though wagers might be placed on any game or sport. Records of the planters' propensity for gambling make their appearance not long after settlement began, and increase throughout colonial times. Even a Dutch sea captain, surely no squeamish observer, calling at Jamestown in 1633, "was astonished at finding so many of the planters inveterate gamblers, even staking their servants." [61] Nearly a half century later, the Huguenot Durand, on a journey with Ralph Wormeley and other fine gentlemen, remarked that his companions spent the whole night in gambling at cards for considerable stakes.[62] It was of course lamentable when gentlemen were so improvident as to lose their estates over the card table, but no social stigma attached to gambling. Cheating at cards, however, was a cardinal sin sufficient to exclude a guilty one from the society of decent men. Indeed, cheating in sports was punished not only by the severity of public opinion but sometimes by the law itself. In the celebrated York County case of 1674, in which a tailor was fined for entering his mare against a gentleman's horse, it is worthy of note that, when it was discovered that this gentleman had connived with the tailor to "fix" the race, the gentleman was put in the stocks.[63]

Love of conviviality resulted in an incredible amount of drinking, and some drunkenness among the gentry, but, on the whole, the tradition that a man should "carry his liquor like a gentleman" prevailed. Considering the amount of strong drink consumed, it is remarkable that there are few records

[60] "Letters from and to George Hume," *The Virginia Magazine of History and Biography*, XX (1912), 413; "Cock Fight, 1767," *ibid.*, X (1902-3), 325; "Letter Book of Francis Jerdone," *William and Mary College Quarterly*, 1st Ser., XI (1902-3), 155.

[61] Edward D. Neill, *Virginia Carolorum* (Albany, 1886), p. 94.

[62] *A Huguenot Exile*, p. 148.

[63] M. N. Stanard, *op. cit.*, p. 252.

of gentlemen who were sots. When Durand rode with Wormeley and other gentlemen, twenty strong, to Colonel William Fitzhugh's, they were royally received and treated to "good wine and all kinds of beverages, so there was a great deal of carousing. He had sent for three fiddlers, a jester, a tight-rope dancer, an acrobat who tumbled around, and they gave us all the entertainment one could wish for."[64] If anyone of the party was ever too drunk to travel, Durand makes no mention of the fact. Whenever the cavalcade stopped on their journey, the punch bowls were brought out, and all drank deeply.

But it was a later and more famous cavalcade, the one led by Governor Spotswood over the Blue Ridge Mountains in 1716, that established a record for its traveling cellar, and perhaps illustrates the attitude of the gentry of that day toward drinking. The party, composed of some of the leading gentlemen of the colony, had as its purpose the exploration of the region across the mountains. Though their objective was serious, they did not propose to make exploration a bore. Hence they diverted themselves with hunting along the way, with stories as merry as those of Chaucer's pilgrims about their campfires, and with an incredible quantity of punch and other liquor. But if any of the party got too drunk, John Fontaine, whose *Journal* describes the pilgrimage, remains discreetly silent. There were proper occasions for their drinking. On September 5 Fontaine was pleased to note that "we drank King George's health, and all the Royal Family's, at the very top of the Appalachian Mountains."[65] On the next day, when they had crossed the "Euphrates" [Shenandoah] River, and had claimed the land beyond in the King's name, there came the grand climax to their celebration: "We had a good dinner, and after it we got the men together, and loaded all their arms, and we drank the

[64] *A Huguenot Exile*, p. 158. See also pp. 129, 138-39, 147, 159.

[65] Maury, *op. cit.*, p. 287. The portion of Fontaine's *Journal* that describes the journey over the Blue Ridge is also reprinted in W. W. Scott, *A History of Orange County, Virginia* (Richmond, Va., 1907), pp. 104-13.

King's health in champagne, and fired a volley; the Princess' health in burgundy, and fired a volley; and all the rest of the Royal Family in claret, and a volley. We had several sorts of liquors, viz., Virginia red wine and white wine, Irish usquebaugh, brandy, shrub, two sorts of rum, champagne, canary, cherry, punch, water, cider, etc. I sent two of the rangers to look for my gun, which I dropped in the mountains; they found it, and brought it to me at night, and I gave them a pistole for their trouble." [66] Yet with all these potations, the explorers were up and in the saddle by seven o'clock the next morning, for this expedition was no mere orgy of drinking and merrymaking. In the party was Robert Beverley, the historian, famous in his day for efforts to establish vineyards in Virginia and to create an industry of wine making. Beverley himself disapproved of excessive drinking, and observed sadly in his *History* that, although in his country "there is the most good nature and hospitality practiced in the world, both towards friends and strangers; but the worst of it is, this generosity is attended now and then with a little too much intemperance." [67] Gentlemen drank deep in that age, and occasionally drank themselves under the table, but in general they

[66] Maury, pp. 288-89. Fontaine has frequent allusions elsewhere to the drinkables consumed. Aug. 29 (p. 284): "We made great fires, and supped, and drank good punch." Aug. 30 (p. 285): "We made large fires, pitched our tents, cut boughs to lie upon, had good liquor, and at ten went to sleep. We always kept a sentry at the Governor's door." They clearly had a good time. On Sept. 9 (p. 290) he notes: "We were very merry, and diverted ourselves with our adventures." A passage paralleling Fontaine's description of the beverages taken on the Blue Ridge expedition is found in William Byrd's *The Secret History of the Line*. See William Byrd, *Histories of the Dividing Line betwixt Virginia and North Carolina*, ed. William K. Boyd (Raleigh, N.C., 1929), pp. 21, 23.

[67] Beverley, p. 254. John Fontaine (Maury, pp. 265-66) asserts that Beverley told him that he had wagered a hundred guineas against a thousand that he could "cultivate a vineyard that would yield at one vintage, seven hundred gallons of wine." Fontaine adds: "I do not in the least doubt but the next year he will make the seven hundred gallons and win the thousand guineas. We were very merry with the wine of his own making, and drank prosperity to the vineyard." Drinking at public gatherings was sometimes an occasion of con-

maintained reasonable decorum and subscribed, at least in theory, to the doctrine of moderation; however, moderation in the seventeenth and eighteenth centuries, one should hasten to add, was gauged by a liberal standard.

The theory of behavior embraced by the Virginia gentleman was implied in the traditional code of his kind that he adapted to his use. Acceptance of the code, however, did not mean that he always succeeded in making his conduct conform to the ideal. But it was something even to give lip service to an ancient ideal. The cardinal virtues that the gentleman was still expected to believe in were the same that had won the praise of Renaissance writers: fortitude, prudence, temperance, justice, liberality, and courtesy. All of these the Virginia gentleman approved as desirable; some he exemplified with considerable zeal.

Fortitude, for example, was a virtue which every planter felt strictly bound to demonstrate in his own actions, for few shortcomings received greater contempt than cowardice. The fear of being thought a coward doubtless led at times to deeds of bravado, but so thoroughly ingrained was the ideal that a gentleman should set an example of courage that it was accepted as a matter of course. And he was also expected to be able to endure hardships and sufferings, particularly those incidental to war, with stoical dignity. For instance, nothing became Colonel Daniel Parke like his death. Horribly tortured by rebels who captured him at Antigua, he was "insulted and reviled by every scoundrel, in the agonies of death, but makes no other return but these mild expressions, 'Gentlemen, you

---

siderable intemperance. The custom of drinking at funerals, for example, seems to have led to abuses. The Reverend Edmund Watts of York County made this provision in his will, dated Feb. 20, 1676: "Imprimis, having observed in the days of my pilgrimage the debauched drinking at burials tending much to the dishonor of God and his true religion, my will is that no strong drink be provided or spent at my burial." (*Tyler's Quarterly Historical and Genealogical Magazine*, I [1919-20], 212.)

have no sense of honor left, pray have some of humanity.' " A few hours after this, he died, "recommending his soul to God, with some pious ejaculations."[68]

The quality of prudence, which may be adumbrated with wisdom, was exemplified in the leadership provided by the ruling class. The members of this aristocratic body were expected to demonstrate a sagacity superior to lesser men's; how well they succeeded, we have already seen. The development of this quality made possible the distinguished leaders of later generations.

Some inkling of how in actual practice the Virginia gentleman failed or succeeded in his effort to live up to the ideal of temperance is revealed by descriptions of his drinking customs. But it is unfortunate that, in the language of our own day, the word temperance has come to connote almost exclusively abstinence from strong drink. The temperance of the gentleman's tradition meant moderation in all things—the moderation prescribed by Aristotle. William Byrd, remonstrating with Mrs. Fleming for being too affectionate toward her husband, observed with unction that "the best things in this world, if constantly used, are apt to be cloying, which a little absence and abstinence would prevent."[69] Although in such matters as drink Virginians had their own ideas of what constituted temperance, the notion of moderation was nevertheless a concept that still profoundly influenced the behavior of gentlemen in the fundamental concerns of life. Perhaps this influence was more or less unconscious—an ideal that was taken for granted as desirable, even when men failed of its attainment.

The sense of justice manifested by the ruling class won praise from observers of Virginia life. Since the administration of law was in the hands of great planters, it is a tribute to their

[68] *The Virginia Magazine of History and Biography*, XX (1912), 379.

[69] William Byrd, *A Progress to the Mines in the Year 1732*, in *A Journey to the Land of Eden and Other Papers*, ed. Mark Van Doren (New York, 1928), p. 320.

integrity and honesty that their decisions were distinguished for wisdom and justice. Indeed, the orderly administration of justice was one of the virtues which gave the colony greatest cause for pride. If officials sometimes betrayed their trust, they were the exception rather than the rule. So complete was the confidence of the public in the just administration of law that Virginians practically never resorted to the sort of vigilantism that so often characterizes frontier life.[70] Durand thought the laws "so wise that there are almost no lawsuits"[71]—a flattering exaggeration that nevertheless indicates the sense of honesty and justice which the colonists had developed. Michel, a few years later, had cause to thank his stars for the scrupulous care with which a country justice of the peace investigated his case when he was arrested and charged with being an escaped servant.[72] In the administration of public affairs and in their private lives, the Virginia aristocracy cultivated the virtue of justice. When one of the ruling class erred in this respect, it was a matter for severe disapprobation by his fellows.

The liberality and courtesy of the Virginia gentry would have been approved by Renaissance advocates of these virtues. As the descriptions of their hospitality show, their generosity was the lavish, openhanded kind that excited the comment of travelers from other regions. And always in their giving they remembered to be gracious and courteous. Niggardliness they held in contempt, and penny pinching was a mark of bad breeding. Since material wealth came easily to the great planters of Virginia, they found it easy to part with their possessions. The continuance of the tradition of benevolence, confined to no class, and transmitted to the colony from England, is

[70] Bruce, *Institutional History*, II, 623-25.

[71] *A Huguenot Exile*, p. 111.

[72] "Report of the Journey of . . . Michel," p. 136. Planters of course took their duties as justices of the peace seriously. Since every gentleman might expect to become a justice of the peace, or a higher judicial officer, he was expected to have some knowledge of the law.

evident in the numerous bequests for the relief of the poor and for other worthy causes.

The recognition of a self-imposed code determining their conduct naturally tended to make gentlemen sensitive to their obligations to that code and quick to resent any imputation that their conduct was not in accord with the customary practice of gentlemen. Though gentlemen were careful to maintain their honor and to protect their reputations, dueling was so rare that it was almost nonexistent in the colonial period.[73] If a few men like Daniel Parke were known as swaggerers ever ready to dare an opponent to a duel, there was no general feeling that a gentleman jeopardized his honor by refusing to accept a challenge. Indeed, public opinion frowned on dueling and looked to the laws of libel and slander to safeguard the good names of honest men.

An aristocracy that was mindful of its obligations to church and state, sensitive about its manners and behavior, and careful to maintain its superiority, would not neglect its intellectual development. Hence we find Virginians of the upper class making provision for the education of their children, employing tutors, and setting up plantation schools. From London booksellers, planters imported works of learning and utility necessary to the education and training of a gentleman. Indeed, their libraries are significant of a desire to duplicate the traditional learning and culture of England. Like the New Englanders, Virginians were determined not to grow barbaric in the wilderness.

[73] See *The Virginia Magazine of History and Biography*, I (1893-94), 216, 347, also pp. 82-83; *ibid.*, II (1894-95), 96-97; *ibid.*, III (1895-96), 89; *ibid.*, V (1897-98), 191; *ibid.*, VII (1899-1900), 139; *ibid.*, X (1902-3), 332; Robert Reid Howison, "Duelling in Virginia," *William and Mary College Quarterly*, 2d Ser., IV (1924), 217-44. See also Evarts B. Greene, "The Code of Honor in Colonial and Revolutionary Times, with Special Reference to New England," *Publications of the Colonial Society of Massachusetts*, XXVI (1924-26), 367-88. Mr. Greene points out that there was less dueling in Virginia than in New England, and that there the duels were for the most part fought by newcomers.

CHAPTER IV

THE PLANTERS' CONCERN OVER EDUCATION

If getting rich by the acquisition of land and the growing of tobacco was a goal pursued by the Virginia colonists with an extraordinary singleness of purpose, material prosperity also increased their desire for a civilized and cultivated way of life—the sort of life some of them had known in England; material possessions stimulated their zeal to safeguard their children against the danger of growing up crude and uncouth in the wilderness. From early in the seventeenth century, therefore, there was a persistent struggle to provide opportunities for education. Virginia planters prosperous enough to look forward to the advancement of their families in the New World were just as concerned over the proper training of their sons and their daughters as were their Puritan brethren of Massachusetts Bay. But the scattered nature of the plantations made the establishment of schools less easy than in the more densely settled townships of New England; as a result, education in the Chesapeake region tended to become an individual rather than a civic enterprise. Though the manner and quality of education in Virginia differed from that of New England, there was nevertheless no general lack of interest in learning among the tobacco planters. The rising landed gentry of Virginia, realizing that their children must have sufficient education to enable them to take care of their estates and dignify the station to which they aspired, provided tutors and plantation schools according to their means, or in rare cases sent their children back to England. Nor were they completely unmindful of their social responsibility to the less prosperous, as is indicated by repeated, though often unsuccessful, efforts to provide facilities for the education of poor children scattered on farms throughout the length and breadth of the colony.

Virginia's lack of towns, rather than any callous neglect or evil policy on the part of the ruling class, was responsible for the breakdown of schemes designed to improve the educational opportunities of the children of the poorer planters. Try as the authorities might, and legislate as they would, it was impossible to support enough schools to be accessible to all the country population. While wealthy planters could afford to hire teachers for their own and their immediate neighbors' children, many poor families were out of range of any school. Hence the Reverend James Blair and two of his colleagues, writing to the Board of Trade in 1697 concerning the dearth of towns, and the amenities that go with town life, could assert of the colony that, "for well-educated children, for an industrious and thriving people, or for an happy government in church and state, and in short, for all other advantages of human improvements, it is certainly . . . one of the poorest, miserablest, and worst countries in all America that is inhabited by Christians."[1] Although the plantation system retarded popular education in Virginia, the ruling class, throughout the colonial period, persisted in its efforts to improve educational facilities.

A strong motive inspiring the efforts aimed to further popular education was the same in Virginia as in New England: the belief in the utility of learning in the furtherance of godliness. Every child, it was felt, should be able to read the Bible, the catechism, and the *Practice of Piety*. Decency and order in the community required that some effort be made to provide a means for the generality of citizens to acquire this ability, even though the inaccessibility of the mass of the people to such schools as were founded made the effort more or less futile.

[1] James Blair, Henry Hartwell, and Edward Chilton, "An Account of the Present State and Government of Virginia," *Collections of the Massachusetts Historical Society*, 1st Ser., V (1798), 125. This tract is also reprinted in the *Calendar of State Papers, Colonial, 1696-1697*, pp. 641-66.

Nevertheless, hopeful philanthropists from time to time established schools which helped somewhat to alleviate the general ignorance, and legislators salved their consciences at intervals with laws providing for the education of orphans and poor children.[2] Meanwhile, as their letters and wills show, the wealthier planters were giving far more thought than is usually supposed to the problem of adequate training for their own children. Economic conditions, rather than conscious plan or Machiavellian design, gave the families of wealth a monopoly, to all practical intents, of educational opportunity.

The efforts, however, to establish schools in the English manner, during the early years of colonization, show a significant desire to reproduce in Virginia the educational advantages of the home country.

Within ten years of the first settlement of Jamestown, an agitation was being made for schools in the colony. King James commanded the bishops to collect money for the founding of schools, and on May 26, 1619, Sir Edwin Sandys, the treasurer of the Virginia Company of London, reported that £1,500, or thereabouts, was on hand for "that pious work."[3] The Virginia Company, under the guidance of Sandys, thereupon set aside ten thousand acres of land for the use of "the university to be planted at Henrico"; they also allotted one thousand

[2] Discussions of education in colonial Virginia may be found in Philip A. Bruce, *Institutional History of Virginia in the Seventeenth Century* (New York, 1910), I, 293-401; Sadie Bell, *The Church, the State, and Education in Virginia* (Philadelphia, 1930), *passim;* Guy Frederick Wells, *Parish Education in Colonial Virginia* ("Teachers College, Columbia University, Contributions to Education," No. 138; New York, 1923); Herbert B. Adams, *The College of William and Mary: A Contribution to the History of Higher Education* ("Circulars of Information of the Bureau of Education," No. 1; Washington, 1887). Many articles on various phases of colonial education are to be found in *The Virginia Magazine of History and Biography* and the *William and Mary College Quarterly.*

[3] *The Records of the Virginia Company of London,* ed. Susan Myra Kingsbury (Washington, 1906), I, 220, 268. See also W. Gordon McCabe, "The First University in America, 1619-1622," *The Virginia Magazine of History and Biography,* XXX (1922), 148 ff.

acres to "the college for the conversion of infidels,"[4] an adjunct of the university. The records of the Virginia Company show that officers intrusted with the creation of the university gave careful thought to the project. On June 14, 1619, the company voted to appoint "a committee of choice gentlemen, and other of his Majesty's Council for Virginia concerning the college, being a weighty business, and so great that an account of their proceedings therein must be given to the state."[5] News of the "sacred work" of the "foundation of the college in Virginia" having got abroad, the company five weeks afterward received a rich anonymous gift of communion plate, a "carpet of crimson velvet," and a "linen damask table cloth" for the collegiate church.[6] A little over a year later a stranger presented "a map of Sir Walter Raleigh's containing a Description of Guiana" and four great books, "whereof one book was a treatise of St. Augustine, of the City of God translated into English; the other three great volumes were the works of Mr. [William] Perkins newly corrected and amended, which books the donor desired they might be sent to the college in Virginia there to remain in safety to the use of the collegiates hereafter."[7] On January 30, 1622, the same stranger presented four more books —a Bible, a Book of Common Prayer, the catechism of Zacharias Ursinus, and "a small Bible richly embroidered."[8] Clearly philanthropists at home hoped to bring up the collegiates in piety and good learning.

Meanwhile other educational ventures were starting. In February, 1620, Sir Edwin Sandys received a box and a letter from an unknown "man of good fashion" who signed himself "Dust and Ashes." The box contained a bag of gold amounting to £550, which Sandys was instructed to use for a school in

[4] *The Records of the Virginia Company*, I, 268.
[5] *Ibid.*, p. 231.
[6] *Ibid.*, pp. 247-48.
[7] *Ibid.*, p. 421.
[8] *Ibid.*, p. 589.

Virginia for the education of "some of the children of the Virginians . . . in Christian religion and good manners."[9] By Virginians the donor meant Indians. Although the colonists showed no enthusiasm for this proposed Indian school, Southampton Hundred was persuaded unwillingly to undertake it, but decided first to increase the endowment by investing the capital funds in an ironworks, which came to naught.[10]

A third school was projected about the same time. In 1621 the Reverend Patrick Copland, chaplain of an East India merchantman, the "Royal James," took up a collection among the gentlemen and mariners of the ship, while it lay off the Cape of Good Hope; the purpose of this charitable endeavor was to benefit the colony of Virginia. The ship's company contributed liberally, and Copland transmitted to the Virginia Company £70 8*s.* 6*d.*; whether to build a church or erect a school was left to the Company's discretion. The officers of the Company decided on October 30, 1621, that there was greater want of a school than of a church, and resolved upon a "public free school, which, being for the education of children and grounding of them in the principles of religion, civility of life, and humane learning, served to carry with it the greatest weight and highest consequence unto the plantations as that whereof both church and commonwealth take their original foundation and happy estate, this being also like to prove a work most acceptable unto the planters, through want whereof they have been hitherto constrained to their great costs to send their children from thence hither to be taught."[11] Accordingly the Company set aside a thousand acres of land in Charles City for the school, sent over carpenters to start work on buildings, and began a search for a proper teacher to undertake the instruc-

[9] *Ibid.*, pp. 313-14, 586.

[10] *Ibid.*, pp. 585-89.

[11] *Ibid.*, p. 539. See also H. Carrington Lancaster, "The East India School Planned for Charles City," *Tyler's Quarterly Historical and Genealogical Magazine,* V (1923-24), 239-40.

tion. The Reverend Mr. Copland received three shares of stock in the Company, in token of his zeal. The East India School, as it was named, was to be a subsidiary of Henrico University.

All of these early educational ventures failed. The disastrous Indian massacre on Good Friday, 1622, which almost wrecked the colony, stopped the development of the college lands, hopelessly impaired the endowments, and completely destroyed enthusiasm for the education of the infidels, which was to have been one phase of the educational program. With the dissolution of the Virginia Company in 1624, the first three educational projects disappeared.

The wording of the Virginia Company's decision to establish the East India School, quoted above, gives one of the earliest indications that the planters themselves were already concerned about the education of their offspring, and that some were sending their children back to England for training. Since many of the colonial records have disappeared, it is impossible to know precisely what steps were taken by the colonists in the initial period to insure the proper training of their children, but we can be certain that so fundamental a matter was not altogether neglected.

Another project for a university in Virginia was conceived about this time by a country gentleman of Warwickshire, one Edward Palmer, who owned lands in Virginia and New England. In 1624 he made a will providing that, in case his issue failed, his property in the New World should be used for the foundation of a "university, and such schools in Virginia, as shall be there erected, and shall be called *Academia Virginiensis et Oxoniensis*." [12] A suggestion that Palmer subscribed at least in part to the plan of education laid down in Henry Peacham's *Compleat Gentleman*, published two years before he made his will, is found in a provision for the instruction of the students

[12] Edward D. Neill, *Virginia Vetusta* (Albany, 1885), p. 183.

of this university in drawing and painting. In their hours of recreation, to avoid idleness, students were to "learn the arts of painting"; and, the benefactor further states, "my will and mind is, that two grinders, the one for oil colors, and the other for water colors, and also colors, oil, and gum waters shall be provided from time to time at the charges of the said college, beseeching God to add a blessing to all these intents."[13] God in his wisdom did not see fit to further the cause of the fine arts in the education of Virginia gentlemen, and this venture, like the others, came to nothing.

In the extant records for the remainder of the seventeenth century, bequests for educational purposes are fairly frequent, and undoubtedly other schools were established, though the records have disappeared. A few schools founded before 1700 survived until later times.

The best-known free school of the seventeenth century was one established by Benjamin Symmes, a moderately well-to-do planter, who in 1635 left by will two hundred acres on the Poquoson River, with the increase and milk of eight cows, for the education of children from Elizabeth City and Kiquotan parishes forever.[14] A little later, by deed dated September 19, 1659, Thomas Eaton founded another school in Elizabeth City County, with a gift of five hundred acres of land and appurtenances, including two negro slaves and cattle.[15] Both the Symmes Free School and the Eaton Free School survived into the nineteenth century, and in 1805 were consolidated into Hampton Academy. These schools were designed to give elementary instruction in reading, writing, and simple arithmetic, with perhaps some attention to Latin, in imitation of the

[13] *Ibid.*, p. 184.

[14] Edward D. Neill, *Virginia Carolorum* (Albany, 1886), pp. 112-13; Lyon G. Tyler, "Education in Colonial Virginia," *William and Mary College Quarterly*, 1st Ser., VI (1897-98), 72-77.

[15] "The Eaton Free School," *William and Mary College Quarterly*, 1st Ser., XI (1902-3), 19-20. See also Bruce, *Institutional History of Virginia*, I, 350-56.

English grammar schools of the same period. Unfortunately no detailed evidence concerning the curricula has come to light.

Planters from time to time provided endowments for other free schools, or for the education of poor children of the parish. As in England, it was customary in the colony for well-to-do men in their wills to make at least a gesture toward philanthropy, to remember the poor, or to give something for schools. In an earlier age, the same men would have founded a chantry, with a provision for perpetual masses for their souls. But among Protestants education gradually acquired a measure of the sanctity of religion and became a proper object of testamentary remembrance. If colonial Virginians were somewhat less zealous than others in this cause, they did not entirely forget educational benefactions.

Captain John Moon, whose will was recorded in Isle of Wight County on August 12, 1655, made charitable bequests to the poor of the parish and ordered the sale of certain cattle to help educate poor children. Henry King, a planter of the same county, bequeathed, by will dated March 2, 1668, one hundred acres of land "to the parish where I now live towards the maintenance of a free school." And Arthur Smyth, also of Isle of Wight, by will dated December 2, 1696, specified that, in case his issue failed, his lands were to be used for "maintaining and encouraging a free school."[16] In other counties whose records are still extant one finds wills bequeathing land or money for educational purposes. William Whittington of Northampton County, in 1659, gave two thousand pounds of tobacco for the use of a free school, "if it should go forward in Northampton."[17] A Quaker, Richard Russell of Lower Norfolk County, by will in 1667, set aside a part of his estate for the education of six poor children, "and after these six

[16] "Isle of Wight County Records," *William and Mary College Quarterly*, VII (1898-99), 222, 236; "Free Schools in Isle of Wight County," *ibid.*, V (1896-97), 112-13.

[17] *The Virginia Magazine of History and Biography*, V (1896-97), 41.

are entered, then if six more comes, I give a part also to enter them in like manner."[18] Frances Pritchard, widow of a Lancaster County boatwright, stipulated by will in 1679 that her estate should be used for a free school if she should have no surviving heirs.[19] The Reverend John Farnefold, minister of St. Stephen's parish in Northumberland County, in 1702 provided for the establishment of a school by a bequest of one hundred acres of land and "what school books I have in my study." The institution, to "be called Winchester School," would be required to take four or five poor children belonging to the parish "to be taught gratis, and have their diet, lodging, and washing, and when they can read the Bible and write a legible hand to dismiss them and take in more."[20] Mrs. Mary Whaley, as a memorial to her son Matthew who had died in 1705 at the age of nine, established the next year in Bruton parish the Mattey School, which survived through various vicissitudes to become, at the end of the nineteenth century, the model school for William and Mary College.[21] Mrs. Whaley specified that the school should teach reading, writing, and arithmetic. Throughout the colonial period other bequests similar to these indicate the planters' recognition of certain obligations to provide public instruction.

An example of this feeling of social responsibility, undoubtedly felt by many planters, is clearly shown in a will made, in 1731, by John Yeates of Nansemond County. A prosperous and philanthropic citizen with children of his own, Yeates had already built two schoolhouses in his parish. His will specifies that the rents and other profits from his estate shall be devoted to a free school or schools "in the Lower Parish of Nansemond County, formerly socalled, being the parish

[18] *Ibid.*, I (1893-94), 326-27.

[19] *Ibid.*, II (1894-95), 97-99.

[20] "Schools in Virginia," *William and Mary College Quarterly*, 1st Ser., XVII (1908-9), 244-47.

[21] Lyon G. Tyler, "Grammar and Mattey Practice and Model School," *ibid.*, 1st Ser., IV (1895-96), 3-14.

I have so long lived in, among such friendly neighbors." He is concerned that "there may be two schoolhouses continued in the same places already fixed, which I have built, so that one schoolhouse will be very convenient for the children of the one side of Bennet's Creek, and the other on the other side thereof, which will complete that part of the parish, as formerly I have done; and by that means, and with God's blessings, the most or all the children of these parts will be educated."[22] Yeates was a man of some learning, given to good cheer as well as piety. To his school or schools, he bequeathed certain unnamed books, to be kept under lock and key, that they might always be available for the school children. To the parish church he gave a great Bible, Bishop Joseph Hall's *Works*, "a sermon book with Divine Contemplations, by the same author, also Bishop Ussher's book in folio, entitled the Sum and Substance of the Christian Religion," and a silver communion service. To the honorable members of the Nansemond County court, his friends, went ten shillings "to drink for my sake." For the gentlemen of the vestry, he provided "a treat" at his house and gave them his lawbooks "as a help at their meetings." Besides many other bequests to his family, friends, and even slaves, this neighborly planter of Nansemond set aside ten pounds sterling "to buy books for the poorer sort of inhabitants," particularly such works as *The Whole Duty of Man*, Testaments, Psalters, and primers. To the vestrymen, he intrusts the duty of purchasing and distributing these good books. Yeates's school foundation remained intact until the War between the States. In 1861 a report stated that the benefactor had left 1,007 acres of land to the foundation; at the time of the report the slaves alone were valued at $40,000. Five years later the Virginia legislature authorized the sale of the lands.[23] Yeates's philanthropy

[22] The will is reprinted in full by W. E. MacClenny, in "Yeates' Free Schools," *William and Mary College Quarterly*, 2d Ser., V (1925), 30-38.

[23] *Ibid.*, pp. 37-38.

stands out as an example of the public spirit felt by certain of the wealthier planting class.

As early as 1661 the conscience of the ruling class was sufficiently aroused over the question of learning for the Virginia Assembly, in March of that year, to pass an act creating a preparatory school and a college. The "want of able and faithful ministers," as the act explicitly states, was a primary motive in stirring the legislative body to action. Hence it was enacted "that for the advance of learning, education of youth, supply of the ministry and promotion of piety there be land taken upon purchases for a college and free school, and that there be, with as much speed as may be convenient, housing erected thereon for entertainment of students and scholars."[24] The Assembly also drew up a petition to the King, asking for letters patent to solicit "well disposed people in England for the erecting of colleges and schools in this country";[25] and members of the Assembly individually subscribed considerable sums to the cause. The commissioners of the county courts were also instructed to make subscriptions. The proposed institution was described as "a college of students of the liberal arts and sciences."[26]

The worthy intention of the Virginia Assembly to create a college and subsidiary schools, like so many other educational projects in the colony, came to nothing. Selfish elements within the government, apparently, let the matter die.[27] The effort, however, is further evidence of an interest among certain of the ruling class in the promotion of learning.

Finally, in the last decade of the seventeenth century, a movement was started that resulted in the foundation of William and Mary College, established by royal charter in 1693. A few years before this date, some of the wealthier planters, aided by

[24] William Waller Hening, *The Statutes at Large, Being a Collection of All the Laws of Virginia*, II (New York, 1823), 25. Some historians, following the old-style calendar, give the date of this act as 1660. [25] *Ibid.*, p. 30. [26] *Ibid.*, p. 37.

[27] Bruce, *The Institutional History of Virginia*, I, 377-79.

English merchants doing business in the colony, had subscribed £2,500 toward an institution of higher learning.[28] In 1691, under the leadership of Governor Francis Nicholson and the commissary of the Bishop of London, the Reverend James Blair, the Assembly sent a memorial to the government in England, asking for financial assistance in erecting a college. The memorial pointed out that Virginia gentlemen had already subscribed liberally and were prepared to give further sums. Although Commissary Blair in person succeeded in persuading the government to allow £2,000 out of the quitrents toward building the college, to give 20,000 acres of land for the endowment, and to authorize an export tax of a penny a pound on tobacco shipped from Virginia and Maryland, his task was not easy. In response to one of Blair's arguments that a college would train ministers to help save the souls of Virginians, Sir Edward Seymour, a Lord of the Treasury, is reported to have blustered, "Souls! Damn your souls! Make tobacco!"[29]

Middle Plantation, soon to be called Williamsburg, was chosen as the site of the college, and on August 8, 1695, the cornerstone of the first building was laid with considerable ceremony, the Governor and the Council being present. Although the development of the college was slow, and for ten years after its foundation it remained little more than a grammar school, by May 1, 1699, five students had advanced sufficiently to deliver eloquent orations in praise of learning, before Governor Nicholson, the honorable members of the Council, and the House of Burgesses. Their object was to impress these notable personages with the progress of learning in Virginia, and to emphasize the advantages of having the capital of the colony located in the college town.[30] These

[28] Adams, *The College of William and Mary*, p. 14. [29] *Ibid.*, p. 15.

[30] "Speeches of Students of the College of William and Mary Delivered May 1, 1699," *William and Mary College Quarterly*, 2d Ser., X (1930), 323-37. The original manuscript of these orations is in the archives of the Society for the Propagation of the Gospel, London. A photostatic reproduction is in the Library of Congress. The names of the orators are not given.

speeches, laboriously prepared and smelling of the lamp, nevertheless give a shrewd insight into the educational ideals of Virginians in the last year of the seventeenth century.

If the state is to be healthy, learning must be encouraged, argues the first of the college orators, as he presents a typically Elizabethan commendation of learning, with particular application to Virginia. "No country can ever flourish and be in repute and esteem without it," he declares. "Learning is of mighty force and efficacy both to secure states and cities from infinite evils and to heap all good things upon them, for how can laws be made, justice be distributed, difference be composed, public speeches be begun or concluded, embassies be managed, and what is fittest and best to be done on all occasions be discovered without the assistance of learning?" With the help of learning, Virginians will be enabled to converse with the most excellent men of all ages, with Plato, Aristotle, Seneca, Cicero, Livy, Tacitus, and with many other writers of infinite value in teaching wisdom and virtue, the orator continues. He also makes a plea for the study of language, lest the speech of Virginians grow corrupt. Because of ignorance "the comeliness of our mother tongue is most intolerably corrupted," so that many persons "can neither write good sense nor true English," the speaker complains. The need of training in proper speech was early recognized by Virginians and became one of the major considerations of aristocratic planters in selecting tutors for their children.[31]

The theme of the second orator's discourse was the advantages of education in Virginia over education abroad. The prestige and good reputation of the colony demand the support

[31] An interesting side light on the concern of an aristocratic planter over the language training of his children, at the end of the colonial period, is to be found in *Philip Vickers Fithian: Journal and Letters, 1767-1774,* ed. John R. Williams (Princeton, 1900), p. 147. Councilor Robert Carter, in whose household Fithian served as tutor, objected to Scotch tutors because their pronunciation was not so good as that of tutors who had been to school on the Continent.

of schools which will make it unnecessary for Virginia children to go to England "or other foreign parts" for their education, the speaker maintains. Education abroad is extremely expensive in time and money, he points out, and the hazards of the sea and disease are very great. Remembering that his audience is composed of men whose financial interest is involved, the speaker emphasizes the drain of money from the colony to pay for English schooling, whereas, if young men are educated in Virginia, the money is spent at home and stays in circulation in the colony. If it was a sign of servitude that the Israelites had no smiths but had to sharpen their tools at the forges of the Philistines, "it is certainly a much greater badge of servitude that we can't have a minister, nor a physician, nor a lawyer, nor a statesman, nor a justice of the peace, nor an ingenious gentleman without going a great deal further to sharpen our wits." The old stock of English gentlemen being dead, the speaker continues, "it is a common complaint that in many counties there are not men enough to be found to fill the bench and to administer justice between man and man, and we insensibly decline to a state of ignorance and abjectness of spirit." Furthermore, when young men go to England for their education, on their return they find themselves unfitted for life in the colony and spend their days cursing the fate that condemns them to live in so uncultivated a society. Virginia therefore must maintain its own schools, the orator patriotically concludes, "for a Virginia education is the most proper and suitable to Virginia children." This early plea for freedom from dependence upon English schools was repeated with increasing insistence later in the colonial period.

That the purpose of education is to produce leaders needed in Virginia is implied or stated by all of the orators. Significantly, the third speaker, who had the task of persuading his audience that many advantages would accrue from locating the capital in the college town, based one of his main arguments on the value to the students of being educated in a center of political and social activity. The students of William and Mary College should learn to bear themselves with confidence among men, he insists. If the college town should remain a quiet country place far from the centers of activity, the utility of the institution would be greatly impaired: "For in such a retired corner of the world, far from business and action, if we make scholars, they are in danger of proving mere scholars, which make a very ridiculous figure, made up of pedantry, disputatiousness, positiveness, and a great many other ill qualities which render them not so fit for action and conversation." No doctrine of learning for learning's sake inspired the educational leaders of Virginia in the colonial period. As in the Elizabethan period, that type of learning which would make a well-rounded man rather than a specialist was the ideal of the gentleman's education. It was assumed that William and Mary College would be an institution where gentlemen's sons might receive this kind of training.

The fourth orator at this May Day celebration mentioned the gifts that had come to the college from various benefactors and pointedly expressed the hope that the governor would continue the favor vouchsafed by the King.

The fifth and last speaker summed up previous arguments, urged continued support of the college, and looked into the future, as is the way of college orators. From a country hitherto ill-equipped with schools of learning, he sees Virginia growing in intellectual grace. "Methinks we see already that happy time," he exclaims, "when we shall surpass the Asiaticans in civility, the Jews in religion, the Greeks in philosophy, the Egyptians in geometry, the Phoenicians in arithmetic, and the Chaldeans in astrology. O happy Virginia!"

Better than most college orators, these student speakers of May Day, 1699, described the educational dreams of their time and revealed the aims and hopes of their college. The Reverend James Blair doubtless had labored long in the composition of their orations, and he must have been pleased at hearing his own ideas well delivered before so august a body.

The ideal of learning implied in these college orations is the traditional ideal of what the well-rounded gentleman ought to know. William and Mary College, as the speakers imagined it, would be an institution where Virginians might become acquainted with what is best and most useful in the arts and sciences. Crabbed pedantry is eschewed, and narrow professionalism has no place in this educational conception. If a strong motive in founding the college was the desire to have a training school for ministers, even that training was not to be narrowly theological. One needs to remember that a professor of mathematics at William and Mary, the Reverend Hugh Jones, reminded clergymen who had an eye on Virginia that ministers were expected to "act like gentlemen," and "be good scholars without becoming cynics, as they may be good Christians without appearing stoics."[32] Students trained at the college, whether they proposed to be preachers or planters, were expected to wear their learning with grace and ease, as was the manner of gentlemen.

A shrewd observation upon the amateur rather than professional interest in learning shown by "the gentlemen of the plantations" is made by Jones in a description of the habits and customs of Virginians. Planters, he points out, are "generally diverted by business or inclination from profound study, and prying into the depth of things, being ripe for management of their affairs before they have laid so good a foundation of learning." Though they are naturally quick and clever, with "a sufficiency of knowledge and fluency of tongue," their learning is "but superficial," and they are more inclined to "read men by business and conversation than to dive into

[32] Hugh Jones, *The Present State of Virginia* (New York, 1865), pp. 96-97.

books." Hence they are "desirous of learning what is absolutely necessary in the shortest and best method." To provide short cuts to learning, Jones himself prepared for Virginia students certain handbooks in English grammar, theology, mathematics, surveying, and navigation.[33] A little farther on, describing in more detail the education of the planters' sons, Jones remarks that "several are sent to England for it, though the Virginians, being naturally of good parts . . . neither require nor admire as much learning as we do in Britain, yet more would be sent over were they not afraid of the smallpox, which most commonly proves fatal to them." English education, Jones observes, is not satisfactory for Virginians, because of the "pedantic methods, too tedious for their volatile genius." His comments are realistic and practical. "Grammar learning, taught after the common roundabout way," proves of small benefit to Virginia youths, "because they are imprisoned and enslaved to what they hate and think useless." Instead of pedantic aridities Jones prescribes "a civil treatment with some liberty." The sons of Virginia gentlemen need, and take to, "polite and mathematical learning," Jones asserts; he thinks, therefore, they should be emancipated from bondage to classical tongues and taught in English "all the arts, sciences, and learned accomplishments of the ancients and moderns." In William and Mary College, Jones foresaw an institution where Virginians would be able to obtain the kind of education they wanted and needed.[34] To bring about improvements toward that end, he appended to *The Present State of Virginia* numerous suggestions on education.[35]

From the end of the seventeenth century onward, most of the sons of the upper class found William and Mary College sufficient for their educational needs, though a few of the wealthier youths went to Oxford or Cambridge, or to the Inns of Court for legal training. In 1701-2 Francis Louis

[33] *Ibid.*, p. 44. [34] *Ibid.*, pp. 45-46. [35] *Ibid.*, pp. 83-112.

Michel observed that the college at Williamsburg had already become an institution whose students were drawn from the families of the upper class, "because most of the people live far away, [and] only the more well-to-do parents, who have the means, can secure boarding for their sons there, which costs yearly twenty guineas." At the time he wrote, Michel estimated the student body at about forty, adding that "before this it was customary for wealthy parents, because of the lack of preceptors or teachers to send their sons to England to study there. But experience showed that not many of them came back. Most of them died of small-pox." [36]

Though only a sprinkling of Virginians in the seventeenth or in the eighteenth century managed to get either a grammar-school or university education in England, enough of the social and intellectual leaders in the colony were trained abroad to prevent the loss of all contact with English educational institutions. After a diligent search, Mrs. Mary Newton Stanard found evidence of less than three dozen Virginia matriculates at Oxford and Cambridge in the period preceding the Revolution,[37] but among these were representatives of such influential families as the Lees, Wormeleys, Carters, Blands, Byrds, Pages, Fitzhughs, Burwells, Corbins, and others who took a leading part in shaping the destinies of the colony. Not all parents shared Hugh Jones's belief that English education was inappropriate for Virginia youths, and only the expense and the grave hazards of the journey prevented more planters' sons from being sent to England for their education. Most Virginia fathers of the upper class still clung to the belief in the value of a classical education, and whenever possible prescribed the

[36] "Report of the Journey of Francis Louis Michel from Berne, Switzerland, to Virginia, October 2, 1701-December 1, 1702," ed. and tr. William J. Hinke, in *The Virginia Magazine of History and Biography*, XXIV (1916), 26.

[37] Mary Newton Stanard, *Colonial Virginia: Its People and Customs* (Philadelphia, 1917), pp. 292-94. See also "Some Virginians Educated in Great Britain," *The Virginia Magazine of History and Biography*, XXI (1913), 196-99.

study of Latin and sometimes Greek for their sons. William Fitzhugh and Robert Carter, for example, had decided opinions on the value of Latin and were insistent that their sons receive the traditional instruction in the classics.[38] Richard Lee II was notable for his Greek, Latin, and Hebrew learning.

If few Virginians had the benefit of education in England, the traditional learning of the English schools was transmitted to the sons of colonists by tutors who had been trained in England. Well-to-do planters employed English tutors for their children and usually set aside a small building for a schoolhouse. There their own and their neighbors' children received instruction. Sometimes planters managed to bring over an indigent but educated young man, under indentures to fulfil his period of servitude as a teacher. The first John Carter, for instance, provided in his will for the purchase of an indentured servant who could teach Latin.[39] Frequently the clergyman of the parish, usually a man trained in one of the English universities, undertook to give children of his parishioners a certain amount of secular instruction. Through the agency of these private teachers, Virginia youths acquired some of the same elements of learning they would have received in an English school.

Haphazard as was the educational system in Virginia during the seventeenth and early eighteenth centuries, the probabilities are that the sons of prosperous planters received about as much schooling as many sons of English squires in the same period. Because Governor Berkeley in 1671, without regard for the truth of what he said, thanked God that Virginia had no free schools and printing press,[40] his statement has been taken as literal proof that the colony was destitute of educational opportunities. Undoubtedly the advantages enjoyed by the mass of children of the poorer sort were meager, and for many non-

[38] See discussions of Fitzhugh and Carter *infra*, Chapters VI and IX.

[39] See the discussions of the Carters *infra*, Chapter IX.

[40] Hening, *Statutes*, II, 511.

existent, but, for those better off in this world's goods, schooling was to be had. Robert Beverley the historian never showed any disposition to flatter his fellow countrymen, but in 1705 he spoke favorably of the "large tracts of land, houses, and other things granted to free schools for the education of children in many parts of the country." These schools, he asserts, were founded by "well inclined gentlemen, and the management of them hath commonly been left to the direction of the county court, or to the vestry of the respective parishes." Where there are no established schools, Beverley adds, "the people join and build schools for their children, where they may learn upon very easy terms."[41]

To the Virginia gentleman of the colonial period, gross ignorance was not only a disgrace but a handicap in the conduct of his business affairs. Without some learning he could neither manage his estate intelligently nor support the dignities and obligations of his position in society. One of the best statements, in this period, of a gentleman's concern over the education of a member of his family is contained in a letter of Nathaniel Burwell to a brother, about the laziness of their half brother, Lewis, then at William and Mary College. The letter, dated June 13, 1718, is worth quoting in full:

> I'm very much concerned for the occasion of your sending, and more to see how insensible Lewis is of his own ignorance, for he can neither read as he ought to do, nor give one letter a true shape when he writes, nor spell one line of English, and is altogether ignorant of arithmetic, so that he'll be noways capable of the management of his own affairs and unfit for any gentleman's conversation, and therefore a scandalous person, and a shame to his relations, not having one single qualification to recommend him. If he would but apply himself heartily one year to write well, learn the mathematics and consequently arithmetic of Mr. Jones, and to translate Latin into English of Mr. Ingles to learn him to spell well, I would then take him home and employ him till

[41] Robert Beverley, *The History of Virginia* (Richmond, 1855), p. 224.

he comes of age in my office and plantation affairs that he might the better be capable to manage his own. And to my knowledge this will be no disservice to him, and a greater than any other method he'll fall into through his own inclination. For my part, 'tis no advantage to me whether he be a blockhead or a man of parts, were he not my brother, but when I have to do with him, to school he shall go, and if he don't go till I can go over, he then shall be forced to go whether he will or not, and be made an example of (while I stand by) before the face of the whole college. As for the pretence of living in the college, the last meeting has taken such care as will effectually provide better eating for the boys, so that need not scare him, and therefore he had better go, by fair means than foul, for go he shall, and send him forthwith.[42]

A gentleman did not need the education of a pedant, but, as Nathaniel Burwell's letter indicates, his position required him to know how to speak and write good English, to be a competent penman, and to have command of enough mathematics to qualify him to manage his accounts and deal with simple problems in surveying. In general it was incumbent upon him to acquire sufficient knowledge to enable him to be intelligent in whatever company he found himself. Latin was still generally believed to be eminently useful—a sort of key to other forms of learning. The gentleman's schooling should give him the kind of training that would fit him to continue his studies after his formal education was finished. For example, the son of a Virginia planter may not have learned much law at William and Mary College, but he was expected to read and interpret hard books, so that, when he became a justice of the peace or a member of the Council, he could refer to his own little collection of lawbooks and understand what he read. Conscious of a class obligation, the Virginia gentleman was obliged to save himself from blockish ignorance. To be a Justice Shallow was to be disgraced. The traditional desire for classical learning, which early manifested itself in the ruling

[42] *William and Mary College Quarterly*, 1st Ser., VII (1898-99), 43-44.

class, gathered force, through the colonial period, to produce the Ciceronian orators and the Latin-quoting statesmen of Revolutionary times. Perhaps their libraries, even more than their schools, will give a further clue to their intellectual training.

CHAPTER V

BOOKS AND THEIR PLACE IN PLANTATION LIFE

IN the treatises of advice published in the seventeenth century for the benefit of emigrants bound for the promised land of Virginia or New England, books find no place on the lists of articles of necessary equipment; nevertheless, many settlers brought with them a few volumes treasured for their utility, piety, or good learning. We may be sure that the emigrants considered these works essential to their well-being, for freight was too high and their little ships too crowded to permit excess baggage. Throughout the first century of colonization, the high cost of all imported products would have deterred Virginia settlers from collecting books for mere ostentation. Books which the planters brought with them or imported later were chosen with a definite notion of their value, and they were often literally read to pieces. It is this fact that gives seventeenth- and early-eighteenth-century book lists unusual significance, for the choice of books provides a clue to the settlers' conception of intellectual and social values. Since these values lie at the foundation of American intellectual and literary history, an understanding of the early colonial attitude toward books is necessary to any study of literary culture in America. The reading habits of these settlers also indicate an important way in which the continuing influence of Tudor and Stuart writers was transmitted to the new country, to be assimilated as part and parcel of the thinking of Americans.

Since there was no permanent printing press in Virginia until William Parks set up his shop at Williamsburg in 1730,[1] books owned by Virginians had to be imported from abroad.

[1] Douglas C. McMurtrie, *The Beginnings of Printing in Virginia* (Lexington, Va., 1935), pp. 7-9.

New England, it is true, was printing books, but the kind of religious works published there attracted few readers in the Chesapeake Bay region, and apparently traffic in books from the northern colonies was almost nonexistent. Like all other imported articles, books were relatively costly, and only the more prosperous planters could afford to accumulate libraries. After the drop in tobacco prices, subsequent to the passage of the Navigation Acts (especially the disastrous Act of 1660), importations of books declined, along with the curtailment of other luxuries. One result was to force the colonists to read the books they already owned, but a still more important effect was to make the ownership of books more and more the exclusive privilege of the wealthier planters. The cultural influence of books, like educational opportunities, was an advantage that could be enjoyed by scarcely any except the well-to-do and the fortunate few who might share their intellectual privileges. If the wills and inventories of the period show a scattering of books owned by humble Virginians, it is nevertheless true that only a small number of aristocratic planters could boast of fairly large libraries. We may be sure, however, that the libraries of the great planters served more than the owners' households. Neighbors and friends consulted these works, and there must have been considerable borrowing of books. An evidence of the practice of lending books to near-by planters may be seen in a catalogue of books owned by Godfrey Pole and kept at the house of James Burwell in 1716. Opposite many titles in the catalogue are the initials or names of borrowers, as for example, "Davenant on Resumptions–Lent Mann Page Esq.," "Annals of Queen Ann, My Lord Bacon's Essays, Puffendorff's History of Europe, Gentleman's Calling–Lent Capt. Randolph," or "Dr. Sherlock on Death–Lent Major Burwell's Lady."[2] More than a quarter of the library had been lent to planters in the vicinity.

[2] The catalogue of Pole's library is printed in *The Virginia Magazine of History and Biography*, XVII (1909), 147-50.

Generalizations about the ownership of books and the reading habits of colonial Virginians are subject to many qualifications, and our conclusions often can be little better than plausible guesses. The evidence is scantier than in most regions, for Virginia, to a greater degree than other sections of the United States, has been ravaged by war and fire. Many county records and private papers have been destroyed. Documents relating to the lives of the settlers during the first fifty years of colonization are particularly scarce. Even where we have inventories of personal property, the references to books are more often than not tantalizingly vague. To know that a planter had "one parcel of old books" or "five great books in folio" is of little help. Hence it is impossible to say that any author then available was not known. Argument from silence is especially vulnerable here. For all we know, the unspecified parcels of old books may have contained quartos and folios of Shakespeare. Moreover, we cannot be certain that a man read a book because he possessed it, although the supposition is reasonable that pioneers did not go to the expense and trouble of gathering books merely for show. What we can do is to reason from the habits of colonists whose records are fairly complete: their letters, diaries, wills, and inventories provide the clues that enable us to make deductions concerning their literary interests.[3]

That from early in the period of settlement books were bought and read by those who could afford them has been amply proved by the diligence of Virginia historians who have ransacked old papers for inventories of libraries.[4] Mrs. Mary Newton Stanard, for instance, discovered proof of "six hun-

[3] In "The Purposeful Reading of Our Colonial Ancestors," *E.L.H., A Journal of English Literary History*, IV (1937), 85-111, I have previously discussed certain phases of the literary interests of early Americans. Portions of that discussion have been used here.

[4] Scattered through *The Virginia Magazine of History and Biography*, the *William and Mary College Quarterly*, *Tyler's Quarterly Historical and Genealogical Magazine*, and the *Lower Norfolk County Antiquary*, are many inventories

dred collections, varying in size from two or three volumes to several thousand."[5] But her investigation, it should be remembered, included the whole colonial era. In Lower Norfolk County in the fifty-year period from 1640 to 1690, records show more than one hundred planters who owned books. Their collections ranged from three or four items to a hundred or more.[6] The total number of book owners in Virginia at the end of the seventeenth century is estimated by Philip A. Bruce at approximately one thousand.[7] This estimate, of course, is a conjecture based on the percentage of owners in the counties where records are fairly complete, and it includes the owner of one book as well as the planter who could boast a library. Even the first settlers on the banks of the James, those mercurial brethren who caused Captain John Smith so much anxiety and trouble, did not come without books, for Smith

---

and wills enumerating books owned in the seventeenth and eighteenth centuries. Valuable studies in book ownership have been made by Philip Alexander Bruce, *Institutional History of Virginia in the Seventeenth Century* (New York, 1910), I, 402-41, and Mary Newton Stanard, *Colonial Virginia: Its People and Customs* (Philadelphia, 1917), pp. 295-307. Useful as these studies are in proving the ownership and distribution of books in the colony, they provide only a slight interpretation of the significance of the choice of books.

The most recent essay on this subject is that by George K. Smart, "Private Libraries in Colonial Virginia," *American Literature*, X (1938), 24-52. Mr. Smart has performed a valuable service by analyzing approximately one hundred private libraries in Virginia in the pre-Revolutionary period, "with particular attention not only to their size but also to what the books in those libraries were, and to draw certain conclusions, which, of course can be only tentative." Many of the libraries which Mr. Smart treats fall in the later eighteenth century, with which I am not at present concerned. The footnotes to his essay contain useful bibliographical suggestions, and the table of classifications of several libraries by subjects is suggestive. I have not seen the unpublished thesis of W. D. Houlette, "Plantation and Parish Libraries in the Old South," at the University of Iowa.

I am afraid I cannot share Mr. Smart's belief (p. 28, n. 15) that many more itemized lists of books will come to light in the Virginia public records. My own efforts to discover lost inventories have given me little ground for optimism on this score.

[5] Stanard, *op. cit.*, p. 296.

[6] Bruce, *op. cit.*, pp. 413 ff.

[7] *Ibid.*, p. 440.

records that Master Robert Hunt, "our preacher," lost his library by fire. Another of the early preachers, the Reverend Richard Buck, who died in 1626, also had a "library of books."[8] If the chaplains' books may be considered merely stock in trade, other, less technical works must have been available. George Sandys, translating Ovid's *Metamorphoses* in the wilderness in 1622, was not without literary aid. And bibulous John Pory, writing to Sir Dudley Carleton in 1619 about the loneliness of Jamestown, announces a resolution "to mind my own business here, and next after my pen, to have some good book always in store, being in solitude the best and choicest company."[9] Virginia planters in the days to come were to find that books were a very present help in combating the uncouthness of a wilderness way of life. Near the end of the century, William Fitzhugh almost paraphrased Pory's observation on the value of literary companionship.[10] A few years after John Pory was resolving always to have a book by him, one Jacob Bradshaw, of Lower Norfolk County, "received his death at the hands of God by lightning and thunder of heaven as he was lying on a chest and reading in a book."[11] Since we usually think of the period of settlement as one of grim struggle, it is pleasant to remember that someone had leisure to spend lying in the shade reading a book, even though he invited the wrath of God.

The early collections of books were small, and, we can be reasonably sure, were chosen with care to suit the needs of their owners. More often than not, the extant inventories do not specify titles. For instance, among the Lower Norfolk County records one finds such inventories as that of Richard

[8] "Minutes of the Council and General Court, 1622-1629," *The Virginia Magazine of History and Biography*, XXV (1917), 225-38.

[9] "Letter of John Pory, 1619," in *Narratives of Early Virginia, 1606-1625*, ed. Lyon G. Tyler (New York, 1907), p. 286.

[10] See *infra*, Chapter VI, on William Fitzhugh.

[11] Quoted from the county records by Bruce, I, 404; the incident is dated 1647.

Waked, in 1648, listing "three Bibles, two and twenty small books, a Bible," or that of Thomas Casson, in 1652, mentioning "a parcel of old books all in pieces," or, in the same year, that of Robert Powes, clerk, who had "two and thirty books," none of which is named.[12] Not only gentlemen-planters but humbler folk sometimes owned a handful of books, usually works of piety or treatises on medicine, for men in every rank of life were anxious to provide for their souls and bodies. Since the collections were small, the books were read and reread, and not infrequently the inventories pathetically suggest that literary legacies were, like Mr. Casson's books, all in pieces. Although the records for the period before 1660 are fragmentary, the evidence is that there were few collections numbering over a hundred books. Ralph Watson, of York, who in 1645 left thirty folios and fifty quartos (titles unnamed), had one of the larger collections.[13] The most extensive inventory of enumerated titles before 1660 is that of the Reverend John Goodborne, an Anglican minister, who sailed for Virginia in 1635, expecting to settle at a plantation called Merchant's Hope. He died on the voyage but his books, numbering one hundred and ninety-one titles, were landed, and became the subject of a lawsuit.[14]

By the later seventeenth and early eighteenth centuries, the libraries of the wealthier planters had grown by gradual accretion and inheritance until men like Ralph Wormeley, Richard Lee, and Robert Carter of Corotoman could take pride in well-chosen collections of two or three hundred titles. By 1736 Dr. Charles Brown of Williamsburg had five hundred and twenty-one works, described in an advertisement in the *Virginia Gazette* as "the finest and most copious in the

[12] *The Lower Norfolk County Virginia Antiquary*, I (1896), 104-6. See also the same journal, I (1896), 121-23; II (1897), 33-36.

[13] Stanard, p. 305.

[14] R. G. Marsden, "A Virginian Minister's Library, 1635," *The American Historical Review*, XI (1905-6), 328-32.

branches of natural philosophy and physic ever offered for sale in the colony."[15] And by 1744 William Byrd of Westover had gathered more than thirty-six hundred separate titles. But Byrd's books represent a collector's library rather than the accumulation of constantly used works. From the second third of the eighteenth century onward, great planters took an increasing pride in their libraries, and their collections were naturally larger in size, but that period is outside the scope of the present inquiry.[16]

A significant fact in the inventories of the late seventeenth century is the constant iteration of the phrase "one parcel of old books," and also of importance is the frequent mention of legacies of "old Latin books." Clearly the earlier settlers had not come without being fortified with learned works. For instance, the inventory, dated 1690, of Samuel Ball, a planter of Lower Norfolk County, enumerated his books as follows: "19 books, some quarto, some octavo, all old," "two English books in folio," "thirty small Latin books, some in folio, some in quarto, all old," "four books in folio," "one book in large octavo, new and thick," "29 books in quarto unbound," "32 old books all English in quarto and octavo." In the previous year, Mrs. Alice Newman of the same county had left "one parcel of old Latin books."[17] Virginia readers undoubtedly continued to read the books their fathers had gathered and to absorb a little of the classical learning in the numerous small collections of "old Latin books" bequeathed them by their parents.

Virginia had no public libraries in the period we are considering. From time to time some philanthropic person worried a little over the state of godliness and learning in the colony, and thought that good books would be a benefit, but no public library was founded. An unknown benefactor in 1620, as has already been noted, gave to the proposed college at Henrico

[15] Stanard, p. 302.

[16] See the excellent survey by Smart, already cited.

[17] *The Lower Norfolk County Virginia Antiquary*, II (1897), 35-36.

a three-volume set of the works of Master William Perkins, a map of America, and a Bible. In 1653 Michael Sparke, the London printer, who had had frequent dealings with the colonies, stipulated in his will that, when money owing him in Virginia and Barbados should be collected, each of those places should receive "one hundred books on the second part of *The Crums of Comfort* with *Groans of the Spirit* and *Handkerchief of Wet Eyes* ready bound to be distributed amongst the poor children there that can read."[18] In 1681-82 Lord Culpeper was commanded to bring over to Virginia "a sufficient number of books of homilies and books of the 39 Articles of the Church of England to be disposed of to every church. And you are to take care that they be duly kept and used therein."[19] In 1701 the Dowager Duchess of Beaufort expressed a desire to contribute £100 or £150 toward the promotion of piety in Virginia and contemplated a gift of good books. To this end she had her secretary write the governor of the colony for suggestions as to proper works for such a purpose.[20] After the founding of William and Mary College, near the end of the seventeenth century, a small library was accumulated there, but the first collection was destroyed by fire. When, in 1724, Hugh Jones published *The Present State of Virginia*, he noted that "The library is better furnished of late than formerly, by the kind gifts of several gentlemen; but yet the number of books is but very small, and the sets upon each branch of learning are very imperfect, and not the best of the sort." He proposed that books should be begged from the superior clergy of England; and he further suggested that "considerable contributions would be made by the clergy,

[18] *The Virginia Magazine of History and Biography*, XX (1912), 75-78. As a side light on Sparke's character, it may be observed that he also made a bequest "To fifty apprentices of the Old Bailey, fifty *Prentices Practice of Piety*. To those invited to my burial and do come, instead of biscuit or plums, to every of them a book of *The Grievances of the Spirit*."

[19] *Ibid.*, XXVII (1919), 334.

[20] *Ibid.*, XXII (1914), 248-49.

burgesses, and gentry of the country, if, upon easy terms, they were allowed the use of the library at certain hours at such times as they shall be at Williamsburg, either for pleasure or upon business."[21]

Virginia, unfortunately, profited little from the zeal of the Reverend Thomas Bray, the most industrious founder of libraries in the colonies. When that indefatigable cleric was appointed commissary of the Church of England for the province of Maryland, in 1696, he already had definite ideas about the value of books in spreading the gospel and stimulating learning among the gentry in his own, as well as in neighboring, colonies. In 1697 he published *An Essay towards Promoting All Necessary and Useful Knowledge, Both Divine and Human, in All Parts of His Majesty's Dominions, Both at Home and Abroad*, in which he stressed the fact that the lending libraries he proposed to establish would serve the "public interest of religion and learning."[22] Particularly in the colonies libraries were needed, Bray believed, for, he says, "I know no good a clergy who are not able to furnish themselves with books in going over can do in a country where none are to be bought when they are there, nor to be had from the merchants, but at excessive rates."[23] The upshot was that Bray so successfully enlisted the support of the influential clergy and business men of England that he was enabled to establish a large library at Annapolis and small libraries in various parishes in Maryland, as well as libraries in New England, New York, New Jersey, Pennsylvania, and the Carolinas. Perhaps because of the lukewarmness of his fellow churchman in Virginia, the Reverend James Blair, Bray's benefactions had slight influence on that colony, though he did propose that Williamsburg should be made one of his depositories of

[21] *The Present State of Virginia* (ed. of 1865), pp. 90-91.

[22] *Rev. Thomas Bray: His Life and Selected Works Relating to Maryland,* ed. Bernard C. Steiner (Baltimore, 1901), p. 60.

[23] *Ibid.*, p. 64.

books designed to reform manners, improve piety, and recover to the unity of the church such schismatics as Quakers, Papists, and Dissenters.[24] Despite the good intentions of Bray, even the library at the college of William and Mary remained undistinguished, and Virginia continued to depend upon its private collections for intellectual sustenance. Although books were never too plentiful, most planters of any pretensions had a few helpful works. The Reverend John Clayton, newly arrived at Jamestown in 1684, wrote back to a friend in England concerning his parishioners: "They have few scholars, so that every one studies to be half physician, half lawyer, and with a natural acuteness would amuse thee. For want of books, they read men the more."[25] And, the Reverend Mr. Clayton might have added, they read the few books they owned with greater attention.

The most noteworthy characteristic of the reading of Virginians, as revealed by the extant lists of their books, was its utility. "Books," observed John Denham, "should to one of these four ends conduce, For wisdom, piety, delight, or use."[26] And, of these four, delight seems to have been the least important consideration with colonial readers. When they came to select their libraries, Virginians in the earlier period were almost as seriously purposeful as their New England brethren. Indeed, sectional patriotism and prejudice have produced too many facile generalizations about the differences in the literary taste of "Puritan" New England and "Cavalier" Virginia. Some significant differences there were, it is true, especially in the later colonial period, but the similarities suggested by

[24] Bernard C. Steiner, "Rev. Thomas Bray and His American Libraries," *The American Historical Review*, II (1896-97), 59-75. See also William D. Houlette, "Parish Libraries and the Work of the Reverend Thomas Bray," *The Library Quarterly*, IV (1934), 588-609.

[25] "John Clayton, of James City, Afterwards of Crofton, Yorkshire," *William and Mary College Quarterly*, 2d Ser., I (1921), 114-15.

[26] "Of Prudence," in *The Poetical Works of Sir John Denham*, ed. Theodore H. Banks, Jr. (New Haven, 1928), p. 193.

their choice of books are frequently striking. The emphasis on religious literature, for example, is not confined to New England, nor were the pious works entirely different for Puritans and Anglicans. The fact is that an extraordinary number of sermons, devotional works, and even treatises on theology were common to both regions. And so it was with books in other fields. The intellectual differences between New Englanders and Virginians were less distinct than some of their descendants would have us believe.

The colonists, whether in Virginia or New England, were bent upon improving their economic and social status, and they brought with them definite ideas of what manner of men they hoped to become. In the new land of opportunity, they might make their fortunes and create for themselves positions of wealth and dignity. Since these settlers were eager to utilize every opportunity for improvement, the more fortunate and the more thoughtful among them did not neglect the stores of knowledge to be found in books. Their little libraries were selected, therefore, to contribute to the serious purpose of their lives—that is, the attainment of prosperity in this world and celestial bliss in the next.

Some literary students of the American seventeenth century have been perturbed over the scarcity of belles-lettres in the luggage of the first settlers. They wring their hands because Shakespeare's plays were neglected and other great poets passed over for dull works of divinity or statecraft. But such critics have rarely taken the trouble to look at the books the colonists actually read, and they forget that these pioneers were more concerned about self-improvement than poetry. Shakespeare, it should be remembered, had not yet been made improving by legions of schoolteachers. Though many of the books listed in colonial libraries seem incredibly dull to the reader of the present day, they nevertheless had a significance and a value to their owners, and, if we hope to understand these men of the seventeenth and eighteenth centuries, we must also understand their books and the implications to be drawn therefrom.

When the colonist began to select books for his five-foot shelf of essential works, he chose items that he proposed to read. He may have borne in mind good advice about reading given by Henry Peacham in *The Compleat Gentleman* (1622), a work some of our ancestors thought necessary to their life in America.[27] Prospective Americans had no inclination to burden themselves with trivial books; they sought help rather than "escape," in their reading. They envisioned in America a projection of English civilization, and they were determined that learning and the cultivation of the mind and spirit should not perish in the wilderness. Books which provided guidance in the way of life that the colonists were marking out for themselves predominated, therefore, in their literary preferences. Instead of idle and frivolous reading matter, the counselors of our seventeenth-century ancestors prescribed good books to "bob us continually on the elbow" and to "importune us to well doing," as one writer expressed it.[28] That reading should tend toward instruction in the proper way of life was the persistent advice of all serious writers, both secular and ecclesiastical. That purpose, for instance, lay behind Peacham's recommendation of Plutarch as a source of moral lessons and rules for living.[29] How earnestly Virginians as well as other colonists heeded Peacham's counsel on reading is manifest in the surviving inventories of their libraries. We need not marvel that plays—even the plays of Shakespeare—poetry, light fiction, and similar categories of literature were little known. If they had been, it would have been more than strange.

As one would naturally assume, a considerable proportion of the books collected by Americans throughout the colonies

[27] Ed. of 1622, p. 52. See Chapter I, pp. 14-15.

[28] B. P., *The Prentice's Practice in Godliness, and His True Freedom* (1608), p. 35.

[29] *The Compleat Gentleman* (1622), p. 52.

were utilitarian works. Since, as John Clayton commented of his fellow Virginians, every man was his own doctor and lawyer, handbooks on medicine and surgery and guides to legal procedure were particularly necessary. Books of surveying and engineering, treatises on various aspects of farming, military manuals, and similar handbooks made up the little collections of works of practical reference. Since more information, practical as well as esoteric, can be found in an encyclopedia than in other books, many libraries had some encyclopedic compilation. A number of seventeenth-century Virginians, for instance, possessed Pierre de La Primaudaye's *The French Academy*, a sort of outline of knowledge, with a strong emphasis on the natural sciences, heavily moralized to take away any taint of damnation which meddling with God's mysteries might have induced.

The zeal to perpetuate learning, to keep alive the desire for knowledge, and to provide the instruments of self-instruction account for many volumes of a textbook character that are common to both Virginia and New England libraries. Works whose value had first been learned in the English grammar schools were brought along to be used by children or to keep the wisdom of the ancients fresh in the minds of adults. Books of rhetoric and logic, collections of aphorisms and the flowers of eloquence, compilations of similes, dictionaries, Latin and Greek grammars, and various sorts of learned handbooks were common. Many were reliable works that the fathers of the earliest settlers might have known, but they continued to find a place in colonial libraries for a century and more. Erasmus, for example, remained popular for generations. Puritan divines in New England and wealthy planters in Virginia owned collections of the adages and colloquies of the great humanist. William Lily's *Grammar*, a Latin textbook dating from early in the sixteenth century, was still being used in Virginia in the eighteenth. The colloquies of Corderius, like those of Erasmus, were read, down through the years, for their wisdom as well as for Latin instruction. Colonial readers, like their brethren at home, prized aphoristic wisdom. This quality in Bacon's essays may help account for their popularity in Virginia.

The humanistic tradition of the Renaissance, with its insistence upon the cultural discipline of Greek and Latin authors, exerted a strong influence upon the choice of books for American libraries, in Virginia and New England alike. Some of the early settlers had a respectable number of classical texts, and, as libraries became larger and more numerous in the later seventeenth and early eighteenth centuries, an increasing emphasis was placed upon Greek and Latin writers, both in originals and translations. Since to know and quote the classics was the mark of a gentleman, it is not surprising to find the libraries of great planters reflecting this interest. Furthermore, the classical tradition of the English schools and universities was also the heritage of colonials, who felt that Greek and Latin authors were essential to the preservation and transmission of the amenities of a cultivated life. Literary style continued in the debt of Cicero and Quintilian; history was still learned from the Latin historians; much information that passed for science was gathered from Aristotle, Aelianus, Pliny, and others; the conduct of life was taught by Plutarch, Seneca, Homer, and Virgil; good morality, in some fashion, was extracted from them all, even from Suetonius' *History of the Twelve Caesars*. Since few, even among the sternest of New England Puritans, were willing to deny that the basis of erudition lay in the classics, every colonist who wanted to be learned—or to appear learned—tried to give the impression of an acquaintance with the literature of Greece and Rome. The tradition that the classics were essential to a well-chosen library, as to a sound education, persisted, and, when the Century of Enlightenment dawned, the bookshelves of Chesapeake Bay planters and Boston scholars were alike graced with the best writings of the ancient world.

As the prevalence of Latin historians in the book lists of the period suggests, historical reading was greatly favored, for it was believed to be highly instructive and useful in providing lessons of benefit to both the individual and the commonwealth. History, Richard Brathwaite had assured the readers of *The English Gentleman* (1630), is "the sweetest recreation of the mind"[30]—a belief that met with general acceptance. Indeed, the value placed upon historical reading was second only to that accorded works of divinity.[31] Whether one proposed to be a preacher in the Bay Colony or a landed gentleman on the Virginia rivers, histories were necessary to one's reading.

Some of the historical works of the Elizabethan period maintained their popularity for a century and more. Sir Walter Raleigh's *History of the World*, especially favored by the Puritans, was also frequently owned by Virginia planters. The colonists, like their kindred in England, no doubt read Raleigh's history, not merely as a compendium of facts about the ancient world, but also as a source of political and moral truths. After the Puritan Revolution, Virginians naturally showed a greater interest than New Englanders in history that reflected the royalist point of view, but they did not exclude standard works, like John Rushworth's *Historical Collections of Private Passages of State . . . [1618-48]*, that were written with parliamentary bias. If historical reading was essential to Englishmen, as educational counselors were careful to point out, it was doubly necessary to settlers on the fringe of the vast American wilderness. Through historical reading they maintained a contact with the great deeds of the past,

[30] Ed. of 1630, p. 220.

[31] When, near the end of his life, Cotton Mather summed up his advice to young preachers, he urged an acquaintance with history as one of the "most needful and useful accomplishments for a man that would serve God as you propose to do." (*Manuductio* [1726], p. 58.)

and out of meditation upon their own relation to human events came a notion that later matured into the idea of manifest destiny.

Books on politics and statecraft found a favored place in the libraries of Virginia planters, as they did in New England. Although political differences that would later become a chasm were already developing in the two regions, both groups nevertheless studied some of the same political theorists. Machiavelli, Guicciardini, and Bodin were not uncommon. Sir Thomas Smith's *The Commonwealth of England and Manner of Government*, a celebrated Elizabethan work that was constantly reprinted for more than a century, was a favorite book in the colonies. Treatises on the ideal commonwealth were available in Sir Thomas More's *Utopia* and Sir Francis Bacon's *New Atlantis*. In America, throughout the seventeenth and early eighteenth centuries, Bacon was a name to conjure with, and his influence upon American thought is the theme for a book. The *New Atlantis*, which was included at the end of the popular *Sylva Sylvarum*, must have been widely read. Not improbably, the *Utopia* and the *New Atlantis* provided the seeds of ideas which politicians were later to elaborate in theories interpreted according to their own peculiar lights. The concern of Virginia readers in current political events is also evident in some of the contemporary tracts and pamphlets which found their way to plantation libraries.

The preponderance of lawbooks, even in the smaller collections, suggests the litigiousness which accompanied the struggle for landed possessions in the colony. Land, the great symbol of aristocratic station and the source of all wealth in Virginia, was the subject of endless lawsuits. In a period when the planter was his own lawyer, his very destiny might depend upon the arguments and precedents furnished by his legal library. But farther-reaching than the mere present usefulness of legal works was the tradition of law which they helped to fix in Virginia. The study of the common law of England had a tremendous influence in the development of ideals of government and liberty; the effect of a long acquaintance with traditional law and its background was evident in the leadership assumed by Virginians after the break with England.

The interest of Virginians in science, outside of medicine, was not particularly noteworthy, although there were a few men, like the second William Byrd, who were scientifically minded. Nearly all of the sizable libraries, however, had some books of natural philosophy, for there was a universal curiosity about botany, astronomy, chemistry, zoology, and related subjects. But this interest was that of the gentleman-amateur rather than the scholar. Some of the scientific works were textbooks which were being used in the universities in the seventeenth century; some were even older books, that had fascinated Elizabethan readers; a few were recent publications. Books of geography and travel, which frequently included scientific observations, were fairly popular.

The emphasis upon social position, and the social aspirations of planters, will help to explain the frequent possession of works of heraldry and treatises on the conduct of the gentleman. Treatises on conduct ranged from Castiglione's *The Book of the Courtier* to more recent manuals of behavior. Although there was a laudable desire to conform to proper etiquette, colonial Americans, even in Virginia, were less concerned with the externals of behavior than with deeper problems of conduct which determined reputation and character. When they sought guidance in this field they usually chose highly moralistic works. In the later seventeenth century, they were likely to turn to two of the most edifying in that genre, *The Whole Duty of Man* and *The Gentleman's Calling*. The degree to which their conduct was patterned on the admonitions of their books is a problem, however, that defies solution.

In our insistence upon the enormous appetite of the Puritans for works of divinity, we sometimes forget the taste of Virginians for religious literature. We fail to remember that Puritans had no monopoly of pious reading in the seventeenth century, and we overlook the fact that religious treatises and books describing the means of attaining the good life were essential to every man who pretended to civilized culture. Sectarian beliefs made a difference in the selection of particular books, but Chesapeake Bay slaveholders and Boston preachers were agreed that every library ought to contain pious reading matter. For example, Colonel Ralph Wormeley, the secretary of the colony of Virginia and a most unpuritan gentleman, given to horse racing and lavish hospitality, collected during the last half of the seventeenth century a library of approximately three hundred and seventy-five titles, of which eighty or more were books devoted to religion and morals. No one ever accused any of the Carters of excessive piety, yet of the books listed in the inventory made in 1690 of the personal property left by Colonel John Carter of Lancaster County, nearly a third were religious works, including several titles by Richard Baxter, the sermons of that favorite Jacobean preacher Nicholas Byfield, and the most ubiquitous of all the devotional books, Lewis Bayly's *The Practice of Piety*.[32] These are not the works that are conventionally supposed to be the reading matter of Cavaliers. Few Virginia inventories fail to record Bibles, prayer books, and a considerable proportion of other religious works, and, if Virginians had more interest in the sermons of Lancelot Andrewes, Jeremy Taylor, John Tillotson, Edward Stillingfleet, and other good Anglicans than their brethren of the Bay Colony displayed, nevertheless a remarkable number of the same sermons and books of devotion were read by both Virginia planters and Boston merchants. Religion

[32] For details of the Wormeley and Carter libraries, see Chapters VII and IX, *infra*.

in the seventeenth and early eighteenth centuries was still a vital part of man's daily existence, and a pattern of life that ignored religion was unthinkable; even reprobates whose personal conduct gave the lie to this belief were not likely to deny the theory. Along with the religious books that made up such a large part of Virginia libraries were to be found a few philosophic works: the writings of the Greek and Roman philosophers; treatises of sixteenth-century thinkers like Pierre Charron; and occasionally copies of the works of Hobbes, Descartes, Locke, and more recent philosophers. In general, however, Virginians demonstrated conservatism in their choice of religious and philosophic works.

Virginia planters did not entirely neglect belles-lettres, or what is sometimes described as "pure literature." Poetry, plays, romances, and sometimes a jestbook found a place in plantation libraries, although in the seventeenth century they were not yet conspicuous. Even so, it is clear that the proportion of belles-lettres to other writings was somewhat larger in Virginia libraries than in those of the northern colonies; it is a mistake, however, to make too much of this difference. Indeed, one can gather, from extant records, more evidence of the intimate acquaintance of New Englanders with the English poets than one can find in Virginia. But that may be accounted for by the New England habit of keeping journals and commonplace books; dwellers in the Chesapeake Bay region were less inclined to set down their thoughts and reactions in writing. If Chaucer, Spenser, Shakespeare, and Milton were not entirely unknown before the mid-eighteenth century, lesser poets are oftener mentioned in Virginia inventories. For example, more planters owned Cowley than Milton, and Butler's *Hudibras* had a greater popularity than any other poem. In general, the most commonly found "literary" works were not books by the greatest authors.

So much for the general nature of literary taste in Virginia.

Specific examples of books deemed desirable provide a further insight into colonial reading habits. The libraries of great planters like Ralph Wormeley, the early Carters, and Richard Lee require separate discussion, but the collections of obscure men are equally revealing. The largest early collection brought to Virginia, that of the Reverend John Goodborne in 1635, is significant for its emphasis upon classic authors. Since it was selected to be the working library of an Anglican clergyman, religious works naturally predominate, but equally notable is the fact that, of the one hundred and ninety-one titles, over twenty-five are those of Greek and Latin writers. Included in the library were Homer's *Iliad*, Plutarch's *Lives* in a Latin and an English version, Thucydides in Latin, Aristotle in Greek and Latin, Pindar, Isocrates, Quintilian, Claudius Aelianus' *De Animalium Natura*, a collection of the minor Greek poets, Virgil in Latin and English (one edition "with pictures"), Horace, Ovid, Plautus, Terence in Latin and English, Juvenal, Persius, Cicero, Seneca, Julius Caesar, Suetonius, Justinus, and a dictionary of poetry. Goodborne also had that invaluable anthology of classical selections, Natalis Comes's *Mythologiae*, a Renaissance compilation that provided many a poor scholar with quotations enough to give him an air of infinite learning. Only classical writers held up the banner of literature in Goodborne's library, for not a single English poet or writer of polite prose found his way there. But the minister was well supplied with works of learning. He had twenty or more grammars, dictionaries, and textbooks to teach Hebrew, Greek, and Latin, the tongues most needful to a preacher, even in that wilderness. He also had a few works of logic, rhetoric, philosophy, physics, and medicine. Erasmus' *Adagia* was among his textbooks, and for pedagogical guidance he had Roger Ascham's *The Schoolmaster* (1570) and John Brinsley's *Ludus Literarius; or, The Grammar School* (1612). Among the theological works, one may be surprised to find the treatises of the Puritan William Ames, the works of John Calvin, and sermons of Puritan preachers like Nicholas Byfield and Richard Stubbes. Goodborne's respect for Erasmus is further attested by a copy of the great Dutch scholar's paraphrases of the New Testament. The fact is that the library of the Anglican Goodborne is not unlike that of John Harvard, dating from the same time.[33] Harvard had fewer classical authors but he admitted a sprinkling of English writers. Goodborne's library must not be taken as typical of the collections gathered by Virginia planters, but it does suggest the kind of books a minister believed necessary to spiritual and intellectual salvation in the colony.

The proportions of subjects in the little library of John Kemp, a planter of Lower Norfolk County, who died in 1648, show what a pioneer regarded as minimum essentials. Though Kemp had only a handful of books, their subjects covered his elementary needs. There were seven medical works, including two copies of Philip Barrough's *The Method of Physic* (1583), John Woodall's *The Surgeon's Mate; or, Military and Domestic Surgery* (1617), and a hoary old book of misinformation, in circulation to this day, *The Problems of Aristotle* (1597); five were books of divinity, including John Calvin's *Institution of Christian Religion*, translated by Thomas Norton (1561), John Brinsley's *The True Watch and Rule of Life* (1637), Thomas Hooker's *The Soul's Vocation; or, Effectual Calling to Christ* (1638), and Lewis Bayly's *The Practice of Piety* (1613); two were legal works: an abridgment of the statutes, and a treatise on the court baron and the court leet, surely suggestive of the planter's sense of legal prerogative. There were also "some small books of small value," concerning the nature of which we can only guess.[34] In select-

[33] For Goodborne's complete list, see Marsden, *op. cit.*, pp. 328-31; for the catalogue of the books given Harvard College by John Harvard, see Thomas Goddard Wright, *Literary Culture in Early New England, 1620-1730* (New Haven, 1920), pp. 265-72.

[34] *The Lower Norfolk County Virginia Antiquary*, I (1896), 104.

ing this small library, Kemp had a thought for his physical, religious, and legal needs in the American wilderness; perhaps the small books of little value were school texts; if so, his collection, inconsiderable as it was, contained the basic elements needed in frontier libraries.

Other small libraries were less austere than Kemp's. For example, Mrs. Sarah Willoughby, the widow of a Lower Norfolk County planter, in 1674 left something over fifty books on a variety of subjects. Although more than a third of her collection was composed of religious works, she also had at least a dozen volumes of the classics, including four volumes of Ovid, the works of Virgil, Cicero, Statius, and Aesop, and several unspecified books of Latin prose and poetry. Of more recent writers, she had *The Familiar Epistles* of Anthony de Guevara (1574), the essays of Montaigne, Pierre Charron's *Of Wisdom* (1606), and Robert Burton's *Anatomy of Melancholy* (1621).[35] In history she had what apparently was a eulogy of Charles II, a life of Louis XIII, Richard Knolles's *The General History of the Turks* (1603), and *The Ancient Ecclesiastical Histories* (1577) of Eusebius. Of textbooks there were a grammar, a "thesaurus poeticus," John Rider's *Dictionary* (1606), and Richard Norwood's *Trigonometry* (1631). Geography and travel were represented by Peter Heylyn's *Cosmography* (1652), George Sandys' *Travels* (1610), dealing with the Near East, and one of Captain John Smith's accounts of Virginia. Science and practical affairs were represented by an unidentified history of animals and minerals, Eucharius Roesslin's work on midwifery, *The Birth of Mankind* (1545), two treatises on navigation, and a book on planting mulberry trees. The religious books consisted of sermons by Richard Sibbes and his contemporaries, William Perkins' *An Exposition of the Lord's Prayer* (1592) and *A Case*

[35] *Ibid.*, I (1896), 122-23. I take "democritus Jur" in the inventory to stand for *The Anatomy of Melancholy* by Democritus, Junior.

of Conscience (1592), several Bibles and Testaments, and a number of small devotional books and tracts. Unlike the libraries of most other planters, Mrs. Willoughby's lacked legal works and, with the exception of one title, was devoid of medical books. There was the usual scarcity of belles-lettres.

But not every Virginian slighted light reading. Among the twenty-three volumes left in 1693 by Nathaniel Hill, a schoolmaster in Henrico County, were sixteen playbooks.[36] Matthew Hubbard, a merchant and planter of York County, left in 1667 a copy of Ben Jonson's plays, John Donne's poems, and a translation of Honoré d'Urfé's romance, *Astrée*, among the twenty-eight books that comprised his library.[37] The rest of Hubbard's books, however, were seriously purposeful. Thirteen titles were religious, including the ever-present *Practice of Piety*, a Latin Bible, a Latin Book of Common Prayer, and William Prynne's *The Antipathy of the English Lordly Prelacy, Both to Regal Monarchy and Civil Unity* (1641). Four medical works and E. W.'s *A Tutor to Astrology* (1657) probably were consulted with equal solemnity in matters of health. Hubbard's social ambitions may have accounted for a copy of John Selden's *Titles of Honor* (1614). An interest in colonial exploration is indicated by a copy of Captain John Smith's *The General History of Virginia* (1624), and, if Hubbard had further geographical curiosity, it may have been partially satisfied by Samuel Purchas' *Pilgrimage* (1613), that curious hodgepodge of geography and religion. Hubbard also owned Rider's *Dictionary*, a French grammar, a copy of Aesop's *Fables*, commonly used as a school text, and *The Swedish Intelligencer* (1632), giving an account of the campaigns of Gustavus Adolphus in his crusade to save Protestantism in Germany.

In addition to two Bibles, one new and one old, William

[36] Stanard, p. 298.

[37] Hubbard's inventory is to be found in the *William and Mary College Quarterly*, 1st Ser., II (1894), 174-75.

Green of Lower Norfolk County left in 1675 four other books: a commentary on the Psalms, an account of the Civil Wars in England, Richard Norwood's *The Seaman's Practice* (1644), and Francis Osborne's *Advice to a Son* (1656), a work full of counsel useful to the founder of a family dynasty.[38]

Of seventeen books left in 1680 by Colonel Southey Littleton, one of the leading planters of Accomac County, four were legal works, including Edmund Wingate's *Body of the Common Law of England* (1655); two were medical; three were religious; six were textbooks, including Norwood's *Trigonometry* and such old favorites as Aesop's *Fables*, Corderius' *Colloquies*, and selections from Plautus; one was a "history of ye New England Warr"; and one was the *Dialogues* of Lucian.[39]

Of the thirty-two books left in 1697 by Captain Thomas Cocke of Princess Anne County, thirteen were religious works. Of these, three were small pocket Bibles; in addition, there were several books of meditations, sermons, explanations of the Scriptures, and pious tracts. Seven of the items were lawbooks and guides to legal procedure. Six were historical works, five being concerned with English history and one with the Turks. William Barriffe's *Military Discipline* (1635) and John Tapp's *The Seaman's Calendar* (1602) provided Captain Cocke with enough military tactics and seamanship for a Virginia militia leader. The one scientific work in his library was a treatise on comets. For light reading he had Richard Head's *The English Rogue* (1665-71), *The Life and Adventures of Lazarillo de Tormes* (1586), "The history of a Coy lady in Octavo," and *The Travels of Ulysses, . . . Related . . . in Homer's Ninth, Tenth, Eleventh, and Twelfth Books of His Odyssey* (1673).[40]

A library displaying a professional interest in the law was

[38] *The Lower Norfolk County Virginia Antiquary*, I (1896), 123.

[39] See the *William and Mary College Quarterly*, 1st Ser., VIII (1900), 230-31.

[40] *Ibid.*, 1st Ser., IV (1895-96), 15. I have been unable to identify "The history of a coy lady."

that of Captain Arthur Spicer, well-to-do planter of the parish of Sitterbourne in Richmond County, who died in 1699. Whether Spicer had any formal legal training is not clear, but, as was the custom of other great planters, he filled the place of attorney for his neighbors, served as justice of the peace, and sat in the House of Burgesses. Like a few other Virginia gentlemen, he provided for the education of his son in England, specifying Charterhouse School as his preference and requesting his friend "King" Carter of Lancaster County to make the necessary arrangements.[41] Perhaps Spicer and Carter had been colleagues in some of the legal battles that constantly vexed the peace of plantation life. Out of a library of over one hundred and twenty titles, Spicer's legal works numbered fifty-three items—a collection unusually large for his time. Most of these were books that could also be found in King Carter's larger collection.[42] As even in certain of the smaller libraries, Sir Francis Bacon's *Elements of the Common Laws of England* (1630) had an honored place among other treatments of the legal tradition upon which Virginia's own system of jurisprudence was founded. Spicer's lawbooks, however, were largely handbooks and guides to procedure. That these lawbooks had been constantly used is indicated by a notation in the inventory that their value was only £5, "being old, broken, and damnified." Next to law, religion, with twenty-nine titles—including Bibles, sermons, and devotional books—occupied the most prominent place in the library. Eight historical works, including Sir Walter Raleigh's *History of the World* (1614), Samuel Clarke's *The Historian's Guide* (1676), Peter Heylyn's *The History of the Sabbath* (1636), Thomas Fuller's *The History of the Holy War* (1639), and the *Eikon Basilike* (1649), then attributed to Charles I, found a place in the collection. Francis Holyoke's *A Large Dictionary*

[41] *Ibid.*, 1st Ser., III (1894-95), 133-34.
[42] See Chapter IX, *infra*.

[of English and Latin] (1677), a Greek lexicon, a grammar, Franco Burgersdijck's *Institutionum Logicarum Libri Duo* (1637), and Comenius' *Janua Linguarum* (1631), supplied the rudiments of learning. Politics, history, and religious controversy were all to be found in one volume, Richard Crakanthorp's *The Defence of Constantine, with a Treatise of the Pope's Temporal Monarchy* (1621), precisely the sort of book to furnish arguments for legal-minded Anglicans. Robert Ward's *Animadversions of War* (1639) supplied information about military science, and three books on medicine and surgery were the only other strictly utilitarian works, unless some of the "parcel of small books of little value" listed in the inventory could be so classified. Among the half dozen items that may be described as belles-lettres, the most interesting volume is Shakespeare's *Macbeth*, very likely a copy of the first quarto of 1673, and, incidentally, one of the rare bits of evidence that Shakespeare was read in the early period. Further literary items were Lady Mary Wroth's *The Countess of Montgomery's Urania* (1621), a popular romance imitative of Sidney's *Arcadia*, another unidentified piece of fiction, listed as "Shearon's Romance," and Madeleine de Scudéry's *Les Conversations sur Divers Subjets* (1686). Of works by the great English literary figures of the seventeenth century, Spicer had Sir Francis Bacon's *Advancement of Learning* (1605) and Sir Thomas Browne's *Religio Medici* (1642). Other English works of the period were Sir Kenelm Digby's *Of Bodies and of Man's Soul* (1669), Sir Matthew Hale's *Contemplations Moral and Divine* (1676), and Gilbert Burnet's *The Life and Death of Sir Matthew Hale* (1682). Spicer's interest in Matthew Hale, a lawyer, who combined in his works piety and a legalistic point of view, was shared by fellow Virginians. The library was unusually poor in the classics, Cicero's orations and an unidentified volume listed as "Socrates' Orations" being the only classical works except textbooks.

Lawbooks helped to swell the size of many planters' libraries, particularly of those who held official positions in the government and needed legal works as part of their stock in trade. One of the larger collections was that of Godfrey Pole, catalogued in 1716.[43] Of one hundred and eleven titles, fifty-six were lawbooks, chiefly collections of statutes, reports, and handbooks of procedure. Since Pole for years was a clerk in the House of Burgesses, and also clerk of Northampton County, his predilection for legal works is understandable. More significant as evidence of his cultural interests was the ownership of the poetical works of Geoffrey Chaucer, Michael Drayton, Abraham Cowley, Edmund Waller, and John Milton. In addition, he had unspecified writings of Erasmus, Bacon's *Essays*, James Howell's *Epistolae Ho-Elianae* (1645), Samuel Butler's *Hudibras*, and Jeremy Taylor's *Holy Living and Holy Dying* (1650-51). Among the classic authors, he owned the works of Homer, Virgil, Horace, Ovid, Juvenal, Persius, Lucan, Martial, Seneca, Suetonius, and Justinus. For piety he had *The Whole Duty of Man*, *The Gentleman's Calling*, and a dozen or so other religious works, mostly devotional books. Historical reading was supplied by three fairly recent popular titles: Samuel Pufendorf's *An Introduction to the History . . . of Europe* (1699), James Howell's *A Survey of the Signory of Venice* (1651), and Abel Boyer's *The History of Queen Anne, Digested into Annals* (1703-13). A fourth history was from the pen of a Virginia writer—Robert Beverley's *The History and Present State of Virginia* (1705). As a socially ambitious member of the colonial aristocracy, he found a peculiar interest in the peerage compiled by Ralph Brooke, York Herald, *A Catalogue and Succession of the Kings, Princes, Dukes . . .* (1622), Gerard Legh's illustrated book on heraldry, *The Accidence of Armory* (1568), and Nicholas Cox's *The Gentleman's Recreation . . . Hunting, Hawking, Fowling,*

[43] *The Virginia Magazine of History and Biography*, XVII (1909), 147-50.

Fishing (1674). The nonprofessional works in Godfrey Pole's library indicate a taste that gradually became more clearly evident in the libraries of Virginia gentlemen later in the eighteenth century: an increasing interest in English belles-lettres and a continued, if not an increased, respect for Greek and Roman writers.

Out of a library of twenty-four titles, left in 1716 by Captain Christopher Cocke of Princess Anne County, there were nine lawbooks, three histories, three medical works, three religious books, three textbooks, two treatises on military science, and one work by a contemporary English literary figure destined to become very influential in the colonies—Joseph Addison's *The Free-Holder; or, Political Essays* (1716).[44] Cocke's inventory was filed on December 10, 1716. Earlier in the year, he had ordered two books hot off the press, the Addison and the first volume of *The Annals of King George* (1716-21), thus demonstrating a speed in the acquisition of new books unusual among colonial readers. One of the textbooks was Edmund Coote's *The English Schoolmaster* (1596), an old but exceedingly popular guide to self-education. Coote's valuable manual was one of a small handful of books offered for sale by a Virginia frontier store in 1679, other items being "two play books," a Bible, *The Academy of Compliments*, and two lawbooks.[45]

Captain Charles Colston, who died in Richmond County in 1724, left a small library consisting of an unitemized parcel of old books and twenty-two listed titles, nine of which were lawbooks of the kind so frequently found in planters' libraries.[46] He had six religious books, five historical works, Elisha Coles's *The English Dictionary* (1676), and *Ovid's Epistles Translated by Several Hands* (1660). Among the religious books were Richard Allestree's *The Art of Contentment* (1675) and the

[44] *William and Mary College Quarterly*, 1st Ser., IV (1895-96), 94.
[45] Stanard, p. 156.
[46] *William and Mary College Quarterly*, 1st Ser., III (1894-95), 132.

works of the Elizabethan preacher, William Perkins. Raleigh's *History of the World* still occupied a respected place among more-recent histories of Europe and America.

Out of approximately one hundred and ten titles listed in 1724 in the inventory of Colonel Daniel McCarty of Westmoreland County, exactly half were lawbooks.[47] Colonel McCarty was a wealthy planter, a member of the House of Burgesses, and influential in his county. The remainder of McCarty's books consisted of fifteen religious works, mostly Bibles and prayer books, ten of the Greek and Latin classics, eight or nine textbooks and dictionaries, two works of travel, a gazetteer, two medical works, one book on manners, a book on military science, and a half dozen works of belles-lettres. Totally lacking are modern histories, scientific treatises, and political and philosophic writings. McCarty's selections represent a working library of a gentleman-planter who had constant need of legal aids; his choice of the classics, consisting of Virgil, Ovid, Horace, Terence, Cornelius Nepos, Juvenal, Caesar, Sallust, and the *Phaedo* of Plato, was dictated by a belief in the educational value of these authors. Indeed, in several instances he had more than one copy of the classics, perhaps keeping a supply in the plantation store for sale to other planters who wanted them for textbooks. A book listed simply as "Erasmus" probably was a copy of the *Colloquies*. The modern literary works consisted of Joseph Addison's stiff tragedy, *Cato* (1713), the plays of Sir Robert Howard, John Banks's tragedy, *The Destruction of Troy* (1679), Francis Quarles's *Emblems* (1635), an old prose romance by Edmund Forde, *Parismus*, with the second part entitled *Parismenos* (1598-99), and the three-volume edition of Abraham Cowley's *Works* (1721). An interest in the slave trade doubtless accounts for William Bosman's *A . . . Description of the Coast of Guinea* (1705). The other travel narrative was Captain Woodes

[47] *Ibid.*, 1st Ser., VIII (1899-1900), 19-20.

Rogers' *A Cruising Voyage Round the World* (1712). Sir Jonas Moore's *Modern Fortification; or, Elements of Military Architecture* (1689) was a work which might still prove useful to a Virginia militia commander. And a man of McCarty's wealth and interest in the amenities of a country estate would find helpful guidance in Leonard Meyer's *English Gardener* (1635). The natural interest of a member of the ruling class in improving human behavior would explain a copy of *An Account of the Societies for Reformation of Manners* (1698). Such were the books that one of the more prosperous gentlemen of Virginia in the first quarter of the eighteenth century deemed necessary to his way of life.

Legal works made up more than half the library of Richard Hickman, clerk of the Council, who died at his home in Williamsburg in 1732.[48] As an important official in that small and aristocratic body which virtually ruled Virginia, he naturally felt the need of such works as Bacon's *Elements of the Common Laws of England* and other expositions of the colony's legal heritage. Of wider philosophic interest was Samuel Pufendorf's *Of the Law of Nature and Nations* (1710). Out of a total of something over one hundred and fifteen titles, sixty-nine were lawbooks. Next to King Carter and William Byrd, Hickman at the time of his death had the best legal library in Virginia. He was better off for case reports than most of his contemporaries, though Edward Coke's *Reports* was fairly common. The proportion of religious reading matter in Hickman's collection is small, only thirteen items being listed—among them Samuel Purchas' pious *Pilgrimage*. Of ten items dealing with learning, two were French dictionaries, one was a treatise on the art of thinking and speaking, one was a method of study, and another was

[48] *Ibid.*, 1st Ser., III (1894-95), 248-51. Some of the entries in this inventory are almost unintelligible; for example, "1 vol praxis Alen Curr Cambell" looks hopeless but it most likely stands for William Brown's *Praxis Almae Curiae Cancellariae* (2 vols., 1694).

John Wilkins' *An Essay towards a Real Character and a Philosophical Language* (1688), an imposing treatise advocating a universal language. Classical history was represented by the works of Tacitus and Lucius Annaeus Florus, and more recent history by a single volume of John Rushworth's *Historical Collections*, five volumes of a serial (begun in 1711) entitled *The Political State of Great Britain*, a life of Columbus, Christopher Helvicus' *The Historical and Chronological Theatre* (1687), Beverley's history of Virginia, and a work listed as "Cabala," which may have been a collection of state papers published in 1654 with that title, or a satire against the nonconformists, published in 1663 and attributed to Sir John Birkenhead.[49] Ralph Brooke's compilation of the peerage was the only other book of a historical nature. A conduct book noted for its practical and worldly wisdom was in the collection—Francis Osborne's *Advice to a Son*. The more literary works consisted of but five titles, though they indicated considerable diversity of taste. There were three volumes of *The Spectator*, Fénelon's *Telemachus* in the original French, a translation of Aristophanes, the first volume of Cowley's *Works*, and John Locke's *An Essay Concerning Human Understanding* (1690). Evidently Hickman was a man whose intellectual interests were not confined to the law, which occupied so much of his attention.

A wider variety of subjects and a smaller proportion of legal works distinguished the library of Edmund Berkeley of Middlesex County, a member of the Council, who died in 1718.[50] Out of a hundred and thirteen titles, only nine were legal books. These, however, were well chosen manuals, of which Michael Dalton's *The Country Justice* was doubtless especially useful to a law-dispensing planter. As in most Vir-

[49] E.g., *Cabala, Mysteries of State, in Letters of the Great Ministers of King James and King Charles* (1654), or *Cabala; or, An Impartial Account of the Nonconformists' Private Designs* (1663), attributed to Sir John Birkenhead.

[50] *William and Mary College Quarterly*, 1st Ser., II (1893-94), 250-51.

ginia libraries there were one or two guides to the proper making of wills and testaments. Virginians, mindful of their family dynasties and their landed possessions, were vastly concerned about the laws of inheritance. Religion, with thirty-two titles, was the best represented subject in the library. Characteristically these religious works were chiefly Bibles, prayer books, devotional manuals, sermons, explanations of the Scriptures, and guides to the good life. Theology proper and controversial writings were almost completely lacking, George Keith's *The Standard of the Quakers Examined* (1702) being one of the few books treating sectarian matters. Berkeley owned the two most popular of devotional books, *The Practice of Piety* and *The Whole Duty of Man*, and he also had an old manual on bringing up a Christian family, Matthew Griffith's *Bethel; or, A Form for Families* (1633). One of the rare instances of a New England book in Virginia was a copy of John Cotton's *Milk for Babes Drawn Out of the Breasts of Both Testaments* (1646). Jeremy Taylor's work was represented by his *Contemplations of the State of Man in This Life* (1684), and there was a copy of Robert Boyle's *Some Considerations Touching the Style of the Holy Scriptures* (1661), a book which many planters owned. Of twenty-one schoolbooks, most were grammars, dictionaries, and introductions to Latin; in fact, the inventory has one uninforming notation of "Eight Lattin Books." Aesop's *Fables*, Norwood's *Trigonometry*, and the *Well-spring of Sciences* (1568), a very popular arithmetic, were the other textbooks listed. Berkeley's fourteen historical works included *A Complete History of England* (1706), Thomas Delaune's *The Present State of London* (1681), Palafox y Mendoza's *The History of the Conquest of China* (1671), Aubert de Vertot D'Aubeuf's *The History of the Revolutions of Sweden* (1711), Josephus' *History of the Jews*, histories of France and Germany, an unidentified history of the whole world, North's translation of Plutarch's *Lives*, and the *Eikon Basilike*. Medical and pharmaceutical titles numbered thirteen and consisted for the most part of old favorites of the early seventeenth century, like Barrough's *Method of Physic* or an even earlier work, Thomas Cogan's *The Haven of Health* (1584). The newest book was William Salmon's *Pharmacopoeia Londinensis; or, The New London Dispensatory* (1678). Though Berkeley was provided with an adequate quantity of medical works, he showed no distrust of outworn handbooks nor any desire for recent treatises. Geographical information was supplied by Peter Heylyn's *Microcosmus, A Little Description of the Great World* (1621), James Wadsworth's anticipation of Baedeker, entitled, *The European Mercury* (1641), and two unidentified topographical descriptions, of England and Switzerland. An interest in music in the Berkeley household is suggested by a copy of John Playford's *A Brief Introduction to the Skill of Music for Song and Viol* (1658). Five works on philosophy and ethics found their way into Berkeley's library; they were Charron's *Of Wisdom*, a favorite in the colony, Plutarch's *Moralia*, probably in Philemon Holland's translation made in 1603, Roger L'Estrange's *Toleration Discussed in Two Dialogues* (1663), John Locke's *An Essay Concerning Human Understanding*, and Henry Lee's pious rejoinder, *Anti-Skepticism; or, Notes upon Each Chapter of . . . Locke's Essay* (1702). Of strictly utilitarian titles, exclusive of medicine, Berkeley had only one, a treatise on horsemanship, listed as "Cavalrie the first Book."

Berkeley's small collection of belles-lettres indicates a stronger leaning toward the drama than is usually evident in colonial libraries. The most significant single item is Shakespeare's *Works*, probably in Nicholas Rowe's edition of 1709. Berkeley's inventory is one of the earliest in Virginia to list the complete works of Shakespeare. But Berkeley's interest did not stop with the greatest of Elizabethan dramatists. He had

Sir William Alexander's *Tragedy of Darius* (1603) and *Julius Caesar* (1607) and the collected writings of the Restoration dramatists, George Farquhar and Thomas Southerne. The first recorded copy in Virginia of Boccaccio's *Decameron* was also in Berkeley's possession. And, as further contributions to literary entertainment, he had the second volume of the facetious Tom Brown's *Works* (1707-11), the old romance of *Valentine and Orson*, a tale of Baltazar Gracian, translated by Paul Rycaut as *The Critic* (1681), the first and fourth volumes of the semifictional epistles of Giovanni Paolo Marana, *The Turkish Spy* (1686), and a curious assortment of questions and answers on a great variety of subjects, from religion to love, bearing the title of *The Athenian Oracle* (1703). A single volume of pastoral verse, Francis Quarles's *The Shepherd's Oracles* (1646), was the only example of nondramatic poetry among the belles-lettres. These, then, were the works which supplied the lighter reading of a wealthy member of the ruling class.

Another book remains to be mentioned—one that we may imagine Berkeley picked out for a purpose—*The Works* (1694) of Henry Booth, second Baron Delamere and first Earl of Warrington. Delamere, who distinguished himself by his opposition to Stuart encroachments on parliamentary rights, was a staunch Whig during the reign of William and Mary, and he included in his *Works*, among other things, his observations on government and liberty and his speeches in Parliament. But of more immediate interest to Berkeley, perhaps, was the introductory essay, written by Delamere as advice to his children. In it he gave a simple, dignified, and common-sense statement of what he conceived to be the proper way for a gentleman to deport himself. His rationale of conduct is precisely that aspired to by Virginia gentlemen of the sort represented by Edmund Berkeley. First of all, Delamere counsels, one should practice piety and daily devotions, "For I have observed any morning that I have hurried over my devotions, the day following has not been prosperous."[51] After one's duty to God comes devotion to the state and public service. Having attained high place, a gentleman should always remember to be modest and to behave "with the like familiarity to all sorts of persons as you did before your promotion." He should be easy of access and not give the appearance of being in a great hurry of business. He should not be credulous enough to believe all he hears. He should not squander his estate, but he ought to be hospitable and generous. In this connection, Berkeley undoubtedly read with approval Delamere's injunction to keep a good cook and "let not the want of a tolerable cook give occasion to have the proverb repeated that *God sends meat and the Devil cooks*." In dealing with servants, one should be generous but "Let not your servants be over-familiar or hail fellow with you, neither keep them at too great a distance from you." Finally, in bringing up one's children, "Let their education be suitable to their quality and what your estate will bear." In study, one should follow inclination rather than drive oneself unwillingly to books. In a long passage on the choice of books, Delamere's counsel reads like the practice of Virginians. First of all he commends works on the law—a large category in most Virginia collections—for law will be the greatest aid in public service. The legal works he mentions are precisely those most frequently found in Virginia libraries: the reports of Coke, Dyer, and others, the works of Sir John Fortescue, and the legal writings of Francis Bacon. Next to a knowledge of the law comes history, and he recommends specifically Plutarch's *Lives*, Grotius' *De Jure Belli et Pacis*, and the works of Machiavelli. Finally, as to light reading, he observes, "To read a play or romance now and then for diversion may do no hurt; but he that spends most of his time in such books will be able to give a

[51] Passages quoted here are from the ed. of 1694, pp. 3-31.

very ill account of it." The book lists of Virginians clearly show that this was their point of view. Delamere's advice to his children summed up much of the wisdom that Virginia planters wished to inculcate in their heirs.

One notable lack prevents Berkeley's collection from being typical of the well-chosen gentleman's library of the period: except for Aesop and Plutarch, no classic authors are listed in the inventory. The eight unspecified Latin books were most likely small school texts, or they would have been enumerated by title. Otherwise, Berkeley's library is a fairly accurate reflection of the intellectual interests of the gentleman-planter in the first quarter of the eighteenth century.

Although a few great planters had larger libraries, deserving separate consideration, the smaller collections that we have discussed here indicate the general characteristics of plantation libraries and the purpose behind the selection of their reading. To the Virginia planter, books represented one of the means to an end; and that end was the fulfilment of a dream of economic and social advancement. The more prosperous planters hoped to become rich enough to be fine gentlemen, and to be a fine gentleman required something more than the mere ownership of landed property, essential as that was. The perpetuation of a cultivated way of life, of the civilized manners and customs of the English gentry, became the goal, therefore, of the leaders among the transplanted Englishmen in Virginia. Far from the centers of the culture they hoped to reproduce in the wilderness, they necessarily depended, to a greater degree than we realize, upon their little libraries. Legal works, which served the utilitarian purpose of aiding in lawsuits, also helped to establish traditional legal procedure and customs. The justice of the peace on the Rappahannock read the same manuals as the justice of the peace in Devonshire, and enjoyed an equal if not greater prestige. Sermons and books of devotions written by English clergymen served the religious needs of Virginians and helped to foster a traditional belief in the social as well as the spiritual value of adherence to the Church. Schoolbooks that handed down the ancient methods and curriculum of the English grammar schools were the favored texts for the instruction of colonial youths. The classics remained the backbone of education and polite learning. Histories and books on statecraft prevented the loss of the sense of historical and institutional continuity between the world the colonists had left and the wilderness of Virginia. The merely utilitarian books—works on agriculture, horsemanship, gardening, or hunting and fishing, for example—transmitted to the new country methods and ways of doing things long established in England. In short, the libraries of the colonists were not repositories of books to be casually read during idle hours; on the contrary, they were potent reservoirs of traditional civilization.

One of the most noteworthy qualities of the book collections of the seventeenth and early eighteenth centuries is their extreme conservatism. Some new books were bought, it is true, but in general Virginians preferred old books tested by time. Nor did they waste money buying many controversial works, whether religious, political, or philosophic. A thinker like John Locke, whose writings swept England with phenomenal rapidity, was soon known in the colony, but, on the whole, new and strange philosophies made slow headway.

In their choice of belles-lettres, Virginians were equally conservative. The literature of Greece and Rome still occupied a larger place than the works of modern writers; there were a dozen copies of Homer and Virgil to one of Shakespeare or Milton. But we should remember that English authors had not yet become apotheosized as "classics," and hence lacked the prestige of the ancients. Furthermore, men still had infinite faith in the power of Greek and Roman writers to provide learning and teach the ways of wisdom. The demand for literature of mere amusement was small, even among the gayer spirits of the colony. This does not mean that there were no frivolous books, or that Virginia readers were a gloom-ridden lot; but it does mean that books were still luxuries, and the more essential works received first consideration when the planter sat down to write an order to a London bookseller. Some literary trifles lightened the somber shelves of Virginia libraries, but they did not materially change the air of purposefulness that Virginians demonstrated in their choice of books. If Cavalier frivolity was a quality of the Virginia aristocracy, as romanticists would have us believe, it was not demonstrated in the planters' libraries. Books were bought to serve the ends of utility, to teach the ways of God and man, to preserve and transmit the spark of learning, and to maintain in Virginians the ancient and honorable traditions of their fathers. Scarce though books were in proportion to the population as a whole, the small libraries of the leaders in the colony were more important, in the perpetuation of English civilization, than we realize. Virginians were not a bookish race, but they depended upon books for part of their instruction in the way they should live. And to their reading we owe in part the kind of world they left to their descendants.

A few of the greater gentlemen who helped establish the cultural pattern of aristocratic Virginia have been chosen for more detailed discussion, because they best exemplify attitudes and qualities of mind characteristic of the ruling class. Other Virginians of their day might have been selected, but the men whose lives are here briefly outlined left documentary evidence sufficient to permit generalizations without too much guesswork. Of this closely related group, William Fitzhugh is an excellent illustration of the transition from a frontier settler to a country gentleman anxious to establish and maintain social and intellectual connections with the mother country.

CHAPTER VI

WILLIAM FITZHUGH: THE EVOLUTION OF AN ARISTOCRAT

In the year 1670 a grave young Englishman of nineteen years, ambitious and eager, equipped with a substantial sum of money and ample self-confidence, stepped for the first time on the shores of Virginia. He was William Fitzhugh, son of Henry Fitzhugh, a woolen draper of Bedford,[1] and, like thousands of others before him, he had come to the New World to seek his fortune. Unlike many pioneers less fortunate than himself, Fitzhugh succeeded in his ventures; indeed, his success was such that he acquired vast acres of tobacco lands, surrounded himself with servants and slaves, married his children into the best families of Virginia, and established a family dynasty that became one of the best-connected and most aristocratic in America. Fitzhugh himself lived and died a respected and prosperous country gentleman, an arch Tory in politics, a devout Anglican in religion, and a diligent apostle of traditional English civilization. His rise is typical of the development of the aristocratic ruling class in Virginia, and his life is particularly significant because his later career can be documented with an extraordinary collection of letters, over four hundred in number, which tell the story of his business dealings, his family affairs, his struggles to carve out

[1] The sketch of William Fitzhugh given in the *Dictionary of American Biography* describes his father as a barrister-at-law. The most recent of the family historians (Victor C. A. FitzHugh, "The Fitzhugh Family," *The Virginia Magazine of History and Biography,* XL [1932], 187-204) shows that he was a woolen draper. In any case, the father must have been fairly prosperous in order to give his son a proper start as a planter. William Fitzhugh had enough initial capital to permit him to take his place almost immediately as one of the upper planters. Other facts about the Fitzhughs are to be found in "The Fitzhugh Family," *ibid.*, VII (1899-1900), 196-99, 317-19, 425-27.

a baronial estate, his social aspirations, his disappointments and achievements, and his intellectual interests.[2] Although success came quickly to William Fitzhugh, he remained an expatriate Englishman until his dying day, always homesick for his native soil. In Virginia he sought to make his life as nearly like that of an English country gentleman as wilderness conditions would permit.

Concerning young William Fitzhugh's life before his arrival in Virginia we can only make conjectures. Because he demonstrated unusual legal learning, the presumption is that he was a member of one of the Inns of Court. There is no evidence that he attended either of the universities. One may be fairly certain, however, that he acquired the rudiments of a classical education in the Free Grammar School of Bedford, one of the better institutions, founded in 1561 by Sir William Harper. Although Fitzhugh maintains that he writes without "elegance and sweetness of style"[3]—as, indeed, is the fact—his letters have an urbanity that bespeaks an education beyond the ordinary. An occasional classical allusion or the turn of a phrase now and then shows the influence of his reading. If the young pioneer was too busy to be an extremely bookish person, he nevertheless gathered a library and depended upon books for companionship. Whatever his early training may have been, he acquired a certain amount of literary taste and appreciation of the cultural amenities.

Soon after his arrival in 1670, the young settler established himself not far from the Potomac River, in Stafford County, then a frontier region. There, in the next few years, he built a comfortable house, planted extensive orchards and

[2] The Fitzhugh letters are reprinted in *The Virginia Magazine of History and Biography*, I (1893-94), 17-55, 105-26, 199-202, 253-77, 391-410; II (1894-95), 15-36, 121-42, 259-75, 370-79; III (1895-96), 1-15, 161-68, 253-61, 368-73; IV (1896-97), 67-74, 176-84, 310-12, 415-20; V (1897-98), 29-33, 169-73, 297-302; VI (1898-99), 60-72, 158-62.

[3] *The Virginia Magazine of History and Biography*, I, 396.

gardens, and named the estate after his native town, Bedford. On May Day, 1674, he married Sarah, daughter of John Tucker, one of the more well-to-do planters of Westmoreland County. Fitzhugh's life was not one sequence of successes, however, and his early struggles brought out those qualities of shrewdness, enterprise, and persistence that characterized his subsequent career. In 1685, writing to his cousin and namesake, a stationer dwelling in Newgate Market, the master of Bedford observes with a certain degree of satisfaction over his accomplishments: "I have a long time in a strange land struggled hard with Fortune's adverse hand, but, thank God, in the end, by God Almighty's blessing upon my mean endeavors (having no friend or relative to lend a supporting hand) have overcome, and, I praise God, live very contentedly and well."[4] A year later, in a letter to his mother, Fitzhugh again expresses satisfaction over his way of life: "Praised be God," he comments, "I neither live in poverty nor pomp, but in a very good indifferency and to a full content."[5]

To the attainment of this golden mean between riches and poverty, Fitzhugh had given years of hard work and close personal attention. No planter, he frequently suggests in his correspondence, can hope to succeed if he neglects the administration of his own affairs. In one letter he observes that "without a constant care and diligent eye, a well made plantation will run to ruin."[6] If any evidence were needed to disprove the fanciful picture of the idleness and frivolity of rich Virginia planters, it is available in Fitzhugh's detailed record of the stern requirements of plantation management.

Since the basis of all riches in Virginia lay in the ownership of tobacco-producing land, Fitzhugh set about acquiring fertile tracts of arable soil between the Potomac and the Rappahannock. The land surrounding his manor house at

[4] *Ibid.*, pp. 276-77.
[5] *Ibid.*, p. 393.
[6] *Ibid.*, III, 260.

Bedford was the first of many pieces of farm and forest land bought in the next two decades. By the time of his death, in 1701, he owned over 54,000 acres of potential tobacco fields. Great tracts of this barony remained undeveloped throughout Fitzhugh's lifetime. In fact, one of the cherished schemes which occupied much of his attention in the 1680's and '90's was the settlement of one tract of over 21,000 acres, in Stafford County, with Huguenot refugees.[7] In his dreams, Fitzhugh saw himself surrounded by a great host of tenants, all industrious and thrifty, who would contribute to the wealth and prestige of the lord of the manor and find for themselves prosperity and freedom from religious persecution. Some Frenchmen settled on his lands, but the colonization venture was not so successful as he had hoped. To the end of his days, Fitzhugh continued his efforts to induce refugees from Europe to settle as tenants on his lands.

But a system of tenantry was not the main source of the Bedford planter's income. Early in his career he became a slaveowner as well as the purchaser of indentured white servants. In his will fifty-one black slaves are listed.[8] These servants, who required little to support them that could not be produced on the plantation, made possible the growing of tobacco at a profit, even in the face of overproduction and low prices. It is easy to understand why Fitzhugh looked upon the advent of a slave ship as a peculiar blessing of providence and why he watched the prices of the Royal African Company with a canny eye. Because of his distance from the first ports of call made by the slave ships, he felt that he suffered a handicap in bidding for the best slaves; hence he wrote to his friend Colonel Ralph Wormeley, on June 19, 1681, requesting the purchase of five or six negroes when

[7] See letters, *ibid.*, I, 408; III, 8. Also, Fairfax Harrison, *Landmarks of Old Prince William* (Richmond, 1924), I, 177-96.

[8] For an abstract of Fitzhugh's will, see *The Virginia Magazine of History and Biography*, II, 276-78.

the next ship anchored in the York River, before they had been picked over and "none left but the refuse."[9] His directions for the purchase of negroes show an anxiety lest he be cheated by the traders, and he insists upon the purchase of only young, healthy specimens. Never is there the least indication that he regards the institution of slavery as anything but a blessing of God.

Although Fitzhugh was concerned to establish his claim to gentility and to maintain himself in the tradition of English gentlemen, not a hint does he ever give that trade and business are incompatible with his social aspirations. The truth is that neither he nor any of his Virginia contemporaries would have understood the snobbish attitude assumed by some of their nineteenth-century descendants toward the so-called "taint of trade." Trade was a necessary concomitant of plantation life, and the greater the planter, the greater his participation in commerce. Fitzhugh bought tobacco from the lesser planters, loaded it at his own wharf, and shipped it to his merchant correspondents in London and Bristol. Sometimes he made a fat profit; occasionally the hazards of the sea or falling prices brought him to the brink of disaster. The ships which carried his tobacco to English ports brought manufactured necessities to Virginia on the return voyage. Some of these imports were sold at the plantation storehouse to his tenants and neighbors.

Business enterprise characterized Fitzhugh's activities in Stafford County. When tobacco prices dropped too low for profitable planting, he was one of those instrumental in curtailing production in the hope of raising the price, and he fostered a scheme to establish towns and encourage manufacturing. "If you can meet with any tradesmen that will come in and live at the town, they may have large privileges and immunities," he writes Captain Francis Partis on July 1, 1680.[10] To Thomas Matthews, of Cherry Point, he writes on July 3,

[9] *Ibid.*, I, 37. [10] *Ibid.*, p. 30.

1681, congratulating him on the report of "great and profitable progress in your linen manufacture," which he regards as a "good example to others."[11] At another time he is enthusiastic about the possibilities of growing olives commercially, and he sends to London for trees. The hope of discovering mineral resources on his plantation was also constantly before him.

Though the art of getting ahead in the world was always close to Fitzhugh's heart, he never forgot that it was a means to an end and not an end in itself. His was not the heart of a shopkeeper. The amenities of life to be found on the plantation at Bedford were the equal of those on many a provincial English manor; but, though the master of the plantation took a pardonable pride in his accomplishment, he still felt a homesickness for his native land. Thanks to his desire to trade his Virginia property for an estate and income in England, we have a detailed description of Bedford. Writing on April 22, 1686, to Dr. Ralph Smith, who married his sister, Fitzhugh expresses the wish to exchange his colonial possessions for land in England bringing in an annual income of three or four hundred pounds. Like a real-estate promoter, he pictures the good qualities of his Virginia possessions:

> The plantation where I now live contains a thousand acres, at least 700 acres of it being rich thicket, the remainder good hearty plantable land, without any waste either by marshes or great swamps. The commodiousness, conveniency, and pleasantness yourself well knows. Upon it there is three quarters well furnished with all necessary houses, grounds and fencing, together with a choice crew of negroes at each plantation, most of them this country born, the remainder as likely as most in Virginia, there being twenty-nine in all, with stocks of cattle and hogs at each quarter. Upon the same land is my own dwelling house furnished with all accomodations for a comfortable and genteel living, as a very good dwelling house with rooms in it, four of the best of them hung [with tapestry] and nine of them plentifully furnished

[11] *Ibid.*, p. 42.

> with all things necessary and convenient, and all houses for use furnished with brick chimneys; four good cellars, a dairy, dovecote, stable, barn, henhouse, kitchen, and all other conveniencies and all in a manner new; a large orchard of about 2500 apple trees, most grafted, well fenced with a locust fence, which is as durable as most brick walls; a garden a hundred foot square, well paled in; a yard wherein is most of the aforesaid necessary houses, pallisadoed in with locust puncheons which is as good as if it were walled in and more lasting than any of our bricks; together with a good stock of cattle, hogs, horses, mares, sheep, etc., and necessary servants belonging to it for the supply and support thereof.
>
> About a mile and [a] half distance a good water grist mill, whose toll I find sufficient to find my own family with wheat and Indian corn for our necessities and occasions. Up the river in this county, three tracts of land more; one of them contains 21,996 acres, another 500 acres, and one other 1000 acres, all good, convenient, and commodious seats, and which in few years will yield a considerable annual income.[12]

The enumeration of possessions lists large stocks of tobacco on hand and emphasizes the productivity of the land.

The vision of pastoral contentment which this description conjures up would have been sufficient, one might think, to induce many a land-hungry London merchant to abandon a career on the Exchange for a new incarnation on the Potomac. Curiously, however, Fitzhugh never consummated a deal to his liking, probably because he was too particular about the security he demanded. A year after his letter to Dr. Smith, he wrote his friend and business agent, Nicholas Hayward of London, declaring that he would be glad to trade his property for an estate even in Scotland or Ireland.[13]

It is worthy of note that his house—containing thirteen rooms—was unusually large for the seventeenth century. As he himself indicates, only the chimneys were of brick, the

[12] *Ibid.*, p. 395.
[13] *Ibid.*, II, 134.

house itself being a rambling frame building which had grown by the gradual accretion of rooms.[14] The tapestry hangings gave an air of luxury which only the better plantation houses could offer. They doubtless represented one of Fitzhugh's extravagances. On one occasion we find him ordering "a suit of tapestry hangings for a room twenty foot long, sixteen foot wide and nine foot high." [15] He also had a considerable number of pictures and maps, as his will indicates. The orders for furniture and silver plate leave no doubt that the owner of Bedford lavished all he could afford upon the furnishing of his home.

Though the plantation was well provided with the necessities of life, and the tobacco fields were fertile, the owner was frequently embarrassed for ready cash. As was the case with some of the wealthiest planters, it was often hard to raise even a small sum in pounds sterling, however abundant crops and livestock might be. On one occasion Fitzhugh had difficulty in raising £10 for his mother in England,[16] and on another he writes rather pathetically to his London agent to send him a riding coat, "if my money holds out." [17] As he says in a letter to his brother Henry, "we live here very plentifully without money." [18] This scarcity of cash in the late seventeenth century helps to explain why the importation of luxuries, including books, was greatly curtailed.

Scarce though cash was, Fitzhugh indulged in several vanities. Among them was an inordinate desire for a vehicle

[14] *Ibid.*, p. 23. In a letter to Nicholas Hayward, dated Jan. 30, 1687, Fitzhugh recommends the procedure in housebuilding which he should follow. He advises Hayward, who is planning a place for his son, to send over indentured servants trained as carpenters and brickmasons, and to build gradually over a period of years. When the servants are not occupied with his own tasks, they can be hired out to his neighbors.

[15] *Ibid.*, I, 121.

[16] *Ibid.*, II, 132, 265.

[17] *Ibid.*, I, 28.

[18] *Ibid.*, II, 17.

described as a calash—a light carriage, which permitted him to ride about the countryside in considerably more style than most of his neighbors. On May 10, 1688, he tells Nicholas Hayward that he is extremely anxious to obtain one not to cost "above £6 or £7 . . . but strong and well geared,"[19] for, he writes a year later, the calash is "a recreative project" and he does "not think it reasonable to give my fancy an unlimited allowance."[20] After playing with the idea of a *chaise roulant*, recommended by the French tutor of his son, at last, on December 19, 1693, he acknowledges the receipt of the long-wished-for calash.[21] For the remaining eight years of his life, let us hope, Fitzhugh enjoyed this recreative vehicle.

Life at Bedford exemplified the ancient ideal of hospitality that had been such a notable quality of the English country gentry in earlier periods. On Fitzhugh's plantation, guests were entertained with the ease that had characterized English squires in the days before they began to give up country pursuits in order to flock to the court in London. At Bedford visitors were warmly welcomed and no crowd of merry-makers was ever too large to be received cordially. A record of the sort of hospitality dispensed has been left by a Huguenot gentleman, one Durand, who visited Fitzhugh during Christmas, 1686, in company with Colonel Ralph Wormeley and a party of planters:

> Monsieur Wormeley is so well beloved and esteemed in this country [Durand wrote in his journal] that all the honest people in the neighborhood came to see him and would not leave him; so we rode twenty strong to Colonel Fichous' [Fitzhugh's], but he has such a large establishment that he did not mind. We were all of us provided with beds, one for two men. He treated us royally. There was good wine and all kinds of beverages, so there was a great deal of carousing. He had sent for three fiddlers, a jester, a tight-rope dancer, an acrobat who tumbled around, and they gave us all the entertainment one could wish for. It was

[19] *Ibid.*, p. 267. [20] *Ibid.*, p. 376. [21] *Ibid.*, IV, 180.

> very cold, yet no one ever thinks of going near the fire, for they never put less than a cartload of wood in the fireplace and the whole room is kept warm. . . . The next day, after they had caroused until afternoon, we decided to cross this river. The Colonel had a quantity of wine and one of his punch-bowls brought to the shore; he lent us his boat.[22]

Fitzhugh was distinguished from the moneygrubbing trader by the ease and grace of life achieved at Bedford. Shrewd though he was in business, and alert to his financial interests, he did not sacrifice the amenities of his existence to the desire for gain. He was never too busy, for instance, to be neighborly. As in all frontier communities, personal services were required more often than in cities, and Fitzhugh was always ready to help in any emergency or need. Likewise, he strove to surround himself with neighbors of similar generosity and good manners. To Nicholas Hayward he wrote on April 22, 1686, to express his pleasure over Hayward's purchase of a tract of land adjoining the Bedford estate—land that he himself had hoped to buy, "for my intention of purchase was to have such neighbors on it as might live quietly and honestly." Hayward's purchase of the land allayed any fear of unacceptable people and gave "assurance of so generous and friendly a neighborhood, either by a trustee for yourself, or by some near and dear relation of yourself." [23] Occasionally Fitzhugh's letters mention the loan of a book from some planter friend,

[22] *A Huguenot Exile in Virginia; or, Voyages of a Frenchman Exiled for His Religion, with a Description of Virginia and Maryland*, ed. and tr. Gilbert Chinard (New York, 1934), pp. 158-59. Durand's *Journal* was published at The Hague in 1687. On June 1, 1688, Fitzhugh wrote Nicholas Hayward his unfavorable comment upon it: "I thank your kindness in Mr. Durand's book, and must agree with you as well as I can understand it, that it's a most weak, unpolite piece, having neither the rules of history nor method of description, and taking it only as a private gentleman's journal, 'tis as barren and defective there too; when I come out in print, [I] do intend to appear more regular and therefore as yet am not provided for such an undertaking." (*The Virginia Magazine of History and Biography*, II, 270-71.)

[23] *Ibid.*, I, 397.

or the exchange of other courtesies. Yet, despite the gaiety of the gatherings of planters and the friendliness of his neighbors, Fitzhugh was often lonely for intellectual companionship. To make up for that lack, he, like Richard Lee and others of his kind, fell back on books. Now and then the sense of isolation from stimulating companions and the provinciality of plantation life almost overwhelmed him, and it was in one of these periods of despondency that he wrote Hayward: "Society that is good and ingenious is very scarce and seldom to be come at except in books. Good education of children is almost impossible, and better be never born than ill-bred. But that which bears the greatest weight with me, for now I look upon myself to be in my declining age, is the want of spiritual helps and comforts, of which this fertile country in everything else is barren and unfruitful." [24] For these reasons Fitzhugh was eager to exchange his plantation and return to England, even though he would be unable to live there "with that great plenty" that he had in Virginia.

Whether he remained in Virginia or returned to England, William Fitzhugh was determined to maintain himself as a gentleman. One of his chief demands in negotiating a trade of his Virginia property for an estate in England was sufficient land and income to enable him to continue that manner of life. Having acquired a degree of prosperity placing him above the average of men, he was intent upon his family's upholding his social position, and he overlooked no opportunity that would help establish the family name among the gentry. When his sister Dorothy contemplated coming to the colony, he wrote to his brother Henry that it was his desire that "she come out handsomely and genteelly and well-clothed, with a maid to wait on her." [25] Later, when Dorothy had become the widow of Dr. Ralph Smith and had married George Luke,

[24] *Ibid.*, II, 25; letter dated Jan. 30, 1687.
[25] *Ibid.*, I, 392; letter dated Apr. 22, 1686.

son of Oliver Luke, a somewhat haughty gentleman of Bedfordshire, Fitzhugh wrote the father that his son had made a good match; he also wrote to Sir Humphrey Winch, uncle of the youth, to assure him that the widow was well-to-do and worthy of marriage into a proud family, "her former husband being a considerable dealer [merchant] here and an able practitioner in physic, both laudable and profitable employs." [26] One of the most prominent gentlemen in the colony, Colonel Nicholas Spencer, secretary of state, had arranged the match, Fitzhugh was careful to point out. Evidently the youth's family had made a row over his marriage, and the brother of the bride felt it incumbent upon him to assert his own family's importance. In the end, Fitzhugh had cause to regret the match, for George Luke proved himself an unmannerly spendthrift, who probably deserved his brother-in-law's later epithet of "foolish little knave." [27]

To improve his brother Henry's position in the world, William hit upon the idea of getting him an appointment as captain of a naval vessel on the Virginia station. Henry, whom his brother addresses as "Captain," had evidently already obtained a post in the navy. The command of a Virginia ship would prove profitable and insure a social position of some consequence in the colony. In 1687 William wrote Henry that he had heard, from his sister, that his "interest and friends are great at Court," and he urged him to use this opportunity to get the desirable commission. The profits, William points out, "might fairly be worth to you a thousand pounds sterling a year, without being at two pence expense." Of the two commanders on the station, "one is a Scot and the other is a fool, and yet they clear better than £500 sterling a year." [28]

[26] *Ibid.*, IV, 71; letter dated July 21, 1692.

[27] *Ibid.*, p. 419; letter to his mother, undated but written in 1695.

[28] *Ibid.*, II, 16; letter dated Jan. 30, 1687. On Apr. 5, 1687, William again wrote Henry, this time proposing that he try to obtain the farm of the Virginia tobacco duties. (*Ibid.*, p. 125.)

Henry's friends at Court were of no avail, however, and he took to drink, to the distress of his brother, who had to foot some of the bills.

The trappings and symbols of gentility were matters of great concern to the planter of Bedford, who was careful to procure an accurately made seal, with his family crest, and a properly painted copy of his coat of arms. In the letter to Henry about the naval commission, he remarks that he would "be heartily glad of your picture and our coat-of-arms, fairly and rightly drawn, not as on the steel seal that came here"—a request that he found occasion to repeat. Over a year later he sent a blazon of his coat of arms to Nicholas Hayward, with a new order for a seal cut in steel; and, lest he lose this seal, he ordered a second "large one upon an ivory stand."[29]

Another symbol of wealth and position—a symbol in which the master of Bedford indulged his vanity to the full—was the acquisition of an extraordinary quantity of silver plate bearing the Fitzhugh crest. Whenever he could raise money over and above the requirements for absolute essentials, Fitzhugh bought silver. Although he salved his business conscience for this extravagance by saying that it was a good investment, there can be no doubt that the planter took more than an investor's pleasure in his goblets, pitchers, salt shakers, dishes, porringers, candlesticks, knives, forks, spoons, tankards, and odd pieces, some very large and heavy. In one expensive order, he specified, among many other silver pieces, two large dishes big enough "for a good joint of meat," a dozen plates, and a three-quart tankard. And he added, "let it all be thus marked *WFS* and that coat-of-arms put upon all pieces that are proper, especially the dishes, plates, and tankards, etc. that I have sent enclosed and blazoned in a letter to Mr. Hayward."[30]

[29] *Ibid.*, p. 272; letter dated June 8, 1688. A reproduction of the Fitzhugh coat of arms is to be found *ibid.*, VII, opposite p. 196.

[30] *Ibid.*, II, 269; letter addressed jointly to the London merchant John Cooper and Nicholas Hayward, dated June 1, 1688. For other orders for silver plate see pp. 140, 274, 377.

Acknowledging the receipt of one shipment of silver plate, Fitzhugh expressed particular pleasure over its timely arrival, "for about two or three days after the receipt of it, I had the honor of the Governor's company at my house for three or four days, who first hanselled it."[31] A visit of the royal governor, accompanied by some of the greatest gentlemen of the colony, was surely an occasion for the Stafford planter's finest hospitality, and we can well imagine his pride in exhibiting one of the largest collections of silver plate in Virginia, all marked "*WFS*" and resplendent with the Fitzhugh crest. To the end of his life, he continued to buy plate. Indeed, he had a servant especially trained as an engraver, in order that he might add the monogram and crest after the silver arrived at the plantation.[32]

Among the problems faced by the heads of families in Virginia was the means of insuring a proper education for their children. The difficulty of providing the necessary schooling for his sons was a reason prompting Fitzhugh's desire to return to England. When that possibility seemed remote, he determined, in 1690, to send his eldest son and namesake back home to school—a dangerous journey for a child. But just as he was planning for the voyage, he met a French Huguenot minister who agreed to teach the lad. The passage, in a letter to Hayward, describing his educational plans for his son is worth quoting in full:

> Sir, this year I was designed to have sent home my eldest son to school there and did intend to request of your care of him and kindness to him but accidentally meeting with a French minister, a sober, learned, and discreet gentleman, whom I persuaded to board and tutor him, which he hath undertaken, in whose family there is nothing but French spoken, which by a continual converse will make him perfect in that tongue, and he takes a great deal of pains and care to teach him Latin, both of which go on hitherto

[31] *Ibid.*, III, 9; letter to Nicholas Hayward, dated July 10, 1690.
[32] *Ibid.*, VI, 71; letter dated July 21, 1698.

very well together, only some books are wanting, as the French *Rudiments of the Latin Grammar*, three of them, three French common prayer books, a French and Latin dictionary, which I desire you will please to send me by the first conveniency.[33]

The child was then hardly four years old! In 1698, when young William was eleven and a half, he was at last sent to England for further training. This time the father placed him in charge of one of his merchant correspondents, George Mason of Bristol, with instructions for him to be put in school near Bristol. Fitzhugh's letter to Mason went into considerable detail about the care of his son. He was to be dressed in accordance with English fashion, but he was not to be decked out in extravagant finery. Instead, he was to be furnished "with what is fit and decent, as befits an honest planter or farmer's son, not with what's rich or gaudy." Quiet decorum, which manifested itself in all of Fitzhugh's conduct, dictated his taste in personal adornment. Though he had as much class-consciousness as many another of the new Virginia aristocracy, his conception of gentility did not permit foolish foppery, and he did not propose that his son and heir should be brought up to have the notions of a London dandy.

A sound classical background, with training in French, seemed to Fitzhugh the desirable sort of education for William. He had made a beginning in this direction under his French tutor, but he needed some instruction in English, the father explains to Mason:

Now, sir, to tell you that he is eleven years and a half old, and can hardly read or write a word of English might make you believe that either he was a dull boy or that I was a very careless and neglectful parent. Indeed, it is neither carelessness in me nor dullness in him, for although he cannot read or write English, yet he can both read, write, and speak French, and has run over the rudiments of the Latin grammar, according to the French method, for he has been a considerable time with a most ingenious French

[33] *Ibid.*, III, 9.

gentleman, a minister who had the government and tutorage of him, and indeed did it singularly well; but the unhealthy fullness of his seat and the sickliness of the child occasioned his remove from thence. Therefore if it could be as Capt. Jones tells me it may, I would have him put to a French schoolmaster to continue his French and learn Latin.[34]

School, the father hoped, would be something more than a stern discipline for the child; and he added a further note to the merchant, that the boy was to be supplied not only with books and clothes but "now and then a little money to buy apples, plums, etc." The classical education that the lad received was not wasted; he grew up to be one of the first gentlemen of Virginia, the lord of the plantation known as Eagle's Nest, and eventually became a member of the Virginia Council—a position his father coveted but never attained. Records of the education of Fitzhugh's other children are lacking, but we can be sure that he gave them as good schooling as he could afford. Five sons survived the father and lived to take their places among the leading planters of the colony. The two older sons probably received the best literary education, for by their father's will his "study of books" was divided equally between them.

Without exception the boys married into the families of important planters. William married Ann, daughter of Richard Lee of Westmoreland County; Henry married Susanna, daughter of Mordecai Cooke, of Gloucester County; Thomas and George married sisters, Ann and Mary, the daughters of Colonel George Mason of Stafford County; and John married Anna Barbara, daughter of Colonel Daniel McCarty of Westmoreland County, Speaker of the House of Burgesses.[35] William Fitzhugh the elder must have taken a patriarchal satisfaction in the contemplation of an established dynasty to carry on his name. To all of his sons he left sufficient land and slaves to insure their social position.

[34] *Ibid.*, VI, 70; letter dated July 21, 1698. [35] *Ibid.*, VII, 317-19.

If the establishment of a family dynasty was a dominating ambition of the first Fitzhugh, the pursuit of that goal did not prevent his sharing in the duties, sometimes onerous and time-consuming, that fell to the lot of the gentry. Indeed, since responsibilities of state were regarded as an obligation of his class, Fitzhugh would not have thought of shirking any service expected of him. At various times he represented Stafford County in the House of Burgesses; he commanded the militia of the county; and he served as judge of the county court. On several occasions he displayed independence and courage of a high degree. In politics he was one of the most conservative of Tories, and he made political enemies who sought without success to disgrace him, charging him on two occasions with misrepresenting claims for personal emoluments. The charges were never substantiated and he was never brought to trial. His political independence, which now and then resulted in conflict with powerful politicians, prevented, he believed, his elevation to the Council.[36]

A man of Fitzhugh's conservative and aristocratic point of view found it difficult to hide his contempt for some of the Whigs who made a great noise in Virginia, following the Revolution of 1688. Earlier than this he had been grieved to find that his brother-in-law, Dr. Ralph Smith, was an "inveterate Whig."[37] During the flurry of excitement in Virginia following the overthrow of James II, feeling ran high between Tories and Whigs. One of the noisiest Whigs in the colony was a certain quarrelsome and blatant preacher named John Waugh, who raised a tumult over a rumored rising of Catholics in Maryland. Because Fitzhugh was a known Tory devoted to the Stuart cause, he came in for a part of Waugh's vituperation. The parson and some of his henchmen had also spread the report that Seneca Indians, with Papists from Mary-

[36] *Ibid.*, III, 256-57.

[37] *Ibid.*, I, 398; letter to Nicholas Hayward, dated Apr. 22, 1686.

land, were about to fall on Virginians in the Northern Neck and murder supporters of the Prince of Orange. Among others preached against was George Brent, Fitzhugh's Catholic law partner. Brent's life was in grave danger and Fitzhugh himself was not safe from the wrath of the rabble. Notwithstanding Fitzhugh's Tory sympathies, the Virginia Council ordered him to muster the militia and to take Brent into his house for safekeeping. Waugh and other leaders of the tumult were arrested by order of the Council and silenced. In a short time the rioting was over and peace once more descended on the disturbed colonies. In the next election, however, Fitzhugh's enemies were strong enough to defeat him and elect his rival, the Whig Martin Scarlet.[38] In the threatened uprising Fitzhugh had demonstrated courage, a sense of fair play, and devotion to law and order.

One of the charges made by Scarlet in his campaign against Fitzhugh was that there was no law or justice in Stafford County except what Fitzhugh said was so,[39] and that Fitzhugh had thwarted the administration of justice. To this charge, the accused hotly replied by pointing to his long record on the bench; since 1686 he had also been presiding magistrate. The truth was that Fitzhugh possessed the greatest store of legal erudition in Virginia, and his technical knowledge had undoubtedly given him a great advantage over planters less well-equipped. He was one of the few Virginians of the time who appear to have had professional training in the law.

Although Fitzhugh served for several years as a judge in the Stafford County court, that office did not prevent his practicing law in other counties and advising clients in cases outside of his jurisdiction. Many of his letters are documents of legal advice, some of the most significant being written to

[38] For a succinct account of Parson Waugh's tumult, see Harrison, *Landmarks of Old Prince William*, I, 127-42. [39] *Ibid.*, p. 133.

Richard Lee, Ralph Wormeley, and Major Robert Beverley. He defended Beverley, in 1682-83, when the latter was arrested and imprisoned for refusing to turn over the journal of the House of Burgesses to the Governor and Council. Fitzhugh based his defense on English common law and argued learnedly for his client's release on a habeas-corpus proceeding. Valuable insights into the place of the common law in Virginia legal practice are to be found in Fitzhugh's letters of advice. To Richard Lee he wrote, in 1679, concerning statute and common law. Before statute law can be interpreted properly, he insists, one must know the common law, "the only guide"; and he adds that a knowledge of the common law "is only to be learned out of ancient authors (for out of the old fields must come the new corn) contrary to opinion of the generality of our judges and practicers of the law here."[40] Significantly, some of the books most frequently found in Virginia libraries were legal works by the old authors whom Fitzhugh commended. A few months after his letter to Lee, Fitzhugh wrote Beverley concerning a point in the law of inheritance, which Beverley had evidently raised in a previous conversation. The answer to his question, his learned friend explains, is to be found "in old authors, which remain in their original languages, to say French and Latin," and he instances Bracton, Britton, and *Fleta* among the works which expound the common-law basis of the point.[41] In the late seventies and early eighties one gets the impression that Fitzhugh was definitely trying to dazzle his contemporaries with his legal learning and was particularly eager to demonstrate his profound knowledge of the common law—something which required more than the handbook learning that any amateur practitioner could acquire. He likes to give erudite citations, as in a letter to Thomas Clayton on April 7, 1679, when he cites such

[40] *The Virginia Magazine of History and Biography*, I, 18.
[41] *Ibid.*, pp. 19-20.

authorities as Sir Edward Coke's *Institutes* and Robert Keilway's and Sir James Dyer's reports, and fortifies his arguments with quotations from Cicero and Magna Charta.[42] Perhaps Fitzhugh's demonstration of the value of legal knowledge, particularly of the expositions of common law hidden away in the Latin and law French of old treatises, did much to stimulate his contemporaries' profounder study of the law. Certainly, from Fitzhugh's time onward, legal libraries multiplied and Virginians followed his advice to base their arguments on the common law. Unconsciously he helped to raise the standard of legal practice.

A further display of the Bedford planter's legal skill and erudition came when he was called upon to defend his friend Beverley. One letter in particular, written January 1, 1683, learnedly expounds the rights of the individual guaranteed by Magna Charta and cites ancient precedents guaranteeing personal liberty.[43] Yet, despite Fitzhugh's learning, the political power of the Council was too great, and Beverley had to beg forgiveness on his knees, before he was granted the freedom assured him by Magna Charta and the precedents found in ancient authors. Nevertheless, the case helped to establish Fitzhugh's reputation as the man most learned in the law in all the colony.

As a leading citizen of Stafford County, Fitzhugh had certain responsibilities of church as well as state. Ecclesiastical duties could not have been uncongenial, for he was a staunch and orthodox communicant in the Church of England. Although the church building, which in his lifetime stood not far from the plantation house at Bedford, has long since disappeared, along with its records, we can safely assume that the master of the plantation was among its most influential wardens. At any rate the duty of finding a clergyman was

[42] *Ibid.*, pp. 22-23.
[43] *Ibid.*, pp. 109-13.

his. To a merchant correspondent in London, one John Cooper, he wrote, in 1690, saying that his brother-in-law George Luke had not only undertaken to bring over from Christ's Hospital "an ingenious boy" educated in arithmetic to be a bookkeeper, but also had promised to find for the church at Bedford "an able, learned, serious, and sober minister, whose allowance here would be large and comfortable."[44] If Luke–evidently an irresponsible young man–should fail in these commissions, Cooper is requested to attend to the matter. The Bishop of London, Fitzhugh points out, would provide the minister with a travel allowance of £20.

Although an interest in the parish church would have been expected of the chief planter of the district, Fitzhugh's interest was more than perfunctory service. In many letters to members of his family there runs an undercurrent of piety that is sincere and genuine. To his mother he writes of religious matters with less reserve than to others. In these letters one gets a glimpse of the spiritual side of a man greatly concerned with the affairs of this world but not forgetful of the duties and rewards of religion and piety. In a note to his agent, John Cooper, he thanks him for sending a letter from his mother, and with it "the welcome Bible";[45] and in a letter to his mother by the same carriage he mentions his religious views: "Before I was ten years old, as I am sure you very well remember, I looked upon this life here as but going to an inn, no permanent being. By God's [aid] I continue the same good thoughts and notions still; therefore am always prepared for my certain dissolution which I can't be persuaded to prolong by a wish." And a postscript adds a comforting assurance to his mother, who was grieving over the death of her daughter Dorothy in Virginia: "My sister died a true penitent of the Church of England."[46] Dorothy's first husband, as may be

[44] *Ibid.*, III, 7; see also pp. 165-66, 258.
[45] *Ibid.*, VI, 65; letter dated June 30, 1698.
[46] *Ibid.*, VI, 66-67.

remembered, was a Whig and possibly a Dissenter, and her second husband a ne'er-do-well. Her brother had reason to be doubly grateful that she had remained faithful to her religion.

Though a firm adherent of the Established Church, Fitzhugh, throughout his career, was tolerant and kindly toward other sects. His neighbor and colleague, George Brent, was a Catholic. He himself had a scheme for bringing in Catholic settlers who might find an asylum in Stafford County, and, as we have seen, his efforts to induce French Huguenots to settle on his lands occupied his attention for several years. If he himself preferred the Anglican establishment, he never gave any indication of a desire to force others to his way of thinking.

In certain of his ethical views, Fitzhugh was perhaps more Aristotelian than Christian. The golden mean between extremes—the doctrine of moderation in all things—guided him in his conduct and was the keystone of his personal code of morality. His belief in moderation was epitomized in a letter written in 1698 to Henry Hartwell, merchant of London, in reply to Hartwell's expression of amazement that the planter had never suffered from gout. "As to your wonder that I have never been troubled therewith," Fitzhugh remarks, "I'll tell you, Sir, I never much frequented Bacchus' orgies and always avoided Ceres' shrine, and never was one of Venus' votaries. To speak [plainly] to you, I never courted unlawful pleasures with women, avoided hard drinking as much as lay in my power, and always avoided feasting and consequently the surfeits occasioned thereby. Tell your doctor this and he will conclude I am not near being his patient yet." [47]

Though a believer in temperance, Fitzhugh was no long-faced killjoy, no unsmiling puritan. When planters gathered for a frolic, he could be as merry as any, but he carried his liquor like a gentleman and regretted excesses of overdrinking. Seventeen years before the letter just cited, he had written to

[47] *Ibid.*, p. 159.

Hartwell, then resident at James City, apologizing for departing from a certain "Bacchanalian banquet" without taking proper leave of his friend. His excuse was "the great absurdity of solecisms committed by Bacchanals, who have privilege by Bacchus himself, the first institutor of the order." [48] For all his code of moderation, the gentleman from Bedford had apparently been a little fuddled and was sorry for it. A few years after this episode, in a letter to Nicholas Hayward in which he laments his brother's heavy drinking, Fitzhugh observes: "I must borrow from the latter part of your letter my excuse for not repeating your health so often as my inclinations lead me by assuring you that what is wanting at Bacchus' orgies shall be supplied at Jove's temple for your good fortune and successes; neither my brain nor my constitution will admit me to go too far in those Bacchanalian exercises." [49] Clearly the master of Bedford was no roistering cavalier of the type conventionally pictured.

The belief in the value of moderation, exemplified here in his attitude toward drink, was a part of his fundamental character, and undoubtedly carried over into other phases of his social relations, concerning which there is no explicit evidence. We may be sure that Fitzhugh took his place at the card table on occasion, but he never gambled away any fortunes. And, if he bet at horse races, as he undoubtedly did, he was careful to keep his bets within his capacity to pay without damaging his credit.

In the safeguarding of his credit, indeed, he was as careful as the most scrupulous merchant. No reckless extravagance, no careless throwing around of bills of exchange, no forgetful negligence of the state of his accounts marred his commercial dealings. His relations with his business correspondents in London and Bristol were remarkably pleasant; only rarely is there

[48] *Ibid.*, I, 38; letter dated June 19, 1681.
[49] *Ibid.*, II, 26; letter dated Jan. 30, 1687.

a note of displeasure because of some failure to follow his instructions. Over a long period his complicated business of selling tobacco and buying commodities was carried on with the same correspondents and there was no dissatisfaction on either side.

The amazing thing about these business dealings is the trust that men placed in each other, without recourse to written contracts. The word of William Fitzhugh was actually his bond and he was eternally vigilant to protect his name. On one occasion, when in an emergency he had consciously overdrawn his account with Nicholas Hayward by giving Colonel Daniel Parke a bill of exchange for £100 sterling—something he had never done before—he hurried to notify Hayward of proper security available in London for the overdraft, though he knew his old friend and correspondent would honor the bill without worry.[50]

A clue to Fitzhugh's own sense of honor in business is to be found in one of his letters to Richard Lee, concerning counsel received from Lee: "I know you are too well practiced in the topics of honor and generosity to render advice other than fair and candid, and as you are not Yorkshire enough to set the course of your advice by the compass of your interest. Sir, I shall always endeavor to manage those parts that God Almighty have given me the use of that the devil may not have the application, and to be sure to keep honesty and integrity at the helm when I launch out into any manner of concerns, and not with North County men thrust them under hatches."[51] From the evidence that survives, Fitzhugh seems to have succeeded better than some of his contemporaries in keeping his honor at the helm.

With all the multifarious duties of business, both private and public, that fell to Fitzhugh's lot, one might think that he

[50] *Ibid.*, IV, 181; letter to Nicholas Hayward, dated Dec. 19, 1693.

[51] *Ibid.*, II, 261; letter dated Jan. 18, 1688.

had no time for intellectual interests, but such was not the case. We have his own statement that he found relief from spiritual loneliness in good books, and his correspondence gives frequent indications that the planter cultivated his mind until the end of his life.

His legal learning was something more than a professional instrument: he found in the law a field of study congenial to his conservative tastes. The gradual development of the legal tradition must have symbolized for him the slow and orderly evolution of the English institutions which he was concerned to perpetuate. The numerous letters discussing legal matters written to Lee, Wormeley, Beverley, and others linger almost lovingly over abstruse points of law, as the writer marshals his citations and displays his erudition. The search for precedents and cases, or the study of the operation of the common law in past ages, must have provided the planter with a not unpleasant relief from such immediate and material worries as the price of tobacco and the high cost of ocean freight. In the law, Fitzhugh, like other planters of his time, found a valuable source of mental exercise. Out of the planters' legal studies developed many ideas that affected their statesmanship and attitudes toward society. As in Fitzhugh's case, the study of law and the interest in law were not only means to an end but an end in themselves.

The inventory of the library at Bedford has apparently perished, but the titles mentioned in the owner's letters give some indication of his literary taste. Closely related to his devotion to the law—the first of his intellectual pursuits—was an interest in history, particularly accounts of recent events. From Wormeley we find him borrowing a copy of John Rushworth's *Historical Collections* and later ordering a complete set for himself. This work supplied him with both legal and historical information for the period of the Puritan Revolution. In one of the last of his extant letters, he orders, besides a set of Rushworth, "secret histories" of Charles II, James II, and William III,[52] and several other books of considerable significance: "all the works of the author of *The Whole Duty of Man*" (which included the popular, pious, and very Anglican devotional book, *The Gentleman's Calling*), George Buchanan's *De jure regni apud Scotos* (1579), "if to be had in English" (which was available in a translation published in 1680); Dr. Thomas Burnet's *The Theory of the Earth . . . The Two First Books Concerning the Deluge and Concerning Paradise* (1684); Sir Robert Bruce Cotton's *An Abstract out of the Records of the Tower Touching the King's Revenue* (1642); *The Remains* (1648) of Sir Francis Bacon, containing the essays, some of the letters, and other miscellaneous pieces; "all the Statutes made since the twenty-second of King Charles the Second to this year"; "Mr. Boyle's letter to a friend concerning specific physic"–probably Robert Boyle's *Of the Reconcileableness of Specific Medicine* (1685); "a large fair printed Bible in quarto"; and "a large common prayer book in folio." The writer adds that all the books, except possibly the Buchanan, are certainly to be found in London, and possibly in Bristol; hence he hopes his correspondent, Edward Hayward, will "not send me word some of them are not to be had."

This little order, the longest in the preserved letters, shows a diversity of interest, for, besides the legal, historical, and pious works, Fitzhugh had included philosophic and scientific items. There are other indications that he had some interest in science, prompted for the most part by a utilitarian desire to discover minerals on his land. Two books of use in that connection were José de Acosta's *The Natural and Moral History of the*

[52] *Ibid.*, VI, 72; letter dated July 21, 1698. The "secret histories" requested were: *The Secret History of the Reigns of King Charles II and King James II* (1690); H. J., *An Historical Account of the Memorable Actions of . . . William III* [n.d.]; and *A Continuation of the Secret History of Whitehall from the Abdication of King James to 1696* (1697).

East and West Indies, translated by Edward Grimestone in 1604, and Robert Boyle's *The Skeptical Chemist* (1661). Writing to Nicholas Hayward about ore that he had sent home for assay, Fitzhugh comments:

> I must confess I had no great opinion at first of the ore, and considerately turning over Josephus A. Costa, in his description of the real good ore of Peru, with all the manner and methods of melting and refining, quite damped my esteem of this ore; it has no substance answering to his account. Till again reading a piece I had by me of Mr. Boyle's, called his *Skeptical Chemist*, there in page 397 and 398, he gives an account of an ingenious mineralist who, out of American mineral earth which the public sayemasters could not bring to fusion and esteemed it useless earth, by a peculiar flux separated from it near a third part of pure gold, which was the occasion that I particularly requested Mr. Boyle might have the experiment.[53]

Since Boyle enjoyed a great reputation in Virginia for both his scientific and his religious writings, it is no wonder that Fitzhugh read his works with respect and wished that the great man himself might make trial of his ore.

That Fitzhugh was not altogether a rationalist and may have been inclined to a belief in magic and alchemy may be suggested by his desire to obtain a copy of "Cornelius Agrippa's *Occult Philosophy*, in English if it be procured, if not then one in Latin."[54] It would not have been strange, in this age, for even so intelligent a man as Fitzhugh to believe in occult mysteries. Certainly, if we can credit an incidental remark, he feared witches; for, speaking of ingratitude, he remarks parenthetically, "which sin, next to the sin of witchcraft, I utterly abominate."[55]

That Fitzhugh respected the classics and believed them the basis of education is clear from the sort of training he desired

[53] *The Virginia Magazine of History and Biography*, III, 8; letter dated July 10, 1690.

[54] *Ibid.*, pp. 257-58; letter dated Oct. 27, 1690.

[55] *Ibid.*, I, 397; letter dated Apr. 22, 1686.

for his son. Nevertheless, he himself preferred Latin books in an English dress, even though his legal citations and other incidental quotations show that he had at least a working knowledge of Latin. When ordering the historical works of Tacitus and Polybius, for instance, as in the foregoing case of Cornelius Agrippa, he specifies English translations.[56] And he also asks for an English version of Virgil, and Horace, Juvenal, and Persius in both Latin and English.[57]

The London and Bristol correspondents of the Bedford planter occasionally sent him books without specific instructions. Writing to George Luke, Fitzhugh observes that "some of the newest books, if they be ingenious, will be mighty acceptable, as will likewise a full account of the news." [58] From time to time he borrowed books from his fellow planters. To Richard Lee, a man who loved his books, he has to write on one occasion: "Last fall, I received a demand of your book, which I neither then was, nor now am capable of restoring because lost; but will honestly satisfy you for them in your reasonable demands." [59] Colonel Lee, it would appear, had firmly asked for the return of borrowed property. A certain Mr. Cannon was luckier, for in a letter to Captain George Brent, the borrower comments: "I have also sent Mr. Cannon's book and thank your kindness in the loan thereof, to whom please give my humble service." [60] By borrowing and by purchase the master of Bedford managed to keep by him a fair number of literary companions. When his old friend and correspondent, Nicholas Hayward, retired from London to a country estate, Fitzhugh expressed the hope that he would turn author and send him some "moral essays." [61]

[56] *Ibid.*, IV, 312.
[57] *Ibid.*, p. 418.
[58] *Ibid.*, III, 255.
[59] *Ibid.*, I, 17; letter dated May 15, 1679.
[60] *Ibid.*, II, 260; letter dated Aug. 10, 1687.
[61] *Ibid.*, IV, 177; letter dated July 23, 1692.

The desire of authorship had long haunted Fitzhugh himself. In the spring of 1687, five years before his request for some of Master Hayward's essays, he had written this friend and confidant, asking his opinion of a proposed "history of Virginia," to be in reality a fulsome promotion pamphlet which Fitzhugh hoped might attract settlers to his acres in Stafford County.

> Sir, I have had it in my thoughts [he informs Hayward] to write a small treatise or History of Virginia, describing its situation, temperature, and fertility, nature of its present inhabitants, with their method and manner of living, the plenty of iron mines almost everywhere in the country, and probable conjectures of the discovery of others (more profitable though perhaps not so useful), together with the prodigious quantity of wood to manage the same, the plenty of all sorts of provisions, the easy and profitable living of the people therein, its regular easy and even government in its several courts of justice together with their respective powers and methods of proceeding, with divers other heads too many to be enumerated, and to observe that brevity as I proposed in the first part of my letter. I have only mentioned this to you, sir, to desire your opinion whether a business of this nature might be of any advantage for the persuading inhabitants hither, and might not be prejudicial to me in my particular concerns, for I have some rough materials towards the building such a work and could quickly supply myself with the remainder and have reason and conveniency to finish the same.[62]

By 1693 Fitzhugh's literary labors had reached the stage where he was almost persuaded to send "a small piece that I have written giving a summary account of Virginia and a succinct digest of our laws," [63] but he thought he ought first to get the approval of the Governor. A few months later he informed Hayward that the digest of the laws had been finished.[64] At last, on July 9, 1694, seven years after he had first broached

[62] *Ibid.*, II, 136; letter dated May 13, 1687.
[63] *Ibid.*, IV, 180; letter dated July 31, 1693.
[64] *Ibid.*, p. 181; letter dated Dec. 19, 1693.

the subject to Hayward, he wrote with enthusiasm about the completed task and sent the manuscript.[65] The motive of profit was not wanting from the writer's purpose in preparing the manuscript, for he describes to Hayward the enthusiasm of his friends over the work and expresses the belief that "some thousands will be suddenly vended" in Virginia and Maryland; hence he suggests that a printer or bookseller "might be induced to give something liberally for the copy of it." The digest of the laws he thinks infinitely superior to John Purvis' *A Complete Collection of All the Laws of Virginia Now in Force* [1684?]. Finally, if the present venture succeeds, he proposes a "large discourse of this country."

Though willing to make a profit on the book, Fitzhugh still had something of the old-fashioned Elizabethan gentleman's reticence about appearing in print, and he very carefully warned Hayward that the book must be published anonymously. There is no indication that the author felt that either the subject or treatment of the material would in any way prove a boomerang; he simply did not want his name vulgarly displayed in bookstalls. Accordingly, he instructed his agent to have the bookseller give out that the manuscript was a "copy that he got by accident."[66] This was an ancient piece of trickery employed by many a genteel author to get his books before the world without violating propriety. The reticence displayed by Fitzhugh over having his name appear on a printed book may suggest the reason for the failure of other Virginians to publish anything over their names. There still lingered a feeling that it was bad taste for a gentleman to rush into print. But Fitzhugh's concern over anonymity was wasted, and he was doomed to disappointment over his book, for it never saw the light—just why is not clear. Perhaps Hugh Newman, the bookseller who was trying to

[65] *Ibid.*, pp. 310-11, 415.
[66] *Ibid.*, V, 297-99.

arrange for the printing, decided that, despite the author's sanguine hopes for a sale of thousands of copies in the colonies, the project was after all a poor business venture. Not only did the book fail to find a publisher, but both manuscripts sent to London disappeared, leaving only Fitzhugh's letters as evidence of his literary efforts.

When William Fitzhugh died in 1701 he was just fifty, twenty years short of the span vouchsafed him in Holy Writ, but he had accomplished more than most of the settlers who had come hopefully to Virginia. He had gathered to himself land, riches, and honor, and he had risen to a place among the small group of nascent aristocrats who ruled the colony. If he himself failed to attain to that Sanhedrin of the ruling class, the Council, his namesake and heir made this final advance to the top of the social hierarchy. The emigrant son of the prosperous woolen draper of Bedford firmly established his family in a social position where it might be envied by less fortunate folk for the next two hundred years.

Fitzhugh's life provides an excellent illustration of the transplantation of the ideal of the English country gentleman to the New World. Though he himself was perhaps more bourgeois than aristocratic in his background, like most Englishmen when they acquired riches he set himself up as a landed gentleman. But his conduct was modeled on counsel of the sort to be found in Richard Brathwaite's *The English Gentleman* (1630), a treatise modified by the very bourgeois influence that Fitzhugh also illustrates. Choosing for imitation qualities of the English country gentry consistent with his own ideals, Fitzhugh adapted the tradition, as he remembered it, to plantation life. He had in him a strain of serious determination that one usually associates with such Puritan gentlemen as Colonel Hutchinson. Little in his career fits the romantic picture of a dashing and gay cavalier, dancing far into the night, and on occasion fighting a duel. Indeed, if we except

Colonel Daniel Parke and one or two other rather rakish fellows, this imaginary type of colonial gentleman was virtually nonexistent. Like most of his colleagues among the greater planters, Fitzhugh was an exceedingly busy man of affairs, but he and his kind never let business become the one absorbing fact in their lives. Fitzhugh took time for a certain grace of living, even though he lived in a backwoods region. If he was less preoccupied with sports and pastimes than a country gentleman in England would have been—for the exactions of plantation life did not permit sufficient leisure—he nevertheless enjoyed social contacts with his neighbors and friends. In everything, he followed a middle course, a path of moderation —neither an ascetic nor a reveler. His ideal was a life of decent decorum. And never did he forget that his mind was a God-given instrument for use. Though Fitzhugh and other Virginia planters lived in the wilderness, they did not lapse into provincial rustics. The cultivation of their intellects saved the planters of the upper class from dull provinciality. As a matter of fact, in their intellectual interests, the members of the ruling class were ahead of many country gentlemen in England. Though Fitzhugh's responsibilities continually multiplied until the end of his life, his interest in books and in intellectual pursuits also increased. Longing at times for the pleasures of a leisurely life in England, where he might have greater opportunities for the less material side of existence, he exerted all his energies to make Bedford in Stafford County a little portion of England, to transmit to Virginia the qualities of life that a gentleman of cultivated mind might have had at home. In this effort, Fitzhugh was typical of the group who composed the upper class of Virginia planters in the seventeenth and early eighteenth centuries. If Fitzhugh needed a model of genteel conduct, he did not have far to seek, for his friend, Ralph Wormeley of Rosegill, was one of the most accomplished men in the colony, a planter who was already an established aristocrat.

CHAPTER VII

RALPH WORMELEY II: A CULTIVATED GENTLEMAN-PLANTER

Two months after William Fitzhugh died at Bedford, his friend and sometime client, Ralph Wormeley, second of his name in Virginia, was also gathered to his fathers. His death, on December 5, 1701, at Rosegill, the family seat in Middlesex County, ended the career of one called by his contemporaries "the greatest man in the government, next the governor."[1] Although Wormeley was not a great statesman, or a great soldier, or the richest man of his time, he was, by the standards of Virginia, a great gentleman, politically powerful and socially one of the elect. He was wellborn, endowed with bodily grace and mental quickness, generous, gay, and hospitable. Of all the planters of the seventeenth century, Wormeley comes nearest to the picture of the fabled Virginia cavalier. Even so, he was far from being a mere seeker after pleasure; in fact, he bore a full burden of civil, military, and religious responsibilities, and took delight in intellectual pursuits as well as in lighter gaieties. The fact that he had the largest and best-selected library brought together in Virginia in the seventeenth century suggests the diversity of his intellectual interests. If William Fitzhugh was the living embodiment of the rules of behavior laid down in Richard Brathwaite's somewhat bourgeois treatise, *The English Gentleman*, Ralph Wormeley was the personification of the ideal

[1] See *The Present State of Virginia and the College* (London, 1727), p. 70. This is a report, written between 1696 and 1698 by Henry Hartwell, James Blair, and Edward Chilton. For an account of the Wormeleys, see "The Wormeley Family," *The Virginia Magazine of History and Biography*, XXXV (1927), 455-56; XXXVI (1928), 98-100, 283-93, 385-89; XXXVII (1929), 82-86. Many references to the Wormeleys are scattered through this journal, as well as the *William and Mary College Quarterly*.

set forth in *The Compleat Gentleman* of Henry Peacham—a more aristocratic guide to conduct.[2] The Renaissance goal of symmetry and proportion in one's personality, of the development of all sides of one's being, was exemplified in this lord of Rosegill.

The Wormeleys, by anybody's standard, were of genteel origin, and they had already reached the top of the social and political ladder in Virginia by the time the second Ralph inherited Rosegill. More convincingly than most colonials, they could trace their ancestry to the landed aristocracy of England—in their case an old family of Yorkshire. The earlier Ralph Wormeley, who reached Virginia in 1636, at once took his place among the leading planters. Established first near the present Yorktown, he was listed in the year of his arrival as one of the justices of York County. When Royalist *émigrés* found their way to Virginia after the execution of King Charles, the elder Wormeley welcomed them to his home on the York River. There, in 1649, Colonel Henry Norwood, a Cavalier officer, found a congenial company of his fellow Royalists. "It fell out," he wrote in an account of his voyage to Virginia, "at that time that Captain Wormeley (of His Majesty's Council) had guests in his house . . . feasting and carousing that were lately come from England, and most of them my intimate acquaintance. . . . Using the common freedom of the country, I thrust myself amongst Captain Wormeley's guests in crossing the creek and had a kind reception from them all, which answered (if not exceeded) my expectations. Sir Thomas Lunsford, Sir Henry Chicheley, Sir Philip Honywood, and Colonel Hammond were the persons I met there, and enjoyed that night with very good cheer."[3] From this

[2] For a discussion of the differences between the conceptions of the gentleman in these two books, see W. Lee Ustick, "Changing Ideals of Aristocratic Character and Conduct in Seventeenth-Century England," *Modern Philology*, XXX (1932-33), 147-66.

[3] Henry Norwood, *A Voyage to Virginia*, in Peter Force's *Tracts* (Washington, 1836-46), III, No. 10, p. 49.

group of Cavaliers so hospitably entertained by his father, young Ralph Wormeley, born in 1650, was to find a stepfather and a father-in-law. Soon after the elder Wormeley died in 1651, his widow married Sir Henry Chicheley, later deputy governor of Virginia. In 1674 young Ralph married Katherine, daughter of Sir Thomas Lunsford. The bride was the widow of Captain Peter Jenings, attorney-general of Virginia. Thus Ralph Wormeley II, one of the most eligible young men of the colony, married into an equally genteel and well-connected family. Shortly before the first Ralph Wormeley's death, he had taken up his residence at Rosegill in Middlesex County. During the lifetime of his son, Rosegill was often to be the social center of the colony.

As a youth of scarcely fifteen Ralph had been sent to England to complete his education. On July 14, 1665, he matriculated at Oriel College, Oxford, but did not take a degree. What his previous education had been, we do not know, but most likely he had received at the hands of tutors the classical training necessary for his entrance to Oriel College. Sir Henry Chicheley looked after his stepson well, and, as the boy was heir to a considerable estate in his own right, he had the best educational opportunities the colony afforded. Although we have no detailed knowledge of his formal schooling other than the record of his matriculation at Oriel, we know that he was one of the best educated native-born Virginians of the seventeenth century. If merely the inventory of his library had survived, it would provide sufficient evidence of his intellectual cultivation and the breadth of his interests. When, years later, in 1690, the Virginia General Assembly was laying plans for schools and a college—plans which materialized in the foundation of the College of William and Mary—Wormeley was named third in a group of eighteen men to be trustees and "founders" of the school and college. These men were chosen, not merely because of their wealth and position, but also for their own interest in learning.[4] The desirability of an English education, impressed upon him by his own experience as a student at Oxford, prompted Wormeley to send his sons to English schools. The boys were still at school in England when their father died, and Robert "King" Carter served as their guardian; his letters concerning their education (which, he feared, would keep them too long in England) provide several significant side lights on the problems of education faced by the planters.[5] Ralph Wormeley's own education equaled—and perhaps slightly surpassed—that received by most of the sons of the country gentry in England. Though born on the York River in what was then a frontier region, his training was not provincial, and, by no stretch of the imagination, was he ever a provincial rustic in ideas and point of view. Because of his very isolation from cultural centers, Wormeley, like many of his colleagues of the upper class, struggled to maintain around him an atmosphere of civilized cultivation.

The life led by Wormeley at Rosegill was in keeping with his inherited position as a member of one of the most important families in the colony. Since his father before him had accumulated a comfortable fortune in land and servants, he was spared the hard work of settling a new plantation and establishing a family seat. His home site, extending along the Rappahannock River, consisted of 5,200 fertile acres, not yet exhausted by too continuous planting in tobacco.[6] Though this estate could

[4] *William and Mary College Quarterly*, VII (1898-99), 162. It is well to remember, however, that Commissary Blair, the president of the new college, and his collaborators in *The Present State of Virginia and the College* took occasion a little later to accuse Wormeley of obstructing the progress of the college by refusing to permit surveys of lands subscribed to the endowment. The authors of this report also acidly observed that "The gentlemen of the Council, who had been the forwardest to subscribe, were the backwardest to pay; then everyone was for finding shifts to evade and elude their subscriptions." (Pp. 69-70.)

[5] Extracts from these letters are to be found in *The Virginia Magazine of History and Biography*, XXXVI (1928), 287-91. See also Chapter IX, *infra*.

[6] *The Virginia Magazine of History and Biography*, XXXIII (1925), 48.

not compare in size with the great acreages acquired by Fitzhugh and the Carters, it was the largest single tract in Middlesex County. Wormeley also owned lands in other counties; for example, he still possessed the ancestral estate on the York River, where his father had lavishly entertained Cavalier refugees, and he owned other tracts up the Rappahannock River. Furthermore, in addition to the revenue from his lands, Wormeley, through most of his mature life, had a considerable income from his various public offices. In short, he was one of the wealthiest men of his time, and, if he left a smaller fortune in land than some of his contemporaries, his descendants could blame his extravagant hospitality and sumptuous manner of life.

The plantation house at Rosegill, on a bluff overlooking the Rappahannock River, was a frame building of nine rooms, with an attic so large that it contained beds enough to accommodate thirty guests.[7] By modern standards, a nine-room house would not be considered a palatial establishment, but in seventeenth-century Virginia it was a mansion. Surrounding the great house were smaller houses, kitchens, storehouses, and servants' quarters. In this domain Wormeley presided like a feudal lord. Besides black slaves, there were at one time eight English servants for the great house, including a shoemaker, a tailor, and a miller.[8] Furniture and hangings were as fine as his London factors could supply. His sideboard was heavy with silver plate, marked with the family crest. When he rode abroad on a fast-pacing horse, men gazed with wonder at his gorgeous equipment. His saddle was of crimson velvet and his saddle blanket was of broadcloth, with silk holsters; the whole outfit had a value of £15 sterling.[9] His personal property was appraised in 1701 at £2,861.[10]

[7] *Ibid.*, III (1895-96), 290.

[8] *William and Mary College Quarterly*, 1st Ser., II (1893-94), 170. See also Philip A. Bruce, *Economic History of Virginia in the Seventeenth Century* (New York, 1907), II, 156.

[9] *Ibid.*, p. 239.

[10] *The Virginia Magazine of History and Biography*, III, 290.

As he contemplated the wealth that was his and surveyed the land that surrounded his manor, the lord of this estate could take comfort in an assurance that his family dynasty was secure. Two sons and three daughters would inherit his lands and possessions and maintain the family position. The two oldest children, Elizabeth and Katherine, were by his first wife. When she died, in 1685, she was buried, with considerable pomp, within the chancel of Christ Church, Middlesex, and in the parish register her name was entered in a manner fitting her station: "The Honorable Lady, Madam Katherine Wormeley, wife to the Honorable Ralph Wormeley, Esquire." A little over eighteen months later, in February, 1687, the sorrowing husband consoled himself with a second wife, Elizabeth Armistead, daughter of Colonel John Armistead of Gloucester County, a member of the Council. Two sons, Ralph and John, and a daughter, Judith, were born of this marriage. Wormeley's second wife outlived him and later married William Churchill.[11] Wormeley was an indulgent father and provided liberally for his children.

Sumptuous as were the surroundings at Rosegill, the plantation was not wholly given over to pleasure. Wormeley had a shrewd eye for the management of his estate and conducted his affairs with businesslike efficiency. Moreover, he sought to set an example to others. When the Virginia Assembly passed an act, in 1682, offering a reward to every planter who would bring into the county court linen and wool cloth of his own manufacture, Wormeley set negro artisans to work and presently demonstrated that both linen and wool could be woven in Virginia. His tanyards turned out great quantities of leather; and he operated a flour mill for profit.[12] Like his friend Fitzhugh, but to a lesser degree, Wormeley was interested in persuading immigrants to settle on his land, on the upper reaches of the Rappahannock. When the French Huguenot

[11] *Ibid.*, XXXVI, 291-92. [12] See Bruce, *op. cit.*, II, 459, 463, 477, 488-89.

Durand came to Virginia in 1686, Wormeley showed him a tract of ten thousand acres, which he offered to sell to the Huguenots. But, so far as there is any record, his efforts to make a profit out of French colonists failed.

Thanks to Durand's visit, however, we have a vivid description of the manner of life at Rosegill, for the Frenchman was vastly impressed and wrote down his opinion of the man and his estate. So great did Wormeley seem to Durand that he described him as a baronet who still possessed estates in England. "He owns twenty-six negro slaves and twenty Christian," he observed. "He holds the highest offices, and owns at least twenty houses in a lovely plain along the Rappahannock River. He has rented his most comfortable house to the Governor. When I reached his place, I thought I was entering a rather large village, but later on was told that all of it belonged to him." [13] The fact was that Francis, Lord Howard of Effingham, then lieutenant governor, had taken up his residence in one of the houses at Rosegill, either as tenant or guest of Wormeley. At any rate, the guests took dinner each day with the Governor, at two in the afternoon. "This is the only meal he takes regularly at home," Durand explained, "the others at Monsieur Wormeley's. He had us served white wine from Spain and claret from Portugal, and Monsieur Wormeley wine from Portugal, cider, and beer." [14] When Durand found the wine so strong that he had to dilute it, the Governor and Wormeley laughed at him; they took theirs straight, and, somewhat to his astonishment, kept an even keel.

During Durand's visit at Rosegill, a meeting of the Council was held. Its members were "fine looking men," Durand thought, and they sat in judgment "booted and with belted sword." But he was amazed when they started gambling after supper. Toward midnight his traveling companion, "Monsieur

[13] *A Huguenot Exile in Virginia*, ed and tr. Gilbert Chinard (New York, 1934), p. 142. [14] Ibid., p. 147.

Parker," begged him to go to bed, as he anticipated an all-night party. "And in truth," Durand comments, "I found them still playing the next morning, and saw that he had won a hundred écus from them." [15]

The meeting of the Council and its attendant gaieties over, Wormeley and several of the company at Rosegill conducted Durand twenty-two leagues up the Rappahannock, to Port Tobago, where Wormeley had a tract of land lying on both sides of the river. The cavalcade rode leisurely along, stopping two nights with planters on the way. Food and drink—great quantities of both—were brought up in Wormeley's boat. Finally, when they had reached their destination, "The gentlemen immediately had bowls of punch prepared, and they began to carouse [*firent grand débauche*], while I went walking, delighted with the sight of those lovely hills, the fountains and brooks flowing out of them, as well as with the quantity of wild grapevines all about. On this side I counted eight or nine houses that Monsieur Wormeley has built on his estates or plantations. His cattle seemed to me fatter and bigger than any I had seen in the county of Gloucester, or elsewhere in the country." [16] Since Colonel Wormeley was one of the colony's grand seigniors, there is something fitting in the fact that even his cattle were fatter than other herds.

When the party finished viewing the rich lands, the fine forests, and the luxuriant wild grapevines which excited the particular interest of the Frenchman, they proposed to visit Colonel Fitzhugh, in near-by Stafford County, and the whole company, twenty strong, marched into Stafford and were hospitably received by Fitzhugh, as we have already seen.[17]

Christmas was now upon them. Durand and Wormeley returned to the plantation at Port Tobago for Christmas Day, but the narrator gives no details of any celebration. After visiting an unnamed justice of the county, they moved on "to the

[15] *Ibid.*, p. 148. [16] *Ibid.*, p. 151. [17] *Ibid.*, p. 158.

house of a captain of cavalry, where we remained some time because Monsieur Wormeley, who is the colonel of this county, wished to see his company."[18] Thus Wormeley remembered his military responsibilities and made an inspection of the militia.

Although one of his contemporaries singled out Wormeley as notable among "the gay part of the gentlemen" in his section,[19] his amusements did not interfere with the serious performance of services to the state. He held many public offices: he was a justice of the county court, commander of the militia in two counties, naval officer on the Rappahannock, receiver of Virginia duties, member of the Council, and secretary of state. And, if he failed in any of these duties, contemporary records are silent. As secretary of state from 1693 until his death, he attained to power, and, although his political position gave him unimpeded opportunities for self-aggrandizement, he seems to have been content with the legitimate perquisites of office—a tribute to his honesty, because the age cynically expected its political rulers to feather their own nests. It is true that the profits from his various offices were ample, but the greed for land among some of his contemporaries was insatiable, and Wormeley might have followed their examples of land-grabbing. Although he obtained title to a few tolerably extensive tracts in frontier colonies, men like Robert Beverley the elder and King Carter must have regarded him as singularly negligent of his opportunities. Wormeley, it appears, had a well developed sense of social responsibility.

[18] *Ibid.*, p. 161.

[19] The comment is in an undated memorandum concerning, among other things, a minister accused of cheating a parishioner out of his shoes. The writer of the memorandum quotes the Governor as saying that the affair had blown over and, unless some other scandal arose, the minister would continue in the good opinion of the gentlemen who had previously countenanced him, including the Governor, Colonel Peter Beverley, Colonel Page, Captain Martin, Colonel Armistead, "and most of the gay part of the gentlemen in Gloucester and about Urbanna, especially Esquire Wormeley." (*William and Mary College Quarterly*, 2d Ser., X [1930], 247.)

But the last statement must not be taken to mean that the lord of Rosegill had any foolish Whig notions, or the slightest sympathy with radicals who might dispute the right of gentlemen to rule Virginia as they saw fit. If anything, he was even more of a Tory than William Fitzhugh, and he hated with consummate wrath such disturbers of the peace as Nathaniel Bacon. During the Bacon rebellion, and afterward, he stood staunchly behind Governor Berkeley and his faction. Indeed, in a report drawn up on October 5, 1677, of persons who suffered in the outbreak, he was listed in this laudatory fashion: "Mr. Ralph Wormeley, a truly honest, loyal gentleman and one of the Council, who by his constant adherence to the governor, was (as we have heard) much worsted and ruined in his estate by the late troubles in Virginia."[20] As a militia commander, Wormeley saw active service in the conflict with the rebels and demonstrated his willingness to suffer for the conservative cause he championed to the end of his days.

Even though he was one of the gayer gentlemen of his time, Wormeley was not unmindful of the demands of religious decorum. If Rosegill echoed with the music of fiddlers playing for a dance on Saturday, or if planters gathered to gamble at cards far into the night, when Sunday came, the master of the plantation and his family went to near-by Christ Church for worship. The two richest and proudest families in the parish were the Wormeleys and the Grymeses. To keep the favor of both families, the vestry decided in 1666 to build a church at a point halfway between the two plantation houses.[21] The original building was replaced in the early eighteenth century, but before its destruction it had become the burial place of members of the Wormeley family, who claimed places within the chancel. Ralph Wormeley served as vestryman, and, for all we know, he may have read the prayers in the

[20] *The Virginia Magazine of History and Biography*, V (1897-98), 66.

[21] Henry Irving Brock, *Colonial Churches in Virginia* (Richmond, 1930), p. 40.

absence of a clergyman. The religious observances of the Church of England were accepted as a necessary part of the life of a leader in the colony.

Manifold as were the activities of the busy secretary of state, he took time to cultivate his mind. His library at Rosegill numbered approximately three hundred and seventy-five separate titles,[22] a larger number than any other Virginian had collected up to that time. These books, moreover, covered a wide range of human interest, and included works on religion, law, statecraft, history, science, medicine, learning, classical literature, more recent belles-lettres, music, and other subjects. This library, collected for use rather than ostentation, is indicative of the character and mental qualities of the owner. Many of the books—in fact, a large proportion of them—were standard works in their respective fields, dating from the late sixteenth and early seventeenth centuries. But until the end of his life Wormeley was buying an occasional new book that interested him. While a guest at Rosegill in 1698, Dr. Cadwallader Colden read in its library Louis Hennepin's *A New Discovery of a Vast Country in America*, published in an English version in that very year.[23] Someone must have borrowed the book, or perhaps Colden carried it away with him, for it was not listed in the inventory made three years later.

As was the case with many other Cavalier gentlemen, con-

[22] The inventory of Wormeley's library, taken from the Middlesex County records, is printed in *The William and Mary College Quarterly*, 1st Ser., II, 169-74. The inventory was carelessly made, and perhaps represents what a semi-literate neighbor set down as another pulled the books from the shelves and dictated the titles. What the scribe heard and wrote sometimes only faintly resembles the correct title: "Lutrox Lives" evidently stands for *Plutarch's Lives*, but other entries are less obvious. For example, "Mathalisco mitis mytholo" is the way the scribe set down *Natalis Comitis Mythologiae* and "courtior of coubaldy" is the entry for *The Courtier of Count Baldassare Castilio* [Castiglione]. A few of the entries have entirely defied my efforts to identify the works. The exact number of titles in the inventory cannot be told because some of the entries specify merely "a Latin book" or "eighteen French books." The list also contains some duplication of titles.

[23] *The Virginia Magazine of History and Biography*, XXX (1922), 329.

trary to the general conception of their characters, Wormeley showed a preference, in his book collecting, for religious works. Nearly eighty titles, or a little more than twenty per cent of his library, consisted of books on religious subjects. They were not books bought merely as a conventional gesture toward religion—books that a gentleman was supposed to own; instead, they too covered a wide range of topics. There were, of course, the usual Bibles, copies of the Books of Common Prayer, catechisms, concordances, annotations on the Scriptures, and similar works. There were also many of the devotional books so often found in Anglican libraries of the seventeenth century, on both sides of the Atlantic: Richard Allestree's *The Whole Duty of Man* (1660), Clement Ellis' *The Gentile Sinner* (1661), Jeremy Taylor's *The Rule and Exercises of Holy Living* (1650) and its sequel, *The Rule and Exercises of Holy Dying* (1651), Thomas Fuller's *The Holy State. The Profane State* (1642), and other similar works. Less orthodox from the Anglican point of view were Richard Baxter's *Confession of His Faith* (1655) and *A Christian Directory* (1673), but Baxter was popular among Virginia churchmen. Although Wormeley owned fewer sermons than Robert Carter, or even Richard Lee, his collection represented some of the favorite Anglican divines of the early seventeenth century: Bishop Lancelot Andrewes, Joseph Hall, Jeremy Taylor, Bishop Gervase Babington, John Boys, dean of Canterbury, and others. Wormeley also had two copies of *The Book of Homilies*, from which useful lessons could be read to the congregation of the parish church. If he needed any theoretical justification of the Church of England, he had Richard Hooker's *Of the Laws of Ecclesiastical Polity* (1594-97), and for theological reasoning he had Archbishop James Ussher's *A Body of Divinity* (1645). If this treatise was not sufficient, Wormeley had the works of the Puritan theologian, William Ames, and of the French Calvinist, Daniel Chamier, as well as a Catholic doctrinal treatise, Henry Turberville's *An Abridgement of Christian Doctrine* (Douai, 1649).

But the leading vestryman of Christ Church was in no danger of being misled by either Dissenters or Catholics, for he had supplied himself with works that neatly disposed of them. Among several tracts against the Catholics the one that he probably found most satisfying was from the pen of Bodley's learned librarian, Thomas James, and bore the title, *A Manuductio; or, Introduction unto Divinity, Containing a Confutation of Papists by Papists* (1625). As an antidote to Dissent, Wormeley had sermons and treatises by staunch Anglicans. Nevertheless, the presence in his library of several defenses of the Quakers may indicate a favorable attitude toward that sect. Among these pro-Quaker tracts, the best-known was Robert Barclay's *An Apology for the True Christian Divinity* (1678). Also present was the work of an enlightened New England apologist for sectaries, Peter Folger's verse defense of Quakers, Baptists, and others, entitled *A Looking Glass for the Times* (1677). A further suggestion of the spirit of toleration was the possession of the *Golden Remains* (1659) of John Hales, a tolerant, conciliatory Anglican who sought peace among religious disputants. Because of the great reputation that John Locke was already acquiring in the colonies, it is worth noting that his treatise, *The Reasonableness of Christianity as Delivered in the Scriptures* (1695), was to be found at Rosegill. An indication that Wormeley, along with many other Virginians, was already thinking of the obligation of Christians towards their negro slaves may be found in his ownership of Morgan Godwin's little book, *The Negroes' and Indians' Advocate, Suing for Their Admission into the Church* (1680), an appeal by a young cleric to the American colonists to remember their pious duty of Christianizing their servants. But, if Wormeley read the book through, he must have found much to infuriate him, for the author appended "A Brief

Account of Religion in Virginia," wherein he roundly criticized Virginians for their negligence of the church and their treatment of the clergy. In one place, Wormeley would have seen Virginia vestries described as "Plebeian Juntos."

As a statesman and as an educated gentleman of the seventeenth century, Wormeley regarded history as one of the most valuable of intellectual disciplines. His collection of sixty historical and biographical works was second in number to his religious books, and at this time was by far the best-selected historical library in Virginia. English history, especially the events of the two preceding generations, occupied the largest place among these books. For English antiquities there were William Camden's *Britannia* (1586) and *Remains* (1605), Richard Verstegan's *The Restitution of Decayed Intelligence* (1605), and Thomas Fuller's *The History of the Worthies of England* (1622). Some of the older-type chronicles jostled newer interpretations of history. Sir Richard Baker's *Chronicle* (1643) and John Clapham's *History of Great Britain* (1606) remained in favor. To make the approach to history easy and to aid the memory, there were such annals as Samuel Clarke's *England's Remembrancer*, appended to a translation from Giovanni Niccolò Doglioni's *Historian's Guide* (1676). Clarke's contribution was a chronicle of events, by exact dates, from the year 1600 to January 10, 1675. In Peter Heylyn's chronicle of the succession of kings, nobles, bishops, and other dignitaries, entitled *An Help to English History* (1641), Wormeley also had another aid to memory. Of specialized English histories there were Sir Robert Howard's *The Life and Reign of King Richard the Second* (1681), Sir Francis Bacon's *The History of the Reign of King Henry the Seventh* (1622), the first two parts of Gilbert Burnet's *History of the Reformation* (1679), and nearly a dozen works treating the seventeenth century. Among these were Rushworth's ubiquitous *Historical Collections*, Lambert Wood's

The Life and Reign of King Charles (1659), and several defenses of the Stuarts. European history was represented by a dozen works dealing with France, Spain, and the Low Countries; the Near East, by three volumes, on the Turks, the Persians, and Scanderbeg, King of Albania. Only one history touched Italy particularly; that was a fairly recent book, *Rome Exactly Described . . . under Pope Alexander the Seventh* (1664). Ancient history was covered by Raleigh's *History of the World*, and by the works of Plutarch, Thucydides, Quintus Curtius, and Lucan. Antiquities of religion and the church were treated in Eusebius' *Historia Ecclesiastica*, Josephus' history of the Jews, Patrick Symson's *The History of the Church* (1624), a history of St. George, a life of St. Augustine, and two or three other works. For the history of the New World, Wormeley had only Captain John Smith's *The General History of Virginia* (1624), Peter Martyr's *The History of the West Indies* (1625), and Richard Ligon's . . . *History of . . . Barbados* (1657). Biography was confined to Plutarch, the saints' lives just mentioned, two or three works on Charles I and Charles II, and Thomas Beard's *The Theatre of God's Judgments* (1597), that ancient and popular compilation of the lives of notable sinners and of the retribution that awaited them.

Since problems of government were unavoidably of concern to a man in Wormeley's position, he naturally showed an interest in books on statecraft. One might have expected to find at Rosegill Machiavelli's *Prince*—that most famous of all treatises on the craft of governing. Instead, there was Cicero's *Prince: The Reasons and Counsels for Settlement and Good Government of a Kingdom Collected Out of Cicero's Works* (1668), a curious little book compiled by William Bellenden and translated by Thomas Rymer. Its dedicatory epistle suggests that it was set forth as a virtuous counterpart of the Italian's devilish work, for it contains maxims "void of all stains and flaws of Machiavellian interest," maxims "raised only upon principles of honor and virtue, which best become a prince." Surely this was an excellent guide for Mr. Secretary Wormeley, the man next in power to the governor. If he failed in statesmanly wisdom, it was not for lack of concise counsel. In his library were Sir Walter Raleigh's *Remains . . . viz., Maxims of State* (1657) and *The Cabinet Council* (1658), a collection of political aphorisms. There were also works of a wider scope: Henri duc de Rohan's *A Treatise of the Interest of the Princes and States of Christendom* (1641), William Penn's *No Cross, No Crown* (1669), John Selden's *The History of Tithes* (1618) and *The Privileges of the Baronage of England* (1642), and John Locke's *Two Treatises of Government* (1690), with its attack on Sir Robert Filmer's theories of absolutism and the divine right of kings. In these works Wormeley had a considerable range of political opinion. But his own political career does not suggest that the liberal views of Penn, Locke, and even of Selden affected his thinking.

Considering Wormeley's place in the government, his legal library was somewhat inadequate. Only about thirty lawbooks found their way to the Rosegill shelves. Of these, the greater portion were handbooks of procedure, statutes, and reports. A half dozen volumes of Virginia laws, including John Purvis' *A Complete Collection of All the Laws of Virginia Now in Force* [1684?]—the compilation so unsatisfactory to William Fitzhugh—and a volume of New England laws, supplied information about colonial legal practice. Though small, Wormeley's law library contained such standard things as Sir Edward Coke's *Reports* and his *Institutes*, Sir Anthony Fitzherbert's *The New Natura Brevium*, probably in the late edition of 1687, and a few other similar works. Of the guides to procedure, there were such manuals as Michael Dalton's *Country Justice* (1618) and *Officium Vicecomitum, The*

Office and Authority of Sheriffs (1623). It is worth noting that Wormeley owned one of the best seventeenth-century expositions of the common law, Sir Francis Bacon's *Elements of the Common Laws of England* (1630). In general, the legal collection at Rosegill was composed of useful, practical works, but it gives no indication that the owner was vastly interested in the law as such, or that he had much legal learning. When Wormeley needed advice on the more esoteric points of law, he turned to his erudite friend William Fitzhugh.

The library at Rosegill was fairly well equipped with textbooks and dictionaries for the study of Greek, Latin, French, and Spanish. Clearly Wormeley children in their respective generations had been brought up in the traditional discipline. Over thirty language books–if one includes English dictionaries–were listed in the inventory. Some of these books were hoary with age and heavy with prestige, for Virginia children, as well as their kindred in England, still pondered the Latin colloquies of Erasmus and Corderius, both of whom were represented at Rosegill. There were also elementary Latin books of Comenius, Charles Hoole's newer text, *An Easy Entrance to the Latin Tongue* (1649), and sundry "rudiments," grammars, and dictionaries of Latin and Greek. The number of French books suggests a considerable emphasis on that language. In addition to a half dozen dictionaries, grammars, and dialogues, there were eighteen French books mentioned without title. These perhaps were works of French literature. A Spanish dictionary indicates an interest in that language. John Florio's *A World of Words* (1598) provided an Italian-English dictionary. The latest English dictionary was Edward Phillips' *New World of English Words* (1658); beside it stood Henry Cockeram's older work, *The English Dictionary* (1623).

The higher reaches of learning were less well represented at Rosegill than were the languages. A single little text on logic, Samuel Smith's *Aditus ad Logicam* (1627), was all that the library had on that subject. Richard Norwood's *Trigonometry* and his *Epitome* (1667) showing the practical application of trigonometry to navigation, Richard Hodges' *Enchiridion Arithmeticon, A Manual of Millions* (1631), and one or two other little mathematical handbooks of a useful and practical nature, were the only books in this branch of learning.

Of books showing an interest in science and related subjects there were about a dozen titles—in addition to a collection of twenty-six medical works. Chemistry was represented by a treatise of Johann Glauber, either his *Opera Chymica* (1658-59) or the translation of his *Works* (1689), and by an unidentified book listed as "the unlearned Keymiss"; natural history by Sir Francis Bacon's *Sylva Sylvarum* (1626); geology by Thomas Burnet's *The Theory of the Earth* (1684); astronomy by John Wilkins' speculation concerning the habitability of the moon, *The Discovery of a World in the Moon* (1638); psychology (among other things) by Robert Burton's *Anatomy of Melancholy* (1621) and an unidentified work listed as "the naturall faculties of man"; and science in general by Robert Boyle's *Some Considerations Touching the Usefulness of Experimental Natural Philosophy* (1664). Conjuring, jugglery, and curiosities of science were explained in a translation from Giovanni Battista della Porta, entitled *Natural Magic* (1658); and the problem of witchcraft was discussed in John Webster's *The Displaying of Supposed Witchcraft* (1677), which refuted traditional ideas of witches and compacts with the devil. One would like to know whether William Fitzhugh ever borrowed this book, for he had implied his own belief in witches. We do not know Wormeley's attitude toward witchcraft, but his possession of a rationalistic treatise on the subject is pleasant to remember.

The medical works were varied in type, ranging from little

books of prescriptions to great folios on anatomy, many of them old works grown obsolete in the course of medical progress. But new theories made slow headway, and Galen's works, Helkiah Crooke's *Description of the Body of Man* (1615), and the works of Ambroise Paré—which Wormeley owned—were still received as invincible authorities. Wormeley had Lazarus Riverius' *The Practice of Physic* (1655) and five of the newer compilations and translations of Nicholas Culpeper, including the so-called *London Pharmacopoeia*. There were also a few treatises from recent writers, as, for example, Walter Charleton's *Inquiries into Human Nature* (1680), a collection of poor anatomical lectures by an ardent Royalist, whose devotion to the Stuarts, in Wormeley's estimation, probably made up for his lack of scientific learning. Among other new books were unspecified works of Sir John Colebatch and the *Practice of Physick* (1684), by Thomas Willis, which included "Two Discourses concerning the Soul of Brutes." In the light of the times, Wormeley's medical collection was diverse and adequate for the understanding of the human body and the treatment of disease.

Wormeley's curiosity about the world at large is suggested by the volumes on geography and travel found in his library. Among the eighteen titles on these subjects were several expensive volumes containing beautiful maps and engravings. Such a book was John Ogilby's *America, Being the Latest and Most Accurate Description of the New World* (1671), a huge folio of nearly seven hundred pages profusely illustrated. Some of the material in Ogilby's compilation was duplicated in Richard Blome's folio, *A Geographical Description of the Four Parts of the World* (1670). In addition to these newer works there were several old favorites, including John Speed's *A Prospect of the Most Famous Parts of the World* (1631), Peter Heylyn's *Microcosmus* (1621), Gerardus Mercator's *Historia Mundi; or, Mercator's Atlas* (1635), and John Pory's translation of Johannes Leo Africanus, *A Geographical History of Africa* (1600). The half dozen works concerned more strictly with travel included George Sandys' *Travels* (1615), describing the Near East, William Lithgow's . . . *Rare Adventures and Painful Peregrinations* (1632), Thomas Gage's *A New Survey of the West Indies* (1655), and a two-volume translation, by John Ogilby, of John Nieuhoff's *The Embassy* (1669-71), describing a visit in 1655 of two Dutch East India Company officials to the Emperor of China. In the volumes of geography and travel at Rosegill one could acquire enough exact information and romantic lore about the great world to prevent the insularity that colonial plantation life might tend to induce.

Something over a dozen utilitarian works covered the main elements of life as lived on a Virginia river plantation. As naval commander of the Rappahannock, Wormeley probably felt a need for his three books on navigation, and, as a militia commander, he could appreciate Robert Anderson's *The Genuine Use and Effects of the Gun, with Tables of Projection* (1674); less immediately practical was Sir Robert Dallington's *Aphorisms Civil and Military* (1613). As a shipper of tobacco, Wormeley found serviceable a book of custom rates and Lewis Roberts' *The Merchant's Map of Commerce* (1638), with its varied information. As an occasional borrower of ready money, he might discover useful arguments in an anonymous treatise, against high interest rates, entitled *Interest of Money Mistaken* (1668). Another, unidentified treatise listed as "the value of money" was perhaps a manual of financial advice. Of general value to a colonial businessman was Thomas Mun's *England's Treasure by Foreign Trade* (1664). In *The English Secretary*, possibly Angell Day's work, first published in 1586, or one of many later manuals with the same title, Wormeley had models to be followed in his letter writing.

Since Wormeley's hospitality was a byword in Virginia, his

household needed a few books on food and drink. One of the most popular cookbooks of the time, William Rabisha's *The Whole Body of Cookery Dissected, Taught, and Fully Manifested* (1661), provided a vast deal of culinary information. Two books by Dr. William Worth of Rotterdam supplied necessary directions for the preparation of beverages; these were *A New Art of Making Wines, Brandy, and Other Spirits* (1691) and *Cerevisiatii Comes; or, The Art of Brewing, and the Right Art of Refining Bottle-Beer and Cider* (1692).

The notable gardens and planting at Rosegill may have been influenced by Wormeley's study of a famous book on the management of a country estate, for he owned two copies of *Maison Rustique; or, The Country Farm* (1616) by Charles Estienne and Jean Liebault, translated from the French by Richard Surflet and edited by Gervase Markham. Although this handsome volume gave a great deal of general information about agriculture—applicable chiefly to France—it was most valuable to a rich Virginia planter for its garden designs and suggestions about ornamental planting. To *Maison Rustique*, seventeenth- and eighteenth-century Virginia homes owed some of the beauty of their landscaping. Wormeley also had another translation from the French, *The French Gardener* (1658), by an enthusiastic English amateur gardener, John Evelyn, which gave directions for growing fruit trees and garden plants, as well as for curing and preserving herbs. One other book was useful to Wormeley the farmer—Robert Almond's *The English Horseman* (1673).

Although our information about music in early Virginia is exceedingly scanty, Englishmen clearly brought with them a love of song and instrumental music. The larger planters frequently had servants trained as fiddlers, so that they could supply the necessary music for dances. Probably there was someone at Rosegill who could play a fiddle, and undoubtedly the ladies and gentlemen who gathered at Wormeley's house on social occasions enjoyed singing themselves. But of the musical entertainments at Rosegill we have no clues except two books of music: John Playford's *A Brief Introduction to the Skill of Music for Song and Viol* (1658)—perhaps the twelfth edition, amended by Henry Purcell and published in 1694—and another, unidentified work listed as "Experiments in Consort."

The only two books which suggest an interest in the pictorial arts were two unidentified works: "the Royall Gravier" and "the Colledges of Oxford." The first may have been a treatise on drawing or a book of engravings; the latter, David Loggan's *Oxonia Illustrata* (1675), containing pictures of the colleges Wormeley had known in his youth, was a volume that he would have been pleased to put on his parlor table.

Wormeley's collection of the classics contained a respectable number of the better-known Greek and Latin writers, but he had no such love of ancient authors as that shown by Richard Lee. Certain Greek and Latin historical works we have already noticed. In addition to these, he owned a book on the philosophy of Pythagoras, Aesop's fables, the works of Virgil, Ovid, Horace, Terence, and Seneca, "the third book of Cicero," and a half dozen unspecified Latin books. He also had the most famous Renaissance anthology of excerpts from the classics, Natalis Comes's *Mythologiae*, frequently reprinted during the sixteenth and seventeenth centuries. Many a man passed for learned by deftly utilizing quotations from this book.

Wormeley's taste in belles-lettres was varied; his selection of poetry, prose fiction, and drama—about twenty-five titles in all—suggests a reader of urbanity and considerable literary judgment. Writers of the late sixteenth and the first half of the seventeenth century predominated. Serious nondramatic poetry was represented by the works of John Donne, George Herbert, Francis Quarles, and Edmund Waller, and *Poems, Elegies, Paradoxes, and Sonnets*, published anonymously in 1657 by

Bishop Henry King. The third part of Samuel Butler's *Hudibras* (1678) and John Oldham's *Satires upon the Jesuits* (1681) showed Wormeley's appreciation of these two popular verse diatribes against Puritans and Catholics, respectively. Small as was this collection of English poetry, and even though it lacked any single scrap by Chaucer, Spenser, Shakespeare, or Milton, it was probably the best in Virginia up to 1701. The collection of plays was likewise the largest then available in the colony. Wormeley owned Ben Jonson's *Every Man in His Humor* (1601), Beaumont and Fletcher's *Fifty Comedies and Tragedies* (1647), James Shirley's *Six New Plays* (1653), William Cartwright's *Comedies, Tragicomedies, with Other Poems* (1651), Sir Aston Cokayne's *The Tragedy of Ovid* (1662), and *The Works of Sir William Davenant* (1673)—surely not a very numerous assortment of plays, but fairly representative of the most popular drama of the two previous generations. The interest in fiction had to be satisfied with Cervantes' *History of . . . Don Quixote* (1612), James Mabbe's translation, from Matthew Aleman, of *The Rogue; or, The Life of Guzman de Alfarache* (1622), and an elaborate romance entitled *The Princess Cloria . . . Imbellished with Divers Political Notions* (1661). An unidentified work listed as "the wife of Donalimpa" may have been a prose tale. The essay was represented by the works of Montaigne and Bacon, Sir William Cornwallis' *Essays of Certain Paradoxes* (1616), and Owen Feltham's *Resolves* (1623). James Howell's *Epistolae Ho-Elianae, Familiar Letters Domestic and Foreign* (1645) was in reality a compilation of informal essays. One solemn discussion of the feminist question, Anne Maria van Schurman's defense of education for women, entitled *The Learned Maid; or, Whether a Maid May Be a Scholar* (1659), was doubtless of interest to the father of three daughters.

Wormeley's library as well as his manner of life exemplified the taste and cultivation of a gentleman brought up in old traditions inherited from Elizabethan England—traditions that still had vigor and influence. It is significant that Wormeley owned the two most famous Renaissance treatises on the rationale of a gentleman's behavior, one Italian, the other English: Castiglione's *Courtier*, translated in 1561 by Sir Thomas Hoby, and Henry Peacham's *Compleat Gentleman*.[24] Both works envision the full development of all sides of man's personality; both regard the cultivated aristocrat as the finest flower of civilization. Undoubtedly Wormeley read with sympathy and agreement most of the philosophy of Castiglione and the practical suggestions of Peacham. Insofar as colonial conditions would permit, he modeled his behavior in accordance with the theories set forth by these congenial counselors.

Wormeley's career illustrates the way of life being developed by the Virginia aristocracy in the later days of the seventeenth century. The first struggle for settlement was over; the arduous labor of carving out estates in the wilderness was past; the ruin from soil exhaustion was not yet imminent for owners of extensive plantations. Planters like Wormeley could concern themselves with the graces and amenities of life. But their responsibilities of plantation management and civil administration were too heavy to permit them to be idlers, whatever their wealth, or to become dilettanti. Although Wormeley's tastes undoubtedly led him to follow the traditional pattern of a country gentleman of the more cultivated type, the very necessities of his place in society forced him to polish the varied facets of his personality. Pleasure-loving though he was, he had to take seriously his multifarious duties; he could not become, had he wanted to, the provincial boor whom Macaulay described as typical of country squires. Upon Wormeley and his kind rested responsibilities for transmitting to a colonial

[24] The inventory lists "the compleat gentleman" without naming the author. There is a possibility that it was a later work, perhaps Jean Gailhard's *The Complete Gentleman* (1678), but the fact that the inventory follows the contemporary spelling of Peacham's title suggests that his book is meant.

society the civilized way of life commended by writers and practiced by gentlemen of the better sort. In this mission, Mr. Secretary Wormeley of Rosegill performed his service well. If his accomplishments were more versatile than profound, he was typical of his time. To set an example of deep erudition was not Wormeley's fortune; that was left for one of his colleagues, the second Richard Lee.

CHAPTER VIII

RICHARD LEE II: A BELATED ELIZABETHAN

VIRGINIA statesmen of the late eighteenth and early nineteenth centuries were distinguished for their polite learning, their classical allusions, and the Ciceronian periods of their oratory. In public speeches, in private letters, and even in the give-and-take of drawing-room conversation, great gentlemen demonstrated their familiar acquaintance with Greek and Roman authors, or with more recent works of the better English and French writers. It was fashionable to give a literary turn to one's speech, whether in an oration or in a conversation, and none followed the fashion so well as Virginia's statesmen. This quality in the culture of the Virginia ruling class, so noticeable in the era of John Marshall and Thomas Jefferson, was no new thing: it was part of a traditional training that went back to the beginning of the colony, to the aspirations of certain planters who set themselves up as country gentlemen in Virginia and reproduced the way of life characteristic of the better type of English gentry. More than that, the traditional ideal of culture had its origin in the Renaissance conception of the well-rounded man who was not complete without the civilizing influence of great literature.

An exemplification of this ideal—indeed, perhaps the best example in the early colonial period—is the second Richard Lee, the squire of Mount Pleasant, Westmoreland County. A consideration of his life and his intellectual interests will throw light on the cultural ideals of the Virginia ruling class. Richard Lee, who was born in 1647 and died in 1714, was of the second generation of the Lees in America. He represented the established line of a prosperous landed family, but he was still conscious of being an Englishman, and he sought to reproduce in his own circle the qualities of English genteel life that seemed to him desirable. Because his descendants played such an important role in the later history of the country, his own part in the transmission of intellectual interests from England to America is of some consequence.

On Richard Lee's tombstone in the family graveyard at Mount Pleasant was carved a Latin epitaph which recorded his two most prominent characteristics: zeal for public service and devotion to learning. It reads, in translation, as follows:

> Here lieth the body of Richard Lee, Esq., born in Virginia, son of Richard Lee, Gentleman, descended of an ancient family of Merton-Regis, in Shropshire. While he exercised the office of magistrate he was a zealous promoter of the public good. He was very skilful in the Greek and Latin languages and other parts of polite learning. He quietly resigned his soul to God, whom he always devoutly worshiped, on the 12th day of March, in the year 1714, in the 68th year of his age.[1]

As a public servant, he discharged numerous offices so faithfully that Governor Alexander Spotswood, in a letter written in 1712, described him as "a gentleman of as fair character as any in the country for his exact justice, honesty, and unexceptionable loyalty in all the stations wherein he has served in this government."[2] Here was official recognition of Lee's

[1] Quoted from Edmund Jennings Lee, *Lee of Virginia, 1642-1892* (Philadelphia, 1895), p. 77. In contemporary quotations, except from the original inventory, spelling, punctuation, and capitalization have been normalized, throughout, in accordance with modern usage. The Latin epitaph, as quoted by E. J. Lee, reads: "Hic conditur corpus Richardi Lee, Armigeri, nati in Virginia, filii Richardi Lee, generosi, et antiqua familia, in Merton-Regis, in comitatu Salopiensi, oriundi. In magistratum obeundo boni publici studiosissimi, in literis Graecis et Latinis et aliis humanioris literaturae disciplinis versatissimi. Deo, quem, summa observantia semper coluit, animam tranquillus reddidit XII. mo. die Martii, anno MDCCXIV, aetat LXVIII." This volume contains nearly all of the known facts concerning the early Lees. The most illuminating interpretation of the founders of the family is that by Burton J. Hendrick, *The Lees of Virginia* (Boston, 1935).

[2] *The Official Letters of Alexander Spotswood,* ed. R. A. Brock (Richmond, 1882-85), I, 178.

service as one of the ruling group, and if later writers, contemplating the erudite works in his library, have been inclined to regard him chiefly as a man of books, they forget the meticulous care with which he performed his duties as colonel of the militia, judge of the county court, collector of customs on the Potomac, and member of the all-powerful Council. The combination of public-spirited gentleman and scholar gives Lee peculiar interest for us.

The second Richard Lee's background fitted him for the role that he was to play in Virginia life. His father, Richard Lee I, the emigrant, was a man of wealth and honor. What the social standing of his family in England may have been is unknown. Genealogists surmise, but without conclusive evidence, that he came of an aristocratic lineage. More important is what he became in Virginia. Soon after his arrival in 1642, he acquired extensive lands, held public office, and was closely associated with Governor Berkeley. In 1651 he took his seat on the Council. His manor house in Gloucester County, significantly named "Paradise," was a gathering place for the gentry of that region. Richard Lee I, furthermore, was a man of business, for his aspirations to be a country gentleman did not prevent his active participation in the tobacco trade. He had an interest in several ships, frequently went himself to London, and at length acquired a landed estate near Stratford-atte-Bowe, a few miles from London, where he probably intended to spend his last days had not fate decreed that he should return to Virginia.[3] Lee sent his eldest son John to Queen's College, Oxford, where he attested his affection for his alma mater by presenting the college with a silver drinking cup. Family historians assert that the second son Richard was also sent to Oxford, but college records do not list a Richard Lee of Virginia in this period. A clause in their father's will had provided for funds "towards the better education of John

[3] For details of Richard Lee I's life, see Hendrick, *op. cit.*, pp. 3-29.

and Richard, equally, to assist the one in his travels for the attainment of a reasonable perfection in the knowledge of physic, the other at the university or the Inns of Court which he shall be most fit for."[4] John did become a doctor of physic, but died young, in 1673. Richard became the scholar of the family.

Richard Lee II grew up in a Tory atmosphere in which intense loyalty to the Stuart line was accepted as a matter of course. His father, the emigrant, continued his allegiance to Charles II after the King's flight from England. Indeed, John Gibbon, author of *Introductio ad Latinam blasoniam* (1682), who spent the greater part of the year 1659 as Lee's guest in Virginia, declared that his host, as secretary of state, after the execution of Charles I, hired a Dutch ship at his own expense, and went to Brussels to procure a new commission for Governor Berkeley from Charles II.[5] If the infant son of Secretary of State Lee was still too young to comprehend such doings, he later absorbed so much of his father's loyalties that he too became a confirmed Jacobite and an ultraconservative.

Of the formal education of Richard Lee II we know little. Most likely his father, following the custom of the times, hired a tutor, or bought an indentured servant who knew Latin—as was the way of his contemporary, Colonel John Carter—and so provided for the instruction of his son in good learning. If he went to England to a grammar school, no records of his attendance have come to light. He may have studied in one of the colleges at Oxford, as did his elder brother John. In any case, whatever his education, he acquired a taste for learning and a knowledge of the learned tongues: Latin, Greek, and Hebrew. The family historian cites the statement of a grandson that

> some great men offered to promote him to the highest dignities in the Church if his father would let him stay in England; but this

[4] E. J. Lee, *op. cit.*, p. 63. [5] *Ibid.*, p. 60.

> offer was refused, as the old gentleman was determined to fix all his children in Virginia . . . Richard spent almost his whole life in study, and usually wrote his notes in Greek, Hebrew, or Latin . . . ; so that he neither diminished nor improved his paternal estate. . . . He was of the Council in Virginia and also other offices of honor and profit, though they yielded little to him.[6]

A descendant might regret an ancestor's failure to utilize opportunities for material aggrandizement, but disinterested observers of human nature can applaud Richard's integrity and devotion to public service and learning.

As a rich proprietor, possessed of land and slaves,[7] Richard Lee was a man of influence and power. Among the planters of Westmoreland County, few could call themselves his equals. Like his father before him, he held the offices that fell to the lord of Mount Pleasant as by natural right, and accepted civil responsibilities without thought of shirking even the most arduous of public duties. Such was the gentleman-planter's code. When in 1676 Nathaniel Bacon rebelled against what he termed the tyranny of Governor Berkeley and the governing coterie, he listed Lee as one of the small circle of Virginia's unjust rulers. Indeed, for his loyalty to the conservative ruling class, Lee suffered seven weeks' imprisonment at Bacon's hands and "received great prejudice in his health by hard usage."[8] Notwithstanding Bacon's accusations, Lee performed his duties to the state with the conscientiousness expected of one of his social position. He could not be disloyal to his class, and he would have denied the charges of tyranny leveled against his group. The desire to lead a contemplative life with his books did not permit him to neglect the active fulfilment of his services to society. In maintaining this balance between the active and the contemplative life, Lee was following an ancient ideal

[6] *Ibid.*, p. 75.

[7] See *ibid.*, pp. 79-81, for the will of Richard Lee II, listing his land and mentioning many slaves by name.

[8] *Ibid.*, p. 76.

of conduct much commended by earlier writers. Unconsciously, perhaps, he was exemplifying in Virginia a manner of life that would have been understood and approved by Sir Philip Sidney.

Of the springs that fed the mixed stream of Richard Lee's life, none was more important than his library. Isolated on a Potomac plantation, far from centers of intellectual activity, he turned to his books for help in replenishing his own inner resources and for practical guidance in the affairs of the day. His library, consisting of nearly three hundred titles, was indicative of the conservative taste, diversity of interests, and scholarly pursuits of the man, but it was not entirely unlike collections owned by contemporaries in his own class. Indeed, it was a good example of the "gentleman's library" of the time, though there was a greater emphasis on learned works and classical authors than was to be found in most similar collections. As in the libraries of other so-called Cavaliers, religious works composed the largest group of books on a single theme. Lee had fifty-eight items in this category. Learned works, chiefly textbooks, were more numerous, but their subject matter was as varied as the field of learning itself. The third largest group was composed of thirty-six standard works of the Greek and Roman writers—a choice of classic authors indicating considerable care in selection. There were also twenty-four lawbooks, twenty works of history and biography, twenty-one medical books, twenty works that may be classified as belles-lettres, and a respectable sprinkling in science and pseudoscience, geography and travel, politics and government, ethics and politics, conduct and heraldry, and certain utilitarian handbooks that a plantation owner might need. On the whole, the library was a well-balanced collection of books needed by a gentleman who proposed to cultivate his intellectual powers.[9]

[9] For the sort of books prized by another Virginia family of the same social class, see "The 'Gentleman's Library' in Early Virginia: The Literary Interests of

The majority of the items were old books in the sense that they were standard works whose place in the reading of cultivated gentlemen had long been recognized. Richard Lee, like many another conservative in that day and in this, did not feel any necessity of keeping up with the latest authors; nor was he concerned with English writers of belles-lettres that later generations have agreed are essential to any library. Chaucer, Spenser, Shakespeare, and Milton found no place among his books. But we must remember that Spenser was always a poet who appealed to a limited group, that Shakespeare had not yet been magnified by innumerable schoolmasters, and that Milton was still a relatively recent poet whose fame had been somewhat dampened by his Puritan affiliations.

Like most of his kind, Richard Lee was a staunch Anglican, and, if his epitaph may be credited, a man of piety. His religious books are the kind that one might expect in the household of a gentleman who believed in maintaining the Established Church and upholding respect for religion in the community. There were Bibles or Testaments in English, Latin, Greek, and French, two copies of the Book of Common Prayer, John Ailmer's versified rendering of the minor prophets, entitled *Musae sacrae* (1652), and other paraphrases of the Scriptures. Lee also had two copies of Henry Hammond's *A Practical Catechism* (1645) and several commentaries and concordances. A volume containing the articles and canons of the Church must have been useful when ecclesiastical questions had to be answered. Among several works of theology and divinity was the *Corpus doctrinae orthodoxae* (1585) by the learned German Zacharias Ursinus—a standard exposition of the Prot-

the First Carters," *The Huntington Library Quarterly*, I (1937-38), 3-61. A useful analysis of the subject matter in a selected group of Virginia collections is to be found in George K. Smart, "Private Libraries in Colonial Virginia," *American Literature*, X (1938), 24-52. See especially the table of percentages of subjects, p. 33.

The complete inventory of Richard Lee's library is reprinted, with identifications of the titles, in *The Huntington Library Quarterly*, II (1938-39), 1-35, where this chapter first appeared.

estant position, frequently found in Anglican as well as Puritan libraries. Of works of religious controversy there were scarcely any, the only one of any consequence being Joseph Wyeth's *Anguis flagellatus; or, A Switch for the Snake* (1699), a reply to an attack made by C. Leslie on the Quakers.

A substantial collection of sermons and religious meditations lent the library an air of piety. Most of the preachers represented were popular Anglican divines of the generation before Lee; they included Bishop Lancelot Andrewes, Griffith Williams, a staunch royalist, Nathaniel Parkhurst, an exponent of cheerful instead of gloomy religion, John White, Henry Greenwood, Isaac Barrow, and others of like quality. Not all the sermons were by orthodox Anglicans, however, for also included was a famous collection by the Presbyterian Samuel Smith, entitled *The Great Assize or Day of Jubilee* (1618). These sermons were so popular that more than thirty editions appeared before the end of the seventeenth century.

Meditations and guides to a religious way of life—a type of writing favored by all classes and sects of readers in this period—were fairly numerous. The best-known work of that kind owned by Lee was Richard Allestree's *The Whole Duty of Man* (1660), a book frequently found in the libraries of Virginia gentlemen. It was a useful guide to devotional exercises and was written with a proper regard for Anglican decorum. Lee also owned a devotional book by George Webb, Bishop of Limerick, which he may have remembered during his imprisonment by Bacon's rebels. It was a manual of religion entitled *The Practice of Quietness, Directing a Christian How to Live Quietly in This Troublesome World*. The work, really a collection of six sermons, first appeared in 1615; a ninth edition was published in 1657. A devotional book containing much practical guidance was Christopher Sutton's *Disce mori; Learn to Die* (1600), a work long popular on both sides of the Atlantic. Not merely did it provide advice concerning the proper preparation for death, but it also contained useful instruction in everyday living. Men are particularly warned against the unchristian practice of going to law—surely a timely bit of counsel for litigious Virginians. Another handbook of piety, Clement Ellis' *The Gentile Sinner; or, England's Brave Gentleman* (1660), a work also quite common in Virginia, helped to instruct the household at Mount Pleasant in the Christian and Anglican way of life. Among other pious meditations were Thomas à Kempis' *Imitation of Christ*, apparently in a Latin edition, Sir Mathew Hale's *Contemplations Moral and Divine* (1676), and Thomas Sherman's *Divine Breathings; or, A Manual of Practical Contemplations* (1680). Such books were not bought merely because one was expected to have a respectable number of religious writings. The chances are that Lee and his wife and children read these works as part of their religious observances. As was the case with other Cavalier planters, Lee demonstrated in the pious books he collected, and doubtless read, the respect for religious decorum that was a part of the code of his class.

Among the miscellaneous religious works at Mount Pleasant were Simon Patrick's *Parable of the Pilgrim* (1665), a piece of religious allegory that Virginians preferred to Bunyan's *Pilgrim's Progress*, and Robert Boyle's *Some Considerations Touching the Style of the Holy Scriptures* (1661), a work often found in colonial libraries, probably because of the great reputation of the author as a Christian philanthropist, as well as a philosopher and scientist.

Though the religious books in the Lee library are more numerous than any other single type of work, the titles are the conventional ones encountered in other collections. The learned works, on the contrary, represent a wider range of scholarly interest than is usually found in similar libraries, although Lee's contemporaries possessed some of the same books.

The skill in languages for which the master of Mount Pleasant was noted in his own time is suggested by numerous textbooks of Greek, Latin, Hebrew, and French. A Greek grammar, two or three Greek lexicons, a Greek and Latin edition of Aesop's *Fables*, and a work on Greek accent were texts which Lee must have used in acquiring or in maintaining his proficiency in that language. He was even better supplied with Latin grammars, lexicons, and readers. Among these last were the colloquies of Erasmus and of Corderius—old and notable instruments for the inculcation of Latin and good lessons of sundry sorts. The Latin grammar prepared by William Lily and John Colet—a textbook Shakespeare used—was one of the grammars specified in Lee's inventory. A Hebrew grammar and a work of Hebrew scholarship by Sebastian Münster helped Lee maintain his knowledge of the sacred tongue. Of modern foreign languages Lee had textbooks only of French. These consisted of a dictionary and two or three grammars, including the much-used text of Claudius Holyband, *The French Schoolmaster* (1573). An English dictionary, Edward Phillips' *The New World of Words* (1658), and George Dalgarno's *Ars signorum* (1661), a book about universal languages, completed Lee's philological resources.

An interest in other branches of learning is indicated by the number of textbooks dealing with rhetoric, logic, oratory, mathematics, and science. In Lee's lifetime some of these books were being used at Harvard College and at the English universities. An elementary introduction to classical rhetoric, the *Progymnasmata* of the fourth-century Greek, Aphthonius Sophista—a favorite manual of the day—may have been used by Lee as a student.[10] He also had an equally popular handbook for rhetorical study, Thomas Farnaby's *Florilegium*

[10] For an indication of the use of the work and similar textbooks at Harvard College and at European universities in the seventeenth century, see Samuel E. Morison, *Harvard College in the Seventeenth Century* (Cambridge, Mass., 1936), I, 177 ff.

(1629), and Charles Butler's *Rhetoricae libri duo* (1598). Of works of logic commonly used in the universities of the seventeenth century, he had texts by Franco Burgersdijck and Marcus Frederik Wendelin. Several treatises on oratory and collections of orations emphasized the importance of that discipline. John Clarke's *Formulae oratoriae* (1632) and Thomas Farnaby's *Phrases oratoriae et poeticae* (1631) provided both precept and illustration for oratorical composition in the classical manner. Latin orations of John Rainolds, a famous professor at Oxford in the last quarter of the sixteenth century, were also among the textbooks on this subject. Although emphasis on oratory was not confined to Virginians, it may be significant, in view of the later qualities of public speech in Virginia, that seventeenth- and eighteenth-century libraries so often contained books on oratory.

Lee's mathematical collection consisted of a half dozen books of arithmetic, including works by Robert Record and Edmund Wingate, Euclid in a Latin and a French text, and John Napier's *Rabdologiae* (1617).

A few titles indicate some interest in science, with the books about evenly divided between ancient and modern works. Beside Aristotle's *De anima*, for example, stood William Harvey's *Exercitationes de generatione animalium* (1651) and René Descartes' *Tractatus de homine et de formatione foetus* (1677). Two medieval works, Sacro Bosco's *Sphaera*, a treatise of astronomy, and the *Opera* of Albertus Magnus, were flanked by Vincent Wing's *Urania practica; or, Practical Astronomy* (1652) and Sir Francis Bacon's *Sylva sylvarum; or, A Natural History* (1626). There were two or three unidentified works on optics and physics. A suggestion that Lee may have had some leanings toward occult science may be found in his ownership of the *Magiae naturalis* (1561) of Giovanni della Porta and an account of the activity of Le Comte de Gabalis, a French dabbler in the occult.

A few textbooks of geography and one or two books of travel supplied information about the great world beyond the colony of Virginia. For example, there were Philippus Cluverius' *Introductionis in universam geographiam* (1651), an *Itinerarium* (1630) of the Low Countries and France by Gottfried Hegenitius and Abraham Ortelius, an *Itinerarium* (1649) of France by Justus Zinzterling, Rutgerus Hermannides' *Britannia Magna* (1661), two books by John Speed, *The Description of England and Wales* (1615) and *A Prospect of the Most Famous Parts of the World* (1631), Peter Heylyn's *Microcosmus* (1621), and *The Travels of Signor Pietro della Valle, a Noble Roman, into East India and Arabia Deserta* (1665).

Other learned works which should be mentioned were commentaries on Aristotle's *Ethics* and on his scientific treatises, and a collection of the works of the Renaissance scholar, Lorenzo Valla. A copy of the statutes of the University of Oxford may be a relic of Lee's attendance there.

No other Virginia library previous to this time had a greater proportion of works of classic authorship than Richard Lee's. His collection of the literature of Greece and Rome was well chosen. As examples of the theories of oratory laid down in his textbooks, he had the orations of Demosthenes and Cicero. Among philosophic works were the writings of Aristotle, Epictetus, and Seneca, and the not always edifying collection of the lives and sayings of the philosophers, compiled by Diogenes Laertius. The historians were amply represented, and included the works of Xenophon, Plutarch, Livy, Sallust, Tacitus, Caesar, Quintus Curtius, Velleius Paterculus, and Suetonius. Of classic poetry, drama, and other belles-lettres, the library contained works of Homer, Hesiod, Lucian, Heliodorus, Virgil, Horace, Ovid, Lucan, Martial, Terence, Claudianus, Juvenal, Persius, and other, less-well-known writings, including a Greek and Latin version of *Aurea Pythagoreorum carmina*, Pliny's epistles, the epigrams of the Alexandrian grammarian Callimachus, and Octavian Mirandula's anthology of classic poetry, *Illustrium poetarum flores* (1598). Altogether, the collection of classics was remarkably complete for a colonial library, and we can be reasonably sure that these books were intended to be read by their owner rather than displayed for purposes of learned ostentation. What proportion were translations, the inventory does not make clear; some were doubtless English versions, but the probability is that most were in their original tongues. Acquaintance with classical writers, so often demonstrated by Virginia leaders, can be attributed to such libraries as Richard Lee's as much as to the educational practices of the time. Few libraries of any importance were without translations of at least a few of the great Greek and Roman writers, and, in a later day, many a Virginian without benefit of university training found it easy to quote from Cicero, Virgil, Ovid, or some other ancient author who suited his purpose.

The lawbooks at Mount Pleasant were the usual works found at this time in a well-selected library of a member of the ruling caste. Although the legal collection was not so extensive as that owned by Robert Carter at Corotoman, it was fairly adequate for a colonial lawmaker and county judge. Whether Lee had any formal legal training is unknown, though the family historian surmises that he might have been a member of one of the Inns of Court. Be that as it may, as a leading citizen of Westmoreland County and a magistrate, he had constantly to face legal problems, for there was not yet a professional class of lawyers in the colony. A dozen or more handbooks on various phases of legal practice must have been in constant use. Such things as Joseph Keble's *An Assistance to the Justices of the Peace, for the Easier Performance of Their Duty* (1683), or George Billinghurst's *Arcana clericalia; or, The Mysteries of Clerkship* (1673-74), or William Bohun's *Institutio legalis; or, An Introduction to the Study and Practice of the Laws of England* (1708-9), provided even the layman with the rudiments of legal knowledge and procedure. Lee also had several works explaining the common law, including Sir Francis Bacon's *The Elements of the Common Laws of England* (1630). A few collections of law reports and two or three dictionaries of legal terms enlarged his equipment. Practically all of the legal works listed in his inventory were also to be found in the library of Robert Carter.[11]

In history and biography, Lee showed an interest in both the ancient and the modern world. Besides the classical historians already mentioned, he owned a French version of Flavius Arrianus' narrative of the wars of Alexander, a French epitome of Roman history by La Mothe le Vayer, Philippe Labbe's *Notitia dignitatum imperii Romani* (1651), an outline of the organization of the Roman Empire, and Ludolph Smids's *Romanorum imperatorum pinacotheca* (1699). The inventory lists the Latin works of Paulus Orosius, a contemporary of St. Jerome's, who wrote among other things *Historiarum adversum paganos*, which proves that the times have always been bad. Among his universal histories were Sir Walter Raleigh's *The History of the World* (1614) and Archbishop James Ussher's *The Annals of the World* (1658), both exceedingly popular works in the seventeenth century. For the Continent, he had a general history of Europe, accounts of the wars of France and of Italy, and a history of the Council of Trent by Paolo Sarpi.

English history in Lee's library is strangely sparse; indeed, the sole work covering the sweep of the English past is an inadequate little book by Lambert Wood, *Florus Anglicus; or, An Exact History of England from the Reign of William the Conqueror to the Death of the Late King* (1657). Sir Fran-

[11] For a more detailed discussion of these lawbooks, see Chapter IX and the titles identified in the article on "The 'Gentleman's Library' in Early Virginia," cited *supra*, n. 9.

cis Bacon's *The History of the Reign of King Henry the Seventh* (1622) and Abel Boyer's *The History of Queen Anne, Digested into Annals* (1703-13) were the only books covering specific reigns. Boyer's eleven-volume work was one of the last bought by Lee before his death. Actions of Parliament during the Puritan Revolution, which had so vitally concerned Lee's father, were described, from the Puritan point of view, in John Rushworth's *Historical Collections* (1659-80), but the curse was taken off this portion of the library by three stout defenses of King Charles I: *Eikon Basilike* (1649), attributed in Lee's lifetime to the King himself, George Bate's *Elenchi motuum nuperorum in Anglia* (1661), and Thomas Forde's *Virtus rediviva; or, A Panegyric on the Late King Charles I* (1660). No other books owned by Lee were primarily concerned with historical events in England. The nearest approach to a narrative of events in the colonies was Sir Dalby Thomas' *An Historical Account of the Rise and Growth of the West India Colonies, and of the Great Advantages They Are to England in Respect to Trade* (1690), a book which a Virginia planter and tobacco merchant would find of considerable timeliness.

The only biography showing an interest in modern history, in addition to the apologia of Charles I, is an English translation of the biography of a French courtier and politician of the early seventeenth century, Guillaume Girard's *The History of the Life of the Duke of Espernon* (1670).

Lee's books on government and politics were precisely the works one would expect a conservative Royalist to own. Sir Thomas Smith's *De republica Anglorum: The Manner of Government of England* (1583) provided a description of the organization of the realm in the reign of Elizabeth and gave Virginia readers in the seventeenth century a link with the past development of the land they still regarded as their mother country. Richard Hooker's *Of the Laws of Ecclesiastical Polity*

(1594-97) justified the Anglican position in church government and confirmed the ecclesiastical ideas shared by Lee and other members of his class. Modern political philosophy justifying Lee's own notions of government by an aristocracy was to be found in Thomas Hobbes's *Philosophical Rudiments Concerning Government and Society* (1651) and *De corpore politico; or, The Elements of Law, Moral and Politic* (1650). If any further bolstering of Lee's monarchical notions was needed, it was to be found in Archbishop James Ussher's *The Power Communicated by God to the Prince, and Obedience Required of the Subject* (1661) and in John Hall's *Of Government and Obedience* (1654). A political allegory of early-seventeenth-century events, James Howell's *Dodona's Grove* (1640), and a treatise attacking the influence of French papists in England, *Europe a Slave unless England Break Her Chains* (1681), completed Mount Pleasant's books of political interest.

The medical collection gathered by Lee was of both scholarly interest and practical use. It is not surprising to find a good classicist owning the works of Galen and Hippocrates, the wisest of the Greek physicians, as well as a text of *De medicina,* by Cornelius Celsus, the greatest of the Roman medical writers. Beside these works of Greek and Roman antiquity stood William Harvey's essay on the circulation of the blood—the Lee library's most advanced modern treatise on medical theory. The rest of the medical works were practical handbooks concerned with anatomy and the treatment of disease. Nearly all of them were medical books commonly found even in small libraries. There was, for instance, Philip Barrough's *The Method of Physic* (1583), frequently reprinted and long popular. The most recent medical works in the library were not very new, for the latest one purchased by Lee was the *Pharmacopoeia Bateana* by George Bate, published in 1694. Lee, like the greater number of his contemporaries, even physicians, was content to use old books long accepted as standard works of medical practice. If he prescribed for members of his household out of one of his newer works, Sir Kenelm Digby's *Choice and Experimented Receipts in Physic and Chirurgery* (1668), they probably fared no better than they would have if he had stuck to Barrough.

Of utilitarian books likely to be needed by a great planter, Lee had but a scant supply. John Wing's *The Art of Surveying* (1699), an unidentified handbook for mariners, a treatise on bookkeeping, one of Gervase Markham's treatises on horsemanship, John French's *The Art of Distillation*, a cookbook, and an almanac supplied all the guidance in the practical concerns of life that the library could boast.

Although not devoid of belles-lettres and the literature of mere entertainment, the library possessed not a single item from the greatest English writers. Lee's taste seems to have run to satires. He owned Erasmus' *The Praise of Folly* (1549), and several later satirical works. Among these were John Barclay's *Euphormionis Lusinini* (1634), a prose allegory admonishing princes and condemning political faction. Lee must have been pleased with its attacks on the Puritans and Jesuits. A celebrated Italian satire, Traiano Boccalini's *La Secretaria de Apollo, che segue gli ragguagli di Parnaso* (1653), also found its way to Mount Pleasant. Although Henry, Earl of Monmouth, translated this work into English in 1656, Lee owned the original Italian version. The most recent satire was Samuel Butler's *Hudibras* (1689), a poem, ridiculing the Puritans, that was popular in Virginia, as one might expect.

Other poetry indicated a fairly catholic taste for both the learned and the amusing, the stately and the satirical. Ariosto's *Orlando Furioso*, probably in Sir John Harington's translation first published in 1591; John Barclay's *Poematum libri duo* (1615), polite Latin verses addressed to Prince Charles and other notables; Abraham Cowley's *Poemata Latina* (1668), learned poems on plants; and John Cleveland's *Poems* (1660), an assortment of amorous, serious, and satirical verses by that Cavalier poet—provided a variety of poetical reading ranging from the epic to love lyrics. Since the prestige of poets like Butler, Cowley, and Cleveland at this time was high, Lee probably prided himself on owning a few of the best of the recent poets. A volume listed simply as "Pains Poems" may have been the *Daily Meditations* (1668) of Philip Pain, a New England poet. Two pastoral plays found a place in the collection: Elkanah Settle's *Pastor fido* (1677), or perhaps its prototype, with the same title, by Guarini, and John Fletcher's *La Fida pastora* (1658). One four-volume picaresque novel, Richard Head's *The English Rogue* (1665-71), was the sole work of prose fiction. Collections of letters found somewhat greater favor, for Lee owned James Howell's *Epistolae Ho-Elianae, Familiar Letters Domestic and Foreign* (1645), really a series of gossipy, familiar essays; *The Letters of Monsieur de Balzac* (1634), a duller but popular collection translated from the French; and Vincent de Voiture's *Letters of Affairs, Love, and Courtship* (1657), presenting Voiture's correspondence with great ladies and nobles of the court of Louis XIV. Lee also had the French version of Voiture's letters. Because of the relations of the Stuarts to the French court, Lee as an ardent Jacobite probably felt a particular interest in gossip about French affairs during the period when Charles II and the Cavalier refugees were in France.

Of frivolous literature, even serious Richard Lee had three items: a collection of humorous and sometimes unedifying verses, entitled *Wit and Drollery* (1661), a jestbook, *Nugae venales* (1648), and Raphael Thorius' *Hymnus tabaci: A Poem in Honor of Tobacco* (1651). Surely no verses in his library could have been read with more heartfelt enthusiasm than this heroic poem, in two books, whose author declared,

> Tobacco, King of Plants I well may call;
> Others have single virtues, this hath all.

In innumerable couplets Thorius commends tobacco and finds infinite good uses for it. Even its ashes are a sovereign dentifrice. We can imagine Lee and his fellow planters of Westmoreland reading the poem with approval.

But Lee allowed himself few books that were not definitely improving to the mind. Any frivolity that his jest-book and his anthology of light verses may have induced was easily purged away by several works of ethics and philosophy. The inventory lists, besides particular titles, a "Collecon of ffrancis Bacon works," probably several of Bacon's books gathered up and bound for Lee. He also had Bacon's *Sermones fidelles ethici, politici, oeconomici* (1641), a collection which contained fifty-six of Bacon's essays, besides other writings. As a complement to Bacon's aphoristic wisdom, the library contained Montaigne's essays, probably in Florio's translation. Besides Montaigne, there were the works of two other French philosophic writers: Pierre Charron's *De la sagesse* (1601) and Antoine Legrand's *An Entire Body of Philosophy* (1694). Although we know little about Lee's inner life and thoughts, it would not have been inconsistent with his Anglicanism if the serious scholar of Westmoreland County leaned toward a skeptical rationalism. Selection of the works of Bacon, Montaigne, Charron, and Legrand would suggest this quality of mind. Charron, who preached a morality based on reason, and Legrand, who had defended Cartesianism at Oxford, with Bacon and Montaigne, found favor with other colonial Americans. The atmosphere which produced the rationalism of Jefferson and the deism of many another eighteenth- and early-nineteenth-century American perhaps owed more to a long period of philosophic preparation than has been generally supposed.

One little group of books on heraldry and the conduct of gentlemen may be significant of the Lees' conception of their position in the social order. The founder of the Lee family in Virginia was conscious of being a gentleman and was concerned to establish a family dynasty with landed property, with wealth, and with the trappings and honors that betoken that station. He laid claim to the coat of arms of certain Lees of Shropshire, and his successors displayed this escutcheon. His son Richard was equally conscious of his gentility and of the obligations that his social position entailed. The first Lees, with their class consciousness, liked to think of themselves as part of the hereditary gentility of England—English country gentlemen living on their Virginia estates. Perhaps that may account for the presence in the Lee library of James Yorke's *The Union of Honor* (1640), a sort of peerage with genealogies, describing the great families of England, and for the possession of John Selden's *Titles of Honor* (1614), an antiquarian history of titles. Lee had a particular personal interest in John Gibbon's *Introductio ad Latinam blasoniam; or, An Essay to a More Correct Blazon in Latin than Formerly Hath Been Used* (1682), because the author—later a member of the College of Heralds—had spent the year 1659 with the elder Richard Lee, and in his work had paid his host a tribute. The younger Lee's copy of Gibbon's book had probably been presented by the author.

For guides to the behavior expected of members of the ruling class, Lee provided his household with two books, Richard Brathwaite's *The English Gentleman* (1630) and H. W.'s *The Accomplished Courtier* (1658). The choice of Brathwaite's work is suggestive of the philosophy of conduct exemplified by the new Virginia aristocracy. In one passage, the author, himself a country gentleman, had observed: "Men in great place (saith one) are thrice servants: servants of the sovereign or state; servants of fame; and servants of business." [12] This passage might have been taken as a motto by the Lees and their kind, for it expresses their own belief in the respon-

[12] *The English Gentleman* (1630), p. 115.

sibilities of the upper class. In the seventeenth century, aristocratic ideals were shifting and were being influenced by the growing commercial spirit of the times. Brathwaite illustrates the changing conception of the place of gentlemen in society, and it is understandable that his work should have been chosen as a useful guide by Virginians, who agreed with his practical suggestions and rules of behavior. *The Accomplished Courtier*, really a translation of Book II of Eustache De Refuge's *Traité de la cour*, was a sort of guide to practical politics, with observations on the conduct courtiers should adopt if they hoped to succeed in their political careers.[13] The treatise was popular with Cavalier readers in England; and, since it carried by implication useful lessons for colonial politicians, Lee naturally regarded it as a book worth owning.

In surveying the Lee library as a whole, one is struck by the proportion of books dating from the early seventeenth century and before. Some of these may have been gathered by Lee's father, though no record of his library has been found. Richard's elder brother John, whose property came to Richard after his death in 1673, owned books valued at four thousand pounds of tobacco—exactly the valuation of his "negro boy Frank and livery suit"[14]—surely not a great collection, but at least a respectable handful of books. In any case, works inherited by Richard would most likely have been standard publications of an earlier day. Hard times may have forced a restriction of book buying during Lee's later years; as was the case with other planters, he was often pinched for ready cash because of the slump in tobacco prices. Whether Richard Lee II chose all the works in his library himself or inherited part of them, they were profoundly influential in determining his character and qualities, and they satisfied his interests and needs. In many respects Lee was a belated Elizabethan, and

[13] See W. Lee Ustick, "The Courtier and the Bookseller: Some Vagaries of Seventeenth-Century Publishing," *The Review of English Studies*, V (1929), 143-54.

[14] E. J. Lee, *op. cit.*, p. 70.

the books he read and provided for his family were the kind that a learned gentleman of the later sixteenth or early seventeenth century would have approved.

The spirit of Elizabethan England lingered with Richard Lee. Oblivious to popular trends in literature or new fashions in learning, he turned to the great minds of the past for inspiration and solace. The desire to know for learning's sake prompted his studies, for he had no urge to write about what he read, no ambition of authorship, no vanity of his own opinions to make him take his pen in hand. Like other thoughtful gentlemen, like many of his spiritual ancestors in the Renaissance, he probably would have felt it indecorous and unbecoming to run to the printing house with his innermost thoughts. An inherited feeling among the educated aristocracy that writing for the public press was not quite proper for a gentleman undoubtedly helps to explain the scantiness of literary production in colonial Virginia. The difficulty was not that Virginians had nothing to say, or that no press at Jamestown or Williamsburg made it convenient for them to print, but that men like Richard Lee and his kind maintained a spiritual and intellectual reticence. They would no more have dissected their emotions or ostentatiously displayed their erudition in the manner of Cotton Mather than they would have appeared at a social gathering stripped of their shirts.

The master of Mount Pleasant, learnedly making notes in Greek, Latin, and Hebrew, thoughtfully pondering the stoical wisdom of Epictetus and Seneca, or contemplating the materialistic aphorisms of Bacon and the gentle skepticism of Montaigne, was a man of two worlds, as indeed the great Elizabethan gentlemen had been. Lee was the heir of all the past, but he was also a participant in a vital world which he was helping to create. In him there was a perfect fusion of the active and the contemplative life. And, if he wrote no scholarly treatise or philosophic essay, Richard Lee, by example and precept, by his personal influence, by the opportunities which his accumulated stores of knowledge gave to others, helped to transmit a part of the Renaissance ideal of civilized life to his colleagues and to his descendants. The influence of the English Renaissance in colonial America was subtle but powerful, and it may account for many mysteries in our intellectual history.

The influence of the classics that was exemplified in the second Richard Lee was further evident in the ideas on education expressed by the early Carters. This family, whose members were too concerned with material pomp and circumstance to follow the narrower path of scholarship pursued by Lee, nevertheless believed in ancient learning and helped to establish and maintain the cultural tradition.

CHAPTER IX

THE LITERATE INTERESTS OF THE FIRST CARTERS

Of the "great gentlemen" of seventeenth- and eighteenth-century Virginia, none took precedence over the Carters. No other clan succeeded so well as the Carters in allying itself with influential families; no family occupied a higher social position; few controlled so much property; and only the second William Byrd exceeded the Carters in elegance of surroundings. The family had a veritable genius for marrying well—and often. During the second half of the seventeenth century, and the generations that immediately followed, they waxed in numbers and riches and power until it was difficult to find a Virginia community in which some family connection of the Carters did not have a dominant voice in affairs. So numerous did they become that their descendants have been estimated at present to number at least 50,000 souls. For many people the name Carter has come to signify the type of Virginia aristocrat of the previous age. Far and wide—and sometimes with more imagination than historical accuracy—descendants have heralded the name and fame of this family, for none of them has ever been accounted a shrinking violet content to bloom unseen—or unheard. Few other families have talked more about the ancient glory of Virginia or done more to inculcate in their descendants a belief in the value of the aristocratic tradition.

The Carters are a good family to study, because they represent so many of the sound, substantial qualities of the English gentry and because they are typical of the Virginia ruling class that developed in the second half of the seventeenth century and came to full power in the eighteenth. They represent a tradition of intelligence and social cultivation. They firmly believed in the value of a classical education, and they were not content to be provincials. If few of them could be described as noted intellectuals, they nevertheless cultivated their minds and gathered libraries which they and their neighbors used. Though some of their collateral descendants rose to the highest posts of political and military honor, most of the Carters were not primarily statesmen; they merely served their state when need arose or opportunity offered, as was the duty of gentlemen. Their chief contribution was made in the establishment and maintenance of an aristocratic social system in Virginia—based on landed wealth, influence, and position. An understanding of the intellectual qualities of the founders of this family, therefore, will go far toward revealing characteristics of the dominant class that firmly established English aristocratic attitudes in Virginia. As a clue to the Carters' intellectual interests, their books are especially significant, for they chose them with care and intended them for use instead of display; moreover, their books are representative of the literary taste and needs of a typical family of the more aristocratic class, and, for that reason, an analysis of their libraries deserves attention.

John Carter, the earliest of his clan in Virginia, was apparently a distressed Royalist who came to Virginia about 1649 and settled first in Upper Norfolk County. Though his background and family connections in England are shadowy, he was evidently a man of some culture and wealth, for early allusions give him the title of "Colonel" and show considerable deference.[1] Soon a member of the House of Burgesses, he promptly took his place as one of the ruling clique and presently was a member of the governing Council. When the succession of Richard Cromwell was proclaimed in the

[1] For biographical facts about the early Carters see Thomas A. Glenn, *Some Colonial Mansions and Those Who Lived in Them* (Philadelphia, 1899), pp.

House of Burgesses in March, 1659, Colonel John Carter was one of those who grumbled about upstart usurpers—grumbled, indeed, so loudly that an order for his arrest was issued.[2] But Richard Cromwell was soon forgotten and Colonel Carter prospered under the restored Stuarts. A manorial establishment called "Corotoman," in Lancaster County, in what was known as the Northern Neck, became the family seat, a center of social life destined to increase in splendor under his sons. In the ripeness of time, after marrying five wives, Colonel Carter died and was buried in the chancel of near-by Christ Church, which the parish had paid him to build. Concern for the continuity of the family name is evident in his will, dated September 15, 1669.[3] To his two oldest sons, John and Robert, went the best portions of his estate. To his last wife—whom he disliked—and her infant son Charles, he left provisionally a third of his property. There may be some ironical significance in his having specified that his wife should have certain pious volumes from his library: "*David's Tears* and Byfield's *Treatise* and the *Whole Duty of Man* and her own books."

To his eldest son, John, he bequeathed most of his books, "only my son Robert to have the sixth part of them in goodness and value." In a codicil he further directed that his son

---

217-94; Charles P. Keith, *The Ancestry of Benjamin Harrison, President of the United States of America, 1889-1893* (Philadelphia, 1893), and the review of this work in *The Virginia Magazine of History and Biography*, II, 229-38; Fairfax Harrison, *Landmarks of Old Prince William* (Richmond, 1924). Further information and references are to be found in the *Dictionary of American Biography, sub* Robert Carter.

Parts of this chapter first appeared in "The 'Gentleman's Library' in Early Virginia: The Literary Interests of the First Carters," *The Huntington Library Quarterly*, I (1937-38), 3-61.

[2] "Arrest of Col. John Carter, the Cavalier," *William and Mary College Quarterly*, VIII (1899-1900), 33.

[3] The will may be found in the Lancaster County Court Records, Wills, 1709-1727, p. 416. There is an abstract in *The Virginia Magazine of History and Biography*, II, 235-36, where it is stated that an inventory of Col. Carter's estate was recorded July 20, 1670. A search of the records has failed to disclose an

Charles should have "Dr. Ussher's *Body of Divinity* when he comes to years of discretion" and Robert should also have copies of "Dr. Ussher's *Body of Divinity* and the *Whole Duty of Man* and the *Practice of Piety* and Doctor Nicholas' (?) *Catechism*." Obviously Colonel Carter had faith in the efficacy of pious treatises in the upbringing of his sons. Significantly, though a staunch Anglican he did not eschew the practical sermons of that popular Puritan preacher, Nicholas Byfield.

John, who inherited five-sixths of the library, was old enough to be named executor of the will, but Robert, later to be known as "King" Carter, was a child of only six at his father's death. Colonel Carter made provision for the boy's education in the classical tradition:

> My will is that my son Robert during his minority have a man or youth servant bought for him that hath been brought up in the Latin School, and that he constantly tend upon him not only to teach him by books in either English or Latin according to his capacity (for my will is that he shall learn both Latin and English and to write), but also to preserve him from harm and from doing evil and as soon as one is free or dead, my will is that he have another bought.

Since it was considered probable that the third son might be apprenticed to business, Carter made provision that, "in case my wife put her son out to apprentice, then so much of her portion be paid as is thought necessary to bind him out to a good trade." John was to maintain the family establishment at Corotoman; Robert was to be educated in such good learning as he could get; and Charles was to go into trade. That was the conventional scheme of things. But John died in 1690, leaving only a daughter, Elizabeth; and Charles died young; so Robert became the progenitor of the Carter dynasty

---

inventory of his library. For some reason, perhaps because the wording of the will revealed the testator's unhappy relations with his fifth wife, it was not recorded until Jan. 9, 1722.

that was to provide Virginia with a multitude of plantation grandees in the next century.

John Carter II inherited, as we have seen, all his father's books except the sixth part that went to Robert and the few pious works received by his father's widow and her infant son. Though the inventory of John Carter II lists only a few more than sixty titles, the library was carefully selected and included standard works in most fields that were of interest to a colonial plantation owner. Many of the books were undoubtedly those his father had brought from England or imported soon after his arrival. Indeed, a large proportion of the books were in print during the first Carter's lifetime, and conceivably might have been in his original library. Some of the titles, however, were of late imprints, showing that John Carter II was buying books almost to the year of his death.[4]

This library is another indication of the Virginia planter's concern over religious problems, for the largest single category of books dealt with that subject, and a goodly number of the volumes were by Puritan authors, though the Carters were orthodox Anglicans.[5] Of the twenty-one religious books (one-third of the whole library), seventeen titles had been in print before the first John Carter died.

The library had, of course, a Bible (listed as "an Old English Bible," without any indication of which translation it may have been), a Greek Testament, and a Book of Common Prayer. To assist the Bible reader, there were a concordance and several works explaining the Scriptures, including the

[4] The list, as it appears in the manuscript inventory, is reprinted in the *William and Mary College Quarterly*, VIII, 18-19. This inventory, like most others recorded with wills, was prepared hurriedly by friends or relatives, and gives only abbreviated titles, often unintelligible. These abbreviated titles have been identified where possible, and expanded, in *The Huntington Library Quarterly*, I, 40-61.

[5] A further discussion of this characteristic of colonial libraries may be found in Louis B. Wright, "The Purposeful Reading of Our Colonial Ancestors," *E.L.H., A Journal of Literary History*, IV (1937), 85-111.

Annotations upon All the Books of the Old and New Testament (1651), published by the authority of the Westminster Assembly, and Giovanni Diodati's *Pious Annotations* (1643), whose author was an erudite Genevan, the uncle of Milton's friend Charles Diodati. These were among the best biblical commentaries then available. Though most of them were compiled by Calvinists, they usually steered clear of disputation and consequently would not have greatly disturbed John Carter's Anglican faith if he had ever taken it into his head to expound the Scriptures to his household (as he may very well have done).

The amount of interest in controversial theology, even in Puritan New England, has been greatly overestimated, and Virginia planters were not likely to be much concerned over the hairsplitting of argumentative preachers. They were interested, however, in treatises that prescribed a way of attaining the good life and perhaps an eternal reward. That explains why nearly everybody who owned any books at all had Lewis Bayly's *Practice of Piety*, a manual which had a thirty-fifth edition in 1635. Though his father's copy of this book had been bequeathed to his younger brother Robert, John procured one for his own household. But the author represented by the largest number of titles in John Carter's library was the nonconformist preacher Richard Baxter, who, as a chaplain in the parliamentary armies, had urged toleration and deplored controversial bickerings. In the folio edition of Baxter's *Christian Directory; or, A Sermon of Practical Theology* (1673) was good advice for all of Carter's household. If that did not suffice, he had five of Baxter's other works, the most important of which were the *Saints' Everlasting Rest* (1650) and the *Poor Man's Family Book* (1674). An interest in the arguments for toleration may be manifest in Carter's possession of a treatise by a Puritan who pleaded with his brethren for a middle-of-the-road policy—John Ball's *Friendly Trial of the*

Grounds Tending to Separation (1640). All the rest of Carter's religious books, with the exception of William Penn's *No Cross, No Crown* (1669), were sermons by Puritan preachers, including the works of his father's favorite, Nicholas Byfield, and a promising treatise, by John Durant, entitled *Sips of Sweetness; or, Consolation for Weak Believers* (1651). Not necessarily a proof of the owner's sympathy with the Puritans' point of view in theology, these books are an indication of the widespread acceptance of their social creed as a practical guide to life. However far readers departed from the paths of righteousness that the preachers marked out for them, they would rarely have argued that the theories of conduct set forth were wrong. Though a gentleman was given latitude to err, he was supposed to subscribe to the doctrine of strict probity.

Next to religion, medicine furnished the largest number of titles in John Carter's library, and in costliness the medical works probably exceeded all others, for the eleven separate works listed included several expensive folios, handsomely printed and illustrated. Limited as this library may seem today, it was selected to present the best available guides to medical practice and was undoubtedly better than many a London practitioner could boast. On an isolated Virginia plantation, the master and his wife assumed responsibility for the health and physical welfare of their servants and neighbors, as indeed was the practice among the gentry of England.

A basis for a knowledge of anatomy, physiology, and the practice of surgery was furnished by Thomas Johnson's translation of the works of Ambroise Paré, the famous French surgeon, of the late sixteenth century, who had popularized Vesalian anatomy. This translation by a London apothecary and herbalist was brought out in a handsome folio edition in 1634. Few works perhaps offered the reader so much of terrible fascination, for here he could see pictured innumerable anatomical specimens, a display of the latest types of artificial eyes and legs, the whole panoply of surgical equipment from scalpels to skull saws, or a patient lying ready to be cut for the stone. If even a seventeenth-century plantation master did not have the temerity to attempt the operation described, any layman could be wonderfully well-informed by the study of Paré's book. He might, in fact, read a section on plastic surgery and learn a technique of face lifting and nose remodeling that would do credit to a modern beauty doctor. The book certainly helped the planter to assist the surgeon when necessary, to undertake simple treatments, and to make rough diagnoses of surgical conditions. A similar work was Helkiah Crooke's *Description of the Body of Man* (1615). Though, a year after Crooke's work was compiled, William Harvey lectured on his discovery of the circulation of the blood, the second edition (1631) did not mention this advance in anatomical knowledge. Paré and Crooke, however, epitomized the best of the older knowledge of physiology, and incorporated such advances as had been made by the great Vesalius in the middle of the sixteenth century; in addition they included later improvements in surgical technique, some of which Paré himself had introduced. With these books, the Virginian was equipped with the best texts then available. Theories like those of Harvey were for London experimentalists, not for Virginia planters.

In addition to these relatively up-to-date books, Carter had some works that had been in use for a century or more. Doubtless midwives on the Rappahannock plantations were still receiving instructions out of Carter's copy of the *Birth of Mankind*—a treatise that had been first translated from the Latin of Eucharius Roesslin, by R. Jonas, in 1540. And Joannes de Vigo, a surgical writer who had set forth his views in the first quarter of the sixteenth century, was also represented in Carter's medical collection.

For the general practice of medicine, Carter had recent

standard works. The best of these was a folio volume on the *Practice of Physic* (1655), compiled by Nicholas Culpeper, the apothecary, and two other collaborators, out of the writings of the French physician Lazare Rivière. To supplement that text, there were two or three volumes of the translated works of Daniel Sennert, an intelligent physician and professor of medicine at the University of Wittenberg during the first third of the seventeenth century. Specific treatises, by this German physician, on dropsy and scurvy are mentioned, as well as the translation, *Institutions . . . of Physic and Chirurgery* (1656), a general discussion of the practice of medicine. Another encyclopedic work on diseases and their treatment summed up the best medical knowledge of the continental physicians of the sixteenth century–the *General Practice of Physic*, a folio volume, by a distinguished Augsburg physician, Christopher Wirsung, first translated into English in 1598, and several times reprinted. Wirsung's book, which maintained its popularity well into the seventeenth century, was one of the best indexed and most convenient of the period. It provided an authoritative text that could be understood by the layman, as the translator pointed out, and was especially useful "for the instruction and safe direction of all those that have not always a good and learned physician at hand." Finally, two English translations of the pharmacopoeia completed the works upon which John Carter depended for medical guidance. Missing from his collection are the cheap little books of popular medicine frequently found, during this period, in the libraries of ordinary citizens on both sides of the Atlantic. Although, as we should expect, Carter showed no interest in new medical theories, his small collection had some of the best of the conservative, standard treatises.

Among the other utilitarian works owned by John Carter, the largest number had to do with phases of farming and country life. Like many country squires of England, he had

Gervase Markham's *Way to Get Wealth* (1631), an omnium gatherum of various treatises published earlier by that diligent author. In this thick octavo, Markham packed information about raising cattle, horses, and fowls, the enrichment of the soil, the growing of various crops, and the planting of orchards. Here the housewife could find directions for preserving, distilling, brewing, and practicing physic and surgery. Furthermore, there was a section on the "knowledge, use, and laudable practice of all the recreations meet for a gentleman." Finally, a sixth division of the book, prepared by William Lawson, described "The making of orchards, planting, and grafting, the office of gardening, and the ornaments, with the best husbanding of bees." It may be of some interest that a passage in the work describes the use of marl in the enrichment of land—a procedure later followed in restoring Virginia soil worn out from overplanting with tobacco. This book provided in the briefest compass the information of greatest practical use to a gentleman-planter, and also supplied advice about his recreations and the design of formal gardens.

Like Ralph Wormeley and other planters, Carter had a copy of Estienne and Liebault's *Maison Rustique; or, The Country Farm* (1616), that magnificent compendium of information on the planning and management of great estates, written originally for aristocratic landowners of France, edited later for English country gentlemen by Gervase Markham, and now found useful by Virginians ambitious to lay out stately gardens. A third work, prepared by Markham, was of undoubted interest to Virginians already developing a taste for horse racing, for *Markham's Masterpiece; or, What Doth a Horseman Lack* (1610) attempted to give a summary of all necessary information about the care and training of horses.

The Carter collection's most recent treatise on farming was Walter Blith's *English Improver; or, A New Survey of Husbandry* (1649), which described the advantages of irrigation, flooding land to increase fertility, rotation of crops, and various forms of manuring, including the application of lime, marl, and ashes to exhausted soils.[6] Blith, in mentioning earlier treatises on husbandry, commends Gervase Markham but says that Estienne and Liebault's work has little value.

If Carter was disappointed by this criticism of one of his handsomest books, he must have been pleased when Blith praised in high terms Francis Bacon's *Sylva Sylvarum; or, A Natural History in Ten Centuries* (1626), the Carter library's only other work concerned with natural science. Since educated colonists shared the characteristic seventeenth-century interest in the curiosities of nature, Bacon's *Sylva Sylvarum*, with its extensive though chaotic observations of natural phenomena, was popular.

As a justice of the peace and commander of the militia in Lancaster County, Colonel John Carter II was necessarily concerned with military affairs—an interest which is reflected in two books on the practical aspects of conducting war and maneuvering troops: John Bingham's translation of the *Tactics of Aelian* (1616), and William Barriffe's *Military Discipline; or, The Young Artilleryman* (1635). These were among the best available printed texts on military tactics as devised by the ancients and the moderns. Whether Carter ever attempted to adapt the maneuvers of the Greek phalanx to conditions of Indian warfare in the Virginia creek swamps is doubtful, but the possession of Aelian's *Tactics*, with its diagrams and plates, shows the persistence of classical theory even in warfare. The suggestions, in Barriffe's book, for the erection and defense of fortifications were more immediately practical.

[6] See Avery O. Craven, *Soil Exhaustion as a Factor in the Agricultural History of Virginia and Maryland, 1606-1860* ("University of Illinois Studies in the Social Sciences," XIII [1925]), pp. 92-94. Professor Craven points out the preoccupation of the Virginia planters with the problem of restoring the fertility of the soil by the use of marl, lime, ashes, etc. Some of the leaders in these agricultural efforts were the later Carters. It is possible that they got their first ideas on the subject from the books mentioned here.

Another book in Carter's library was directly valuable to a gentleman establishing himself in the wilderness. It was an unidentified work on architecture. One would like to know whether it was some version of the works of Vitruvius, the Roman architect whose theories did so much to modify architectural design, particularly in the seventeenth century.

Of schoolbooks surprisingly few are listed, and no Latin textbooks are recorded, though the will of John Carter II mentioned the bequest of all his law and Latin books to his brother Robert.[7] Perhaps, by the time of his death, the textbooks had been passed on to his brother or other relatives who had greater need for them. Either John Carter II or his father was determined that Greek should not die out at Corotoman, for, in addition to the Greek New Testament previously mentioned, the library contained "An English Greek Lexicon" and Eilhard Lubin's *Clavis Graecae linguae* (1620), a guide to the learning of the Greek language. There also remained "Spanish and French Dialogues," "A Spanish and English Dictionary," James Howell's *French-English Dictionary* (1650), based on dictionaries compiled by Randle Cotgrave and Robert Sherwood, Noah Bridges' *Vulgar Arithmetic* (1653), and Thomas Spencer's *Art of Logic* (1628). The last-named book acquainted Virginia students with the Ramean attack on Aristotle, which stirred the seventeenth century profoundly. The library contained two of the best English dictionaries then available, Thomas Blount's *Glossographia* (2d ed., 1661) and Edward Phillips' *New World of English Words* (1658).

One instructive book, useful in the education of a gentleman, was King James I's *Basilikon Doron* (1603), devised for the instruction of his son, Prince Henry. This little volume, which was widely read by seventeenth-century Americans, even in Puritan New England, suggested ideals of conduct

[7] *The Virginia Magazine of History and Biography*, II, 237.

congenial to a Royalist planter of Virginia. Among many other pieces of practical advice, the treatise urged a youth of gentle blood to be versed in history and to be well acquainted with all the liberal arts and sciences, but only as an amateur, not as a "passe-maister," lest too much concentration upon learned matters distract him from his calling as a member of the governing group. With few exceptions, the best of the ruling class of Virginia in the late seventeenth and early eighteenth centuries exemplified that practice.

To fulfil the injunction in *Basilikon Doron* to read history, John Carter II had less than a half dozen titles. One would have expected more. The sole representative of recent English history consisted of the first three parts of John Rushworth's *Historical Collections* (1659-80). If his political observations gave recent history with too much Puritan bias, there is no evidence that Carter tried to correct the impression with any other historical work. An offset, however, to any taint of parliamentary prejudice that might have come from reading Rushworth was provided by *Eikon Basilike: The Portraiture of His Sacred Majesty in His Solitudes and Sufferings* (1649).

The only additional historical works in the Carter library were Josephus' *History of the Jews*, probably in Thomas Lodge's early seventeenth-century translation, and Plutarch's *Lives*, almost certainly in Sir Thomas North's version. Every man who wanted to be intelligent about Old Testament matters felt that he ought to own Josephus' *History;* an acquaintance with Plutarch was already considered desirable in the gentleman's education. No such good reason explains the other biographical work, a book describing notable examples of a certain variety of sinners—John Reynolds' *Triumphs of God's Revenge against . . . Murder* (1621-24). Surprisingly enough, Sir Richard Baker's *Chronicle of the Kings of England* (1643), a volume which seventeenth-century satirists pictured on the parlor table of every English squire, was absent.

One other book, faintly historical, occupying a place between history and belles-lettres, found its way into the Carter library. It was James Howell's *Dodona's Grove; or, The Vocal Forest* (1640), a prose allegory designating England, Scotland, Wales, Ireland, and several continental countries under fanciful names and describing political events of recent interest. The story emphasizes the fiasco resulting from James I's scheme for a Spanish marriage of Prince Charles, and touches on the Gunpowder Plot, the Overbury murder, the assassination of Buckingham, and other fairly recent events.

Three romances were the only books that could be described as belonging to modern belles-lettres. They were English translations of *Cassandra* and *Cleopatra* by La Calprenède, and *The Countess of Montgomery's Urania* (1621) by Lady Mary Wroth, Sir Philip Sidney's niece. All three recount fantastic adventures in some unreal opera land, Lady Mary's novel being written in imitation of Sidney's *Arcadia*.

Of classical authors, in addition to Aelian and Plutarch, previously mentioned, Carter had Homer's *Iliad*, probably in George Chapman's translation, published complete in 1611; Virgil's *Works*, translated by John Ogilby and published in 1649; and Ovid's *Historical Epistles*, in one of the several English versions of the period.[8]

From the late years of the seventeenth century until his death, in 1732, at the age of sixty-nine, Robert Carter, known by the sobriquet of "King" Carter, was the richest and one of the most influential men in Virginia. After the death of his elder brother, he came into possession of Corotoman, where he maintained a family seat that rivaled the splendor of many an English noble's estate. But Corotoman was only the chief

[8] In 1700 the Duke of Bedford's library at Woburn contained only "one hundred and fifty-two books, including manuscript volumes." Most lesser English gentlemen had fewer books. See Gladys Scott Thomson, *Life in a Noble Household, 1641-1700* (London, 1937), pp. 262-79.

manor, the center and heart of the great man's possessions. Other vast areas were acquired as plantations for his twelve children, and when King Carter died he left, according to a contemporary account, "about 300,000 acres of land, about 1000 negroes and £10,000 in money."[9] In the enormous array of personal property inventoried at his death, a library of more than two hundred and sixty titles was enumerated.[10] This collection of books, which included the best law library in the American colonies at that time—with perhaps the exception of the one then being gathered by William Byrd II at Westover[11]—gives a valuable clue to the intellectual interests of a Virginia grandee at the end of the seventeenth and the beginning of the eighteenth century.

Most of the coveted offices in the colony of Virginia were held at some time by King Carter. In 1691-92, at the age of twenty-eight, he was a member of the House of Burgesses; in 1696 and 1699 he was speaker of the House; in 1699 he became a member of the Council; and for the rest of his life he was one of that small body of men who ruled Virginia. During his first six years in the Council, he was colonial treasurer, and during his last six years he was president of the Council. As the leading citizen of the Northern Neck, he was colonel and commander in chief of Lancaster and Northumberland counties and naval officer of the Rappahannock River

[9] *The Virginia Magazine of History and Biography*, XXXII (1924), 19.

[10] See *ibid.*, VI (1898-99), 145-52, 260-68, for the inventory of King Carter's personal property, including his books, which are listed by abbreviated titles. Some of the titles are so fragmentary that it has been impossible to identify them.

[11] Charles Warren, *A History of the American Bar* (Cambridge, 1912), p. 7: "Even in England at the end of the seventeenth century, hardly more than seventy law books had been published, of which not more than ten or fifteen were known in the colonies, and less than one hundred volumes of law reports, of which not over thirty were in use in the colonies." This statement needs modification, but it serves to emphasize the importance of Carter's library. Warren points out (p. 162) that the largest colonial library "in the middle of the eighteenth century, that of William Byrd the younger, in Virginia, contained only 350 volumes of law and statutes out of a total of 3625."

district. But the office which enabled him to grow rich in lands was that of agent for the Fairfaxes, the noble family who held by royal patent the proprietorship of all the Northern Neck region. This post Carter held for two terms, 1702-11 and 1722-32. During those years he laid the foundation of one of the most important family dynasties in colonial America —a foundation of immense plantations that made his sons fine gentlemen beyond the most extravagant dreams of the first settlers.

Undoubtedly King Carter consciously sought to imitate the best of the English gentry. His early training was designed to make him follow the tradition. As we have seen, his father was determined that he should have a classical education, even if an indentured servant able to teach Latin had to be purchased. In his youth Robert spent six years in England, where he was sent in care of a merchant, a certain "old Mr. Baily." [12] What school he attended is unknown. Somewhere he learned that it was not enough merely to be rich and to exercise political power. An aristocrat, especially an aristocrat in a new country, had an obligation to encourage the things of the mind and spirit. And, if King Carter sinned grievously in exalting his pride instead of piety, he nevertheless rebuilt Christ Church at his own cost, with a grand avenue connecting Corotoman with the house of God. There the lord of the manor had a magnificent pew for himself and his family, and he decreed that one-fourth of the remaining pews should be reserved for his tenants and servants.[13] Following English

[12] In the manuscript Letter Book of Robert Carter in the Huntington Library (Brock Collection, Fairfax Papers, Box 1) there is a letter to William Dawkins, dated July 14, 1720, in which Carter complains of his own sons' expenses. In conclusion he says: "The world is strangely altered sure since I was young. I lived with old Mr. Baily six years. I never stood my brother in £30 in any one year of the time." See also *The Virginia Magazine of History and Biography*, XXXII, 18.

[13] Henry Irving Brock, *Colonial Churches in Virginia* (Richmond, 1930), p. 46; Bishop William Meade, *Old Churches, Ministers, and Families of Virginia* (2 vols., Philadelphia, 1857), II, 116-21.

precedent, he kept the disposition of the living of Christ Church in his own hands. He also took time from the materialistic architecture of his fortune to serve as trustee, member of the board of visitors, and rector of the College of William and Mary. If he remembered English custom, he recalled that only great lords became chancellors of the universities, and he saw himself as the Virginia counterpart of a university chancellor while serving as rector of the college at Williamsburg.

He founded a scholarship at William and Mary and lived to see more of his descendants enrolled in the college than came from any other family in Virginia.[14] First among his claims to honor, as recorded in his high-flown Latin epitaph, was the statement that as "Rector of William and Mary, he sustained that institution in its most trying times."[15] King Carter would have liked that tribute; he may have composed it himself.

The reverence in which the lord of Corotoman held the classical discipline made him send his five sons to England for an education. In a letter dated January 28, 1724, to William Dawkins, one of his agents in London, Carter expressed some displeasure at the failure of his son Landon's schoolmaster, one Solomon Low, to follow the older methods of teaching Latin. This letter reveals the Virginian's eagerness to perpetuate the sort of learning that conservative Englishmen had found desirable:

> I could wish Mr. Low had kept in the old way of teaching the Latin tongue and had made my boys perfect in their understanding of Lily's *Grammar* and of the old school books that we and our forefathers learned. There is one book which did me the most service of any that I was acquainted with, to-wit: the *Janua Linguarum Trilinguis* in Latin, English, and Greek, writ by John

[14] Fairfax Harrison, "The Will of Charles Carter of Cleve," *The Virginia Magazine of History and Biography*, XXXI (1923), 40-41, in a note on King Carter.

[15] Meade, *op. cit.*, II, 122.

> Comenius, the best stock of Latin words and in the best sense to suit the genius of boys, even to their manhood, of any book that ever I met with in my life; it is so very much in my esteem that I would desire you to give positive directions to Mr. Low that my son Landon be made a perfect master of this book in all the three languages, that he may be so perfect to be able with his eye upon one of the languages to repeat the others. 'Tis so pretty a compendium of all the arts and sciences and writ in so handsome a style to captivate the genius of youth that I resolve to be pleased in this matter and am so much fixed in it that if Mr. Low will not answer my desire I will have my boy removed to another school and I think if he is, the next place shall be Eton, whither Lewis Burwell is gone. Mr. Low's school is valuable upon the good and orderly government of it, the care he takes of boys' morals, but if they do not meet with a thorough improvement in their learning, such as will stick by them and be useful to them in their riper years, all our cost is thrown away and the greatest part of their work is to be done after they have left the school. It is not reading a few scraps from the poets and the other classics that make boys understand the scope and design of the authors. I have had so good a character of the genius of Landon in his aptness to take learning as well as of the strength of his memory that I have reason to think if he falls into good hands he may be an absolute master of the languages before he arrives to 18 years of age; he is a younger brother; I would make learning a part of his portion, which is all I shall say concerning him at present, leaving the rest to your kind care and consideration.[16]

From the classics, Carter expected his sons to acquire something more than tags of poetry. In the wisdom of the ancients was to be found a way of life suitable for young Virginians to imitate.

The bringing up of his children in learning, good manners, and godliness was constantly on Robert Carter's mind. His correspondence is full of admonitions to them to use their time profitably. As a practical man of affairs he was also concerned

[16] Letter quoted from note in Harrison's "The Will of Charles Carter of Cleve," *loc. cit.*

that they realize the value of money. To William Dawkins, who was intrusted with the direction of his children's education in England, he wrote long and earnestly—and sometimes wrathfully—about their progress. A letter to another correspondent, Richard Perry, on July 13, 1720, thanked him for a good report of his sons, for "to have spent so much money upon a dunce or a blockhead had been most intolerable." Even in the education of his boys he wanted "a pennyworth for my penny." [17] On the same date Carter wrote his son John, reproving him for his large expenses and urging frugality. John, it seems, had complained that one of the Randolphs was wearing finer clothes than he and had done him some disservice. To this the father replied that he had bandied no words with young Randolph, who had never appeared in Virginia in finer clothes than a Carter, and that to his mind the youth was a "rank Tory, a proud, humble parasite, a fawning sycophant to his patron, with all the other requisites to a servile courtier"; in short, he writes, Randolph's qualities are "as much reverse to my nature as white is to black" [18]—a statement that may suggest something of Carter's own qualities.

Carter's desire that his sons be brought up in the Established Church is clear from a letter to Dawkins on July 14, 1720. Very significantly, he expresses his disapproval of High Church tendencies and emphasizes his concern for a practical religion. His words epitomize the development of the Virginia church, which had become something of a disgrace in the minds of certain prelates in England. "The health of my sons and their improvement in learning and manners is one of the greatest blessings I can meet with in this world," the planter writes. "Let others take what courses they please in bringing up their posterity, I resolve the principles of our holy religion shall be instilled into mine betimes; as I am of the Church of England

[17] Huntington MSS, Fairfax Papers, Box 1.
[18] *Ibid.*

way, so I desire they should be; but the highflown up top notions and the great stress that is laid upon ceremonies, any farther than decency and conformity, is what I cannot come into the reason of. Practical godliness is the substance; these are but the shell."[19] Although he has no patience with High Church ritualism, he stands for conformity and "decency" of observances. In Carter's letters there are many expressions of piety and a genuine interest in religion—a quality that previous accounts of this somewhat haughty aristocrat have neglected to point out.

For all his practical religion, the great man of Corotoman was not beyond violent rages in which pride and arrogance showed themselves. When poor William Dawkins made the mistake of paying £20 for a pair of earrings for one of Carter's daughters, the planter flew into a fit. What particularly annoyed him was that Dawkins had deigned to say banteringly that he had taken a certain Mrs. Heath to be a pattern in purchasing the earrings on Carter's account. To this the Virginian replied that henceforth he would be obliged if Dawkins would let him be the master of his own money. Furthermore, he added, "you talk vainly to me of making Mrs. Heath my pattern; had I but one daughter and she the descendant of two successive muckworms, perhaps a parallel might not be improper. My circumstances are other ways. I must cut my coat according to my cloth, and bless God I am able to do so well as I do."[20] At Carter's letter Dawkins himself took offense, and made the further mistake of calling the irate writer to task for using so inelegant an expression as muckworm. Dawkins' reply gave Carter an opportunity to display his acquaintance with the sermon literature of the day, and to point out that his reference to muckworms was a literary allusion that Dawkins might have known had he been better read. So revealing is the letter that it is worth quoting at

[19] *Ibid.* [20] *Ibid.*, dated July 13, 1720.

length, for the writer lets himself go and vents several grievances against Dawkins:

The affair of my children is handled as if they were dependent upon your charity for their maintenance. What they have, I doubt not I shall pay for even to a farthing. You may believe when I committed them to your care, I had a respect to your friendship and an opinion of your prudence and expected you would be so far from counting it a trouble that you would look upon it as an obligation and a pledge of my friendship. Before I sent them, I consulted you what their maintenance might stand me in. You tell me you believed £40 per annum apiece (?). To put you in remembrance of this, forsooth must pass for unkindness, and wear the harsh name of bringing you under an obligation. Seeing you are a gentleman of such a tender, touchy, elevated nature that cannot endure a plain style and think me so much your debtor for the oversight you have of my children, I have taken care to ease you of that burden. My son hath orders from me to remove them to another person who will treat me and them with more civility. If you want not me, I shall let you know I want you as little. Do me but justice with the concern of mine you have in your hands, and I shall not value how soon I shut up all correspondency with you.

Your next paragraph is a note above Elah sure. You were then sitting in your master's chair of state, with your rope-makers and carmen about you, and looking upon me as one of your dependents and inferiors. I shall come a little to particulars. You had laid out my money upon several things much beyond my orders. Among the rest you had laid me out £20 extraordinary upon a pair of ear rings, and tell me in a way of banter, or rather tantalizing, Mrs. Heath had a pair cost a thousand pound. This brought in the word muckworm, which is so offensive to your nice stomach. I had not the least thought of throwing any reflection upon the memory of the dead nor the living. Neither doth the sentence carry any such import to my understanding, and if you want the skill to measure the force of words, you should keep a dictionary by you. But that you may have a true idea of the scope of the word muckworm, I shall recommend to your perusal the fifth part of Doctor Scott's *Christian Life*, where he's treating of the excellency of the soul;

there you'll find the signification of this word and how applicable it is to the best of us all. I knew Mr. Bayley, both father and son, better than you did. I lived in the family and have a very good respect for their memories, and have been often concerned in the vindication of their characters from aspersions that have been let fly at them, and yet after all, I think it no injury to them to say they were too much muckworms, that is, in other words, too great lovers of this world. And by the way, I wish both you and I were more mortified to it than we are. The thoughts of having a little more white and yellow earth than our neighbors would not puff us up with so much vanity and insolence, nor make us so uneasy when we meet with plain dealing. I have a great value for Mrs. Heath, both for her own sake and her father's, and if it lay in my way, I would requite her ten fold for any respects she has shown to my children, but let me tell you, I esteem her more for the ornaments of her mind, her humility, prudence, affability, piety, charity, than for the fine trappings of her person. These are but of short duration and will quite vanish away when a winding sheet comes to be her portion. But her virtues and graces will keep her company into the other world. We are but stewards of God's building: the more he lends us, the larger accounts he expects from us, and happy they that make a right use of their Master's talents.

Now pray upon the whole, where was your prudence, or rather manners, to use me with language that was hardly fit for your footman if you keep one. You might remember I was your master's equal and all along have lived in as good rank and fashion as he did, even when you were something like Graves' cabin boy, and am old enough to be your father, not to mention any more reasons that justly give me a title to your deference. I shall conclude with telling you that I resolve to live in a calm, quiet air the rest of my days and will be treated with respect by those that do my business. If you are so overgrown and tumified with the little success you have had in the world, I would have you vent your vanities upon those that are to be gainers by you and not upon

Your humble servant.[21]

[21] *Ibid.*, dated Feb. 23, 1720/21. Carter spells the name Bayley, as here, and also Baily.

By the same ship Carter wrote his son John to remove the children from Dawkins' house and place them in charge of a certain Thomas Evans, a man of "very gentlemanly behavior." The father had first thought of two honest merchants, Micajah Perry and his son, but had decided against intrusting his children to them, for "old Mr. Perry is too much a senior for such a business."

When gout had laid him low, shortly after these letters were dispatched, Robert Carter's wrath cooled. He then wrote John to see whether Dawkins seemed sorry for the affair, and if he appeared repentant to leave the children there. Dawkins was small of stature, Carter explained, and little men are prone to lose their tempers! Having discovered that he was sufficiently contrite, Carter forgot the incident and for years maintained the most cordial relations with this trusted agent.

The proper training of his posterity was a matter that Robert Carter, throughout his life, kept constantly before him. He wanted his sons to be worthy of their name and he took care that they should be amply provided with the land and wealth to maintain their dignity as gentlemen of one of the first families in the colony. His will, a long and complicated document, dated October 11, 1726, entailed immense tracts of land on his sons and provided liberally for his daughters.[22] Specific mention was made of the education of the younger sons, Landon and George. Landon was to be kept in school until he was seventeen and then "disposed of in such a manner as my executor, his brother [John] shall judge most conducive to his future well being." George was to remain at the College of William and Mary so long as his brothers thought fit.[23] Later, the father decided that George had in him the makings of a learned man; in a codicil to the will, dated June 9, 1730, he directed that after two more years

[22] See Harrison, *Landmarks*, I, 252-53. The will is reprinted in *The Virginia Magazine of History and Biography*, V (1897-98), 408-28; VI (1898-99), 1-22.

[23] *Ibid.*, V, 424.

George should be sent to the University of Cambridge, or, if his brothers thought best, to one of the Inns of Court.[24] A final alteration in his opinion concerning George's education—and universities in general—is evident in another codicil, dated July 23, 1730: "And whereas I have ordered my son George an university education, I have seen such bad effects of it that I leave the care of him to the disposal of his brothers, particularly my son John, and after a year's stay more at the College, if he thinks fit, to breed him up in the Secretary's office."[25] What had happened in the preceding month to change the testator's opinion of university education—or of George's prospects of profiting from it—is unknown.

In his attitude toward every aspect of life, Robert Carter is typical of the realistic, practical type of aristocrat that Virginia developed in the early generations of settlement. He and his group valued the tradition of gentility, and they were eager to perpetuate the usable elements of that tradition; but they were never fooled by romantic notions of aristocracy, and were unhampered by any suggestions of an aristocratic code that was obsolete or alien to the practical necessities of Virginia. For example, the code-consciousness and the fripperies of the French aristocracy of the period would have been dismissed by Robert Carter as nonsense. As he was constantly reiterating, he was a plain-dealing man, albeit one acutely class-conscious. But his class consciousness did not prevent his being an industrious and astute businessman, for shrewd oversight of his tobacco sales, his purchases of commodities or securities, his land transactions, and the multifarious details connected with his great plantations were a part of the responsibilities of his kind. His letters to his own sons drive home his ideas of what a Virginia youth should learn. Carter is extremely suspicious of the vanities of London, and writes John that he wishes he would "mind less the pleasures of the town"[26] and

[24] *Ibid.*, VI, 17. [25] *Ibid.*, p. 21.

[26] Huntington MSS, Fairfax Papers, Box 1; letter dated May 27, 1721.

stick closer to his duties. One of his worries about his wards, the sons of his friend Ralph Wormeley, was that they were learning foolish extravagance and acquiring vain notions in their English school.[27] The Virginia planter, aristocrat though he might be, was of necessity strongly imbued with qualities usually attributed to the bourgeoisie.

In an era of land-grabbing and land speculation, Carter's greed for real property exceeded that of most of his contemporaries. During his two long terms as agent for the proprietors of the Northern Neck, he had unusual opportunities for the acquisition of large tracts of virgin territory. But, though he granted himself and members of his family great acreages of proprietary lands, all was done legally, according to the custom of the times. The Fairfaxes' agent was careful about the legal aspects of his office, and he was anxious to avoid litigation. His letters contain frequent allusions to the desirability of staying out of the courts; perhaps his knowledge of the ins and outs of the law made him doubly anxious to steer clear of the tribulations that lawsuits invariably entailed. Even when necessity demanded recourse to the law, he always disliked it.

If this ruler of vast estates appears at times as an exacting man of business, he also had traits of kindness and magnanimity that indicate a social conscience. Concerning a lawsuit brought by an absentee landowner, one Mr. Cary, Carter comments: "If he recovers to the outermost [lines of the survey], it will be a very hard fate to several poor families whose ancestors before them have lived and died in quiet possession of these lands, and if Cary be a man of honor and circumstance—I believe if he were upon the spot—he would be contented to take his land without disturbing these poor

[27] See the excerpts from his letters concerning the Wormeley boys, in *The Virginia Magazine of History and Biography*, XXXVI (1928), 287-91; also the *William and Mary College Quarterly*, 1st Ser., XVII (1908-9), 252-64.

people."[28] When his own agent, William Dawkins, wanted someone to proceed against improvident Richard Lee III for the collection of a debt, Carter refused because he would not "go into harsh measures" against the son of an old and intimate friend.[29] He even regretted having to sue Edmund Jenings, whom he had no cause to love, because his affairs were desperate; indeed, he waited for positive orders from William Cage, the English trustee of the Fairfaxes, before taking "these harsh measures."[30] When too ill with the gout to ride his horse, he went in his coach to visit the sick slaves of his home quarters;[31] no doubt it was the part of self-interest to keep his slaves in good health, but the regard which he had for dependents displays genuine sympathy and humanity. In his will, for example, he provided against the separation of husband and wife in the division of slaves.[32] At his death he left a bequest of £40 to the poor of the parish and £10 to the minister.[33]

A part of Robert Carter's latter-day reputation for overbearing selfishness and greed has resulted from venomous remarks by his enemy, Governor Francis Nicholson.[34] Actually, from his correspondence, he appears a much more charitable person than he has been made out to be.

Something of King Carter's intellectual quality is revealed by the books at Corotoman, for, although part of them were inherited, the titles indicate many additions almost to the end of his life. The world of the intellect and the world of affairs beyond the confines of Virginia interested the planter. In a letter to Ralph Smith, a bookseller, dated February 14, 1720/21, he wrote:

> In the news-packets I have had from you for sometime, you have only sent me the *Mercuries*. You send to Colonel Page the *Evening*

[28] Huntington MSS, Fairfax Papers, Box 1; letter to John Carter, dated July 13, 1720. [29] *Ibid.;* letter dated July 15, 1720.

[30] *Ibid.;* letter to William Cage, dated July 4, 1723.

[31] *Ibid.;* no addressee except "Honorable Sir"; letter dated Mar. 3, 1720/21.

[32] *The Virginia Magazine of History and Biography*, V, 419, 420.

[33] *Ibid.*, VI, 7. [34] *Ibid.*, VIII (1900-1901), 55-56, 136-38.

> *Post* and the *Quarterly Register*, published at the charge of the Fire Office. These two papers I desire you will let me have for the future, and what ingenious pamphlets you think worth reading. I am told *Queen Anne's Reign* is in print. If it be, pray let me have it. Doctor Scott's *Works*, they say are printed all together in a large volume, which I would also have, and Doctor Wellwood's *Memoirs or Secret History*. I would likewise have Bohun's *Precedents of Proceedings in Parliament* if I have not forgot the name and title of the book. These books Mr. Perry will take care to pay you for and convey to me.[35]

The library at Corotoman obviously represented not only the sort of collection a gentleman thought he ought to have, but was also of practical value for the planter and his household.

Over one-third of the Corotoman library, or approximately one hundred titles, were lawbooks, comprising a selection of legal works designed to provide an adequate knowledge of the background and practice of English law. Since professional lawyers were few and frequently of low repute in the colonies,[36] even till past the middle of the eighteenth century, the better-educated Virginia planters had to conduct their own and their less capable neighbors' legal business. As agent for the proprietors of the Northern Neck, and as a great landowner in his own right, Robert Carter was in peculiar need of a knowledge of the law. Although there is no evidence that he ever received any formal legal training, he acquired sufficient skill to carry on his business with unusual shrewdness. Without doubt his library provided the answer to many a tough legal question which he had to argue in the Virginia courts, for here were to be found most of the standard works then available on the common law, on chancery law, and on the law merchant. If the common law of England had greater prestige and authority in colonial Virginia than it had in New England,[37] this may have been a result of the legal learning exemplified

[35] Huntington MSS, Fairfax Papers, Box 1.

[36] Warren, *op. cit.*, pp. 7-9, 39 ff.

[37] *Ibid.*, pp. 10-15, 39-41.

in the books owned and used by such leaders as Robert Carter.

Although a few of the titles of the lawbooks are so fragmentary that they cannot be identified and dated, about thirty were certainly works in print before 1650; approximately fifty were first published between 1650 and 1700; and twenty were brought out in the next three decades. Probably Robert Carter inherited some of these books, but most of them were works that he himself bought. Clearly he had an interest in maintaining a good working library of lawbooks, and he did his best to keep it up to date. A few of the works treated the historical development of the common law and provided some conception of the philosophy of English law, but in the main they were concerned with legal procedure, practice, and precedent. King Carter's neighbors could find at Corotoman a fairly ample supply of manuals, reports, and books of statutes. But, since many of the older works were written in Latin or Norman-French, not every planter could make use of them—a situation which helped keep the practice of law in the hands of the better-educated members of the upper class.[38]

The books for the period before 1650 show a careful selection with a view to the needs that any Virginia gentleman might encounter. Among the early works are relatively simple introductions to the study of law, such as the guides written by William Fulbecke and Sir Henry Finch, the latter's discourse on the law being regarded as one of the best elementary texts before the publication of Blackstone's commentaries. The library contained two manuals that most conscientious country gentlemen of England felt they needed, and usually owned: Michael Dalton's famous treatises on the duties of the justice of the peace and the sheriff. Models for drawing up legal instruments were supplied by a well-known manual compiled by William West and entitled *Symboleography* (1603). Mat-

[38] *Ibid.*, p. 22. Parliament in 1649 first required English to be used in legal works and proceedings.

ters pertaining to the civil law were explained in Henry Swinburne's treatise on wills, a work of particular utility because it was written in language simple enough for the ordinary understanding.[39] These and similar guides of the previous age were still being used by Virginians of Carter's period, as they were likewise used for generations by country justices in England.

Among the library's expositions of the common law were some of the best works to be had in the sixteenth and early seventeenth centuries. The oldest books in point of composition were two treatises of medieval law—one by an author generally referred to as Henry de Bracton, on the laws and customs of England (a work described as "the crown and flower" of medieval English jurisprudence), and the other work simply designated "Britton," from the supposed name of the mythological compiler.[40] Also available were Sir Anthony Fitzherbert's *Abridgment*, the first monumental epitome of case law; his *New Natura Brevium*, a highly praised treatise on writs; Sir Robert Brook's *Abridgment* (1573), a work of larger compass than Fitzherbert's, citing more than twenty thousand cases; Edmund Plowden's *Commentaries* (1571), outstanding among law reports of that period, and containing useful expositions by the compiler; a legal treatise by John Perkins, recommended in the title as a "profitable book"—so profitable, indeed, that it was printed at intervals from 1530 until 1827;

[39] In an epistle to the reader, of *A Brief Treatise of Testaments and Last Wills* (1590), Swinburne avows that he wrote his book "To this ende and purpose especially, that euerie subiect of this realme, though he be but of meane capacitie, may with little labour, and lesse charge, take a sensible view (as in a glasse) of those Ciuill and Ecclesiasticall lawes testamentarie now in force." Furthermore, he translated it into English, "preferring publique commoditie before particular vtilitie." To planters on the Rappahannock, anxious over their wills, this consideration must have been grateful.

[40] See Percy H. Winfield, *The Chief Sources of English Legal History* (Cambridge, Mass., 1925), pp. 258-64. Bracton's name was really Henry of Bratton, but he is known in legal history by the first appellation. His work was compiled between 1250 and 1258.

Sir John Fortescue's *Learned Commendation of the Politic Laws of England* (1567),[41] a patriotic eulogy of the common law, with many interesting digressions—a very popular work, remarkable because of its readability; and the dictionary of legal terms compiled in Norman-French and English by John Rastell, about 1525, and often reprinted.

Some of the statutes printed before 1650 were in the library, as well as two works, likewise published before that date, giving the transactions of the court of chancery. Strangely, the *Reports* compiled by Edward Coke, the best legal reporter of the early seventeenth century, is lacking, but his *Institutes*, a monumental exposition of the common law,[42] was there. Carter also had Coke's commentary on Sir Thomas Littleton's *Tenures*, which included a reprint of the text. Littleton's *Tenures* was a widely used compilation of the law governing real property—a document which Coke himself described as an "ornament of the common law, and the most perfect and absolute work that ever was written in any human science." [43] The absence of Coke's original *Reports* is the most serious gap in Carter's collection of early legal books—a collection that is otherwise noteworthy among colonial libraries for its comprehensiveness.

One more of the earlier books deserves mention. This is a treatise on the law merchant, by Gerard de Malynes, first published in 1622. Since there were few good works on the international aspects of mercantile law, Robert Carter and his fellow Virginia planters concerned with shipping and other widely scattered business dealings must have found many helpful suggestions in Malynes' little volume.

The books in the Corotoman library that were printed between 1650 and 1700 indicate much the same legal interest

[41] Fortescue's book was first written, in Latin, between 1463 and 1471. For a brief analysis, see Winfield, *op. cit.*, pp. 316-17.

[42] See Winfield, *op. cit.*, pp. 333-37.

[43] Quoted by Winfield, p. 309.

as the earlier volumes. Reports are more numerous, as would be expected from the development in the reporting of case law after Sir Edward Coke's time; the number of manuals is larger; and there are some of the best discussions, for that period, of the basis of English common law.

Although Coke's original *Reports* was lacking among the earlier lawbooks, the library had a later abridgment, probably the widely used one compiled by Sir Thomas Ireland. The work of Coke's predecessor in reporting, Sir James Dyer, was also available in an abridgment. Eighteen other compilations gave the library a respectable collection of reports, though it lacked William Sheppard's encyclopedic *Epitome* of the common and statute laws.[44] Statute law was supplied, however, by Edmund Wingate's *Abridgment* (1655) and four additional compilations. There was also William Rawlin's *Laws of Barbados* (1699), a helpful work for a Virginia planter doing business in the Caribbean.

Over a dozen manuals published in the second half of the seventeenth century provided information on special problems in the practice of law. If Michael Dalton's old guide for the justice of the peace was still not obsolete, at least a newer book was also there—William Sheppard's *Whole Office of the Country Justice of Peace* (1652). Furthermore, there were several "Clerk's Guides," "Complete Attorneys," and similar handbooks providing practical aid. Henry Swinburne's earlier book on wills was supplemented now by John Godolphin's *Orphan's Legacy* (1674), expounding the law as it affected wills and testaments, executors and administrators, legacies and devises. Virginia planters, eager to establish their families properly and to keep out of lawsuits, must have prized a book of that sort.

Expositions of the common law were supplied by several

[44] See John D. Cowley, *A Bibliography of Abridgments, Digests, Dictionaries, and Indexes of English Law to the Year 1800* (Selden Society; London, 1932), p. lii.

notable works of the period. Two books by Edmund Wingate, *The Body of the Common Law* (1655) and *Maxims* (1658), provided not only the substance but the theoretical explanation of this field of English jurisprudence. A treatise, by George Dawson, on the origin of the laws of England also helped to give a philosophic understanding of the growth of legal institutions. Two essays by John Selden, written earlier but brought out in Carter's time in versions owned by him, discussed the laws and customs of the Britons, Saxons, and Norsemen, and gave a reasoned comment on constitutional development.

A knowledge of certain phases of the law merchant and of other elements of international law was obtainable in Charles Molloy's *De Jure Maritimo et Navali; or, A Treatise of Affairs Maritime and of Commerce* (1676), which has a chapter "Of Planters," dealing with international law respecting colonization—a subject naturally of concern to the Virginians.

A few miscellaneous works of legal interest date from this period. A critique of several recent trials, written by Sir John Hawles, was of some interest to legally and politically minded Virginians; and, if an account of an early victim of the Popish Plot, in the *Trial of William Staley, Goldsmith, for Speaking Treasonable Words against His Most Sacred Majesty* (1678), impresses a modern reader as a description of a miscarriage of justice, it was probably interpreted by royalistic Virginians as a warning to seditious folk. As sometime rector of the College of William and Mary, Robert Carter found enlightening facts in James Harrington's *Defense of the Rights and Privileges of the University of Oxford* (1690).

The latest lawbooks in King Carter's library, those printed after 1700, consist largely of reports, but there were also listed two recent abridgments of the common law, a new book on estates, and several miscellaneous works. William Bohun's *Institutio Legalis; or, An Introduction to the Study and Prac-*

tice of the Laws of England (1708-9), one of the important books of the period, furnished instruction in the scholarly approach to English jurisprudence. Some explanation of constitutional development in England was provided by the same author's reports of debates in Parliament dealing with the election of members. Two compilations made after 1700 supply information about colonial laws: an *Abridgment of the Laws in Force and Use in Her Majesty's Plantations* (1704) and a collection of the laws of Massachusetts. These two works, and an earlier work on the laws of Barbados (already mentioned), were the only treatments of colonial law included in the Corotoman library. That Robert Carter was scantily provided with texts of colonial laws was not his fault, for the colonies were dilatory about publishing their statutes. Not until 1733, the year after the planter of Corotoman died, did Virginia bring out a definitive official collection of its laws.[45]

A professional lawyer, experienced in the practice of English courts, would have discovered many gaps in the library of Robert Carter, but a Virginia planter probably found this collection more than adequate for his needs. Not merely did the library supply the necessary works for the utilitarian practice of law, but it also contained books which taught the reader the continuity of English legal tradition and the development of the constitutional form of government. The ideas implicit in the legal books in Robert Carter's library were full of significance for the future growth of American political thought. If we cannot estimate the influence of such reading upon our colonial ancestors, at least we know that the sources of many ideas that later developed more fully can be found in these volumes.

It would have been more than strange if Robert Carter, a member of the governing Council and a holder of other important offices, had not been interested in the theory of gov-

[45] Warren, *op. cit.*, p. 161.

ernment. An indication that he and his family had some concern for political theory is suggested by several books, in addition to legal works, that have to do with questions of government and the state. Royalist though he was, he owned copies of the *Sovereign Power of Parliaments and Kingdoms* (1643) by William Prynne, the parliamentarian lawyer, and *Discourses Concerning Government* (1698) by Algernon Sidney, the republican. He also owned Nathaniel Bacon's *Historical and Political Discourse of the Laws and Government of England* (1689), a discussion of constitutional history "pervaded by a strong spirit of hostility to the claims of the royal prerogatives and to hierarchical pretensions."[46] But, if any radical ideas were engendered by these treatises, Carter had as an antidote Sir Robert Filmer's *Observations Concerning the Original of Government* (1652), a Royalist work arguing for the patriarchal origin of government—a book, however, unflatteringly described by John Locke as "glib nonsense." Realistic political advice, of a sort appealing to a politician of Carter's type, was supplied by Machiavelli's *Works* and by a Spanish treatise, Bartolome Felippe's *Tractado del conseio y de los conseieros de los principes* (1589). A passage in the last-named book urges the retirement of a ruler's advisers at the age of sixty and almost anticipates recent arguments for early retirement of Supreme Court justices. Additional political and worldly wisdom was contained in Sir Robert Dallington's *Aphorisms, Civil and Military* (1613), chiefly based on Francesco Guicciardini's maxims of state.

Since the instructive quality of historical reading was so highly regarded that almost every treatise on the education of the gentleman prescribed its study, one is not surprised to find forty titles of historical and biographical works in the library. These ranged from ancient history to the best of contemporary books.

[46] *Dictionary of National Biography, sub* Bacon.

Greek and Roman historical writers were represented by works in translation. Great as was Carter's own respect for Latin, he seems to have preferred even Caesar's *Commentaries* in an English version.[47]

Looking back from our vantage point in time, we might surmise that certain ideas of liberty were suggested to colonial Americans by their classical reading. For example, one might easily insist that Virginians who read Carter's copy of Cornelius Nepos' *Lives of Illustrious Men* (1684) were stirred by these biographies of Greek, Carthaginian, and Persian patriots, that the germ of Patrick Henry's later oratorical patriotism could be found in such reading. But this would be mere speculation. All we can say is that, in pondering the antiquities of Greece and Rome, seventeenth- and early-eighteenth-century Virginia leaders followed the fashion of the age, and that classical learning is later evident in their oratory and political writings. Plutarch's *Lives*, the historical works of Tacitus, Josephus' *History of the Jews*, Humphrey Prideaux' *Old and New Testament Connected in the History of the Jews and Neighboring Nations* (1716-18), and Laurence Echard's *Roman History* (1698-99) comprised the rest of a collection of ancient histories sufficient for any educated gentleman of that day, either in Virginia or England.

English history, ancient and modern, was amply represented at Corotoman. The antiquities of Britain could be studied in William Camden's renowned *Britannia* (1586) and in *Cottoni posthuma* (1651), a series of antiquarian essays by Sir Robert Bruce Cotton. Although old-fashioned chronicle history could be read in Sir Richard Baker's *Chronicle of the Kings of England* (1643), most of the English histories were of the newer sort, and many were concerned with relatively modern events. Sir William Temple, who seems to have been one of

[47] The inventory lists titles by a catchword on the title-page. Books in a foreign language are given with a foreign catchword. The Greek and Roman works here cited are listed in English and hence were probably translations.

Carter's favorite authors, supplied an interpretation of British tradition down through the Norman conquest, in his *Introduction to the History of England* (1695), a work which laments the poverty of previous English histories. Temple is careful to emphasize the sterling virtues of the ancient Saxons —a thesis that became popular with Americans. Events of contemporary history in which Temple had a part were chronicled in Temple's *Letters*, his *Memoirs*, and the *Life and Character of Sir William Temple, Written by a Particular Friend* (1728).

Histories describing the events of the Puritan Revolution in England, from Puritan and Royalist points of view, stood beside each other, with calm impartiality, on the Corotoman shelves. John Rushworth's *Historical Collections*, Bulstrode Whitelock's *Memorials of the English Affairs* (1682), and the *Memoirs of Edmund Ludlow* (1698-99) presented the parliamentary side; while the Earl of Clarendon's *History of the Rebellion* (1702-4) and Sir Edward Walker's *Historical Discourses* (1705) supplied historical information and opinion pleasing to the stoutest Tory. Walker's book, principally about King Charles I "of ever blessed memory," as the title-page piously observes, was a gathering of the Royalist author's essays. Bishop Gilbert Burnet's *History of His Own Time* (1724) and the *History of the Reformation* (1679-1715) gave a somewhat Whiggish interpretation to modern English history. James Wellwood's *Memoirs . . . for the Last Hundred Years Preceding the Revolution of 1688* (1700) had an initial chapter of "The excellencies of the English Constitution, and the various changes that have happened in it"—a matter of some interest to colonial settlers establishing a government in a new country.

More recent history brought the story of English affairs down to Carter's own time. The court of Queen Anne seems particularly to have interested him, for he had two lives of the Queen. He also owned the *Complete History of England* compiled by Bishop White Kennet and others and published in an expensive three-volume folio edition in 1706. More expensive still was a fifteen-volume *History of England* (1725-31), written by Paul de Rapin-Thoyras in French and translated by Nicholas Tindal. As in some of the other histories of the period, interest in the growth of the English form of government is indicated—in this case, by a section, in the preface, on the "Origin and Nature of the English Constitution." Virginia leaders did not lack information about this important element in our common background.

For the history of the rest of the world, Carter had to depend upon a half dozen books: a universal history in Latin, an anonymous general history of Europe, two histories by Samuel Pufendorf covering the rest of the world, including America, Thomas Fuller's Protestant account of the Crusades in his *History of the Holy War* (1639), and a report by John Freind of Peterborough's fairly recent campaign in Spain. With the exception of a section in one of Pufendorf's works, the only other book about the New World even faintly historical was A. O. Exquemelin's *Buccaneers of America* (1684). If this seems strange we should remember that Virginia gentlemen were still Englishmen living in the colonies and not yet Americans consciously curious about the past of their nation.

A half dozen other titles more or less concerned with historical events completed Carter's history library. Among these books were the *Eikon Basilike* (1649), the pseudo-autobiography of Charles I; John Toland's *Amyntor* (1699), which refuted King Charles's authorship of *Eikon Basilike;* and a life of the Earl of Shaftesbury.

The influence of historical works, especially English histories, upon colonial leaders who were setting the social and intellectual patterns of the new country was particularly important. Though they felt at times that their land was an outpost —sometimes a lonely outpost—of English civilization, they never forgot that they belonged to a tradition that stretched into the dim past. Even when economic and political events caused a break with the mother country, the new nation still felt that it had a part in the common heritage. The reading of histories like those in the library at Corotoman was a constant reminder to colonial Americans of the continuity of this inheritance.

Of religious books a collection that would have been a credit to a minister of the gospel graced the library at Corotoman. In all there were fifty-five titles, some of them in several volumes, ranging from the Bible and the prayer book to religious allegory. Fifteen of these books concern controversies of one sort and another; eleven are works of devotion or Christian ethics; seven are collections of sermons; six deal with theology and Christian philosophy; and there are a few of a miscellaneous nature. Some were written by Anglicans, others by Puritan preachers.

To what extent these pious works represent the personal interest of the Carter household we can only guess, but Robert Carter's letters prove that he read his religious books and remembered them well enough to quote them aptly. It is conventional to consider the so-called Cavaliers of Virginia a worldly group of materialistic aristocrats, as undoubtedly they were; and by modern standards they were not the sort of people to indulge in profound religious study. But we should not forget that the age of faith was sufficiently close to leave men of that period—even the most materialistic of them—with a respect for religion. The country gentlemen of Virginia, furthermore, were expected to set a standard for the community, to assume a moral as well as a political leadership. In their eyes the church, with all it stood for, was still something to be supported and defended. Religious books were therefore a necessary part of every gentleman's library, and we need not be surprised that Robert Carter, who had handsomely rebuilt Christ Church at his own expense, should have one of the best religious libraries in the colony.

Since the clergymen of the country were usually poor men who could afford few books, the libraries of the planters often took the place of a parish library. To all intents and purposes the rector of Christ Church was the chaplain of the great manor of Corotoman, whose library supplied his professional needs.

The controversial books in the Carter library were not concerned with fine points of theological reasoning but with recent disputes about the prerogatives of the Church of England. Matthew Tindal, who styled himself a "Christian deist," in 1706 wrote a pamphlet, entitled *The Rights of the Christian Church Asserted*, that attacked the High Church position. His treatise provoked a number of replies in support of the privileges of the Anglican Establishment. Robert Carter, as a defender of the Church in Virginia, naturally was interested in the problem, and we find in his library Tindal's provocative essay and replies by William Wotton, George Hickes, Samuel Hill, and John Turner, all of whom were careful to point out the wickedness of Tindal's deistic and unchristian views.

Another controversy, over the problem of conformity, interested Carter so much that he bought the books pertaining to it. Edmund Calamy, in his abridgment of the life of Richard Baxter, published in 1702, took occasion in one chapter to argue against the necessity of conformity. When his position was attacked, he replied with a *Defence of Moderate Nonconformity*. One of those who attempted to rebuke Calamy was Benjamin Hoadly, Bishop of Bangor. Carter had the relevant works of both Calamy and Hoadly—an apparent indication of a desire to know both sides of a then famous quarrel. Moreover, he had one of Hoadly's later pamphlets, *An Answer to . . . the Committee of the Lower House* (1718), containing a statement of Hoadly's views after he had made a complete about-face and had become a Whig and an extreme latitudinarian.

Robert Carter, for all his high-and-mighty notions about other things, was a moderate in church polity, for it was well-nigh impossible for an isolated Virginia parish church to maintain the forms and rituals of high Anglicanism, and Carter had the common sense to know that the Established Church in Virginia of necessity had to adapt itself to frontier conditions. But clearly, from his books on the subject, he regarded this problem as one deserving careful attention.

Carter had practically no books of strictly theological controversy. In this connection, it might be well to reiterate that the interest in theological dogma, as such, was far less widespread in the seventeenth and early eighteenth centuries than is generally supposed. A book confuting the papists, and one of Edward Stillingfleet's treatises defending the doctrine of the Trinity against a supposed attack by John Locke, were practically the only other controversial works, aside from incidental allusions in sermons and similar writings.

Like scores of other colonial Americans, both Puritan and Anglican, Carter had one of the numerous collected editions of the sermons and essays of William Perkins, perhaps the most popular Puritan preacher of the late sixteenth century. Since Perkins taught a "practical" theology, or common sense applied to ethical and religious problems of everyday life, his sermons were naturally regarded with favor by colonial readers. The influence of Perkins' ideas upon American conceptions of morality, and even of business practice, is a theme for a separate study.

The remaining collections of sermons were by Anglicans of the late seventeenth or early eighteenth century. Fifteen volumes of the sermons of John Tillotson, Archbishop of Canterbury, found a place on the Corotoman shelves. There were also collected editions of the sermons of Ralph Brownrig, the Calvinistic Bishop of Exeter; of Richard Fiddes, a "literary" preacher and friend of Swift; of Robert South, a preacher better known for his humor than for his piety; and of James Blair, president of the College of William and Mary.

The Carter library's books of devotion and Christian ethics were of the sort to teach good morality and to instruct a gentleman in the proper understanding of his relation to God. Though a few nonconformist authors were included, the majority of these books were by orthodox churchmen. The mere titles of two of them would have been sufficient to recommend them to a Virginia planter conscious of his social position; they were *The Gentleman's Calling* (1660) by Richard Allestree and *A Gentleman's Religion* (1693) by Edward Synge, Archbishop of Tuam in Ireland.

Of these two, Allestree's book is the more significant for its social teaching, since Synge contents himself with explaining the principles of faith and the reasonableness of religion. Allestree, on the other hand, emphasizes the social responsibilities of gentlemen, urging them to remember that by reason of their higher station, better education, greater wealth, authority, reputation, privileges, and leisure they must set an example to the rest of mankind. This social doctrine coincided with the views of Robert Carter and the other great planters, who needed no persuasion to believe that they were the ordained leaders of the community. Belief in the sin of idleness, frequently said to have been a Puritan obsession, was also strongly emphasized by Allestree, who pointed out that gentlemen, no less than plain mechanics, must diligently pursue both their spiritual and temporal callings, putting aside all temptations to unprofitable idleness. This book, which was widely read for generations, was important in crystallizing certain social conceptions, because it confirmed, and gave authority for, notions already acceptable.

Instruction in the attainment of a life pleasing to God was the burden of the remaining devotional works, which included a collection of prayers for domestic crises; a book by William

Vickers on the proper preparation for receiving the Holy Communion; an orthodox Anglican treatise, in five volumes, by John Scott, called *The Christian Life;* the curious and edifying *Contemplations Moral and Divine* (1682) by the jurist, Sir Matthew Hale; and a few other similar books. One wonders whether religion or an interest in the law prompted Carter to purchase Hale's volume, which embodied the lawyer's Sunday-evening meditations. Robert Carter, like his brother, had a copy of Richard Baxter's *Right Method for a Settled Peace of Conscience and Spiritual Comfort* (1653), a book which must have held out hope to many a troubled Anglican, even though its author was a nonconformist.

Among the theological writings expounding the doctrines of Christianity, Carter had a volume which was probably the famous treatise by Philippe de Mornay, *On the Truth of the Christian Religion* (1581). This book, popular for generations after its first translation, not only gave a philosophic defense of Christian dogma, but, in the opinion of Christians of that age, successfully disposed of "atheists, epicures, paynims, Jews, Mahumetists, and other infidels." Since a translation of one of Hugo de Grotius' works had a similar title, we cannot be certain which book was meant by the Carter inventory, for Grotius was also often listed in colonial library catalogues.

Carter did not lack for explanations of Christian doctrine, inasmuch as his collection embraced volumes ranging from Archbishop James Ussher's *Body of Divinity* (1645), a relatively simple question-and-answer book, to Latin treatises by such learned Protestant theologians as Zacharias Ursinus, Marcus Frederik Wendelin, and Dudley Fenner. Even though the last three authors were strongly Calvinistic in some points of their theology, their works were nevertheless regarded as important expositions of the fundamental Protestant position, and were standard treatises in Protestant theological libraries.

Since the ability to interpret the Scriptures correctly was

regarded as a mark of education and intellectual capacity, the library at Corotoman naturally had works useful for the study of the Bible: a concordance, Thomas Haynes's *General View*, several volumes of annotations, including one by Giovanni Diodati, the Genevan Protestant, and *Some Considerations Touching the Style of the Holy Scriptures* (1661) by Robert Boyle. Curiously, the only catechism in the library was a Presbyterian work, published under authority of the Westminster Assembly in 1648. The possession of two copies of this catechism need not argue that the owner had Presbyterian leanings, for the Westminster catechism was received with respect by various Protestant faiths.

If some of the serious works on religion were too deep and dull for ordinary readers, Carter had one volume that even the simplest member of his household could understand: a pious allegory by Simon Patrick, Bishop of Ely, entitled *Parable of the Pilgrim* (1665), somewhat anticipating the manner of *Pilgrim's Progress*.

The collection of religious books at Corotoman contained works that any Anglican gentleman was conventionally supposed to own. But more than that, it contained sufficient resources for the ecclesiastical needs of Christ Church parish and its rector. Robert Carter, it may be repeated, occupied the place of a lord temporal and spiritual in the Northern Neck.

In philosophy, this library was anything but distinguished. An English translation of Pierre Charron's early-seventeenth-century treatise, *Of Wisdom*, made available the mildly skeptical belief of that French Catholic theologian, who insisted that man, recognizing his limitations, must base his morality on reason and accept the guidance of authority. Virginians of Carter's generation would have found little that was novel or unacceptable in such a doctrine. But, for those who were not ready to place too much dependence upon pure reason, the library had a copy of Blaise Pascal's *Thoughts*, which exalted faith and mystical revelation. Two treatises by Sir Matthew Hale, one on the primitive origin of mankind and the other on the knowledge of God in the light of nature, provided a certain amount of the sort of speculation that the age found stimulating. Although these books suggest that Hale was clearly a better jurist than speculative thinker, his works seem to have found considerable favor with colonial readers. His legalistic ability in rationalizing the Mosaic account of Creation, without getting too far from orthodoxy, helps to explain his popularity. The only other book that need be mentioned in the present connection is Samuel Palmer's *Moral Essays* (1710), a curious assortment of brief discussions of well-known proverbs. Palmer took such aphorisms as "If you have not a capon, feed on an onion," and "No alchemy like to thrift; or, a penny saved is a penny got," and set forth cogent explanations that appealed to the practical common sense of his readers. Franklin must have known this popular compilation of proverbial wisdom.

If Robert Carter had any scientific interest, his library failed to show it, for, aside from eight medical works, one or two old commentaries on Aristotle, probably used as textbooks, and John Evelyn's *Sylva* (1664), describing the propagation of forest and fruit trees, he had nothing of a scientific nature. Even the medical collection was not quite so good as the one his brother John had owned more than forty years before. Old books which had occupied a prominent place in John's library still constituted the best of Robert's medical collection. Helkiah Crooke's huge treatise on anatomy and related subjects, Christopher Wirsung's *Practice of Physic*, Lazare Rivière's book with a similar title, and the *London Pharmacopoeia* were the library's most comprehensive works on medicine. The only new medical books were Dr. Richard Mead's *Mechanical Account of Poisons* (1702), devoting considerable space to snakebites, and Dr. George Cheyne's *Essay of Health and Long*

Life (1724), advocating temperance in diet and drink—themes of considerable moment to Virginians of the early eighteenth century. The failure of Robert Carter to keep his medical library up to date was probably a result of the improvement in medical practice in his later years. As frontier conditions disappeared from the older-settled regions, physicians became more numerous and more skilful, and the need for medical knowledge at home grew less imperative.

Utilitarian works were also lacking. Not a single agricultural treatise, such as John Carter owned, was to be found in Robert's library. As a military leader, however, he did have two copies of Robert Ward's *Animadversions of War* (1639), which, in addition to instructions concerning fortifications and military tactics, had a section on the articles of war and laws to be observed during war. Perhaps Carter's interest in the law gave this book an added importance to him.

The schoolbooks listed in the library show the continuing vitality of works that had been in constant use in English grammar schools since the early sixteenth century. The Latin colloquies of Erasmus and Corderius had undoubtedly been studied by Robert Carter in his own youth, and the copies listed in his inventory were still being used in the instruction of his children. Such books as these constituted one medium through which a little of the spirit of Erasmus and other Humanists of the Renaissance was transmitted to the New World.

Comenius, the great Czech educator of the seventeenth century, whose influence was particularly strong in New England, was represented by one textbook, the famous *Janua linguarum*, the "gate of tongues," many times revised and reprinted—a work strongly recommended by Carter in a letter previously quoted. In addition to these texts, there were several other guides, almost as well known, for the study of Latin grammar and composition. John Smith's *Mystery of Rhetoric*

Unveiled (1656), a book reprinted at intervals for the next seventy-five years, was the only representative of more advanced study in that discipline.

The Corotoman library contained two textbooks in logic used at Harvard throughout the seventeenth century and later, and probably equally familiar at William and Mary: Bartholomaeus Keckermann's *Systema logicae* and Franco Burgersdijck's *Institutionum logicarum*, both standard college texts which sought to introduce students to the use of reason. A copy of Aristotle's *Metaphysica*, certain commentaries on Aristotle (already mentioned), and an unidentified work on metaphysics, which may have been Burgersdijck's popular *Institutiones metaphysicae*, comprised the rest of the books designed to transmit the learned tradition of the universities.

Two books on arithmetic, a copy of Herman Moll's popular geography, and a fairly adequate collection of dictionaries provided means of instruction in less esoteric branches of learning. For the translation of foreign languages, Carter had dictionaries of Greek, Latin, French, Italian, and Spanish. His English dictionaries included the newest good book available, Nathan Bailey's *Etymological English Dictionary* (1721). And encyclopedic information of an endless variety was to be found in the *Great Historical, Geographical, Genealogical, and Poetical Dictionary*, edited by Jeremy Collier and published in two great folio volumes in 1701. If this work was not accurate enough for the scholars of the day, it was adequate for ordinary needs. Scientific and utilitarian information was supplied by John Harris' *Lexicon technicum* (1704), which promised to explain "not only the terms of arts, but the arts themselves." Surely no alert mind in the Carter household needed to grow up in ignorance of the arts and sciences, or of other fields of learning, with voluminous encyclopedias such as these available.

Greek and Roman literature was represented by only four authors besides the historians already mentioned—a scarcity that is surprising in view of Robert Carter's professed adherence to the classical tradition in education. The inventory lists "Horace," "Terence," "Homer's Iliads," and "Ovid's Metamorphosis." Whether the works of these writers were in their original languages or in translation, we cannot be certain, but probably at least the last two were in translation, for Chapman's Homer and George Sandys's version of Ovid's *Metamorphoses* were fairly common in colonial libraries. Since the plays of Terence still occupied a high place in the estimation of schoolmasters, the copy of Terence at Corotoman may have been a schoolbook. The poetry of Horace, which enjoyed a tremendous popularity throughout the eighteenth century, was already regarded as essential to the library of any gentleman who pretended to cultivated sophistication. The omission of the works of Virgil is an unexpected lack.

Robert Carter's taste for belles-lettres and other modern literature seems to have been reasonably catholic, with a leaning, however, to moralistic books. He found room in his library for such diverse works as the rambling French romances of La Calprenède and Scudery; the mixture of learning, wit, and bawdry found in the writings of John Oldham and the second Duke of Buckingham; essays on health and long life, popular discontents, and ancient and modern learning, by Sir William Temple; and a long heroic poem on the life of Christ, by Samuel Wesley.

The oldest belletristic work at Corotoman was *The Countess of Montgomery's Urania* (1621), by Lady Mary Wroth, a pastoral romance describing the fantastic adventures of shepherds and shepherdesses in a Grecian setting. This novel was widely read in America. Colonists whose forests were peopled with yelling Indians perhaps found a sort of "escape" in the decorous chivalry and dainty gallantries of the inhabitants of *Urania*'s unreal world. At any rate, this was a popular work until well into the eighteenth century.

One other romance was read by the Carter household: a two-volume religious novel, by the Reverend Nathaniel Ingelo, entitled *Bentivolio and Urania* (1660-64). Probably many a book buyer thought he was getting a sequel to Lady Mary Wroth's novel when he ordered the Reverend Mr. Ingelo's pious, allegorical, and edifying romance, with its learned preface justifying fiction as an instrument of salvation. The second volume has a digression giving "a short story of the life" and a "brief synopsis of the sacred doctrine, of our dearest Saviour."

A fine folio edition of the *Works* (1668) of Abraham Cowley occupied a favored place among the Corotoman books. In the writings of that solemn poet, Virginians could find an abundance of moral and historical instruction. His Pindaric odes and the "Davideis, a Sacred Poem of the Troubles of David," were highly edifying if not vastly entertaining. Among his "Discourses" in verse and prose occurs "Of Liberty," whose sentiments appealed to some later Virginians, if not to Robert Carter, for Cowley begins his little essay by observing: "The liberty of a people consists in being governed by laws which they have made themselves, under whatsoever form it be of government. The liberty of a private man in being master of his own time and actions, as far as may consist with the laws of God and his country." Though the great baron of the Northern Neck may have subscribed in principle to such a doctrine of self-government, he probably cared little for Cowley's austere notion of liberty, as expressed at the close of his little discourse:

> For the few hours of life allotted me,
> Give me (great God) but bread and liberty,
> I'll beg no more: if more thou'rt pleased to give,
> I'll thankfully that overplus receive:
> If beyond this more be freely sent,
> I'll thank for this, and go away content.

Robert was less humble. He demanded liberty for himself and took what he needed of lands and material blessings. But, if he did not exemplify all these sentiments, he may have foreseen that the germ of many a political speech was hidden away in his copy of Cowley's works.

Three entries in the inventory enumerate copies of the *Reformation of Manners*, probably Daniel Defoe's satirical poem by that title, published in 1702. Its moralistic tone, particularly its castigation of the sins of London, would have recommended it to provincial or colonial readers, who always liked to see metropolitan iniquities rebuked.

The most recent publication of a strictly literary nature was Joseph Addison's *Works* (1721). Although Addison's Whig politics may not have appealed to many a Tory gentleman of England, the decorous sentiments of his essays won universal approval. Since his satires of boobery and coarseness in behavior are credited with going a long way toward the reform of manners in England, they probably had a similar influence in the colonies. Certainly his works were widely read in eighteenth-century America, both in Thomas Tickell's collected edition and in bound volumes of the *Tatler* and *Spectator* papers. Scarcely a gentleman's library in Virginia, from Robert Carter's day until our own, was without Addison. And this august apostle of the decorous and the correct was almost as well known among the socially elect of the other colonies. It is clear that the great Mr. Addison helped to shape American notions of the proper conduct of the gentleman in the period when gentlemen were self-consciously aware of an obligation to their station. Robert Carter was precisely the sort of man to read Addison and recommend him to his friends.

So much for the books owned by the first Carters. The omissions may disappoint the present-day student of their literary culture. If they knew anything of the works of Chaucer, Spenser, Shakespeare, or Milton, their inventories do not disclose it. Of the whole realm of drama, only Terence, and one or two plays, such as Addison's *Cato*, imbedded in collected works, were available. Other poetry was also scarce; and fiction was represented by not more than a half dozen romances. Entertainment was clearly not the objective that prompted the accumulation of these books. On the contrary, the Carters' libraries, like most other colonial book collections, show a consistent utility. Books were bought to provide their owners with practical knowledge or to teach them wisdom.

The works mentioned in the foregoing discussion show a conscious selection by the Carters. Though some libraries grow by chance, the books of colonial Americans were, for the most part, a result of reasoned choice. As John Carter the emigrant, and John and Robert his sons, deliberately set out to establish themselves as fine gentlemen in the New World, they did not neglect the things of the mind and spirit. Even while they were greedily gathering about themselves the material evidences of great station—lands, servants, tenants, money, better houses, and all the trappings of gentility—they were determined to preserve their intellectual superiority. Although far removed from the civilization of the England they had left, they were also determined to reproduce in their own new world the society they would have chosen at home. To this end, as well as for strictly utilitarian purposes, their libraries were selected.

Just as New Englanders were intent upon educating their children lest they grow barbarous for lack of learning, so the Virginia leaders insisted upon transmitting to their descendants a tradition of humane culture. In the isolated plantation houses scattered along the Virginia rivers, the collections of carefully chosen books were an essential medium in the dissemination of cultural ideals. Many of the Virginia gentlemen of the late seventeenth and early eighteenth centuries showed a greater concern over the cultivation of their minds than some of their counterparts in England, for the obligation and the necessity were greater in the new country; and, by the same token, their libraries were often more wisely chosen.

The old idea that a gentleman should fit himself to serve the state persisted in Robert Carter's thinking, and he was solicitous that learning should be preserved in order that the colony might have intelligent leaders. In a letter written to Francis Lee, a Virginia merchant in London, on June 15, 1702, he expresses pleasure over the educational progress of his wards, the sons of Colonel Ralph Wormeley, and hopes that their generation will be better educated to serve their country:

> Am glad to learn my cousins Ralph Wormeley and John Wormeley thrive so fast in their learning; no doubt the continuance of careful education will render them accomplished men qualified to preserve the character of their father, and fit for the service of their country, which, to my sorrow I will complain to you, having drawn your first breath here, does at this time labor under a very thick cloud of ignorance. Pray God send in the next generation it may flourish under a set of better polished patriots.[48]

To help in the development of the kind of "polished patriots," within his own family, who would do him credit as intelligent leaders in Virginia, Robert Carter maintained a library of useful works.

Among Carter's social equals there was one patriot whose polish was not to the liking of the lord of Corotoman. This man was Robert Beverley the historian, who took pleasure in flouting the vanities of some of his contemporaries. His career, in many ways, offers a contrast to that of Robert Carter.

[48] "Robert Carter and the Wormeley Estate," *William and Mary College Quarterly*, 1st Ser., XVII, 255.

CHAPTER X

ROBERT BEVERLEY II: HISTORIAN AND ICONOCLAST

Of all the great Virginia planters who flourished in the late seventeenth and early eighteenth centuries, Robert Beverley the younger was the least compatible with his colleagues and departed further from the conventional pattern of a Cavalier gentleman. Amidst a group of Tories, he chose to be a Whig. Among planters who sought to reproduce the manners and style of English country squires, he was first a Virginian and then an Englishman; or, as he himself once remarked—apropos of his prose style—"I am an Indian, and don't pretend to be exact in my language." [1] In other things besides language Beverley liked to think of himself as a forthright "Indian." Taking a sardonic pleasure in mocking the smugness of his fellow planters, at times he must have been a thorn in their flesh. With an almost avaricious appetite for fees from the public treasury, he nevertheless was sincerely a patriot, vigorously defending Virginia against the calumny of others, sometimes with more fervor than wisdom. Though he once described himself as "yeoman" [2]—probably out of sheer perversity—he was descended from a genteel family; his father was one of the wealthiest men in the colony; and he himself accumulated a great estate, with Beverley Park in King and Queen County as the heart and center of his barony. Though Beverley was deliberately an individualist—like many another American—he did not depart entirely from the conventions of gentility; and, though his politics kept him on the peripheral outskirts of power, he was distinctly a member of the gov-

[1] Preface to the 1705 ed. of *The History and Present State of Virginia.*

[2] Philip Alexander Bruce, *Social Life of Virginia in the Seventeenth Century* (2d ed., Lynchburg, Va., 1927), p. 121.

erning group. But—what is of greatest interest to posterity—he was the first native son to make a distinguished contribution to literature.

The individualism of Robert Beverley the younger was a natural inheritance from a father whose own divergence from the normal pattern of his kind made him a storm center in Virginia politics. Major Robert Beverley the elder, who arrived in Virginia about 1663, quickly took his place among the leading planters, accumulated property, held public office, and was politically active from the day he stepped on the shores of the colony until his death in 1687.[3] In that time he had incurred the enmity of many members of his own class, gathered about him some loyal adherents among the lesser planters, helped suppress the Bacon rebels, led a riotous party himself, and was committed to prison. All in all, Major Beverley's career was exciting and turbulent, and his namesake must have been "conditioned" in his childhood to habits of outspoken independence and forthright action.

Major Beverley was descended from a family of the small gentry of Yorkshire. On his arrival he had sufficient capital to enable him to acquire a comfortable seat in Middlesex County, and he continued to add to his landed possessions until at his death he held more than fifty thousand acres of land, chiefly in frontier counties.[4] His personal property, valued at approximately £5,000, included expensive furniture, a quantity of silver plate marked with the family crest, and forty-two slaves.[5] In twenty-four years he had become one of the richest planters of his time. To share this property he

[3] The best account of the elder Beverley is that by W. G. Stanard, "Major Robert Beverley and His Descendants," *The Virginia Magazine of History and Biography*, II (1894-95), 405-13; III (1895-96), 47-52, 169-76, 261-71, 383-92. See also [Fairfax Harrison] "Robert Beverley, the Historian of Virginia," *ibid.*, XXXVI (1928), 333-44.

[4] *Ibid.*, II, 412.

[5] P. A. Bruce, *Economic History of Virginia in the Seventeenth Century* (New York, 1907), II, 88, 251, 254.

left a family of nine children by two wives.[6] Robert was the second son by his first wife.

Before Bacon's rebellion in 1676, Major Beverley had already become an influential citizen. He had been elected clerk of the House of Burgesses in 1670 and had served as a justice of the peace in Middlesex County. When danger from the Bacon rebels threatened, he was made a member of the Council and proved one of Governor Berkeley's most loyal supporters, leading a troop into the field and capturing some of the most active of Bacon's followers. Indeed, he seems to have been overly zealous. The royal commissioners sent to investigate the rebellion quoted Beverley as saying that "he had not plundered enough, so that the rebellion ended too soon for his purpose"; and the commissioners added that he had "been the evil instrument that fomented the ill humors between the two governors there on the place, and was a great occasion for their clashing and difference."[7] This last was an allusion to Beverley's continued adherence to the cause of Governor Berkeley after Herbert Jeffreys had been sent to replace him.

Thenceforth, Beverley was the leader of a "people's party" or a Whig group in Virginia politics. Distrustful of the governors who succeeded Berkeley, he was constantly opposing their policies. When Governor Jeffreys and the royal commissioners demanded the Journals of the House of Burgesses in 1677, Beverley as secretary saucily refused, saying he would not comply without the consent of their masters (meaning the House of Burgesses)—a reply that caused the Governor to complain of his impudence.[8] After the commissioners had seized the books by force, the House of Burgesses, prompted by Beverley, passed a resolution of remonstrance which aroused the anger of King Charles himself. The upshot was that the Privy Council ordered the removal of Beverley and

[6] *The Virginia Magazine of History and Biography*, III, 169-70.

[7] *Ibid.*, II, 406-7.

[8] *Ibid.*, XXIII (1915), 152.

Edward Hill from the Council because of their "evil fame." Meanwhile the House of Burgesses, in which Beverley had a strong following, loyally supported him. He was re-elected clerk of the House on June 8, 1680, and was regarded as a leader against the oppression of the clique adhering to the various royal governors. Governor Culpeper, with unusual perception of the trend of public opinion, persuaded the English government to reinstate both Beverley and Hill.

But Major Beverley's troubles had only begun. When tobacco prices fell to a disastrous level in the spring of 1682, a movement to curtail production by refusing to plant tobacco for one year gained considerable headway. This movement was favored by many small planters and was led in part by Major Beverley. Because the assembly called by Deputy Governor Chicheley failed to give government authority for the cessation of tobacco culture, a group of planters took the matter into their own hands and set out to cut down tobacco plants wherever they found them. For his part in that foray, Major Beverley was arrested and imprisoned on board a ship, accused of "being the prime actor" in the plant cutting.[9] On being transferred to the custody of the sheriff of York, Beverley escaped and returned to his own home in Middlesex, where he was retaken but again escaped, only to be brought back once more into custody. One gets the impression that his arrest was something of a farce, though Fitzhugh's habeas-corpus plea failed to gain his client's release. Later, other charges of a frivolous nature—namely, that he had broken open letters directed to the secretary of the colony—were preferred against him. After considerable persecution, he was finally driven, on May 3, 1684, to plead on bended knee for the forgiveness of the Council—surely a bitter pill for the proud and irascible old clerk of the House of Burgesses. A year before, Major Beverley, being called before the General Court, had prepared

[9] *Ibid.*, II, 409.

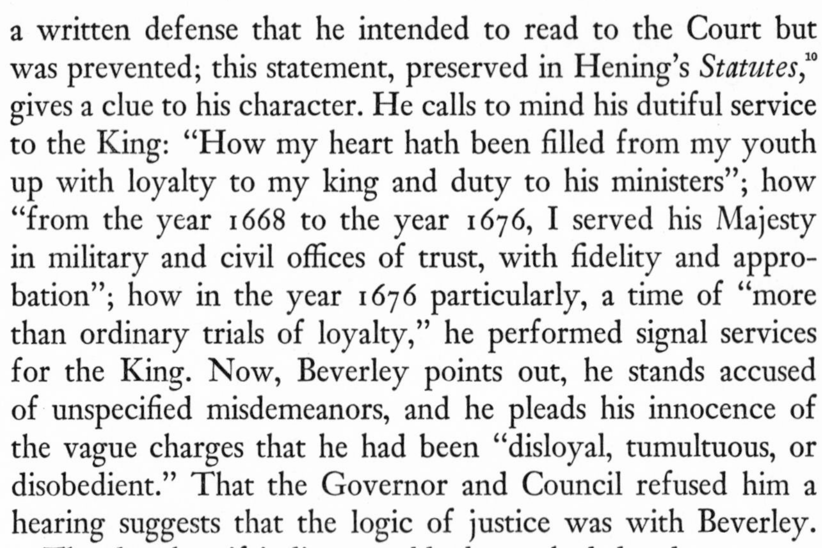

a written defense that he intended to read to the Court but was prevented; this statement, preserved in Hening's *Statutes*,[10] gives a clue to his character. He calls to mind his dutiful service to the King: "How my heart hath been filled from my youth up with loyalty to my king and duty to his ministers"; how "from the year 1668 to the year 1676, I served his Majesty in military and civil offices of trust, with fidelity and approbation"; how in the year 1676 particularly, a time of "more than ordinary trials of loyalty," he performed signal services for the King. Now, Beverley points out, he stands accused of unspecified misdemeanors, and he pleads his innocence of the vague charges that he had been "disloyal, tumultuous, or disobedient." That the Governor and Council refused him a hearing suggests that the logic of justice was with Beverley.

The doughty if indiscreet old planter had dared to oppose the policies of his class, and for that crime he was punished as a "trouble-maker." Undoubtedly Beverley's hostility to the governing clique, interpreted by the aristocratic group as a betrayal of his class, was the source of most of his woe. Apparently he took a sardonic pleasure in his own rebelliousness, and we know that his tactless utterances were not conducive to increasing his popularity with the great gentry of the colony. Especially when drink had overcome him, Beverley was likely to talk too much; as a contemporary observed, it was expected that "some idle words should fall from him in his cups, which when so taken he is not *compos mentis*."[11]

Many of the qualities of the father were repeated in the son, and Robert the historian lived out his life not altogether in harmony with his brethren in the colony.

The younger Robert Beverley was born about 1673, at his father's plantation house in Middlesex County. His mother was the daughter of a merchant of Hull and the widow of

[10] William Waller Hening, *The Statutes at Large, Being a Collection of All the Laws of Virginia*, III (Philadelphia, 1823), 557-60.

[11] *The Virginia Magazine of History and Biography*, II, 410.

George Keeble, one of the pioneer settlers in Middlesex.[12] Of his childhood we know next to nothing. In his youth he was sent to school in England, but what school he attended is unknown. In 1694 his father's executors paid to two London merchants, Micajah Perry and Thomas Lane, the sum of £40 "for entertaining and accomodating Major Beverley's sons, Harry, John, and Robert Beverley." [13] Perry and Lane most likely had the responsibility of placing the boys in a proper school, since Virginia planters sometimes left such details to the discretion of trusted mercantile correspondents in England. It has been supposed that Robert attended Beverly Grammar School in Yorkshire, because some of his descendants were educated there.

After the youth's return to Virginia, when he was about nineteen years old, he set out to learn the ways of Virginia law by becoming a volunteer scrivener in the office of the colonial secretary of state, then Christopher Robinson, who had been his father's friend. In 1693 Ralph Wormeley succeeded Robinson and may also have helped to guide the young novice. But Beverley needed little advice to make him worldly-wise, and he was not long content to remain a volunteer scrivener. On April 24, 1695, the Journals of the House of Burgesses record that "The petition of Robert Beverley for an allowance for his public services as clerk attending the Secretary's office was read and referred to the consideration of the Committee for Public Claims." [14] How often were Beverley's claims for compensation to echo in the meetings of committees of the House of Burgesses during the years to come! At the outset of his career, this petition is symbolical of his lifelong anxiety over fees. Significantly, perhaps, Bev-

[12] *The Dictionary of American Biography* contains a brief sketch of Robert Beverley, Jr., written by Fairfax Harrison. His account in *The Virginia Magazine of History and Biography*, XXXVI, 333-44, is more detailed.

[13] *Ibid.*, II, 413.

[14] *Journals of the House of Burgesses*, 1695-1702, p. 10.

erley became secretary of the Committee for Public Claims on March 8, 1693. And presently we find him serving as clerk of the General Court, clerk of the Council, and clerk of the General Assembly.[15]

Beverley had inherited from his father a plantation in Gloucester County; a little later his landed wealth was increased by six thousand acres when his younger half-brothers, John and Thomas, died, leaving him an estate, in the frontier region of King and Queen County, named by their father Beverley Park.[16] But since Beverley found it convenient to live near the seat of government, in 1694 he bought a lot in Jamestown and settled his residence there. His landed property in King and Queen County gave him a claim, however, on the post of clerk of the county, which he obtained through the favor of Mr. Secretary of State Wormeley in 1699. In the same year he was elected to the House of Burgesses from Jamestown, but, because the capital was too poor to pay its representative the allowance usually granted members from the counties, Beverley complained and demanded his fee—whereupon Jamestown decided to do without representation by Beverley, or anyone else, in the session of 1703-5.

Meanwhile, in 1697, by making a brilliant marriage with Ursula Byrd, sixteen-year-old daughter of the first William Byrd, Beverley proved that the political opposition aroused by his father had not impaired his own social position. His bride had received the advantages of an English education. At the age of four, Ursula, with her sister Susan and a maid, had been sent to England, where apparently she remained until after the Treaty of Ryswick, in 1697, had made ocean travel safe again.[17] Immediately on her return she married Beverley; and in less than a year she died at the birth of her

[15] *Executive Journals of the Council of Colonial Virginia* (Richmond, 1925-30), I, 285, 350, 353.

[16] *The Virginia Magazine of History and Biography*, XXXVI, 335-36.

[17] *Ibid.*, XXXV (1927), 243-44.

son William, who lived to become the owner of a great estate called Blandfield and a member of the Council—an office to which his father aspired but never attained. Robert Beverley never remarried.

The increase of his estate became one of the main concerns of the young politician of Jamestown. To his already extensive holdings, he added lands and houses in Elizabeth City. But so curious is the working of fate that the acquisition of this property not only caused his political downfall but was indirectly responsible for his writing the history of Virginia.

Having become involved in litigation over the title to the Elizabeth City estate, the new owner went to England in June, 1703, to prosecute an appeal to the Privy Council. There he remained for eighteen months and lost the suit. More unfortunate still, he meddled in politics at home by writing letters making satirical attacks on Governor Francis Nicholson and Robert Quarry, the surveyor-general of customs. If the letters are indiscreet and biting in their sarcasm, they nevertheless show that Beverley was inspired by a patriotic desire to arouse the House of Burgesses over what he sincerely believed to be the dangerous machinations of Nicholson and Quarry against the liberties of Virginians.

What had stirred the patriotic fervor of the young colonial were the reports he heard in London of Nicholson's and Quarry's contemptuous remarks about the Council, the House of Burgesses, and Virginia gentlemen generally. Furthermore, he had reason to believe that the Governor and the Surveyor of Customs were plotting to gain dictatorial powers over the colony and to impose their wills by means of a standing army. He also disliked their efforts to raise money and men in Virginia to defend New York against the French and Indians. In an open letter, copies of which he sent to several Virginia leaders,[18] Beverley mentioned a dozen or more of the principal

[18] Two letters, the first directed to Major David Gwyn, inclosing a second called by Beverley a "Narrative," are reprinted in the *Executive Journals of the Council of Colonial Virginia*, II, 391-95.

planters—including Robert Carter, Philip Ludwell, William Byrd, and himself—who had been abused and slandered in reports sent back to England by the two officials. Virginians had been represented as "obstinate people of Commonwealth principles," who "must be corrected and lowered in time"; the Council, as "vain, cowardly, disloyal to her Majesty, and perjured, not regarding their oaths"; the House of Burgesses, as "a pack of rude, unthinking, willful, obstinate people, without any regard to her Majesty or her interest, and *it's laid as a crime to them that they think themselves entitled to the liberties of Englishmen.*" [19] And he adds, "but what I take to be the most dangerous, and comes nearest to the loss of our lives and liberties, as well as estates, is the many inventions and unsuspecting arguments that are constantly used in all letters and memorials to obtain a standing force [army], and a title of captain general over all the plantations on the [American] continent." Beverley concludes with the pious wish that "my country would but lay their head and heart to consider and would but believe what is really true of the designs against them." Nicholson he calls "our Duke" and describes as proud, domineering, and dictatorial; Quarry is compared with his predecessor "old [Edward] Randolph," and called "ten times worse; nay the devil himself, were he in his room, could not do us more mischief." The Council heard this outpouring of sarcastic if patriotic invective, and appeared not altogether incredulous; when it met on September 24, 1704, Nicholson asked their advice concerning so impudent an utterance, "Whereupon the Council declare that it is their opinion that it will not affect the peace of the country." But Nicholson was furious and caused his ideas about Beverley to be inscribed in the official journals as follows:

> As to Mr. Beverley's letter and narrative, they are part false, part scandalous, and part malicious, but I could not expect otherwise

[19] Italics are mine.

> from a man of his universal ill character; but I suppose his pride, ambition, vanity, unsettledness in all his conditions and his poverty might make him hope to make a sedition in the country. The advice I give him is to get himself close-shaved and make friends with the governors of her Majesty's hospital of Bethlem to get a place there; and there he may meet with real chains instead of imaginary ones that I was preparing for her Majesty's loyal and dutiful subjects of Virginia.

The Governor forthwith discharged the offending Beverley from his lucrative office of clerk of King and Queen County.

The House of Burgesses, however, listened sympathetically to the charges against Nicholson and Quarry. Since Quarry was no favorite anyway, the House was induced by Beverley's letters to send an address to the crown complaining against him. Quickly came back a vindication of Quarry and a rebuke to the House for preferring "groundless" charges, tending only to "fomenting divisions amongst our subjects."[20] Beverley's chances for political advancement having been ruined by this fiasco, he returned to Virginia and shook from his feet the dust of both Jamestown and the new capital at Williamsburg. For the rest of his days, he lived the life of a somewhat Spartan gentleman at Beverley Park. During the session of 1706 he sat in the House of Burgesses for King and Queen County, but henceforth he was content to watch the intrigues of Virginia politics with satirical aloofness.

Had Beverley not gone to England to prosecute his case, most likely he would not have written *The History and Present State of Virginia*, published first in London, in 1705. And had he not written this earliest enduring work by a native Virginian, his fame would have been no greater than many another litigious planter's. Though Beverley's journey was politically disastrous and economically ruinous, he achieved thereby a permanent place among significant American authors.

[20] *Calendar of State Papers, America and West Indies, 1706-08*, pp. 22, 28.

The reasons for his writing the history are set forth in the preface to the second edition, of 1722. "In the year 1703, my affairs calling me to England," Beverley remarks, "I was soon after my arrival complimented by my bookseller with an intimation that there was prepared for printing a general account of all her Majesty's plantations in America." The bookseller desired him to "overlook it before it was put to the press," and Beverley agreed to criticize the part on Virginia. Soon afterward the bookseller brought "about six sheets of paper written, which contained the account of Virginia and Carolina. This it seems was to have answered [for] a part of Mr. Oldmixon's *British Empire in America*." So inaccurate was the account that, after trying to correct it, Beverley gave up and offered to write a new history himself; but he refused to allow the publisher to "mingle it with Oldmixon's other account of the plantations," because of the inaccuracies in the Englishman's work. When John Oldmixon's *The British Empire in America* finally appeared, in 1708, with a section on Virginia, its treatment of that colony was so unsatisfactory that Beverley, in the preface to the 1722 edition of his own work, printed four pages of corrections, with page references to Oldmixon.

From early manhood Beverley had taken an interest in the history of Virginia. "My first business in the world being among the public records of my country," he says in the 1722 preface, "the active thoughts of my youth put me upon taking notes of the general administration of the government, but with no other design than the gratification of my own inquisitive mind." This inquisitive mind had also led him to make many observations of Indian life and of the natural history of his country. Furthermore, he had read widely in the literature of travel and history and had compared Virginia with the descriptions of the great world, ancient and modern. With such a preparation, Beverley was ready in 1703 to begin a descriptive narrative of Virginia, which he quickly completed and published.

The History and Present State of Virginia attracted considerable attention in England and created some excitement at home. Interest in France was so great that, two years after publication in England, a French translation was printed at Orleans and sold in Paris; there followed a pirated edition of this French version, published the same year, 1707, at Amsterdam, and a second pirated edition, published in 1712, also at Amsterdam.[21] Perhaps the curiosity of French Huguenots about the new Promised Land accounts for the demand for three editions in French.

Beverley's history was read with more wrath than favor by some of his Virginia colleagues. The caustic irony, evident in his letters about Nicholson and Quarry, makes his book eminently readable today, but its perusal must have been an unpleasing experience to members of the ruling clique, as well as to certain of the more complacent planters, since the writer was unsparing in his criticism of the shortcomings of his contemporaries. For his "freedom to represent the mismanagement of several gentlemen," the author remarks in the preface of 1705, he should not be blamed, because "it is their fault that acted such irregularities, and not mine that report them to the world. If men will please to be unjust, run counter to the royal instructions, oppress the people, and offer violence to all the laws of a country, they ought to be known and abhorred by mankind."

If personal animosities prompted part of Beverley's acid comments upon Virginia's rulers, he also was moved by a genuine love of his country and a zeal for justice. Robert Beverley was intensely Virginian. No longer did he feel that his primary allegiance was to England. In him appears a definite and vocal patriotism for his native country. The phrase "my country," often repeated in his writings, is indicative of his attitude. Beverley's concern over justice for Virginia is evident in the

[21] *The Virginia Magazine of History and Biography*, XXXVI, 342-43.

dedication of the first edition of his history to Robert Harley, then Speaker of the House of Commons. He praises Harley for the friendly and wise interest he has taken in the colonies. "While some people," the writer points out, "upon very mistaken principles of policy are for loading those countries with heavy impositions and oppressing them with rapacious and arbitrary governors, you, sir, who are a better judge of their importance, are for milder methods, and for extending the blessings of justice and property to all the English dominions." Harley's attitude, Beverley thinks, is "directed by unbiased reason and the real advantage of England." Virginia, he insists, asks no other treatment than to be governed by such a policy as is "due to a loyal people whose lives are devoted to the benefit of their mother country." Beverley never forgets that he is a subject of the English sovereign, but he is eternally conscious that he is also a free citizen of Virginia.

The lack of any accurate description of his country, or any intelligent account of its institutions, has induced him to try to give a faithful picture of Virginia, Beverley remarks in the preface of 1705. Previous descriptions have not been true, "or so much as well invented." Therefore, he has mentioned nothing that he cannot "make good by very authentic testimony." Although he is passionately devoted to the interest of Virginia, he does not believe that a patriot should hide his country's faults. Hence, he has "shown the small improvements that the English have made since they have been in possession, and pointed at several great advantages which they might secure to themselves by a due spirit of industry and management."

The history is divided into four parts; the first gives a running narrative of the settlement of the colony up to the writer's own time; the second is a description of the natural history of the region; the third is an account of the Indians; and the fourth is a discussion of the form of government, with some description of the laws and public offices. It was in this last portion that Beverley gave most offense to his contemporaries. Although the historical narrative is too sketchy to be of great value, the natural-history portions and the descriptions of the Indians are exceedingly valuable, as are the comments on the manners and customs of the day. And Beverley's history, besides being a mine of information for the social historian, is also an entertaining and amusing book, written with verve, clarity, and a shrewd sense of humor. The author never betrays the naïveté of a provincial; throughout the book he shows the urbanity of a widely read and experienced citizen of the world—surely a rare quality in an American writer of the early eighteenth century.

But, since Virginia politicians relished criticism, even from one of their own kind, as little as other folk, Beverley's history did not win him many friends among the ruling set; hence, when he returned from England, he settled down at Beverley Park on what was then the frontier and prepared to make the most of his plantation, without benefit of political sinecures.

While other planters were sedulously trying to duplicate the manners and customs of English country gentlemen, the proprietor of Beverley Park chose to be a gentleman with a difference. If his brother-in-law, William Byrd of Westover, was eager to make his establishment a replica of an English lord's estate, Beverley was content to dwell in austere simplicity, pursuing his own life with an individualistic disregard for trends and fashions. When even small planters were able to afford imported furniture from London, he furnished his house with wooden stools of plantation manufacture.[22] Having criticized his countrymen for being such "abominable ill-husbands, that though their country be over-run with wood, yet they have all their wooden-ware from England,"[23] Beverley doubtless felt that he ought to set an example by making his own furniture.

[22] Bruce, *Social Life*, p. 121.

[23] *The History and Present State of Virginia* (1705), Bk. IV, p. 58.

Though he had only one son to inherit his wealth, for the rest of his life Robert Beverley labored to increase his estate by land speculations and by the thrifty operation of his plantations. To those who crossed him in his business dealings, he was not above meanness and harshness. In fact, from some of his contemporaries he earned the reputation of being overbearing.[24] Yet he does not appear to have been disliked as a neighbor. Indeed, he was capable of convivial gaiety and was a gracious host.

When that able administrator, Alexander Spotswood, became lieutenant-governor in 1710, under the nominal governorship of the Earl of Orkney, Beverley's political fortunes improved slightly. He won the favor of the new executive sufficiently to receive two or three minor appointments: he was made one of the tobacco agents under the act of 1714 for the inspection of tobacco; later he was a member of a committee for licensing attorneys; and in 1718 he was appointed presiding officer of the King and Queen County court.[25] Since Spotswood was vastly concerned with the development of the frontier, he doubtless recognized in Beverley a vigorous personality who could further his interests in the opening of the new country to the west.

Beverley was one of the gentlemen participating in the famous expedition, led by Spotswood, across the Blue Ridge Mountains into the Shenandoah Valley, in August, 1716—an expedition as convivial as it was spectacular in its accomplishment. On the way to the mountains, the Governor's party had stopped for the night at Beverley Park, where they had made merry with wine of Beverley's own vintage.[26] The next morning their host joined them for the rest of their joyous adventure.

[24] *The Virginia Magazine of History and Biography*, XXXVI, 342.

[25] *Ibid.*, p. 339.

[26] See *ibid.*, p. 340, for proof that it was Robert, not his brother Harry, who accompanied Spotswood. See also "The Ultra Montane Expedition," *William and Mary College Quarterly*, 1st Ser., VII (1898-99), 30-37.

To the journal of John Fontaine, a Frenchman who accompanied the Spotswood expedition, we are indebted for details of the journey, and from the same source comes information about Beverley's life on his plantation, for Fontaine had visited Beverley Park nearly a year before and had written down his impressions.

One of Beverley's enthusiasms during his later years was the belief that Virginia could be made an important wine-producing country. He planted vineyards that were his greatest pride, and made large quantities of wine. Though his neighbors were so doubtful of his success that they took one hundred guineas on a ten-to-one wager with Beverley that he could not produce seven hundred gallons of wine in seven years' time, the planter himself was confident, when Fontaine visited him, that he would win the stake of a thousand guineas after the next vintage.[27] Because Beverley followed Spanish methods of wine making rather than French, Fontaine was skeptical of his judgment, but he "drank very heartily of the wine," even though he did not relish the taste as much as he could wish.

That Beverley conscientiously set out to demonstrate to his less thrifty contemporaries that a Virginia gentleman could and should make his own land supply his wants is suggested by a passage in Fontaine's journal, dated November 14, 1715: "This man lives well; but though rich, he has nothing in or about his house but what is necessary. He hath good beds in his house, but no curtains; and instead of cane chairs, he hath stools made of wood. He lives upon the product of his land." Yet Beverley was not penurious and was invariably hospitable. Fontaine was graciously entertained and not permitted to depart until the rainy weather had ended. On November 16 the rain let up sufficiently for host and guest to divert themselves with hunting, followed by more potations from the

[27] Ann Maury, *Memoirs of a Huguenot Family* (New York, 1872), pp. 264-67. For other side lights on Beverley's interest in wine making, see *The History and Present State of Virginia* (1705), Bk. II, pp. 19, 21; Bk. IV, p. 46.

vineyard. But, the next day being Sunday, "About ten of the clock, we mounted our horses, Mr. Beverley with us, and we went about seven miles to his parish church, where we had a good sermon from a Frenchman named Mr. De Latané, who is a minister of this parish. After service, we returned to Mr. Beverley's house and finished the day there." Though Beverley was pleased to flout some of the conventions of his fellow planters, he observed the proprieties of religious worship expected of a country gentleman.

The traditional hospitality of Virginians, which Fontaine enjoyed, received Beverley's praise in his history. "If there happen to be a churl that either out of covetousness or ill-nature won't comply with this generous custom," the writer remarks, "he has a mark of infamy set upon him, and is abhorred by all. But I must confess (and am heartily sorry for the occasion) that this good neighborhood has of late been much depraved by the present governor, who practices the detestable politics of governing by parties, by which feuds and heart-burnings have been kindled in the minds of the people, and friendship, hospitality, and good neighborhood have been extremely discouraged." [28]

Although Beverley's enthusiasm for the produce of his own vines may seem to indicate a partiality for the wine cup, he was not given to excess in drinking, or in anything else. In fact, he was an advocate of temperance in all things. To intemperance he attributes the report of Virginia's sickliness—a charge often made by sailors who "imprudently fall to drinking cold water, or perhaps new cider," or who eat too much and "so fall into fluxes, fevers, and the belly-ache, and then to spare their own indiscretion, they in their tarpaulin language cry 'God damn the country.'" [29] Moderation is the way to health, Beverley believes, and, "by the most impartial observation I can make, if people will be persuaded to be temperate,

[28] *The History and Present State of Virginia* (1705), Bk. IV, pp. 76-77.
[29] *Ibid.*, Bk. IV, p. 61.

and take due care of themselves, I believe it [Virginia] is as healthy a country as any under Heaven."

Fontaine's journal, with its allusions to hunting, suggests some of the pleasures followed by the owner of Beverley Park. If hunting had not yet developed the conventions of a society sport, it undoubtedly furnished a pleasant diversion for many a planter. Though Beverley refers to himself as only a "small sportsman,"[30] he shot ducks and turkeys, hunted deer and bear, and–what must have been rare sport–rode "full speed after wolves in the woods."[31] Fishing was one of his favorite amusements, and he delighted in all types of the sport. "I have set in the shade at the heads of the rivers angling," he boasts, "and spent as much time in taking the fish off the hook as in waiting for their taking it."[32] We know that Beverley did not confine his fishing to rod and line, for he makes an allusion elsewhere to a strange fish he caught one day while "hauling a seine upon the salts."[33] So much satisfaction did Beverley derive from these outdoor enjoyments that he remarks somewhat enviously of the Indians, that "by their pleasure alone, they supplied all their necessities."[34]

Beverley found delight in the observation of nature. The world about him was not something to be conquered and subdued, but rather something to be investigated, appreciated, and enjoyed. We should remember that his estate was already a settled plantation when he occupied it, and that he was spared the necessity of rough pioneering. To the development of the natural beauties of his place he could give his attention. Detailed descriptions of the grounds at Beverley Park are lacking, but we can be certain that the owner was proud of his gardens and trees. Almost lyrical is his praise of Virginia gardens and the "merry birds" that make up a "rural consort," especially the mockingbirds "who love society so well that

[30] *Ibid.*, Bk. II, p. 37. [31] *Ibid.*, Bk. IV, p. 73. [32] *Ibid.*, p. 74.
[33] *Ibid.*, Bk. II, p. 32. [34] *Ibid.*, Bk. I, p. 4.

whenever they see mankind, they will perch upon a twig very near them, and sing the sweetest wild airs in the world," or fly along ahead of a traveler and "by their music make a man forget the fatigues of his journey." [35] "Have you pleasure in a garden?" Beverley asks, and answers by describing the perfection of Virginia gardens, which any man must love. "All things thrive in it most surprisingly. You can't walk by a bed of flowers but besides the entertainment of their beauty, your eyes will be saluted with the charming colors of the humming bird which revels among the flowers, and licks off the dew and honey from their tender leaves on which it only feeds. Its size is not half so large as an English wren, and its color is a glorious shining mixture of scarlet, green, and gold. Colonel Byrd, in his garden, which is the finest in that country, has a summer house set round with the Indian honeysuckle, which all the summer is continually full of sweet flowers in which these birds delight exceedingly. Upon these flowers I have seen ten or a dozen of these beautiful creatures together, which sported about me so familiarly that with their little wings they often fanned my face." [36]

These words were not a mere conventional tribute to natural beauty, but an expression of genuine love of nature. Beverley's own garden must have been one of his delights. When he is describing the sarsaparilla vine with its bright red berries, he thinks it suitable for "divers ornamental uses." His zest for experiment, as exemplified in his vine-growing, no doubt led him to adapt native plants to his garden.

There was more than a little of scientific speculation in Beverley's observations of nature, though he was conscious of his lack of scientific training. His treatment of the natural history of Virginia was briefer than the author wished, because of his "want of skill in the works of nature." But he voices a hope that his book "will be sufficient to give a handle to a more complete undertaking." [37]

[35] *Ibid.*, Bk. IV, pp. 61-62. [36] *Ibid.*, p. 62. [37] *Ibid.*, preface.

Beverley's curiosity about the natural world was immense, and he anticipated Thoreau in the patience with which he studied the habits of birds and beasts. His willingness to experiment led him on one occasion to eat a rattlesnake, "which was dainty food," he assures us.[38] The cunning of animals fascinated him. Beavers, for example, struck him as peculiarly shrewd creatures. They live, the author reports, "in a regular form of government, something like monarchy," and have such a "deal of policy" that they can defeat "all the subtlety and stratagems of the hunter."[39]

During Beverley's last years, he busied himself with the pleasures of his own little realm and with the revision of his history. Although he was still not an old man—for he was only forty-nine when he died—experience had mellowed him, and he set about purging his work of statements likely to offend. To that end he deleted most of the pungent comment on his contemporaries and "set down the succession of the governors with the more general incidents of their government, without reflection upon the private conduct of any person."[40] If the second edition, published in the year of his death, 1722, was less readable in consequence, it shows a commendable sense of fair play. He was unwilling to hand on to posterity remarks that he realized were partly a result of his own prejudice. For, in the first edition of his book, Beverley had not spared the subjects of his dislikes, particularly the recent governors. Governor Francis Nicholson was described as a hateful tyrant, ready to hang Virginia citizens, "with Magna Charta about their necks," if they protested on the ground of their natural rights.[41] The founding of Williamsburg was merely a wild project of this governor.[42] But one wonders whether the fact that Beverley owned real estate in the old capital of Jamestown might not have affected his views on Williamsburg. Thomas, Lord

[38] *Ibid.*, Bk. IV, p. 65. [39] *Ibid.*, pp. 74-75. [40] Ed. of 1722, preface.
[41] Ed. of 1705, Bk. I, p. 100; see also pp. 98-99. [42] *Ibid.*, Bk. I, p. 79.

Culpeper, was pictured as chiefly intent upon suppressing the liberties of Virginians—even their freedom of appeal to the throne.[43] Francis, Lord Howard of Effingham, was held up as an example of greed.[44] And Sir Edmund Andros was blamed for complicating the procedure of Virginia law by insisting too meticulously upon English precedents.[45] Only old Governor Berkeley, his father's friend, was praised wholeheartedly.[46] All of the personal malice that had found its way into the book was toned down in the 1722 edition.

Another project that occupied Beverley's later life was a compilation of the laws of Virginia—a task completed shortly before his death. The work was brought out in London, in 1722, by the same booksellers who published the new version of the history.[47] The little book, which bore the title of *An Abridgment of the Public Laws of Virginia*, was dedicated to Alexander Spotswood in words that praised him in the highest terms for protecting the laws and liberties of the country, suppressing the pirate Teach, reviving the College of William and Mary, encouraging teachers to instruct the Indians in religion and letters, and extending the frontier settlements. Finally, the author concludes with the assertion that Spotswood's administration is an honor to Great Britain and the "greatest happiness that ever befell Virginia, raising it from need and indigence to a flourishing plenty and prosperity, with an increase of virtue and good manners." Spotswood had recognized Beverley's merits and had won him for a friend. The

[43] *Ibid.*, p. 81; see also Bk. IV, pp. 4-5.

[44] *Ibid.*, Bk. I, p. 89.

[45] *Ibid.*, p. 95.

[46] *Ibid.*, p. 50.

[47] The full title of the compilation is *An Abridgement Of The Publick Laws of Virginia, In Force and Use, June 10. 1720. To which is added, for the Ease of the Justices and Military Officers, &c. Precedents of all Matters to be issued by them, peculiar to those Laws; and varying from the Precedents in England.* London: Printed for F. Fayram and J. Clarke at the Royal-Exchange; and T. Bickerton in Paternoster Row. 1722. For a discussion, see *The Virginia Magazine of History and Biography*, XXXVI, 344.

compilation of laws is a workmanlike manual that must have been useful to every justice of the peace and planter. The only other work known to have been composed by Beverley is a small manuscript note, on a map drawn by one Lamhatty, a Creek Indian, describing a journey from Virginia to the Gulf.[48] This note is an illustration of Beverley's long-continued interest in the Indians.

Beverley died on April 21, 1722, and was buried in the family graveyard at Beverley Park. Though we know he left a will, it and the inventory of his property have long since disappeared, with other records of King and Queen County, but such legal records as have survived show that he passed on to his son William one of the greatest estates of the early eighteenth century.[49] The accumulation of wealth had taken much of Beverley's energy, but something stronger than avarice prompted him. It was his love of his land—the sentiment of a man who had roots deep in the soil. When John Fontaine wanted a tract of three thousand acres of Beverley's Rappahannock land, he refused to sell but offered a lease for nine hundred and ninety-nine years.[50] Apparently he wanted to feel that this good Virginia soil would remain in his and his heirs' possession.

Because the inventory of Beverley's property is lost, we do not know the extent of his library, or the range of his literary interests, but his own style has a polish that could have come only from familiar acquaintance with good books. Allusions in the history clearly show that he had read widely in works of travel, geography, and history, both of classical and modern writers. Conditions in Virginia suggest to him similar situations in other parts of the world. The eating habits of the Indians, for example, remind him of the strange foods sold in the markets of Fess, and of the diet of the Arabians, Lybians,

[48] See *ibid.*, pp. 343-44.
[49] *Ibid.*, p. 341.
[50] Maury, *Memoirs of a Huguenot Family*, p. 267.

Parthians, and Ethiopians. A broth made "of the head and umbles of a deer" seems "to resemble the *jus nigrum* of the Spartans."[51] Constantly he is drawing parallels from his reading. Of classical authors on natural history, he cites Pliny and Aelian. Concerning the New World, he quotes from Samuel Purchas, Alexander Whittaker, Captain John Smith, Thomas Hariot, Father Louis Hennepin, Peter Martyr, Sir Josiah Child, and the voyages of Theodor de Bry. These were works well known to English readers; but Beverley also consulted out-of-the-way books, and quotes such men as Pierre Belon, who in the mid-sixteenth century composed treatises on natural history; Adam Olearius, German author of many seventeenth-century travel narratives; Joannes de Laet, who wrote and compiled works of geographical and historical interest; and Ferdinand Verbiest, who in 1695 published a narration of the voyage of the Emperor of China into eastern Tartary. Sir Francis Bacon is cited two or three times as an authority on natural history, and Sir Walter Raleigh's *History of the World* is mentioned with admiration. When Beverley is heaping invective on Governor Nicholson, he finds a parallel in Machiavelli's principle of "divide and rule."[52] In short, Beverley's own book shows an acquaintance with many authors, though never does he sound pedantic or drag in allusions by the hair. He writes with the ease of a man who had digested his learning.

Beverley's intellectual curiosity extended beyond the authority of books. The scientific attitude demonstrated in his first-hand observations of nature was even more clearly shown in his zeal to present an accurate picture of Indian life. His history's section on the Virginia Indians is not only one of the most valuable portions of the book, but also gives a further revelation of the intellectual qualities of the author. In order to gain first-hand knowledge of the habits and customs of

[51] *The History and Present State of Virginia* (1705), Bk. III, p. 14. See also Bk. II, p. 27.

[52] *Ibid.*, Bk. I, p. 99.

these people, he visited their villages and won their friendship. Having experienced difficulty in learning about their religious beliefs, he welcomed an opportunity to spend an evening plying an intelligent Indian with hard cider until his tongue was loosened sufficiently to talk about his gods and devils.[53] Far from conventional in his attitudes generally, Beverley once more proved his original point of view in discussing the relations of the English with the Indians. Unlike the usual Englishman, who believed the Indians were devils incarnate, Virginia's first historian commended them for their virtues. Intermarriage between the settlers and the Indians he thought desirable, and he stoutly defended Indian women against charges of customary unchastity before marriage. "Indeed," he comments, "I believe this story to be an aspersion cast on those innocent creatures by reason of the freedom they take in conversation, which uncharitable Christians interpret as criminal upon no other ground than the guilt of their own consciences."[54]

So far convinced was Beverley of the good qualities of the Indians that he doubted whether the white settlers had brought any great improvement to the land. The Indians lived an idyllic life and enjoyed the natural produce of the country "without the curse of industry, their diversion alone and not their labor supplying their necessities." The change that had come since the country was settled by white men awoke no enthusiasm in the author's breast. "And indeed all that the English have done since their going thither has been only to make some of these native pleasures more scarce by an inordinate and unseasonable use of them, hardly making improvements equivalent to that damage."[55]

Though Beverley was critical and unconventional in his personal views, he was not intolerant. In fact, he was vigor-

[53] *Ibid.*, Bk. III, p. 32.
[54] *Ibid.*, p. 9.
[55] *Ibid.*, Bk. II, p. 40.

ously opposed to religious persecution of any sort and proclaimed the value of religious freedom. To his country's credit, Beverley asserts, "Christians of all nations have equal freedom there, and upon their arrival become *ipso facto* entitled to all the liberties and privileges of the country, provided they take the oaths of obedience to the crown and government."[56] Colonel William Byrd, brother-in-law of the writer, receives praise for his generosity to distressed Huguenot refugees.[57] If Beverley was a protagonist of religious toleration, that does not mean that he had no definite religious views himself or was free from prejudice. He clearly disliked priestcraft, as he demonstrates in a passage comparing the cunning of Indian and Romish priests.[58] As an Anglican himself, he probably took a sly pleasure in pointing out that "those counties where the Presbyterian meetings are, produce very mean tobacco."[59]

One quality in Beverley, evident throughout his history—a quality obvious all his life—was his devotion to Virginia. Although he could criticize his contemporaries with sardonic irony, he never doubted the goodness of this land. He was a Virginian and proud of it. When others found fault with the colony, he defended her vigorously. When the charge was made that Virginians mistreated their servants, Beverley hotly denied the libel and cited benign laws that had been enacted to protect the lives and rights of servants.[60] Reproaches heaped on the colony had come from "unfit and unequal judges," travelers from England who knew little of the real genius of the country—a complaint that Americans were to make for the next two hundred years. Even the laziness of Virginians, a fault that Beverley himself had criticized, comes from the "exceeding plenty of good things with which nature

[56] *Ibid.*, Bk. IV, pp. 44-45; see also Bk. I, p. 59.
[57] *Ibid.*, Bk. IV, pp. 46-47.
[58] *Ibid.*, Bk. III, p. 44; see also p. 33.
[59] *Ibid.*, Bk. IV, p. 27.
[60] *Ibid.*, pp. 36-39.

has blest them; for where God Almighty is so merciful as to work for people, they never work for themselves." [61]

In Robert Beverley Virginia had a native son whose originality and iconoclastic views sometimes irritated his contemporaries; but in this vigorous writer the colony had a voice that proclaimed her dawning intellectual and political maturity. Robert Beverley and his brother-in-law, William Byrd of Westover, were the most vigorous writers that Virginia produced in the pre-Revolutionary period.

[61] *Ibid.*, p. 60.

CHAPTER XI

THE BYRDS' PROGRESS FROM TRADE TO GENTEEL ELEGANCE

If no other records had survived except those of the Byrd family, they alone would have made it possible for later generations to understand the social development of Virginia and to trace the evolution of an aristocracy that attained a mellow splendor. Although the Byrds were richer and more influential than some others of the ruling families, they were typical of the group who controlled the colony and established the pattern of life followed by the colonial gentry. Indeed, the first three generations of Byrds went through a cycle that was to be repeated many times in the evolution of later American families: the first William Byrd, by shrewd business acumen, accumulated a fortune and established his family as a power in the land; the second William Byrd became an elegant ornament of that family, but inherited enough of his father's business judgment to hold on to his property and even to add to his possessions; the third William Byrd, by his vices and bad management, squandered the fortune. With only the first two Byrds are we concerned.

William Byrd the elder—the emigrant who established the name in Virginia—was the son of John Byrd, a London goldsmith of moderate means, who had married Grace Stegg, daughter of Captain Thomas Stegg.[1] Captain Stegg, a merchant and ship captain engaged in the Virginia trade, had residences on both sides of the Atlantic and was already a man of promi-

[1] More has been written about the Byrds than about any other early colonial Virginia family. Accounts of the lives of William Byrd I and II are to be found in the excellent introduction to John Spencer Bassett, *The Writings of Colonel William Byrd* (New York, 1901); in the respective articles on them by Thomas J. Wertenbaker in the *Dictionary of American Biography;* in Richmond Croom

nence in the colony when his daughter married the goldsmith. When Parliament wanted an honest and capable commissioner to subdue Virginia to its will, Captain Stegg was chosen. Returning from Virginia, in 1651, with the colony's submission to Parliament, he was lost at sea. His substantial Virginia property went to his son Thomas, who also rejoiced in the title of captain. The year after the elder Captain Stegg was drowned, his grandson William Byrd was born; and sometime before 1670 he went to live with his uncle, Captain Thomas Stegg the younger, who made the boy his heir. Thus the first William Byrd inherited rich properties, in land and houses, near the falls of the James River, where the city of Richmond was one day to stand.

Not only did young Byrd fall heir to a settled estate of considerable value, but also he succeeded to an established social position. His uncle's friends had included, among others, Governor Berkeley and members of the powerful Ludwell family. Anyone could have foretold that William Byrd would one day achieve a position of power in the colony.

Further to establish his position, Byrd in 1673 made a good marriage, to Mary Horsmanden,[2] the daughter of a Cavalier officer who had fled to Virginia during the Puritan regime. A year after his marriage his first child, William, was born, and the Byrd dynasty was assured. In due time, four other children were born: Susan, who married a London merchant; Ursula, who married Robert Beverley the historian; Mary, who died unmarried; and Warham, who died in childhood. Mrs. Byrd died in 1699, five years before her husband's death.

Beatty, *William Byrd of Westover* (Boston and New York, 1932); and in *The Virginia Magazine of History and Biography*, XXXV (1927), 221-45, 372-89. Many of the letters of both Byrds are to be found in the same journal, especially Vols. IX, XXIV-XXVIII, XXXII, XXXV-XXXVIII, *passim.* See also the letters in *The Virginia Historical Register and Literary Advertiser*, I (1848) and II (1849), *passim.*

[2] The name seems to have had several variant spellings, including Horsemanden and Horsmonden.

Included in Byrd's inheritance in Henrico County at the falls of the James was a store of trading goods used in traffic with the Indians. At that time the Stegg plantation was a distant outpost, and it continued to be within the range of Indian forays until near the end of Byrd's life. But the very fact of its nearness to the Indians enabled him to develop the trade with them that his uncle had begun. For nearly thirty-five years after he came into possession of the property, Byrd made his plantation the center for traffic with the red men. His traders pushed their way hundreds of miles to the south, following trails that led them deep into the Cherokee and Catawba country of South Carolina. In addition to the usual trinkets used in trade, his pack trains carried to distant Indian villages blue cloth, kettles, hatchets, rum, guns, and ammunition; and they brought back furs, deerskins, rare herbs, and minerals that Byrd hoped might prove of value. Although the savages were a constant menace, occasionally murdering his own traders, Byrd worried little over the fact that he himself provided them with rum and firearms.[3] If they did not buy such supplies from him, they would procure them from other traders, and Byrd saw no reason to lose the fat profits of the traffic.

But the Indian trade was only part of Byrd's business undertakings. He bought and sold tobacco, imported black slaves and white indentured servants, and supplied many planters with the imported English goods they used. He traded with New England shippers for rum, molasses, sugar, and barrel staves. To Eliakim Hutchinson of Boston we find him writing, in 1689, requesting a shipment of "rum, sugar, Madeira wine, turnery, earthenware, or anything else you may judge convenient for this country, fish excepted."[4] Always in orders

[3] For letters by William Byrd mentioning the sale of arms to Indians, see *The Virginia Magazine of History and Biography*, XXIV (1916), 234, 353. Accounts of killing of traders are given in letters, *ibid.*, XXV (1917), 51-52; XXVI (1918), 128.

[4] *Ibid.*, XXVI, 23; see also p. 258.

to New England he warned that he wanted none of their codfish. Incredible quantities of rum are mentioned in numerous letters to his mercantile correspondents in New England, Barbados, and London. For instance, in one letter, to John Thomas & Company of Barbados, he ordered 4,000 gallons of rum, along with 5,000 pounds of muscovado, 6,000 pounds of sugar, and eight or ten tons of molasses.[5] Slaves and rum were his most lucrative imports. In fact, his cargoes sometimes combined the two commodities, as is indicated by a letter to Perry & Lane of London, requesting a large supply of slaves and 1,000 gallons of rum.[6] Occasionally the importer had cause to rue the slave trade—for example, in 1686, when the new slaves brought smallpox into his very household, resulting in the death of some of his house servants and a neighbor then staying with the Byrds.[7]

Though Byrd was a shrewd and enterprising trader, his correspondence never suggests that he was given to trickery, meanness, or sharp practice. If he sold rum and guns to the Indians and slaves to his neighbors, the transactions were honest and legitimate. He is constantly cautioning his correspondents against sending him shoddy goods. The trading cloth must be just the right color; the guns to be sold the Indians must have the right kind of locks; the negroes must all be prime workers, young and healthy. Byrd knows that it is sound business to handle goods that will not jeopardize his reputation. He is disturbed when his customers complain that kettles in a recent shipment had holes in them, and he writes a protest to his agent.[8] His letters are filled with complaints about the failure

[5] *Ibid.*, XXV, 253.

[6] *Ibid.*, XXIV, 232. The letter as printed here specifies 506 negroes. I have had no opportunity of seeing the original letter, but this may be a misprint or a slip of the pen. The investment required for importing so large a number of negroes, even for quick resale, was larger than Byrd probably could have managed at this time.

[7] *Ibid.*, XXV, 134. The neighbor was Mrs. John Brodnax.

[8] *Ibid.*, p. 52.

of his agents in London to supply the proper sort of goods; he is alert to efforts to overcharge him; but he is also careful to report any articles not charged against him in his invoices.

By his diligence and shrewdness William Byrd grew prosperous in trade. When the details of business became too heavy for him to manage alone, he sent to Christ's Hospital for a likely apprentice[9]—one trained, as those youths were, in the elements of mathematics and bookkeeping. When he was little more than thirty years old, Byrd was already one of the chief businessmen of the colony—soundly established and well-thought-of by his contemporaries. That alone attests his reputation for fair dealing.

With one eye intent upon trade, William Byrd kept the other on political offices, which he filled from time to time. From some of these he gained a neat profit; others he held because it was his duty to the state. Early in his career he narrowly averted political catastrophe by becoming involved with Nathaniel Bacon the rebel. At the inception of the revolt, Byrd led a part of Bacon's followers against the Indians. One of the chief grievances of Bacon's frontier adherents was that Governor Berkeley had done nothing to put a stop to Indian attacks. On that score, Byrd, as an Indian trader and one of the frontier planters himself, was in sympathy with the agitator, but, when Bacon began idealistically to plead for constitutional reforms, Byrd parted company with him. As a practical businessman, the trading planter had nothing to do with political daydreams; he wanted protection from the savages.[10] Having left the Bacon faction, Byrd quickly made his peace with the Governor, and thereafter trod cautiously and surely along the path that led to political power. In 1677 he became a member of the House of Burgesses, and six years later took his seat on the Council, becoming president of that body in 1703. In 1687 he went to England to seek an appoint-

[9] *Ibid.*, p. 50; see also *ibid.*, XXVIII, 22.

[10] Bassett, *op. cit.*, pp. xx-xxi.

ment as auditor-general of Virginia—a lucrative post. Although he received the appointment, he was engaged in a long dispute with one Robert Ayleway, who asserted a prior claim to the office and had to be bought off.[11] In addition to these offices, Byrd commanded the militia of Henrico County. Being colonel of the county military forces was something more than an honor, and Byrd was responsible for the safety of the outlying plantations. Because of his knowledge of the Indians he was sent in 1685 to Albany, New York, to negotiate a treaty with the Iroquois, who were regarded as a menace to the peace of the southern tribes. He also served as a member of the building committee of the newly established William and Mary College, and had the contract to construct the college chapel.[12]

All the while, this busy man was accumulating land. If his land hunger was not so great as that of some of his contemporaries, he nevertheless did very well by himself. At his death, his holdings consisted of 26,231 acres.[13] Some of the land was situated at the falls of the James River, where he built a house and named the place Belvidere; some was in scattered tracts in other parts of Henrico County; and one fine estate was at Westover on the James, in Charles City County. The Westover property became Byrd's particular pride. There he erected in 1690 a wooden mansion, which his son later replaced with a brick house. For his new home he imported fine furniture, but his thrifty habits did not let him run riot with expense. In an order for house furnishings—including a dozen "best Russia leather chairs," and one small, one middling, and one large oval table—he specifies a "looking glass for a chamber to be handsome and neat, but cheap." [14]

The gardens of Westover—later to be extended and further

[11] *Ibid.*, pp. xxiii-xxiv.

[12] *Ibid.*, p. xxviii.

[13] *Ibid.*, p. xxxv.

[14] *The Virginia Magazine of History and Biography*, XXVI, 391. Concerning the building of Byrd's house at Westover, see also pp. 128, 129, 130.

improved by his son—were laid out soon after the house was completed. Byrd took great pleasure in his flowers and rare shrubs; his letters frequently mention shipments of bulbs and plants from England. In fact, one of his intellectual interests was botany, in which he had some proficiency. When he visited England in 1687, he met Jacob Bobart, keeper of the botanical gardens at Oxford and Sherardian professor of botany, who sent him a gift of trees and plants for experimentation.[15] Byrd was intimately acquainted with John Banister, the naturalist, who was at work on a natural history of Virginia when he was accidentally killed. Byrd himself made many observations of plant and animal life and was interested in the mineralogy of the colony. From time to time he sent samples of ores and other rocks to England for examination in the hope of discovering commercially valuable minerals.

During his later years Byrd devoted his spare time to the cultivation of the graces of life and to satisfying his intellectual curiosity concerning the world about him. As might be expected, much of his interest was intensely practical, and his scientific reading was prompted by a desire to learn profitable secrets of nature. To John Clinton of London, "who had formerly devised me to some books," Byrd in 1686 sent a fine Indian outfit for his little son, with an urgent request that Clinton procure "a treatise or two of minerals and stones, the fittest you find for my purpose, either of Mr. Boyle's or any other English author; also Salmon's *Polygraphice*, the last edition."[16] A little later he is writing for a copy of Thomas Burnet's *The Theory of the Earth* (1684),[17] a work that mixed piety and geology in a fashion satisfactory to a devout believer in the Scriptures.

[15] *Ibid.*, pp. 255-56.

[16] *Ibid.*, XXV, 129-30. "Mr. Boyle's" treatise was Robert Boyle's *An Essay about the Origin and Virtue of Gems* (1672); "Salmon's Polygraphice" was William Salmon's *Polygraphice; or, The Art of Drawing, Engraving, . . . Varnishing . . . and Dyeing* (1672).

[17] *Ibid.*, XXVI, 31.

Because no inventory of the first William Byrd's library has been discovered, we can only make conjectures concerning the sort of books he preferred. It is clear, however, that the foundation of the great library gathered by his son was laid by the elder Byrd. At intervals, in the letters to his agents abroad, he mentions books, though not many are cited by title. In one letter he wants "*The Turkish Spy*, all but the first volume"[18]—an indication that he had previously received the beginning of this popular series of publications. On another occasion he orders Pierre Jurieu's *The Accomplishment of the Scripture Prophecies; or, The Approaching Deliverance of the Church* (1687)[19]—a work, by a French Protestant controversialist regarded as almost the equal of Calvin, that had been translated into English and published only three years before Byrd sent for it. The purchase suggests an anti-Catholic point of view, though there is not much in his letters to indicate any violent religious bias. What his other books were, we do not know, but he must have had a fair collection. In 1690 he complained to Perry & Lane that he had been charged twice for an item of books amounting to £35 14*s.*[20]

That Byrd had a strain of sincere piety is evident from his letters. His expressions of gratitude to God for good fortune are more than conventional utterances, and his advice to his children emphasize the value of devotion to religion. If young William Byrd absorbed too much of the rationalistic notions of the London wits, it was not because his father had not endeavored to bring him up in the fear of the Lord.[21]

The elder William Byrd's concern over the proper education of his children, that they might become ornaments to the family, is evident in the care which he took to send them

[18] *Ibid. Letters Written by a Turkish Spy*, by Giovanni Paolo Marana, appeared in an English translation, in eight volumes, in 1687-93.

[19] *Ibid.*, p. 391.

[20] *Ibid.*, p. 133.

[21] See Bassett, pp. xxxviii-xxxix.

to English schools. As mere infants, William, Susan, and Ursula were sent to England. The girls were placed in a school at Hackney and later were taken into the household of their uncle, Daniel Horsmanden—an arrangement that proved unsatisfactory to all concerned. Because war with France made ocean travel hazardous, the children were compelled to remain in England longer than intended; in fact, Susan married and settled there, and Ursula had turned sixteen before she again set foot in Virginia. The planter and his wife were agreed that their children should be given every opportunity to acquire the polish and culture of English ladies and gentlemen. In 1685, when Ursula was four years old, Byrd wrote his father-in-law: "My wife hath all this year urged me to send little Nutty [Ursula] home to you, to which I have at last condescended, and hope you'll please to excuse the trouble. I must confess she could learn nothing good here in a great family of negroes."[22] William was placed under the tutelage of a famous schoolmaster, Christopher Glasscock,[23] headmaster of Felsted Grammar School in Essex. Felsted School had a fine reputation for its emphasis on both learning and piety. There the sons of Oliver Cromwell had gone, and, if Byrd knew this he doubtless felt—Royalist though he was—that he was making no mistake in the selection of a school considered good enough for the Protector's children. That he was pleased by the choice is made clear in a letter to the headmaster on March 31, 1685, expressing his "hearty thanks" for William's excellent instruction and hoping that the boy would not "be discouraged in his fair proceedings."[24] Though Byrd was anxious for his son to acquire good learning, that did not

[22] *The Virginia Historical Register*, II, 79.

[23] The name of Byrd's schoolmaster is given by his biographers as Christopher Glassock. No English schoolmaster at this period by that name can be found. Without doubt Glassock is a misinterpretation of the name of Christopher Glasscock.

[24] *The Virginia Historical Register*, II, 80. The name is here printed "Glassock" instead of Glasscock.

mean at all that his purpose was to make a mere scholar of him; hence, when the lad was about sixteen, he sent him to Holland—probably in the care of one of his mercantile correspondents—to learn about business and trade. From Holland the boy presently returned, at his own request, with instructions from his father to report to Perry & Lane in London, "there to learn what may be farther fitting for you"; Perry & Lane had been requested, the father wrote, "to employ you about business wherein I hope you will endeavor to acquaint yourself that you may be no stranger to it when necessity will require you to attend to it."[25] Byrd had no intention of bringing up a son who would have the polish of a gentleman and yet lack the training needed to carry the burden of business that was a necessary concomitant of a great planter's life.

Although the elder William Byrd was proud of his wealth, power, and position in Virginia, he had no false notions of factitious grandeur. He possessed, to a remarkable degree, the quality of realistic hard sense which characterized the ruling class of his day. Occasionally, he fell a victim to the vanity of fashion, as when, in 1689, he sent his old sword to Perry & Lane with an order to exchange it for a newfangled "small silver-hilted rapier"; but in general he was too shrewd and wise to be swayed by the fripperies of life. He was determined to found his family on a sound basis of wealth, and he hoped that his son, whatever his cultural attainments might be, would have the good judgment to manage his business affairs with discretion.

In order that the name of Byrd should carry proper dignity in Virginia, the founder of the family, when he died in 1704, left his entire estate to his eldest son and namesake. The law of primogeniture was never seriously regarded in Virginia, where a father felt that he had land enough for all of his heirs,

[25] Quoted by Bassett, p. xliv. See also *The Virginia Magazine of History and Biography*, XXVI, 128-29.

but Byrd wanted to concentrate his family fortune on the bearer of his name. Hence, in his will, he cut off his two surviving daughters with a few hundred pounds and left the rest of his great estate to William, who was made executor.[26] This beneficiary was later to prove worthy of his father's faith, for few Virginia families attained to such glory or landed greatness as that of the second William Byrd.

The new lord of Westover was already a man of distinction when he came into his inheritance. Although he was only a few months more than thirty years old, he had served in the House of Burgesses and had represented the colony as agent in London. Furthermore, in the years spent in England he had made friends with some of the important figures in the social, political, and intellectual world. When he hurried home in 1705, he was an experienced and urbane gentleman, equally at ease in a drawing room, law court, or meeting of the General Assembly. Moreover, he was still one of the most eligible bachelors in all Virginia. His arrival at the Westover landing, in the spring, must have been an event of more than usual interest to the little social world where his doings abroad were the envy of the stay-at-homes.

A large part of Byrd's life before his return to Virginia in 1705 had been spent abroad in varied activities that had given him a well-rounded education. Academic learning, business training, and social opportunities had all gone into the experience of the young man who was to become the most accomplished Virginian of his time. When he came back to London from Holland in 1690 and went into the counting-house of Perry & Lane, he had no intention of staying there long; after learning something of the ways of business he entered the Middle Temple, in April, 1692, and in due course was admitted to the bar.[27] On a visit home in 1696 he was elected for the first time to the House of Burgesses.

[26] *The Virginia Magazine of History and Biography*, XXXV, 235-37.
[27] Bassett, p. xliv.

The years spent as a member of the Middle Temple were among the gayest of his life. With other young blades of his circle, he indulged in his share of gallantries and sowed the usual crop of wild oats. A hint at his rakehell days is found in one of Byrd's letters, written over forty years later, to his friend, Judge Benjamin Lynde, of Salem, Massachusetts, who had shared his adventures at the Middle Temple. "But matrimony has atoned sufficiently for such backsliding," Byrd observes, "and now I suppose you have so little fellow feeling left for the naughty jades that you can order them a good whipping without relenting. But though I should be mistaken, I hope your conscience, with the aid of three score and ten, has gained a complete victory over your constitution, which is almost the case of, sir, your, &c." [28] During young Byrd's residence at the Middle Temple, the atmosphere of Restoration gallantry had not yet been entirely dispelled by the chill wind of respectability that blew from Holland on the accession of William and Mary. The Virginian could still attend a theater only little "improved" since the heyday of the broadest Restoration comedies. Indeed, Byrd was intimately acquainted with William Wycherley, one of the boldest of the comedy writers, and quoted his plays. The great William Congreve was still at the Middle Temple when Byrd entered, as was Nicholas Rowe. Other wits of the theatrical world were also known to him,[29] and he was probably more familiar with the characters in Restoration plays than with the names of some of his living neighbors in Virginia.[30] Certainly Byrd was a constant theatergoer, and his interest in the drama persisted

[28] *The Virginia Magazine of History and Biography*, IX (1901-2), 244.

[29] See Beatty, *op. cit.*, p. 44.

[30] Among the manuscripts in the Brock Collection in the Huntington Library are nine volumes of transcripts of Byrd papers, for the most part copies of the letters of William Byrd II. Vol. 9 of this collection (BR 188) is a transcript of a literary piece called "The Female Creed," a prose travesty in the Restoration spirit, probably written by Byrd. In it are numerous literary allusions which suggest that the writer had been reading Restoration plays.

for the rest of his life. Many years later, while stormbound at the Randolph home at Tuckahoe, he amused the company by discussing comedies and reading aloud three acts from the second part of *The Beggar's Opera,* which Mrs. Randolph had in her own library.[31]

If Byrd could count among his London acquaintances a few of the rakes and scapegraces of the day, he also had for his intimates men of learning and influence. Sir Robert Southwell, distinguished diplomat and virtuoso, was his patron and adviser. Through him he met Sir William Petty and many other learned men of the time. Southwell's sponsorship resulted in Byrd's election on April 29, 1696, at the age of twenty-two, to the Royal Society[32]—a remarkable honor for a colonial youth. Membership in the Royal Society brought him into further contact with scholars, as well as with a few of the nobility who chose to patronize scientific learning. Charles Boyle, who succeeded his brother in 1703 as the fourth Earl of Orrery, was one of Byrd's lifelong friends. They were all chosen from "the best people." Byrd maintained a correspondence with them after his return to Virginia, and, with considerable pride in his own social success, collected their portraits and hung them in his picture gallery at Westover. There, gazing on the likenesses of Sir Robert Southwell, Sir Wilfred Lawson, Sir Charles Wager, Lord Oxford, Lord Egmont, the Earl of Orrery, the Marquis of Halifax, the Duke of Argyle, Lady Elizabeth Southwell, Lady Betty Cromwell,

[31] The passage describing this incident is found in *A Progress to the Mines in the Year 1732* (in *Writings,* ed. Bassett, pp. 341-42). Byrd described the popularity of *The Beggar's Opera,* "which had diverted the town for 40 nights successively, and gained four thousand pounds to the author," and then related several gossipy bits of information concerning the play. "After having acquainted my company with the history of the play, I read three acts of it, and left Mrs. Fleming and Mr. Randolph to finish it, who read as well as most actors do at a rehearsal. Thus we killed the time and triumphed over the bad weather."

[32] Maude H. Woodfin, "William Byrd and the Royal Society," *The Virginia Magazine of History and Biography,* XL (1932), 23-34, 111-23.

and other fine ladies and gentlemen,[33] the Virginian could remember the days of his social triumph in England and count himself an American counterpart of those noble persons. So much did he prize his friendship with Southwell and Boyle that years afterward the author of his lengthy epitaph thought fit to memorialize this intimacy.[34]

While he was still a very young man, Byrd began the long political career that was to make him a powerful figure in the ruling circle of Virginia. The year of his entry into the Royal Society also saw his election to the House of Burgesses. The following year, having returned to England, he represented the colony before the Board of Trade and defended Governor Andros, at the Lambeth Conference, against attacks from Commissary James Blair, who complained that the Governor was indifferent to the needs of the Anglican Establishment and the new College of William and Mary. Though Byrd's defense was no match for the Scotch logic of Blair, he gained useful experience,[35] and in October, 1698, he received a salaried appointment as agent for Virginia. But, because he went over the head of Governor Nicholson, in 1702, to present an address to the King from the Council and Burgesses, protesting against raising troops and money to defend the frontiers of New York, the Board of Trade objected to his agency, the government rebuked the Council, and Byrd ceased his official duties in London. In 1706 he obtained the post of receiver-general for the crown in Virginia—a profitable appointment, that paid him at first a three per cent, and later a five per cent, commission on receipts. In 1708 Byrd was appointed to membership on the Council—an office of dignity that he held until his death. In the last year of his life, as senior member of the Council he became its president—an honor that would have come much earlier but for the longevity of old Commissary

[33] Bassett, p. lxxxi.

[34] *Ibid.*, p. xli; and Beatty, *op. cit.*, pp. 210-11, where the epitaph is reproduced.

[35] Bassett, p. xlv.

Blair, who, though deaf and obstinate, presided over the Council till the age of eighty-seven. Blair, who had thwarted Byrd in the defense of Andros at the Lambeth Conference, was long a stumbling block to his highest advancement in Virginia politics.

The gay bachelor who, in 1705, had set the hearts of Virginia maidens aflutter on his inheritance of Westover, in 1706 took a wife. She was Lucy Parke, daughter of Colonel Daniel Parke. Socially, Lucy Parke was all that could be wished, but the match was a financial disaster for her husband. When Daniel Parke was killed in the uprising at Antigua in 1710, he left his English and Virginia estates to his elder daughter Frances, wife of John Custis, and bequeathed Lucy a mere thousand pounds. Parke's debts were to be paid by selling some of the real estate. Byrd, always land-hungry, agreed with Custis, the executor, to take over the lands that would have to be sold and to assume the debts. This bargain proved a grave error, for Parke owed his London agent, Micajah Perry, more than his son-in-law realized, and there were also other debts. Byrd's efforts to meet the demands of Parke's creditors kept him pressed for ready money during most of his later life.[36]

Four children were born to Lucy and William Byrd, but two died in infancy. The oldest child, Evelyn, was sent to England to be educated and was regarded as one of the beauties of the day. According to a romantic tradition, the Earl of Peterborough sought her hand in marriage, but her father would not permit the match. Two recently discovered letters by Byrd, in the University of North Carolina letter book, clearly prove that another nobleman and not Peterborough was Evelyn's suitor. These letters, one written to the daughter and the other to her lover, an unidentified baronet, forbid the marriage.[36a] Evelyn never married, and died at the age of thirty.

[36] See *ibid.*, pp. l-li, for details of the deal.

[36a] In the University of North Carolina letter book, Byrd disguised most of the

The other surviving child, a daughter, Wilhelmina, married Thomas Chamberlayne of New Kent County. Mrs. Byrd died in London in 1716. About 1724 Byrd took as his second wife Maria Taylor, daughter of an English gentleman of Kensington. Four children were born to them. The first daughter of this match, Anne, married Charles Carter of Cleve; the next daughter, Maria, married Landon Carter of Sabine Hall; and the third daughter, Jane, married John Page of North End, Gloucester County. The fourth child was a son, named, after his father, William. He became the heir of Westover, but dissipated the property, turned Tory during the Revolution, and ended his life by his own hand in 1777.[37]

When Byrd married in 1706, he hoped to settle down at Westover to the life of a country gentleman. He was ready to forego the gaieties of London for quieter rural pleasures. But just when he had established himself comfortably as a squire on the James River, with a young family about him, he

---

names. He addresses his daughter as "Amasia," and the baronet as "Erranti." The letter to his daughter is dated July 20, 1723. In it Byrd reminds Evelyn of her promise by word of mouth and by letter to have no further "converse of correspondence with the baronet." He rebukes her for seeing him in the country and orders her not "to meet, speak, or write to that gentleman," or to give him an opportunity "to see, speak, or write to you." After forbidding her "to enter into any promise or engagement with him of marriage or inclination," he solemnly vows to cut her off without "one brass farthing" if she disobeys. The letter ends on a pleading note, with Byrd begging his daughter not to wreck her happiness by an unfortunate match. This letter was followed by one to "Erranti" under the same date. He informs the baronet that he has learned of his following his daughter into the country, "with a pompous equipage." Byrd warns him that in a new will, made since the baronet's attentions to his daughter became known, he has bequeathed her "a splendid shilling if she marries any man that tempts her to disobedience." Sarcastically, Byrd remarks: "I fear your circumstances are not flourishing enough to maintain a wife in much splendor that has nothing, and just such a fortune as that my daughter will prove if she ventures to marry without my consent."

Sir Charles Mordaunt, Peterborough's grandson and successor, has been suggested as Evelyn's suitor. This seems hardly possible, for on Dec. 1, 1720, Mordaunt married a daughter of Sir John Conyers. She lived until Mar., 1726.

[37] *The Virginia Magazine of History and Biography*, XXXII (1924), 37.

once more had to go back to England. About 1713 he came into conflict with Lieutenant-Governor Spotswood over the question of the manner of collecting quitrents, and he also led the Council in opposition to Spotswood's efforts to set up courts of oyer and terminer—a procedure designed to weaken the power of the oligarchic Council. The struggle between Spotswood and the Council was long and bitter. In 1715 Byrd went to England, partly on private business and partly to take up the cudgels against Spotswood, before the Board of Trade. Not until five years later was he able to return to his home on the James. In the meantime, Spotswood had attempted to procure his removal from the Council, but Byrd had circumvented him, and, when the planter came back in 1720, he brought a command to the various factions to make peace.[38] To the credit of both Byrd and Spotswood, they reconciled their differences and became friends.

Byrd's leadership of the Council in the fight with the royal governor over questions of prerogative helped to increase the dignity and prestige of that governing body. As one historian has observed, "instead of throwing the Councillors, who through abilities and position were the natural leaders of the community, into an inane espousal of the rights of the crown, it developed in them a strong colony sense. They felt that they were Virginians first of all."[39] Though Byrd was strongly imbued with a love of English institutions and English manners, he did not forget that he was one of Virginia's rulers, and he exerted his best efforts to defend the colony against any encroachment from outside authority, even the authority of the King's representative.

If Byrd was looking forward to a peaceful life at Westover when he came home in 1720, he was doomed to disappointment. In the fall of that year, the Assembly passed an address

[38] Bassett, pp. lv-lxxv, gives a detailed account of the controversies.

[39] *Ibid.*, p. liii.

to the King and again appointed Byrd colonial agent, with instructions to go back to London. There he stayed until 1726, when he returned to spend the rest of his life as the lord of Westover. The long years in England had given him further opportunities of making friends with important people, and he had become the best-known American of his time in the drawing rooms of fashionable English society. But by 1726 he was tired of London and eager to resume his residence on the James.

Byrd quickly adapted himself to the pleasant life on his estate, but one of his prominence could not avoid devoting a portion of his time to public responsibilities. He at once resumed his duties as a Councilor. When the vexed question of the boundary between Virginia and North Carolina had to be settled in 1728, he was chosen to head the Virginia Boundary Commission. His racy account of the survey, in the *History of the Dividing Line*, assured him a distinguished place in the history of colonial letters. Byrd acquitted himself so well in surveying the North Carolina boundary that eight years later, in 1736, he headed the commission appointed to survey the Northern Neck. These were his two most arduous labors in his later years, but, as senior member of the Council next to old Commissary Blair, he had many judicial and executive tasks to perform. Because of Blair's deafness, Byrd had to preside over the General Court. In short, he was the most distinguished and experienced of Virginia's elder statesmen.

More important than his political influence, however, was the example Byrd set as an aristocrat and fine gentleman. Having had greater opportunities than any contemporary Virginian to mingle in the beau monde and cultivate the graces of aristocracy, he thought of himself as the colonial equivalent of such noblemen as his friend the Earl of Orrery, and he sought to reproduce at Westover the kind of life he had learned to appreciate in his circle of aristocratic English friends.

About 1735 Byrd rebuilt the family mansion, erecting a handsome brick house, essentially the same as that standing today, though damage by fire and war has required reconstruction and renovation. For a model Byrd may have followed the design of Drayton Court, the Northamptonshire seat of the Earl of Peterborough,[40] mistakenly believed to have been a suitor for his daughter's hand. The new manor house, with its extensive gardens and expanse of greensward sloping gently down to the river, became one of the show places of Virginia. From England the owner imported the finest Georgian furniture, a huge quantity of cut glass and silver, and everything else needed to equip his house after the latest fashion. The picture gallery, as we have already observed, contained not only family portraits but pictures of as many of Byrd's noble friends as he could procure.

The way of life followed by Byrd—as by others of his class—was patriarchal. Surrounded by his dependents, the great planter ruled his domain like a potentate and dispensed hospitality with the generosity of a prince. But this power and this habit of hospitality implied responsibilities that prevented the lords of these baronies from sitting in idle ease. The rich planter's life in the early eighteenth century has had few better descriptions than those found in Byrd's own letters. To the Earl of Orrery, he wrote on July 5, 1726:

> I have a large family of my own, and my doors are open to everybody, yet I have no bills to pay, and half a crown will rest undisturbed in my pocket for many moons together. Like one of the patriarchs, I have my flocks and my herds, my bondmen and bondwomen, and every sort of trade amongst my own servants, so that I live in a kind of independence of everyone but Providence. However, this sort of life is without expense, yet it is attended with a great deal of trouble. I must take care to keep all my people to their duty, to set all the springs in motion, and to make every-

[40] Edith Tunis Sale, *Manors of Virginia in Colonial Times* (Philadelphia, 1909), p. 137.

> one draw his equal share to carry the machine forward. But then 'tis an amusement in this silent country and a continual exercise of our patience and economy. Another thing, my lord, that recommends this country very much: we sit securely under our vines and our fig trees without any danger to our property. We have neither public robbers nor private, which your lordship will think very strange when we have often needy governors and pilfering convicts sent amongst us. . . . Thus, my lord, we are very happy in our Canaans, if we could but forget the onions and fleshpots of Egypt.[41]

Five years later Byrd wrote to John Boyle, heir of the Earl of Orrery, almost the same description, and added: "We are all of one religion and one party in politics. . . . The merchants of England take care that none of us grow very rich, and the felicity of the climate hinders us from being very poor. . . . We have no beggars but for places, which for want of favorites, court mistresses, and first ministers are never sold."[42]

Though the peace and plenty on the James compensated for the gay and bustling life Byrd remembered on the Thames, he sometimes yearned for the high living he had enjoyed in England. To the end of his days he kept up a correspondence with his English friends, and through their letters to him he lived over his experiences abroad.[43] To Orrery and his son he was constantly writing; with Lord Egmont he remained on terms of intimacy, praising extravagantly the portrait he had received from his lordship;[44] and to Sir Robert Walpole, the great prime minister, he wrote familiarly, advising him to maintain a big navy—and also sent him a little of the herb ginseng, which Byrd believed a sovereign remedy against most of the ills of the world.[45] Far away in Virginia though he might be, Byrd never lapsed into a provincial; indeed, he

[41] *The Virginia Magazine of History and Biography*, XXXII, 27.
[42] *Ibid.*, p. 35; letter dated June, 1731.
[43] *Ibid.*, XXXVI (1928), 216.
[44] *Ibid.*, p. 219.
[45] *Ibid.*, pp. 356-58.

displayed the sophisticated urbanity that he had acquired during his years in London. Writing to a certain Mrs. Taylor, widow of his second wife's brother, he playfully remarks that he is outside the latitude of news, for " 'tis a mighty misfortune for an epistolizer not to live near some great city like London or Paris, where people play the fool in a wellbred way, and furnish their neighbors with discourse."[46] But he never lacked for sprightly comment, and even to this day his letters are a pleasure to read.

Byrd's life at Westover was by no means given over to mere material things. He never forgot that he was a member of the Royal Society, and he took care that the learned world should also remember the fact. Three years before his death he wrote to Sir Hans Sloane, the president: "I take it a little unkindly, sir, that my name is left out of the yearly list of the Royal Society, of which I have the honor to be one of its ancientest members. I suppose my long absence has made your secretaries rank me in the number of the dead, but pray let them know I am alive, and by the help of ginseng hope to survive some years longer."[47] For more than thirty years Byrd had corresponded with Sloane, one of the most distinguished of British physicians and botanists, and had supplied him with animal, vegetable, and mineral specimens from Virginia. From 1697, when he contributed his first paper to the Society—on the curious phenomenon of a negro with a dappled skin[48]—until his death, Byrd kept up his scientific interests and was in frequent communication with the English virtuosi. It was fashionable in this period for gentlemen to play at being scientists, but in Byrd's case fashion was joined to a natural bent. A man whose activities were so varied could hardly

[46] *Ibid.*, IX, 229.

[47] "Letters of William Byrd II and Sir Hans Sloane Relative to Plants and Minerals in Virginia," *William and Mary College Quarterly*, 2d Ser., I (1921), 186-200.

[48] Woodfin, *op. cit.*, pp. 28-29.

be ranked among the great scientific minds, but Byrd may be regarded as one of the more serious amateurs of his day.

Throughout a long life he maintained an interest in literature. His education and associations in England had given him a wide acquaintance with many writers, both living and dead. In spite of multifarious duties and the bustle that only one who has lived on a sprawling plantation can appreciate, he managed to find time for systematic study at Westover. An insight into his scholarly interests is to be found in an intimate and personal diary, which he kept in shorthand. A part of this diary, dating from February 6, 1709, to September 29, 1712, was recently discovered in the Huntington Library; it shows that in these years he was an early riser, and, after saying his prayers, frequently read a chapter of Hebrew, a hundred or more verses from Homer, or a chapter in a Greek version of Josephus—a ritual that provided for mind and soul. Later in the day he indulged in other studies. Sometimes he notes the reading of Latin books, and he mentions time given to Italian, geometry, and law. Occasionally, he read a sermon or some other religious work. Dr. Tillotson seems to have been a favorite. All in all, he was as versatile in his learning as that later genius of Virginia, Thomas Jefferson.

Byrd collected books more avidly than any Virginian before him. His library, numbering over thirty-six hundred titles,[49] was the largest in the colony, and was equaled in North America by only that of his New England contemporary, Cotton Mather.

Generalizations about Byrd's reading, based on the catalogue of his books, cannot be very convincing, for his library represents the accumulation of a book collector, the first of his kind in Virginia. One can assume with some degree of assurance that smaller collections, bought for their utility by persons

[49] A catalogue of the library was made in 1777 by J. Stretch, just before the library was sold. Bassett, pp. 413-43, reprints this catalogue.

not interested in the magnificence of their libraries, were read by their owners, but the very size of the Westover collection, and the fact that Byrd had to employ a librarian, one William Proctor, to look after it,[50] probably prevented intimate acquaintance with all his books. Yet it is safe to assume that the main lines of his collecting followed his personal likings and interests. Furthermore, in his time he was probably the best-read man in Virginia and his taste was more catholic than that of most of his contemporaries. If he cannot have read every book he owned, he undoubtedly was familiar with many a volume, as allusions in his letters and writings indicate, though, unlike his brother-in-book-collecting, Cotton Mather, he was no pedant and did not lard his writings with evidence of his erudition. As became a gentleman, he wore his learning with grace.

The breadth of Byrd's interest could be discerned at once by anyone who entered his library, for that estimable man, Mr. Proctor, had carefully arranged the collection by subject matter, and had numbered the cases and shelves. The sales catalogue of 1777 followed this classification, but by that time many books had been put back in the wrong places and a few works published after Byrd's death had been added. In the first four cases stood a collection of more than two hundred and fifty works of history, biography, voyages, and travels, many of them fine folios illustrated and furnished with maps. Next in order came the lawbooks, including all the most useful works, though the legal collection by no means dominated the library. Immediately after the lawbooks there was a case containing over a hundred and thirty medical works, both ancient and modern. The section classified as "Entertainment, Poetry, Translations, &c." was one of the largest and most important. Here were to be found most of the great names in English literature, particularly recent writers, many of whom Byrd

[50] See a humorous letter from Byrd to his librarian, in Bassett, pp. 399-400.

had known personally. The works of the Elizabethan and Restoration dramatists were more completely represented than in any other American library. Next to the literature of entertainment were cases containing upwards of a hundred and fifty works of divinity, about equal in number to the books of law. The religious works included many sermons and books of devotions, a little controversial material, and several Bibles, in Hebrew, Greek, Latin, French, Dutch, and English. Of books in modern European languages, there were more than two hundred in French, "Chiefly of Entertainment," as the classification states. In this section were novels and plays, as well as poetry and French translations of the classics.

Of Greek and Latin authors in the original languages there were nearly three hundred works, including the latest edited texts. Byrd's classical library had not only all the better-known writers of antiquity but also most of the minor authors then available. The cases of miscellaneous works contained books on almost every phase of man's life and intellectual pursuits. There were many scientific and mathematical treatises, ancient and modern; a large number of books of architecture, including the works of Vitruvius, Palladio, and more recent writers on that subject; a sizable collection of books on drawing and painting; collections of music, including examples of Italian and English operas; many books of philosophy, classical and modern—among them the works of Hobbes, Descartes, Boyle, Shaftesbury, Locke, and other relatively recent writers; twenty or more works on gardening and agriculture; an ample assortment of other utilitarian books, such as treatises on distilling, cookery, and related subjects; a scattering of textbooks on language, rhetoric, mathematics, and logic; a few books on behavior, including *The Courtier's Calling* and *The Gentleman's Recreation*—in short, almost any book that a cultivated and thoughtful aristocrat might want was available at Westover.

The Byrd library indicates no particular hobby or obsession of the collector; instead, it suggests the wide range of interest that a versatile gentleman was expected to have. As a carefully balanced collection of the best literature and learning of the day it had no equal in America. Moreover, there were few items that conceivably the owner might not have wanted to consult. The mere presence of so many good books in the house of an influential and hospitable planter undoubtedly had an effect on the cultural development of his contemporaries. What the great man of Westover did, others would try to imitate; furthermore, the books gathered there served not only the owner but also his friends and neighbors. From Byrd's time onward, libraries among the wealthy planters became more numerous and larger, and the probability is that his example encouraged others to buy books and display them in their homes.

If Byrd himself had an ambition to be a man of letters, it was the well-bred and somewhat casual ambition affected by a gentleman. He never rushed into print with anything, and, though he took care to rewrite the *History of the Dividing Line* with some idea of publishing it, he never finished the work to suit his taste, and the manuscript remained unprinted until 1841.[61] From a rough journal kept on the surveying expedition, he prepared a narrative, probably for the amusement of some of his English friends, entitled *The Secret History of the Line*. In this account, which was not published until Professor William K. Boyd's edition in 1929, fictitious names were given the persons mentioned, and some of the incidents, particularly the quarrels and a few cases of violence offered women by members of the surveying crew, were described with more detail than appears in the better-known version.

[61] For a history of the manuscript and the printing of Byrd's work, see William Byrd's *Histories of the Dividing Line betwixt Virginia and North Carolina*, ed. William K. Boyd. (Raleigh: The North Carolina Historical Commission, 1929), p. xvi.

As many a gentleman before him had done, Byrd apparently wrote an account for private circulation among his friends, and at that time was not considering publication.

The news of the narrative got around in England, and his friends urged publication. Lord Egmont, for instance, in 1736 wrote in praise of the history and another account of Byrd's travel into the border country, which the writer called *A Journey to the Land of Eden*. Egmont begged him to give these works to the world, but Byrd answered that " 'tis a sign you never saw them that you judge so favorably"; and he added that he was too busy to prepare anything for the press, "for I am always engaged in some project for improving our infant colony." [52] The projects then engaging him were schemes to found a city at the falls of the James and to settle his land on the Roanoke River with Switzers. Other friends wrote urging him to print his works, but to all of them he replied evasively that he had not yet found time to complete any literary pieces.[53] Nevertheless, he did revise *The Secret History*, substituting real names for the fictitious ones, and toning down passages that might give offense. Clearly, Byrd intended sometime to bring out the *History of the Dividing Line*, but he never got around to putting the finishing touches on it. In the same way he wrote out *A Journey to the Land of Eden, Anno 1733* and *A Progress to the Mines in the Year*

[52] *The Virginia Magazine of History and Biography*, XXXVI, 217.

[53] See Bassett, p. lxxix. In a letter to Peter Collison, July 18, 1736 (*The Virginia Magazine of History and Biography*, XXXVI, 355), Byrd comments: "But now I come to the most difficult part of your letter to answer, that I mean wherein you desire a sight of my *History of the Line*. I own it goes against me to deny you such a trifle, but I have one infirmity, never to venture anything unfinished out of my hands. The bashful bears hide their cubs till they have licked them into shape, nor am I too proud to follow the example of those modest animals." He offers to send him his rough journal, but adds: "This is only the skeleton and ground work of what I intend, which may sometime or other come to be filled up with vessels and flesh, and have a decent skin drawn over all, to keep things tight in their places and prevent their looking frightful. . . . I must only desire you not to suffer this journal to go out of your hands nor a copy of it unless Sir Charles Wager should have a fancy to see it."

1732. Both of these are pleasing and entertaining accounts of trips he made to inspect his frontier properties.

Further evidences of Byrd's literary efforts are to be found in two unpublished notebooks in the University of North Carolina library. These notebooks, containing journal entries for the years 1739-41, are also filled with odds and ends of literary exercises: letters addressed to various persons under classical names, "characters" drawn in the manner of the seventeenth-century character writers, scraps of poetry, a version of the classical story of the Matron of Ephesus, and a series of love letters to one Mrs. Smith, designated as Sabina. The letters to Sabina are a part of a genuine, and unfortunate, courtship,[53a] but many of the other letters suggest that Byrd was writing for the sake of the composition.

Byrd wrote in the sophisticated and urbane manner of the Londoners of his day. The man who had known Wycherley, Congreve, Swift, Pope, and many another well-known author was not likely to lapse into provincial solecisms. Moreover, his style has a gaiety and sprightliness that no other American of his generation attained. Had he been less involved in "projects" and more intent upon a literary reputation, he might have become an author of note, who could have influenced others to regard their pens as a way to the attainment of honor. But, as already noted, Byrd's works were not published until long after his death and, except upon the few who may have read the manuscripts, they exerted no appreciable contemporary influence. Like other great planters, he was too busy with the

[53a] One letter, addressed to the father of Mrs. Smith, under the name of "Vigilante," is of particular interest because Byrd evaluates his Virginia possessions in pounds sterling. At that time, 1717, he lists 43,000 acres of land and 220 slaves. He points out that the yield from his plantations varies according to the price of tobacco, but he shows that his annual income is satisfactory: "In the year 1715 they produced clear of all charge £1716:5. In the year 1716 they cleared no more than £1535:14:11. But this year they will yield more than £1800."

In a letter that follows, addressed to "Lord Tipparari," he estimates the value of his Virginia property at £33,000.

innumerable duties and obligations of his class to follow the craft of letters.[54]

Byrd's social attitudes constantly appear in his correspondence and his writings. Though he was by nature a kindly and gracious man, there was never the least taint of democratic equalitarianism in his thinking. He was conscious of his own superiority—so conscious, in fact, that he rarely saw any need of asserting it. The lordly disdain that he felt toward tradesmen who imitated the dress and manners of their betters is illustrated in a letter to an unnamed London agent, dated June 27, 1729:

> You will herewith receive the invoice for my family, and beg you will please to employ your interest with the tradesmen not to send all the refuse of their shops to Virginia. Desire them to keep them for the customers that never pay them. 'Tis hard we must take all the worst of their people and the worst of their goods too. But now shopkeepers have left off their bands, and their frugality, and their spouses must be maintained in splendor, 'tis very fit the sweat of our brows should help to support them in it. Luxury is bad enough amongst people of quality, but when it gets among that order of men that stand behind counters, they must turn cheats and pickpockets to get it, and then the Lord have mercy on those who are obliged to trust to their honesty.[55]

When roughing it in the wilderness with his party of surveyors Byrd maintained an instinctive reserve that set him apart from common men. For example, there were familiarities which he did not permit himself, even in the freedom from social restraints experienced by campers on the borders of the Dismal

[54] "The Female Creed," perhaps written by Byrd (see *supra*, n. 30), suggests that the writer was consciously trying to imitate the manner and style of certain frivolous writings of the day. There are other evidences of Byrd's literary efforts. He had known John Oldmixon, author of *The British Empire in America* (1708), when he was at Middle Temple, and had written out for him a brief history of Virginia, which that author utilized in his own account of the colony. (See *The Virginia Magazine of History and Biography*, XXXV, 374-75.)

[55] Huntington Library manuscripts, Brock Collection (BR 188, Vol. V, n.p.).

Swamp. When some of the party made a harmless but coarse jest at the prudery of the chaplain, Byrd preserved a dignified and serious mien. "I left the company in good time," he says in *The Secret History*, "taking as little pleasure in their low wit as in their low liquor, which was rum punch."[56] Although he knew how to keep his distance—a sort of spiritual aloofness—from the rest of his party, he readily shared their hardships. "For want of our tent," he remarks of one incident on the survey, "we were obliged to shelter ourselves in this wretched hovel, where we were almost devoured by vermin of various kinds. However, we were above complaining, being all philosophers enough to improve such slender distresses into mirth and good humor."[57] Throughout his life Byrd held to a strict belief in the superiority of his class. When, in *A Progress to the Mines*, he reports the unfortunate marriage of a planter's daughter to her uncle's overseer, he takes occasion to observe: "Had she run away with a gentleman or a pretty fellow, there might have been some excuse for her, though he were of inferior fortune; but to stoop to a dirty plebeian, without any kind of merit, is the lowest prostitution."[58]

Byrd's sense of superiority and his adherence to a code of gentlemanly behavior had in them nothing of priggishness. Combined with his belief in the value of social distinctions was a healthy lustiness and a fund of common sense. Furthermore, he had too much of kindly toleration, as well as too much of calm assurance of his own position, to become a snob.

In his ethical views, Byrd represented the better type of gentleman of his time. Consciously or unconsciously he exemplified a dictum laid down in many a courtesy book—the command to heed Aristotle's doctrine of the golden mean. In his letters and other writings there is evidence of his consistent belief in the principle of temperance and moderation in all

[56] Byrd, *Histories of the Dividing Line*, ed. Boyd, pp. 111, 113.

[57] *Ibid.*, p. 40.

[58] Bassett, p. 338.

things; in his private life he exemplified that belief. The unpleasant prohibitions of Puritanism and the violent excesses of license were equally distasteful. But as "a man of sense," as a thoroughgoing rationalist of the day, he had a broad tolerance for the shortcomings of his fellows. No missionary zeal could burn in his soul, and he could report with a sense of amusement the moral lapses of members of his surveying party when they encountered freehearted country wenches or tempting Indian squaws. As the leader, Byrd himself held aloof from these temptations, yet without any attitude of being "holier than thou." Indeed, he was not altogether a Galahad, as his shorthand diary reveals.[58a] But before his men Byrd could not afford to show a weakness for women. There were some things a gentleman kept decently hidden from public notice. Even his sins must be committed in accordance with convention.

The gallantry that Byrd had learned as a young man in London never left him, and his attitude remained that of the cavalier quickly attracted by the smoldering eye of a charming woman. Many of his letters portray him as the passionate and romantic lover. One group, smacking of the artificiality of French romance, were signed "Veramour" and addressed to "Facetia"; they recount his passion for an unknown young woman in the summer and fall of 1703, three years before his first marriage. Another group, addressed to "Charmante," describe an equally passionate attachment for an unidentified enchantress, in 1722, two years before his second marriage,

[58a] Since the discovery of the portions of Byrd's intimate journals in the Huntington Library and at the University of North Carolina, a third part, also in shorthand, has turned up in the Virginia Historical Society. This covers the period from Dec. 13, 1717, to May 12, 1721, when Byrd was in England. At the time, he was a widower, and was paying court to various ladies, including the Mrs. Smith mentioned in the University of North Carolina letter book. He also kept a mistress, and notes, after a visit on Dec. 14, 1717, the payment of a fee of two guineas. The Virginia Historical Society has permitted me to have a photostat of this part of the diary, for purposes of study only. I do not have permission to quote verbatim from the document.

when Byrd was fast approaching his forty-ninth year.[59] Some of the letters to Charmante have all the artificial pastoralism of a painting by Boucher.[60] Gallantry, tinged with some of the hard brutality of the Restoration, is evident in a third group of love letters—the series addressed to Sabina, in the University of North Carolina notebooks. All of these letters show studied care in their composition. Byrd knew how to convey his passion in the approved literary manner of the day. He also kept up a correspondence with Mrs. Taylor. His letters to her suggest a particular pleasure in her friendship, and occasionally they show a hearty delight in a good story and a bit of scandal not altogether edifying.[61] But there is no suggestion that the relations between Byrd and Mrs. Taylor were ever anything but proper.

If anyone had seriously suggested to Byrd that drinking of alcoholic liquors should be prohibited among gentlemen, he would have regarded such a proposal as barbarous and uncivilized. But, in an age when drunkenness did not place a man beyond the pale, he himself stood for moderation in this, as in other things. On the rare occasions when he was intemperate he notes the fact in his diary; for example, on September 12, 1709—the day that he was sworn a member of the Council—he notes: "we went to the President's where I drank too much French wine and played at cards and I lost 20 shillings. I went home about 12 o'clock at night. I neglected to say my prayers and had good health, good thoughts, and good humor, thanks be to God Almighty." After a somewhat lavish entertainment, tendered by a "plain man worth £20,000," near Norfolk, during the survey of the boundary line, Byrd observes that "the parson and I returned to our quarters in good time and good order, but my man Tom broke the rules of hospitality

[59] For accounts of these two affairs, see Beatty, pp. 34 ff., 104 ff.

[60] See, e.g., letters in *The Virginia Magazine of History and Biography*, XXXV, 383 ff., especially p. 385.

[61] See letter to Mrs. Taylor, dated Oct. 10, 1735, in Bassett, pp. 394-96.

by getting extremely drunk in a civil house."[62] The intemperate servingman, we may be sure, received an appropriate reprimand from his master. When preparing for the survey, the Virginia commissioners took care to have ample quantities of strong drink, and informed their North Carolina colleagues that "we shall be provided with much wine and rum as just [to] enable us and our men to drink every night to the success of the following day; and, because we understand there are many Gentiles on your frontier who never had an opportunity of being baptized, we shall have a chaplain with us to make them Christians."[63] Thus everything was to be performed fittingly, with good cheer and clear consciences.

Byrd was ahead of most of his contemporaries in his attitude toward negro slavery and the rum traffic. Though he owned his full share of negroes, and occasionally even followed in his father's footsteps as an importer of African slaves, he realized that slavery was an evil and dangerous institution. His sense of decency was also outraged by the sanctimonious piety of the New England traders who brought in enough of both rum and slaves to be the ruin of the country. When Oglethorpe prohibited rum and slavery in Georgia, Byrd expressed his approval. Writing to his friend Lord Egmont, one of Oglethorpe's partners, Byrd observes that Georgia will have much ado to keep out negroes and rum, for "the saints of New England, I fear, will find out some trick to evade your act of Parliament."[64] These "foul traders," Byrd continues, "import so

[62] Byrd, *Histories of the Dividing Line*, ed. Boyd, p. 39; from *The Secret History*.
[63] *Ibid*., p. 21.
[64] *The Virginia Magazine of History and Biography*, XXXVI, 220-21; letter dated July 12, 1736. All the quotations cited here are from this letter. Byrd felt bitter about the traffic of New England ship captains who invaded the Virginia rivers. In a letter, dated Feb. 20, 1736, to his friend, Judge Benjamin Lynde, of Salem, he comments: "Some of these banditti anchor near my estate, for the advantage of traffiquing with my slaves, from whom they are sure to have good pennyworths. I am now prosecuting one of them, whose name is Grant, for this crime, and have evidence sufficient to convict him. I wish you would be so kind

many negroes hither that I fear this colony will sometime or other be confounded by the name of New Guinea." A further remark about the influence of negro slaves upon the planters shows Byrd's realistic perception of a subtle danger. "I am sensible of many bad consequences of multiplying these Ethiopians amongst us," he comments to Egmont. "They blow up the pride and ruin the industry of our white people, who seeing a rank of poor creatures below them, detest work for fear it should make them look like slaves. . . . Another unhappy effect of many negroes is the necessity of being severe. Numbers make them insolent, and then foul means must do what fair will not." The debasing effect of slavery upon the owners, as well as the positive danger from their increasing numbers, was seen as clearly by this slaveholder as by any latter-day social historian. Rum, a commodity that the elder William Byrd had imported in huge quantities, received the peculiar condemnation of his son. "I entirely agree with your lordship in the detestation you seem to feel for that diabolical liquor rum, which does more mischief to people's industry and morals than anything except gin and the Pope," he assures Egmont. "Thrice happy Georgia if it be in the power of any law to keep out so great an enemy to health, industry, and virtue. The new settlers there had much better plant vineyards like Noah, and get drunk with their own wine." There is scarcely need to point out, however, that his objection to rum was not based on puritanical considerations, but upon the abuse of rum drinking by the poorer elements in the population—a factor that has induced hard-drinking Southern aristocrats in later times to vote for prohibition. Byrd, of course, was no prohibitionist. His complaint was against the social disintegration that had come to the mass of the population through the importation of cheap rum.

---

as to hang up all your felons at home, and not send them abroad to discredit their country in this manner." (*The Virginia Magazine of History and Biography*, IX, 243-44.)

Swearing was scarcely a vice in Byrd's opinion, though he would have depended upon a gentleman's taste as to the time and place for oaths. He himself had the good sense to know how to make effective use of a few resounding oaths properly delivered. When provoked because of some disobedience and rascality among his men, he swore at them so furiously on one occasion that, "by the good grace of my oaths, I might have passed for an officer in his Majesty's Guards." [65] If swearing was scarcely a sin at all, lying, on the other hand, was an offense as heinous as thievery. A gentleman's word was literally his bond, but Byrd was wise enough to know that gentlemen did not always live up to their professions. Hence, when one of his fellow commissioners insisted that "a gentleman should be believed on his bare word without evidence and a poor man condemned without trial," he commented that this procedure "agreed not at all with my notions of justice." [66] Justice was the greatest of the obligations of a true gentleman to both his equals and his inferiors.

One would hardly pick William Byrd as a man of religion, for he seems the very essence of worldly rationalism. But, for all that, he still believed that decency and order in society demanded adherence to the Anglican Establishment. Religion, no doubt, was scarcely a mystical experience for him, but it was nevertheless an essential part of the society to which he belonged. That he insisted upon a chaplain—his friend the Reverend Peter Fontaine—accompanying the party that surveyed the boundary is in itself worthy of remark. Though at times in *The Secret History* he makes a joke at the expense of the parson, he never speaks lightly of religion. Even in the wilderness, when Sunday came Byrd put on clean clothes and attended divine service.[67] In the daily entries of his earlier diary he is careful to note the routine of his private devotions,

[65] Byrd, *Histories of the Dividing Line*, ed. Boyd, p. 59.
[66] *Ibid.*, p. 89.
[67] *Ibid.*, p. 71; see also pp. 174, 287.

morning and evening, though now and then he confesses to forgetting to say his prayers. On the first leaf of the little notebook containing the shorthand entries of the diary,[68] there is a religious creed in Byrd's handwriting. Most of the statements of belief are orthodox and conventional, such as any good Anglican would have made, but a few imply a leaning toward the rationalism that characterized eighteenth-century intellectuals. "I believe that God made man . . . [and] insp[ire]d him with a reasonable soul to distinguish betwe[en] good and evil," the credo reads; "that the law of nature taught him to [follow] the good and avoid the evil because the good tends manifestly to his happiness and preservation, but the evil to his [misery] and destruction." Finally, after expressing an orthodox belief in Christ and the Resurrection, the assertion of faith concludes without mentioning the conventional heaven or hell; instead, it affirms "that those who have led good and holy lives here will be rewarded with unspeakable happiness hereafter. But those who have obstinately and impenitently rebelled against God and their own consciences shall go into a state of sorrow and misery." Surely this was a faith that a cultivated and rational gentleman during the Century of Enlightenment could well have accepted.

William Byrd II, who died in 1744 and was buried in the garden he loved at Westover, was the herald of the eighteenth-century order of Virginia gentlemen—gentlemen in the grand manner, who made the Virginia aristocracy famous throughout the land. Though at times the pressure of "the usurers" of London—his creditors—sometimes embarrassed the great planter and kept his purse light, he accumulated a princely domain. At his death he held title to 179,000 acres of the best land in the colony.[69] Only two years before his end he patented 105,000

[68] Huntington Library manuscripts, Brock Collection (BR 61). Miss Norma Cuthbert, of the Department of Manuscripts of the Huntington Library, was the first to observe that this creed was in Byrd's handwriting. I am indebted to her for calling it to my attention.

[69] Bassett, p. lxxxiii.

acres in the rich valley of the Dan River stretching to the North Carolina line. Like the nobles of England whom he knew, admired, and perhaps envied, he sought to enhance his greatness by the acquisition of land. He, of course, was not the only rich landed aristocrat of the first part of the century, for there were others even wealthier, but he was the most cultivated of them all, and he lived in greater elegance and with more fitting grace than any of his contemporaries. A generation later there would be many like him, but Byrd was the forerunner of a type. In the second William Byrd, the aristocracy that had been slowly evolving during the seventeenth century attained a brilliant exemplification, and, though Virginia gentlemen before him had exhibited aristocratic qualities like his, the best attributes of his class shone in him with peculiar radiance. The way of life marked out by the lord of Westover was the pattern followed by other gentlemen of Virginia in succeeding generations.

CHAPTER XII

THE VITALITY OF THE TRADITION

WHEN great gentlemen like Robert Carter of Corotoman or William Byrd of Westover surveyed their social order in the first third of the eighteenth century, they must have found many elements pleasing to them. Virginia had reached the first stage of its maturity as a settled and assured commonwealth. It was already a proud state—if not in name, at least in practice and spirit—and its leaders were an intelligent body of aristocrats who had developed a strong sense of social and political responsibility. In the period treated in the preceding discussion, Virginia came of age. In the succeeding generations before the Revolution, the ruling aristocracy reached its greatest splendor and power. Economic disaster had not yet overtaken the tobacco plantations of the tidewater region, and the great houses of the gentry were the centers of a society characterized by a remarkable degree of intelligence and cultivation. Indeed, the intellectual training and powers of this society make it noteworthy in the history of America—or of any other country.

A vivid and accurate picture of the aristocracy on the eve of the Revolution is implicit in the diary kept by Philip Fithian, an eager young ministerial student from Princeton, who lived as a tutor in the household of Robert Carter of Nomini Hall.[1] This Robert Carter—called "Councilor" Carter by his contemporaries—grandson of "King" Carter, surpassed even his ancestor in the magnificence of his surroundings and his zeal for classical culture. He had what Fithian described as an "overgrown library of books," containing among many other

[1] *Philip Vickers Fithian: Journal and Letters, 1767-1774,* ed. John Rogers Williams (Princeton, 1900).

items "all the Latin and Greek classics," a "vast number of books on divinity," and "the works of almost all the late famous writers as Locke, Addison, Young, Pope, Swift, Dryden, &c." [2] Careful of every phase of his children's education, Carter particularly emphasized the value of correct diction. For that reason he avoided Scotch and English tutors, preferring "young gentlemen educated in good schools on the Continent" as models for his children to imitate.[3] Cultivated Americans were already suspicious of the affected dialects that Englishmen often represented as the true mother speech. Carter's meticulous care in the training of his children is indicative of his educational ideals. In this interest in intellectual cultivation Councilor Carter was representative of his class. Fithian, in a letter to John Peck, his successor as tutor, emphasizes the inflated opinion that Virginia aristocrats have of their superior "worth and precedency," but he points out that they place an enormous value "upon posts of honor and mental acquirements." Their respect for learning is very high, he insists. Because of Peck's sound education at Nassau Hall, the new tutor can expect to "be rated, without any more questions asked, either about your family, your estate, your business, or your intention, at £10,000; and you might come and go and converse and keep company, according to this value; and you would be despised and slighted if you rated yourself a farthing cheaper." [4]

The Virginia gentry composed an aristocracy not only of wealth and position but of intelligence and learning. In this latter aspect of its development it had transcended its counterpart in eighteenth-century England, where learning among the country gentry had fallen behind the ideal of earlier generations.

The flowering of the aristocracy in the years preceding the

[2] *Ibid.*, p. 279; letter to the Reverend Enoch Green, dated Dec. 1, 1773.

[3] *Ibid.*, p. 147; entry dated Apr. 6, 1774. [4] *Ibid.*, p. 287; letter dated Aug. 12, 1774.

Revolution was of tremendous importance in the subsequent history of the country. From the ranks of the men who had used their leisure to cultivate their minds came leaders who shaped the destinies of the country in 1776 and in 1787. The Federal Constitution was the work of gentlemen cognizant of their duty to serve the highest interests of the state. The tremendous influence of the Virginia aristocrats in the Convention has recently been emphasized by an authority on the history of the Constitution. "Virginia was the first to appoint delegates to the Federal Convention," Dr. Max Farrand comments, "and what a deputation it was from the social point of view!—George Washington, Edmund Randolph, George Mason, John Blair, James Madison, Chancellor Wythe, and Dr. McClurg. The last-named were not perhaps of the same high inheritance, but by virtue of their positions and accomplishments they were accepted without question as members of the upper class. The example set by Virginia was followed, to a greater or less degree, by all the other states, and in consequence attendance at the Federal Convention was a recognition of one's importance and, by inference, of one's social standing as well. Virtually every delegate to the Convention was of the 'class of men denominated *gentlemen*.' "[5] These men were not sent from heaven in an hour of need to work a miracle. The statesmen who molded opinion in that critical period were gentlemen with all the background that their social station connoted. They had been educated in the humanistic tradition, and they had the wisdom of the ancients, as well as the resources of their own heritage, to guide them in the task of making a new nation.

The Elizabethan ideal of the complete gentleman—an ideal that did not neglect the cultivation of the intellect—characterized the aristocrats of 1787. These men, imbued with a

[5] Max Farrand, "If James Madison Had Had a Sense of Humor," *The Pennsylvania Magazine of History and Biography*, LXII (1938), 134-35.

zeal for service to the state and mentally equipped with a sound cultural background, were spiritually akin to the great gentlemen of the age of Sir Philip Sidney. Indeed, they were closer to the Elizabethans in spirit and training than to the English country gentlemen of a few generations later. An English writer, Mr. Esmé Wingfield-Stratford, commenting sadly on the frequent stupidity of leadership demonstrated by the English gentry during the nineteenth century and since, finds a reason for the ineffectiveness of the upper class in its emphasis upon conformity to what he calls "public-school virtues," with a consequent exclusion of intellectual qualities.[6] The fox-hunting gentleman of the Georgian period, and later, did not know enough. It was not sufficient that in his behavior he respected all public-school taboos, that he knew precisely how to assume the pose of reticent modesty, that he refused to thrust himself forward, that he was courageous, that he was ready to shoulder the white man's burden and die fighting for glory and empire; none of this sufficed when he consciously subscribed to a cult of anti-intellectualism and was suspicious of too much concern about brains. "The English gentleman [of this type] was unsurpassed as a figurehead," Wingfield-Stratford wryly observes.[7] It was otherwise with the Virginia aristocrats of the late eighteenth century, who had brought an earlier and higher ideal of the essential qualities of the gentleman to extraordinary development in the fresh soil of the New World. They were true heirs of the English Renaissance.

Brilliant as were the social and intellectual attainments of the Virginia aristocracy of the eighteenth century, the elements of disaster were latent in the economic system which supported it, and its eclipse might have been predicted. The exhaustion of the soil of tidewater Virginia, wasteful methods of farming, loss of markets during the Revolution, the grow-

[6] Esmé Wingfield-Stratford, *The Making of a Gentleman* (London, 1938); see especially pp. 311-27. [7] *Ibid.*, p. 316.

ing unprofitableness of slave labor—all these things combined to prepare the way for the ultimate destruction of the aristocracy in the later nineteenth century. Preoccupied with public service and social responsibilities in the early days of the nation, the gentry devoted less time to their private business or else displayed less business acumen than their forefathers. Gradually economic ruin overtook the aristocracy. Thomas Jefferson's struggles to keep out of bankruptcy are well known, but his plight was typical of that suffered by many of his kind. The devastation of the War between the States, and its aftermath, gave the final blow. Since then the aristocracy of Virginia has been merely a memory of former grandeur.

But despite the destruction of the social order which produced the most public-spirited aristocracy this country has known, the ideals and traditions of Virginia gentlemen have shown an amazing vitality and capacity for adaptation and survival in uncongenial environments. Not even generations of poverty following a destructive war have been able to obliterate the inner consciousness of social responsibility, of a pride in family and class, and an assurance of inherited position and spiritual superiority among remnants of the aristocracy. Although raiding armies wiped out the family fortune in 1863, a descendant of one of the old families of tidewater Virginia remained a very great lady until the day of her death; though the pressure of economic necessity forced her grandchildren into many strange trades and occupations, she never let one of them forget that he came of a long and distinguished line of gentlemen who had ably served the state; and each grandchild was brought up to believe that there was a higher calling than mere getting and spending, that a gentleman should cultivate his mind and rise superior to the common herd. Another aristocrat, a soldier who had fought in the sixties on most of the battlefields of Virginia and had lost everything but his reputation and sense of superiority, held fast to his heritage of gentility, though he was frequently hard pressed to pay the tax collector. With wealth and servants merely a memory, he often harnessed a mule and plowed his own vegetable garden. But, even when engaged in such manual labors, he retained the manner and dignity of his class and never once discarded his black string tie, his white collar and cuffs, or his waistcoat. And, if he sweated as other men, his grandchildren cannot remember it.

These men and women had a calm assurance of their position and of their dignity and its obligations. For their poverty and the uncongenial tasks that it imposed they never apologized or explained. No explanation was necessary. Intelligent and informed persons already understood. To one brought up in their tradition, the impulse to assert one's social superiority is ungenteel and shocking, carrying with it the proof of snobbery. "For the psychological kink that we call snobbery," Wingfield-Stratford shrewdly remarks, "is no more than an obsessive preoccupation with class or social distinctions, and this may affect duke or dustman." [8] Few people were more conscious of their social position than the Virginians, but the best of them had no obsession that would make them want to impress other men by asserting that position. Any man worth impressing would know a gentleman when he saw one.

The influence of the Virginia ideal of gentility was far-reaching, as Dr. Farrand has implied in his discussion of the Federal Convention. That influence is not yet dead. It survives in descendants of the men who had a part in establishing the tradition, and it is manifest in others who have recognized and emulated the best of its ideals of leadership and social responsibility. Though the muddy waters of political and economic confusion threaten to engulf all intelligence, the belief in the value of an intellectual and a socially-conscious leadership remains alive. Perhaps the aristocracy of the seventeenth and eighteenth centuries may yet teach us important lessons in leadership.

[8] *Ibid.*, p. 275.

INDEX